Additional praise for *The Strategy Pathfinder*

"The unique micro-cases in this book will surely spark energetic discussion in the classroom. The diversity of international companies and strategic issues in the cases provides an unusually broad set of examples from which to draw."

Constance E. Helfat, Dartmouth College

"*The Strategy Pathfinder* represents a refreshing and engaging method for teaching strategy. The processes and cases, which define the book, provide excellent learning materials that bring a real-life experience to students."

Stuart Sanderson, Bradford University

About the Authors

Duncan Angwin is associate professor in strategic management at Warwick Business School, University of Warwick, where he has won several awards for teaching excellence and research publications. He is also associate fellow at Saïd Business School, Oxford, visiting professor at ENPC, Paris, and lectures for Georgetown University, USA. He is Associate Chair for Strategy and Practice at the Strategic Management Society and maintains close links with industry.

Stephen Cummings is Professor of Strategic Management at Victoria Management School, Victoria University of Wellington, New Zealand and regularly lectures at other universities in Asia, Africa and Europe. He is the author of *Recreating Strategy* and the co-editor (with David Wilson) of *Images of Strategy*.

Chris Smith is senior lecturer in strategy and Director of the Singapore MBA program for the Adelaide Graduate School of Business, University of Adelaide (South Australia).

◀ ◀ ◀ STRATEGY IS . . .

"A combination of the words stratos, *which meant 'army' (or more correctly an army spread out over the ground), and* agein, *meaning 'to lead'."*
Greek Language (6th century BC)

". . . the great work of the organization. In situations of life or death, it is the Tao of survival or extinction."
Sun Tzu (5th century BC)

". . . the determination of the long-run goals and objectives of an enterprise, and the adoption of courses of action and the allocation of resources necessary for carrying out these goals."
Alfred Chandler (1962)

". . . the plan enabling a company to gain, as efficiently as possible, a sustainable edge over its competitors."
Kenichi Ohmae (1983)

". . . a pattern of resource allocation that enables firms to maintain or improve their performance."
Jay Barney (1997)

". . . a firm's theory *about how to gain competitive advantages."*
Peter F. Drucker (1994)

". . . a pattern of behavior that emerges over time."
Henry Mintzberg (1987)

In reading this book on paths through strategy, many other views of strategy will also become apparent.

THE STRATEGY
PATHFINDER

CORE CONCEPTS AND MICRO-CASES

DUNCAN ANGWIN — STEPHEN CUMMINGS — CHRIS SMITH

Blackwell
Publishing

© 2007 by Duncan Angwin, Stephen Cummings, Chris Smith

BLACKWELL PUBLISHING
350 Main Street, Malden, MA 02148-5020, USA
9600 Garsington Road, Oxford OX4 2DQ, UK
550 Swanston Street, Carlton, Victoria 3053, Australia

First published 2007 by Blackwell Publishing Ltd

1   2007

Library of Congress Cataloging-in-Publication Data

Angwin, Duncan.
The strategy pathfinder : core concepts and micro-cases / Duncan Angwin,
Stephen Cummings, Chris Smith.
p.   cm.
Includes bibliographical references and index.
ISBN-13: 978-1-4051-2613-7 (pbk. : alk. paper)
ISBN-10: 1-4051-2613-2 (pbk. : alk. paper)
1. Strategic planning.   2. Strategic planning—Case studies.
I. Cummings, Stephen.   II. Smith, Chris.   III. Title.

HD30.28.A5315 2007
658.4′012—dc22
2005032596

A catalogue record for this title is available from the British Library.

Set in 10/12.5pt Book Antique
by Graphicraft Limited, Hong Kong
Printed and bound in the United Kingdom
by TJ International Ltd, Padstow, Cornwall

For further information on Blackwell Publishing,
visit our website: www.blackwellpublishing.com

Contents

The Strategy Pathfinder
User's Guide

Strategy texts often come across as rather dry and sterile products that seem to view the reader as a consumer: "read this, then replicate it." We think that business today is too complex, too varied, and too interesting for this approach to work well. We wrote *The Strategy Pathfinder* to put strategy making into the hands of the reader, to make you a "producer" of strategy, and to subsequently breathe the life back into the subject. *The Strategy Pathfinder* represents a different way to learn about strategy. It is founded on four learning principles based on our combined 50 years of experience teaching MBAs and undergraduates across five continents.

1. Less means more

Unlike conventional strategy texts *The Strategy Pathfinder* isn't a pile of theories and concepts 1,400 pages long. By synthesizing and presenting essential pathways through the complexities of the strategy jungle, the Pathfinder's contents can comfortably be covered in a module or short course, enabling you to build momentum and stay enthused. The short chapters are designed to stimulate interest and raise curiosity as well as being digestible in moments. At the end of each chapter we have a Pathfinder Compass that relates core themes to leading strategy textbooks that readers may have to hand. To encourage readers to explore topics more deeply and pursue other routes through strategy, we provide an extensive list of pertinent references at the end of the book, which includes classic articles on most aspects of the subject.

2. Strategy cases should hit you like strategy problems in real life, not like academic exercises

The Strategy Pathfinder isn't weighed down by enormous cases that throw in every detail but are very time consuming to handle and can be poorly focused and difficult to relate to. It is built around "micro-cases" on real-life problems faced by real companies and real executives. We believe these micro-cases have greater immediacy than large cases and are both more engaging and more like the strategy situations that people encounter in reality than the traditional Harvard-style cases. They are more real because, like life, they hit you with a problem and then *you* have to go about forming a viewpoint, and testing these against the opinions of others, before deciding on recommendations about how best to proceed. Conventional cases tend to hand you the case on a plate, suggesting that all you need is contained in the same 20 pages of charts, tables, and text placed fully formed before you and your peers. This is also why micro-cases are more engaging. They force you to think about past experiences, do more research, surf the Internet and form your own opinions. In other words, you take ownership. They make you a producer of strategy, rather than a consumer. Also, because they are brief, you can be interacting and arguing about them with others in a matter of minutes.

At the end of the first micro-case in every chapter (apart from the last one on maverick strategies, where the emphasis is on you thinking differently) we provide some ideas on how you might have gone about answering the questions. After that, the questions and possible solutions are for you to debate with yourself, your colleagues, classmates, or peers.

Note that the cases have been prepared solely to promote classroom discussion and learning. They are not intended to illustrate either effective or ineffective strategy management or implementation.

3. There is no such thing as local versus international cases

Today's strategists are just as likely to work for, or with, companies from another country as they are to work with companies from their own homeland. Furthermore, as national barriers diminish, all business has become international business – your competitors/suppliers/customers could come from anywhere. Therefore, strategists need to be comfortable with problems from all parts of the globe. Thus, while many of our micro-cases are from our main base, Europe, there are also many cases from Africa, the Americas, Asia, and Oceania.

4. Symbols and colors can provide a structure that aids learning

The Strategy Pathfinder provides a number of familiar symbols and colors to aid knowing where you are along the way and remembering what you have covered.

- Using a geographic symbol, we depict the main location of each case with a globe-style silhouette representing its continent of origin:

- Europe
- Americas
- Asia
- Africa
- Oceania
- General

- In the following Strategy Pathways section, each chapter is depicted as a train line with the micro-cases as stops along the way, showing the geographic location of the cases and naming the company the case focuses on. In some instances, where the case focuses on an industry rather than a particular company, the industry name is given. The earlier cases on the line are more tightly tailored to chapter material whereas later ones are more stretching.

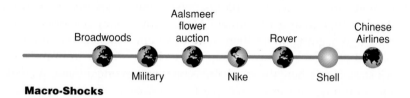

Macro-Shocks

- Each of our chapters is represented by a coloured organizer showing the chapter title and number. Then the micro-cases in each chapter are headed up by a mini-organizer that gives the number of the case and provides an image that represents the subject matter. The geographic symbol on the click-wheel shows the location of the case. Many of the representative images are cryptic in nature, which we hope will arouse curiosity in the reader. They may also be useful slides in lectures to encourage case recall. (The images can be downloaded from the website for this book: www.blackwellpublishing/angwin.) The forwards and backwards symbols on both organizers imply that the reader can move in either direction.

- At the end of each chapter, before the micro-cases, a pathfinder compass provides directions to corresponding sections in leading strategy textbooks where you can find out more about the aspects of strategy covered in the chapter.

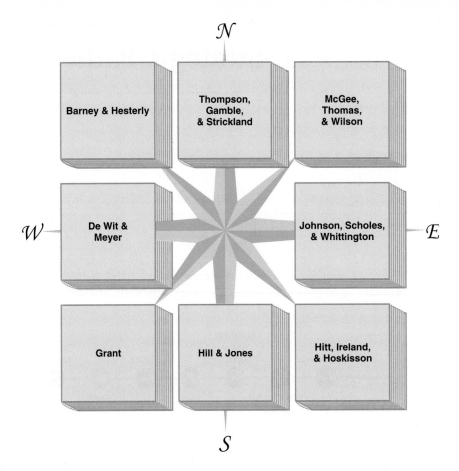

$\mathcal{N}$

| Barney & Hesterly | Thompson, Gamble, & Strickland | McGee, Thomas, & Wilson |

$\mathcal{W}$ — De Wit & Meyer — Johnson, Scholes, & Whittington — $\mathcal{E}$

| Grant | Hill & Jones | Hitt, Ireland, & Hoskisson |

$\mathcal{S}$

The core textbooks in the pathfinder compasses are:

Barney, J. B. and Hesterly, W. S. (2006) *Strategic Management and Competitive Advantage: Concepts and Cases*. New Jersey: Pearson/Prentice Hall.

De Wit, B. and Meyer, R. (2004) *Strategy: Process, Content, Context; An International Perspective*, 3rd edn. Thomson.

Grant, R. M. (2005) *Contemporary Strategy Analysis*, 5th edn. Oxford: Blackwell Publishers.

Hill, C. W. L. and Jones, G. R. (2004) *Strategic Management Theory: An Integrated Approach*, 6th edn. Boston and New York: Houghton Mifflin Company.

Hitt, M. A., Ireland, R. D., and Hoskisson, R. E. (2005) *Strategic Management: Competitiveness and Globalization Concepts*, 6th edn. Thomson/South-Western.

Johnson, G., Scholes, K., and Whittington, R. (2005) *Exploring Corporate Strategy: Text and Cases*, 7th edn. Financial Times/Prentice Hall.

McGee, J., Thomas, H., and Wilson, D. (2005) *Strategy: Analysis and Practice*. McGraw-Hill.

Thompson, A. A., Gamble, J. E., and Strickland, A. J. III (2006) *Strategy Winning in the Marketplace: Core Concepts, Analytical Tools, Cases*, McGraw-Hill, and

Thompson, A. A., Strickland, A. J. III, Gamble, J. E. (2007) *Crafting & Executing Strategy: Text and Readings*, 15th edn. McGraw-Hill.

Additional compasses are presented on the website for this book (www. blackwellpublishing/angwin), providing directions to other major strategy textbooks.

- Finally, we provide an integrating diagram on page xiii that shows how our 11 strategy paths may be combined into the overall strategic path of an organization over time.

Strategic Pathways

1. Macro-Shocks

PEST/ESTEMPLE – systems thinking – levels of analysis – scenarios – forecasting – SWOT – impact matrix – chaos theory – turbulence – Icarus paradox – strategic drift – corporate agility – organizational ecology – incrementalism – punctuated equilibrium

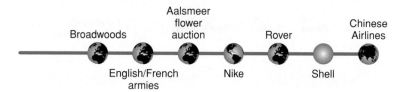

2. Movers & Shakers

Chain of ownership – principals/agents – corporate governance – market for corporate control – stakeholder analysis – management consultants – government influences – role of the CEO – executive rewards – executive responsibilities – power/interest groups – CSR

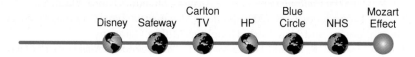

3. Industry Terrain

Industry margins – perfect/imperfect competition – industry life cycle – CSFs – industry structure – forces of industry – value net – dynamics of industry – industry maps (peaks and troughs) – co-opetition – complementors

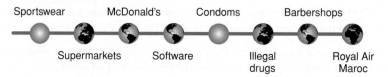

4. The Big Picture

Corporate strategy – M-form – diversification – organizational structure – strategic choice – conglomerates – portfolio management – BCG matrix – parenting advantage – transferring skills – core competences – M&A – diversification matrix

5. Perfect Positioning

Cost advantage – differentiation advantage – focus advantage – segmentation – generic strategy matrix – strategy clock – game theory – value chain – strategic groups – resource-based view – CASIS/VRIO analysis

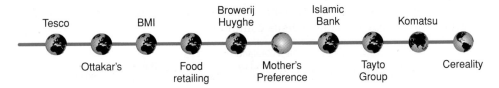

6. Living Strategy

Organic approaches – relationships/networks – knowledge society – learning organization – the living organization – strategic stories – communities of practice – social capital – capabilities – emergent strategy – strategy as practice – balanced scorecard

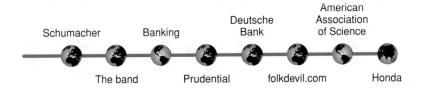

7. Corporate Character

National culture – Porter Diamond – 7-S framework – organization culture – cultural web – identity – image – branding – reputation – vision and mission

8. Crossing Borders

Internationalization – globalization – expansion strategies – theory of absolute advantage – theory of comparative advantage – HOS model – international product life cycle – eclectic theory – country clusters – national culture frameworks – Porter Diamond – leveraging national competitive advantage – international business structures

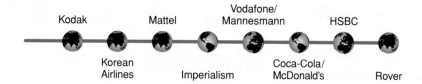

Kodak   Mattel   Vodafone/Mannesmann   HSBC
Korean Airlines   Imperialism   Coca-Cola/McDonald's   Rover

9. Guiding Change

Managing change frameworks – levels of change – degrees of change – styles of change – turnarounds – post-acquisition integration – instigators of change – resistance to change – change versus continuity

Pringle   ICI   New Zealand Social Policy Agency   Reliant   Baraka College   The Churches

10. Sustain Ability

Sustainable competitive advantage – corporate social responsibility – corporate environmental integrity – corporate social equity – corporate economic prosperity – triple bottom line

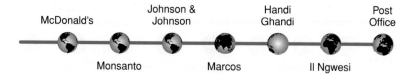

McDonald's   Johnson & Johnson   Handi Ghandi   Post Office
Monsanto   Marcos   Il Ngwesi

11. Maverick Strategies

Value innovation – S-curves – diversity management – next practice – blue ocean thinking – unique moments – entrepreneurs – value chimera – organigraphs – different strategy schools

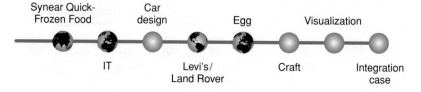

Synear Quick-Frozen Food   Car design   Egg   Visualization
IT   Levi's/Land Rover   Craft   Integration case

The Strategy Paths Combined

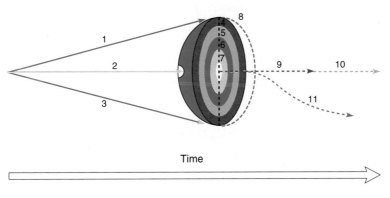

Time

1	Macro-Shocks	7	Corporate Character
2	Movers & Shakers	8	Crossing Borders
3	Industry Terrain	9	Guiding Change
4	The Big Picture	10	Sustain Ability
5	Perfect Positioning	11	Maverick Strategies
6	Living Strategy		

The strategy paths in this book may fit together dynamically as shown above. *Macroshocks*, or pulses from the external environment, pressure from influential *movers & shakers*, and the shape of the *industry terrain* can determine a firm's strategy over time. Within the firm, corporate strategy, or the *big picture*, attempts to accommodate these pressures and maneuver the firm mindful of its *positioning* in markets, its shape as a *living* entity, and its core *character*. Decisions need to be made about growing or expanding the firm across *borders*, and internal *change* must be managed to enable success to be *sustained* over time. Increasingly, however, risks have to be taken and molds broken. To stay "in the game" firms need to develop *maverick strategies* to create new business opportunities or change the shape of existing ones.

WE WOULD LIKE TO THANK OUR STUDENTS AT THE FOLLOWING
UNIVERSITIES WHO HAVE HELPED DEVELOP, CRITIQUE, AND TEST THE
MICRO-CASES AND PATHWAYS IN THIS BOOK:

UNIVERSITY OF WARWICK, UK
ADELAIDE UNIVERSITY, AUSTRALIA
VICTORIA UNIVERSITY OF WELLINGTON, NEW ZEALAND
UNIVERSITY OF GEORGETOWN, USA
VLERICK BUSINESS SCHOOL, BELGIUM
ÉCOLE NATIONALE DES PONTS ET CHAUSSEÉS, PARIS, FRANCE
ECOLE HASSANIA, CASABLANCA, MOROCCO
CHINESE UNIVERSITY OF HONG KONG, CHINA

Does the flap of a butterfly's wings in Brazil set off a tornado in Texas?

R. C. Hilborn (1994) Chaos and Nonlinear Dynamics

We will never be able to escape from the ultimate dilemma that all our knowledge is about the past, and all our decisions are about the future.

Ian Wilson (2000) From Scenario Thinking to Strategic Action

As I turned on the television on September 11, 2001, to check share prices, the first image to come onto the screen was a speeding object smashing into a skyscraper. I thought it was just a daytime drama, until, with a deep sense of shock, I realized it was for real!

One reason for the intensity of the shock was that it seemed so unlikely that an airliner would crash into the World Trade Center. It was a major, catastrophic, unanticipated event. Its shock waves have resounded around the world, impacting on people, businesses, organizations, and governments, across multiple geographic regions, with differing intensities at different times.

What happened on 9/11 is just one example of **macro-shock**, which can be defined as a major event in the broad context within which business is embedded, and over which businesses can exert little, if any, control. Businesses and their strategies do not operate in a vacuum. They are *open* systems that take resources and information *from* the environment and transform them into products and services that are fed back *into* the environment. This general systems theory perspective emphasizes the interconnectedness of the firm and multiple levels of the environment. For instance, Canada's top mutual funds, Chile's copper mines, and Europe's steel companies are all outperforming expectations because of events on the other side of the world, namely the recent surge in China's economy. Some of these key interactions (or forces) in the business environment are illustrated in figure 1.1.

Businesses are subject to a wide range of shocks from such forces. Industry-level shocks and the actions of competitors, suppliers, customers (discussed in chapter 3 Industry Terrain and chapter 5 Perfect Positioning), together with shocks internal to the business (see chapter 9 Guiding Change), can all have major consequences for the firm, but in this chapter we focus on the broad macro-environment beyond these levels, where firms have little direct control over the forces that determine the shape of their industries and businesses. (The interaction between firms and institutions, where firms may have some influence through lobbying, for instance, is explored in chapter 2 Movers & Shakers.)

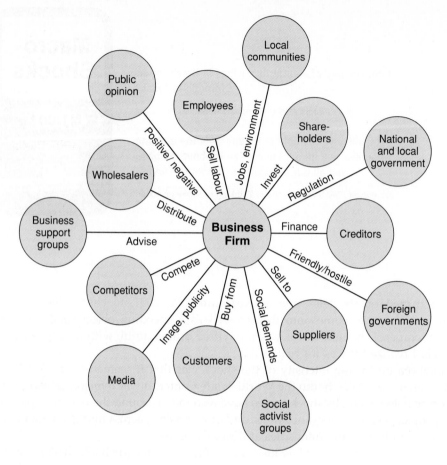

Figure 1.1 Some of the many interactions between businesses and their environment (Source: Davis and Frederick (1984))

The Consequences of Macro-Shock

The 9/11 disaster had a differential impact on firms and industries. For some the effect was direct and specific. The wholesale broking firm Cantor Index, located in the World Trade Center, lost 658 employees on that day. Its business suffered immediate and direct damage. The impact also had a direct effect on other industries, such as US airlines, which experienced a significant slump in sales because of fears over the safety of flying. For other industries the effect was indirect, emphasizing the connectedness point made earlier. Theme parks in the USA, for instance, suffered from the fall in air passengers, and other support industries, such as catering and insurance, were also hit. For some industries, therefore, 9/11 had an immediate effect and for others the impact was delayed. In some instances the duration of the effect was short lived, while for others the effects still linger – there has been no sustained recovery in North American and transatlantic aviation markets so far.

The 9/11 shock, although a while ago, still reverberates around the world, triggering other after-shocks. This seismic characterization as an earthquake sending a major disruptive pulse or pulses into the environment lends itself to linear analysis of consequences. The pulses, or ripples, tend to follow a predictable entropic pattern, allowing their consequences for the environment to be anticipated. On the other hand, some would suggest that as 9/11 occurred in a social system, the decay effects may be different to an earthquake, and indeed may escalate, which would make the prediction of consequences altogether more complex.

Both viewpoints make assumptions about the importance of the 9/11 event that may not be accepted by all. Some would downplay the importance of the effect of 9/11 on businesses by pointing to contextual forces at work before the event itself. The aviation industry was already struggling with the consequences of deregulation, greater competition, and soaring fuel prices as well as a US economy that had already experienced several quarters of recession and the bursting of the tech bubble. Indeed, Wall Street had declined 24% for the month before 9/11 and only lost a relatively small 8% two weeks before the event and a further 7% on resumption of trading.

Predicting Macro-Shocks

It is fairly safe to say that most businesses did not anticipate or plan for 9/11, even though there is some evidence that the US Government was aware that something of this sort might occur. Why should it be so difficult to predict such events? As our opening quotation about butterflies and tornados suggests, major events may have their origins in rather obscure and minor happenings. One wonders what tiny far-away environmental ripples ultimately led to 9/11?

Edward Lorenz, in trying to predict weather patterns at MIT during the 1960s, is widely credited with recognizing that very small differences in initial conditions are rapidly amplified by evolution into complex patterns. By rounding the numbers in his calculations, from six to three places, widely divergent trajectories arose rapidly in his predictions from reality. Such observed complexity has led to the term "chaos" being applied, implying prediction of the future is impossible. Ian Stewart in his book *Does God Play Dice?*[1] takes a more optimistic view, observing that chaos and order, rather than being polar opposites, are in fact intertwined so that irregular behaviour is governed by a deterministic system. Such systems are not truly random and so for small parts of the complexity some order can be determined.

Fortunately not all macro-shocks fall into the category of being very difficult to predict. For instance, it is widely known that world oil resources are depleting rapidly and will cease to be a major energy source this century. This will be a huge shock to the way businesses operate and will require fundamental shifts in organizations' strategy. However, businesses are aware of this coming change and Honda and Toyota are already committing vast resources to R&D to produce alternative ways to power cars. The interconnectedness of these firms, as shown in figure 1.1, could result in major changes throughout the entire value chain, from supplier relationships to customer perceptions of what makes a good car. In this instance, some firms are clearly anticipating a macro-shock and are adjusting to compensate for a new reality.

Perceiving Macro-Shocks or Detecting the External Environment

Some car firms do not appear to be taking any substantial measures in anticipation of an impending oil crisis. This may in part be explained by individual firms' propensity for perceiving macro-shocks. As we shall see later in the book (chapter 9 Guiding Change), firms can be so bounded in their perceptions, often when they are at the peak of their success, that they fail to perceive, or through arrogance choose to ignore, changes and trends that do not fit their conception of how the world will be. Danny Miller has likened this situation to the Icarus Paradox, where the Greek boy, learning how to fly successfully with wings of feathers and wax made by his doting father, flew too close to the sun with disastrous consequences. As some of the subsequent cases show, firms that have successful strategies but which fail to adjust to a changing macro-context can suffer terrible damage and may even be doomed. One remembers IBM, once the most creditworthy institution on the planet, being brought to its knees by a major *technological* change – the rise of the desktop PC – which decimated the mainframe business. In the UK, Marks & Spencer was the greatest retailer in the nation's history and yet failed to perceive, or at least acknowledge, changing *social* tastes and fashions in the high street. Profits crashed, its share price plummeted, swathes of senior executives "left," and the firm was subjected to a takeover bid.

Other firms have invested significant resources in attempting to understand how the macro-environment may change. Royal Dutch/Shell is famous for its development of scenario planning techniques, and benefited from being able to anticipate the effects of the 1973 oil crisis by selling off its excess oil supplies before the worldwide glut in 1981. This raises the question: how should firms view the macro-environment?

> The environment is not a very mysterious concept. It means the surroundings of an organization; the climate in which the organization functions. The concept becomes challenging when we try to move from simple description of the environment to analysis of its properties.[2]

Ginter and Duncan's article, quoted above, provides a good example of R. J. Reynolds' activities in detecting the implications of the US Surgeon General's report on the harmful effects of smoking. Firms should engage continually in four activities:

1. **scanning** for warning signs, macro-changes, and trends that will affect the firm
2. **monitoring** for specific trends and patterns
3. **forecasting** to develop projections of anticipated outcomes of those trends
4. **assessing** to determine timing and effects of macro-changes on the firm

Analyzing Macro-Environmental Drivers

Which areas of the macro-environment should be scanned, monitored, forecasted, and assessed? For the purposes of strategic analysis, and under what might be termed the **outside-in** analytical framework, the complexity of interaction of

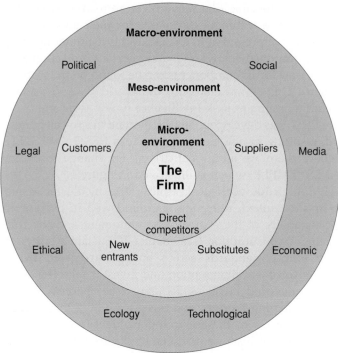

Figure 1.2 Conceptual decomposition of the business and its environment to structure strategic analysis

an organization with its external environment may be decomposed into macro influences, meso influences (firms and consumers influencing the industry) and micro influences (firms competing in the same industry as the focal firm). Competitive strategy embraces the micro and meso levels and is the bridge between the company and the environment in which it operates. The degree of influence of a large focal company is greatest at the centre of figure 1.2 – where decisions are made about the firm's strategies, resource policies, and configuration – and then declines outwards across successive boundaries. (The strength of this influence, or bargaining power, will vary by firm as discussed in chapter 5 Perfect Positioning.)

Adopting this outside-in approach is useful to avoid myopia, or seeing the world in the firm's own image. A common conceptual tool for embracing the macro-environment is **PEST analysis**, which stands for political, economic, social, and technological issues. The value of the technique is in identifying drivers for change in the broad context that could affect the firm's industry and the firm itself. PEST is a *process* technique as it makes explicit how forces in the macro-environment will change over time, rather than offering a snap-shot view – a criticism often directed at many other strategy frameworks. PEST's other advantage is as a handy acronym that helps strategists avoid *partial* coverage of a large macro-territory. Indeed it has been remarked that the worst failing of a strategist is not to see the whole picture, or the "elephant issue!" There can be a natural tendency for analysis to be skewed towards economic and financial issues, perhaps because they are more tractable (data may be more readily available and there are convenient tools and techniques available for their analysis) and there are significant institutional pressures to engage in this legitimating language. PEST and its derivatives (outlined below) offer an important protection against this bias. Good sources of data for its components can be found on the websites of the Economist Intelligence Unit (www.eiu.com), the World Bank (www.worldbank.org), and Business Environment Risk Intelligence (www.beri.com).

Since PEST was developed, other important macro-categories have been acknowledged, resulting in new acronyms such as PESTLE, PESTEL and STEEPLE. As we believe there are additional drivers for change to be considered, we have coined **ESTEMPLE**, which is illustrated in figure 1.3.

ESTEMPLE adds ecological, ethical, and media factors to our appreciation of the macro-context, reflecting a groundswell in current concerns regarding: the sustainability of the ecological environment and the role of the firm in its management/consumption (see chapter 10 Sustain Ability); the need to address different ethical standards across borders, triggered by stakeholder actions (such as government intervention and investor sell-offs), altering codes of practice, and influenced business decisions (see chapters 7, 8, and 10, Corporate Character, Crossing Borders, and Sustain Ability); the growing body of research that shows that the media are an independent force in influencing and shaping social opinion. For instance, national media are important in generating national solidarity and shaping perceptions of threat[3] when, for example, foreign firms launch hostile takeover bids. Through dramatizing risk to the loss of national resources, jobs, identities, and culture, national media are defining the nation and mobilizing response.[4] The importance of the media is evident when markets are moved and corporate policies and actions influenced contrary to the dictates of rational economics.

Planning For the Future

Clearly all these issues are present continuously in the macro-context, but the important question for the strategist is which ones will be relevant, how might these change over time, and which of these factors, or collection of factors, will drive change in the business context? The extent to which the strategist can make sense of all this data will be influenced by the turbulence of the context. This will determine the extent to which future environmental configuration(s) can be predicted and hence the ability of firms to anticipate effectively.

As shown in figure 1.4, the turbulence of the environment can be conceived in three dimensions[5] of:

1. **dynamism** (intensity and frequency of change)
2. **complexity** (number relatedness and diversity of factors)
3. **unpredictability** (cyclicality of change and clarity of data)

Clearly where an environment is highly dynamic, very complex, and unpredictable, attempting to anticipate and plan for specific change is largely a waste of time and resources. In these situations of considerable ambiguity, firms have to explore their

Drivers	Time
Economic	Health and direction of the economy(ies) in which the firm competes. Relevant variables: GDP levels, inflation, interest rates, money supply, unemployment, disposable income. Scan linked economies; monitor currency fluctuations and exchange rates.
Social	Demographic variables: population size, age structure, geographic distribution, ethnic mix, and income distribution. It also includes tastes, fashions, attitudes, and values. These are the cornerstone of society and often drive all the other macro-categories.
Technological	Primarily new products, processes, and materials. Includes the institutions and activities involved in creating new knowledge and translating it into new outputs, products, processes, and materials. Government support and initiatives can be very influential.
Ecological	Reflects concern for the sustainability of the physical environment. Issues include: greenhouse effect, CO_2 emissions, genetic engineering. Factors for consideration include environmental policies, waste disposal, and energy consumption.
Media	An increasingly important influence on business, politics, and society as opinion former and shaper. The media is affecting outcomes in ways unascribable to other macro-drivers.
Political	Issues: government stability, alignment at the international level, taxation and fiscal policies, foreign trade regulation, social welfare policies, attitudes towards competition and state ownership. All governments' policies are to further their own country's interests.
Legal	Factors include employment law, health and safety, product safety, monopolies and mergers legislation.
Ethical	Codes are rising in importance and affect the ways businesses operate internationally. They have directly affected the financial performance of many international businesses.

Figure 1.3   Conceptual decomposition of the macro-environment using ESTEMPLE

contexts, scan for weak signals, and indeed try to be active in creating the future. However, where sense can begin to be made of the environment, with patterns detected or several potential futures identified, firms can begin to anticipate and plan for the future. A technique for dealing with an alternate future, or a range of futures,[6] is **scenario planning**. This is the construction of detailed plausible

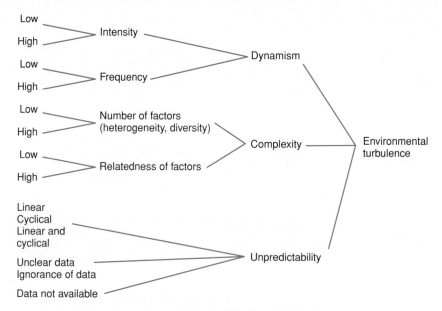

Figure 1.4 Dimensions of environmental turbulence (Source: Volberda (1998))

alternative views about the future based on groupings of key environmental drivers. Scenarios are *not predictive* but consider equally plausible futures that allow managers to explore a set of possibilities and increase their perceptiveness of the key forces at work in the environment. This can facilitate contingency planning. For Royal Dutch/Shell, scenario development had two goals: (1) a protective goal to enable the firm to anticipate and understand the risks involved in doing its business, and (2) an entrepreneurial goal to discover new strategic options. In creating "macrocosms" Royal Dutch/Shell used scenarios as a fundamental aid to changing mental models of future opportunities and risk.[7]

If the environment is more predictable in nature, or clear enough, then **forecasting** through extrapolation can allow a more precisely configured view of the future and more tightly specified planning. Here we may use an **impact matrix** to quantify the probability of an external shock happening and the extent to which it is likely to impact upon firm performance. Where environments are largely static, firms can plan for the future with confidence and rely on precedents to guide their decisions.[8]

In "Strategy under Uncertainty," published in *The Harvard Business Review* in 1997, Hugh Courtney, Jane Kirkland, and Patrick Viguerie show which strategy tools might be appropriate for different levels of environmental uncertainty (see table 1.1).

Scenarios in Practice

Of course, the techniques and tools described are not ends in themselves. They are planning tools to improve the quality of executive decision-making. Some techniques, such as single-point forecasting, lend themselves easily to integration

Table 1.1 Appropriate strategy tools

	Clear enough future	Alternate futures	A range of futures	True ambiguity
What can be known	A single forecast precise enough for determining strategy	A few discrete outcomes that define the future	A range of possible outcomes but no natural scenarios	No basis to forecast the future
Analytic tools	Traditional strategy tool kit	Decision analysis; Option valuation models; Game theory; Scenario planning	Latent demand research; Technology forecasting; Scenario planning	Analogies and pattern recognition; Nonlinear dynamic models

Adapted from Courtney, Kirkland, and Viguerie (1997)

with central planning. However, managers are apt to be confused with the multi-point forecasting of scenarios, complaining that three or four forecasts are less helpful than one. This is to misunderstand the purpose of scenarios: full-blown strategies should not be developed for each scenario and then each tested against the other by some financial means such as DCF to see which scenario is the best (even if a management team were willing to do this, which is highly unlikely). The temptation should also be resisted of assigning probabilities to scenarios as this is more the preserve of forecasting and would negate the exercise. The aim is to develop a strategy within the framework of alternative futures provided by the scenarios. The strategy can then be tested against the scenarios for its resilience and management can be forewarned of possible vulnerabilities.[9] Ian Wilson, in his article "From Scenario Thinking to Strategic Action" published in *Technological Forecasting and Social Change* (2000), highlights how scenarios can be used to strengthen strategy formation and suggests four levels of sophistication from sensitivity/risk assessment for a specific strategic decision to the development of a strategy resilient to a wide range of business conditions. A fuller treatment of scenario development is contained in Van der Heijden's (1996) classic work, *Scenarios: The Art of Strategic Conversation*, published by Wiley.

The Flexible Firm and Fitting With the Environment

We are told that the world is becoming an increasingly turbulent place and that the ability of firms to respond is determined by whether they have rigid or flexible organizational forms and prevailing social structures. Rigidity is often the result of the drive for efficiencies in complex operations in stable environments whereas flexibility and the ability to respond to change are more characteristic of organizations in emerging new industries. The real challenge is where macro-forces demand change and yet the firm is structurally rigid and therefore resistant to alteration.[10] These structural rigidities impede change and cause **strategic drift**,[11] where the firm begins to fall out of alignment with the changing business context. One of the most heavily used tools to assess this matching of the firm to its environment is **SWOT analysis**, in which a firm's *internal* strengths and weaknesses are explicitly matched against *external* opportunities and threats. In revealing mismatches between the firm and its environment, strategic options can be generated to enhance the **fitness** of the firm.

SWOT analysis does not discriminate between different layers of the external environment and so includes meso and micro levels, which we shall cover later in the book. It is critical to remember that SWOT is not just about generating lists of factors, as the analysis only has value if there is an explicit comparison, or **fitting**, of strengths against opportunities and threats and weaknesses against opportunities and threats. While many students and practitioners may well use SWOT as a starting place for their analysis, the technique has many weaknesses used in this way, not least the issue of how strengths and weaknesses are actually determined. For instance, are the strengths identified strengths in relation to other internal factors or those of competitors? Our preference is to use the technique only as the culmination of other more focused analysis.

Underlying much of the discussion so far about the firm changing in response to/anticipation of macro-shocks is the notion of **fit**, or fitness of strategy. Much of the writing on firm strategy is the extent to which the firm "fits" with the context (c.f. strategic gap analysis), or whether its "fit" will improve or deteriorate over time. This external consonance is important on the basis that misalignment will lead to firm underperformance. For organizational ecologists, firms cannot change easily because of structural rigidities and organizational routines (of which more later) and so lack fit with the environment, which will lead to failure through liquidation or acquisition. Some companies, however, can and do change. Nokia of Finland, for instance, started life as a timber company, moved into white goods manufacturing, and latterly has been hugely successful in mobile phones. However, such change is difficult, often requiring substantial changes in competencies. To some extent the issue is whether the gradual change of a company – or "logical incrementalism"[12] – is fast enough to accommodate step changes in the environment or macro-shocks. Such "punctuated equilibrium"[13] may force radical and comprehensive change in the company or its demise.

One of the most influential business books of the last decade is *Competing for the Future* by Gary Hamel and C. K. Prahalad. They argue that too many companies focus on competing in the present and do not devote enough time to creating the future. They argue that firms need to go beyond the static analysis of *fitting* their environment and instead should *stretch* and *leverage* their resources to redefine both the company and its context. For them, the key is not to anticipate the future but to create it. This suggests a philosophical shift from a more deterministic viewpoint, in which the macro-environment determines the success or failure of organizations, to an individualist view where managers can make a difference and can influence and shape the future context. For Gary Hamel: "The company that is evolving slowly is already on its way to extinction."[14] His solution is that revolution must be met with revolution. This discontinuous renewal perspective echoes Michael Hammer's "Reengineering Work: Don't Automate, Obliterate," which advocates that managers should take bold steps and dare to accept high risk. It is an all-or-nothing proposition with an uncertain result. In contrast, Masaaki Imai's famous book, *Kaizen: The Key to Japan's Competitive Success*, argues that continuous improvement best explains the competitive strength of so many of Japan's companies. This view stresses the importance of evolution and learning. For Imai, Western companies have an unhealthy obsession with one-shot solutions and revolutionary change. We can see that views on what constitutes "good" strategy, and consequently how one should view and relate to the macro-context, are fiercely debated. The aim of this book is to enable readers to make their own informed choices.

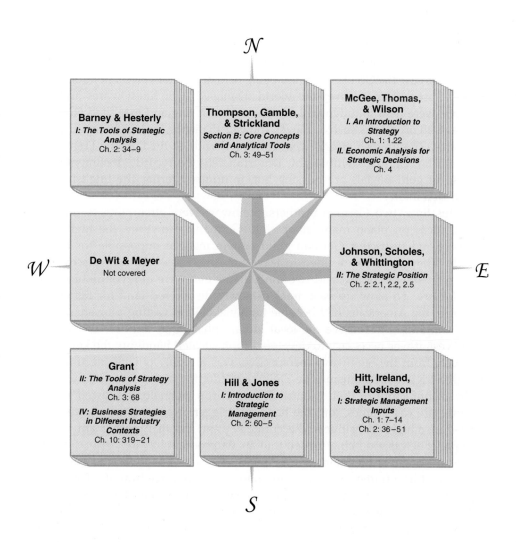

Ironclads versus canoes

In 1843, Broadwoods, England, was the greatest instrument manufacturer in the world. Admired for its association with the great composers, such as Ludwig van Beethoven, it had a highly skilled workforce and a reputation for producing the finest of pianos. But by 2000, Broadwoods was just a shell company, outsourcing all piano production to Asia and licensing piano tuners for instrument maintenance. What had gone wrong for this world-class firm?

In 1851 there was a census, which showed that Broadwoods was one of just 12 factories in London, employing over 300 people. These craftsmen fashioned and adjusted by hand all the 3,800 pieces that went into making a Broadwoods piano. The instrument consisted of a wooden frame strengthened by sophisticated wooden braces and some metal tension bars. This allowed the piano frame to take up to 16 tons of force from its strings, of which there was one per note. The firm produced around 2,500 pianos per year, which was 15% of total English production. Broadwoods' own output was 2.5 times greater than its nearest rival.

1851 also saw the Great Exhibition being held at Crystal Palace, London, where manufacturers from all over the world displayed their finest wares and competitions were held to judge which were superior. England exhibited 66 pianos, France, with producers such as Pleyel, showed 45 pianos, and Germany displayed 26 pianos. The English efforts were rewarded with 12 medals, the French with nine and the Germans with eight. Unfortunately the records documenting the number of gold medals are missing but, in numeric terms, the English pianos appear dominant.

At this time, two German brothers, Steinway, were attempting to introduce radical ideas on piano manufacture into Germany. However, the highly conservative and restrictive German guild system made it impossible for them to operate. They therefore decided to leave for America where they discovered a more sympathetic context and two innovations that were to revolutionize piano manufacture. To plow up vast areas of newly discovered land for agricultural purposes, the Americans had become highly skilled in casting plowshares from iron. In addition, to remove the local Indian inhabitants, and to survive in the Wild West, it was necessary to develop a sophisticated handgun, the key feature of which, from the Steinways' perspective, was a highly reliable, accurate, and sensitive trigger mechanism. The Steinways adopted both of these innovations in the manufacture of their pianos. The cast iron technology allowed them to manufacture cast frames, and the handgun trigger arrangements allowed them to produce a highly sensitive and accurate key and hammer mechanism – a good example of a weapon being turned into an art product!

The advantage of the Steinways' "American system," as it became called, was that the cast iron frame could tolerate up to 30 tons of force from its strings. This allowed the use of much heavier strings, which could generate a far more powerful and richer tone as well as more compact pianos. This was particularly important for upright pianos, which, up until this time, had really been grand pianos on their side. The new hammer mechanism gave greater sensitivity to the pianist and its precise vertical movement greatly reduced the clatter of key mechanisms associated with pianos of that era. Overall these innovations also allowed cost savings of some 30%.

The next big piano exhibition was again in London in 1862. Although the jury was accustomed to pre-Steinway sounds, two gold medals were awarded to Steinway pianos, one gold medal to a copy of a Steinway, and one to a Broadwoods as a *souvenir des travaux passes*. Nevertheless, the leading industry paper at the time, the *London Musical Standard*, wrote: "We [meaning the English piano industry] have no reason to dread competition in the manufacture of music instruments."

In 1873 the tables were completely turned on the English at the next big exhibition, which was staged in Vienna. England exhibited 12 instruments, France 34, and Germany 129. The Steinways' American system was now adopted by all successful European firms and its dominance was epitomized in an advertisement at the time "as a MODERN IRONCLAD WARSHIP to a CANOE." In 1878 at another exhibition there was a modest square piano, which was barely noticed. It came from Japan and its makers were Yamaha.

A reasonable indicator of Broadwoods' performance in overseas markets can be seen in Australian import figures for English pianos from 1862 to 1902, among which Broadwoods was the most prominent manufacturer. In 1862, Australia imported 100 pianos from England and just five from Germany. By 1886, imports from each country were running at similar levels of 230 per year. However, by 1902 over 500 pianos were being imported from Germany alone, compared with just 35 from England.

At this time, the managers of Broadwoods were described as "sleepers" not "thrusters," and "gentlemen" rather than "players." When one director died in 1881, he left a huge fortune of £424,000 and his obituary declared: "He took no share in the active portion of the business but was, however, an enthusiastic yachtsman." A new board member, appointed in 1890, was educated at Cambridge University and Eton College. He was a keen farmer, oarsman, and swimmer – "few could equal him at plunging." He travelled extensively, "shot his tiger," but apparently visited no piano factories.

---

1. *Using an ESTEMPLE analysis, identify the macro-environmental drivers for change in the piano industry.*
2. *Construct an impact matrix to show how these changes affected Broadwoods and its main competitor, Steinway.*

◄ ◄ ◄ Ironclads versus canoes: Some Ideas . . .

The ironclad versus canoes case shows the calamitous decline of the once world-beating firm of Broadwoods. As such it resonates with other major collapses in corporate history, such as the fall of IBM, Marks & Spencer, and Rover Cars. The way in which the ironclad victory case can be analyzed is transferable to these other disasters.

1. Using an ESTEMPLE analysis, identify the macro-environmental drivers for change in the piano industry.

In assessing Broadwoods' evolution over time, we detect a slow but sustained drift away from its previously strong environmental fit. An **ESTEMPLE** analysis shows substantial changes in the macro-environment. Changes in **technology** in the agriculture and military industries began to be adopted in the piano industry, radically altering the way in which the piano was constructed. It was now possible to produce pianos with enhanced abilities at lower cost. The **social** context was also propitious. The Steinways found American society to be far more tolerant of their ideas than the German craft system. Their "American system," with its greater volume and richer tone suited music being composed at the time, which relied increasingly on the rich sonorities of the instrument in complex harmonies and its percussive sounds. It is instructive that this new type of "romantic" music, pioneered by Beethoven some 50 years earlier, had now moved beyond the abilities of contemporary instruments, which he regarded as inadequate and lacking in powerful tone. Customers were also becoming more demanding, wanting more product for their money. Interestingly one might argue that the **media** in the case are more backward- than forward-looking, and worked toward preserving the status quo and the maintenance of Broadwoods' reputation. It is possible that in this time of a weakening British Empire, there was some patriotism behind these sentiments. **Politically** and **economically**, the decline of the Empire at the turn of the century might be seen as a contributory factor in the decline in Broadwoods' export sales.

Against this shifting macro-context, Broadwoods had barely changed its structure, competitive model, or product. Indeed, it was very late in introducing a cast iron frame, as well as over-stringing, long after it had become commonplace in the industry. Broadwoods hardly invested in R&D and relied heavily on its superior craft skills. Its management was passive rather than active, more interested in external unrelated activities, and not sensitive to a changing context. In this sense Broadwoods displays sustained **strategic drift**.

Broadwoods' problem was that its original competitive advantage – a wide range of products with a very highly skilled labor content – had become a **core rigidity**. The new manufacturing methods and procedures introduced by Steinway struck at the very heart of the Broadwoods model and undermined the value of their cherished assets. To move towards the Steinway system would have necessitated the removal of large amounts of skilled labor and the reduction in importance of many who remained in the company.

2. Construct an impact matrix to show how these changes affected Broadwoods and its main competitor, Steinway.

A simple **impact matrix** (see figure 1-1.1) shows the ways in which Broadwoods and Steinway were affected by macro-shocks.

Another useful way of conceiving of Broadwoods' situation is in a model of industry evolution (see figure 1-1.2). Here we can see that Broadwoods stalled in a game of diminishing returns over product evolution, whereas Steinway had pushed forwards into improving the manufacturing process, which was being copied by competitors.

Key macro-influences	Broadwoods	Steinway
Innovations in technology – iron frame – heavier strings – superior key action	Low investment in R&D ––	High investment in R&D and willingness to experiment ++
Convergence of customer requirements	Many diverse products ––	Central product planning ++
Customers want more value for money	High labor costs ––	Beginnings of automation ++
European establishment norms – UK music press favored Broadwoods – Establishment used to "Broadwoods sound"	Technicians well respected Links with great composers ++	Up-starts ––
Political/Social – Decay of the British Empire	Contracting markets –	Opportunity +
Total	–5	+5

Figure 1-1.1   Impact matrix

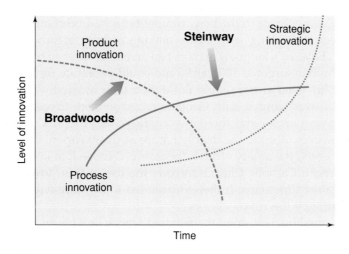

Figure 1-1.2   Industry evolution

Shock and awe

The French mounted knight had dominated the battlefields of Europe for centuries. His heavy armor, powerful weapons, and maneuverability made him virtually invincible and capable of wrecking the organization of opponents, ripping holes in enemy lines and intimidating advances. His military power was echoed in the economic and political power of a French elite knightly class that had developed an elaborate code of chivalry and military conduct.

In 1346, however, King Edward III of England was conducting a successful campaign through Normandy where he had met little resistance. In moving his 8,000 men northwards to link up with Flemish allies, he was suddenly confronted by a far larger French army at Crécy.

Edward arranged his forces around a hilltop from which he could observe the lay of the land. With his rear protected by forest and high ground, the enemy would try a frontal attack across open fields. To repulse the assault, Edward placed his yeoman archers to the fore. The English had learnt just how effective archers' bows could be from bitter experiences in their border conflicts with the Welsh and Scottish. The English had begun to put this learning to good use by diverting a good portion of their increased wealth garnered from subduing their Celtic neighbours toward the development of technology such as the longbow. To encourage competence in the bow, competitions had been introduced around the English counties along with edicts making archery a compulsory activity. Subsequently, Edward's longbow archers had an effective range of 300 yards, were able to hit a human target at 100 yards, and could penetrate three inches of oak. With a direct hit, even armor would not deflect their arrows.

French lines were fronted with Genoese crossbowmen. Crossbow bolts could pierce the heaviest armor and these mercenaries could fire at a rate of two bolts a minute. However, despite the deadly nature of this weapon, the French nobility bitterly resented the ability of such "peasantry." Indeed, in keeping with these beliefs, the French Catholic Church forbade the use of this "lowly" weapon by Christians against Christians. It therefore tended to be marginalized and under-utilized in battle by the ruling classes.

Behind the crossbowmen stood the armored French knights on heavy warhorses supported by footmen. However, at Crécy, the narrow road to the battlefield was heavily congested. Supply carts and necessary equipment could not get through to serve the lines ahead.

The Genoese were the first to fire, but their volley fell short. Before they could reload and advance, the English let loose barrage after barrage of arrows. The Genoese, normally protected by large wooden shields, were vulnerable as most of their shields were still in the supply carts. Hundreds were killed, defenceless against the hail of arrows.

A wave of French knights then charged over the Genoese ramparts, aiming to crash through the English line and break their formation. But they too were engulfed in lethal English arrows. Although the rounded surfaces on the French armor deflected the deadly tips, flat surfaces, chain mail, and open helmets did not, and the horses, being much less well protected, fell with their riders. Once grounded, the French knights were virtually defenceless against the English footmen who slaughtered them with axes and daggers.

The French made repeated assaults, but by the end of the day it was said that 16,000 Frenchmen had perished to England's 300. The scale of the defeat was such that nearly every noble family in France was affected directly.

The new technology of the massed English archers had changed the landscape of war. However, the French responded to this blow to their pride and chivalry by investing further in armor. Chain mail was replaced by armor plate and warhorses also had armor plate covering vital areas. The plates became thicker and helmets had visors added. While their operational elements were reinforced, France's strategic approach to warfare remained unchanged.

Almost 70 years later, in October 1415, Henry V led the English on another campaign in France. After capturing Harfleur and proceeding towards Calais, dwindling supplies, poor weather, and casualties weakened Henry's army. Large numbers of French knights began to converge on Henry's position, detecting the weakening condition of their foe. At Agincourt the French army was four times the size of the English force and now blocked their path. Henry was forced to fight.

The French were supremely confident of defeating the English through their superior numbers, the weakened condition of the English, and the superb quality of their knights. Their commander, who was not of noble birth, intended to send foot soldiers into battle first and then carry out a flanking maneuver with the knights to destroy the English archers. However, Henry assembled his army on plow land made muddy by recent rain and placed his archers in the narrowest part of the battlefield, where sharpened stakes were set in the ground with bowmen and men at arms arranged amongst them so they could crouch, "hedgehog-like," upon an assault by the French. This maneuver prevented the French from outflanking the English archers, as either side of them was thick forest, and forced a frontal assault across muddy fields.

To intimidate the English archers, the French promised to cut both of their bow fingers off to prevent them from ever drawing a bow again. The English archers now taunted the French by waving those two fingers in the air. This show of defiance so enraged the French knights, vastly superior in number, that they charged across the muddy field without their commander's approval. Hail after hail of English arrows followed and, as before, knights and horses were cut down. The huge numbers of knights also meant that those behind continued to press forward, preventing those in front from maneuvering, crushing those that had fallen, and impaling others on the English stakes: "so great was the undisciplined violence and pressure [of the second French line] that the living fell on top of the dead." In this carnage the English men at arms then came forward to finish off the floundering French knights. The French losses were again immense, with an estimated 6,000 dead in the first 90 minutes of battle. In total the English lost just 150 men.

Despite these huge defeats, French nobles continued to patronize the armorers of Europe for a further 130 years. The incremental changes to armor only made the knights slightly less vulnerable to arrows, while making them slower, less maneuverable, and thus easier targets. Indeed, the French investment in armor continued well beyond the point when firearms made it totally obsolete.

1. *Why did the French lose at Crécy?*
2. *Why did the French lose at Agincourt?*
3. *What can we conclude about how the French approach to battle changed over this time period?*
4. *What can we learn about differing views shown in this case on what is strategy?*

Flower power

You're about to land at Amsterdam's Schiphol airport. As you survey the flat Dutch landscape below, your eye catches sight of what seems like row upon row of low lying buildings, covering an area of what must be the equivalent of 100 football fields. If you have ever experienced this sight and wondered what was housed in those buildings, it is VBA – the Aalsmeer Flower Auction. Buy a bunch of flowers anywhere in the world, be it San Francisco, London, Singapore or Tokyo, and it is likely that they passed through VBA but a day or two before. In just a few short years VBA has virtually cornered the world's flower auction market. It has done so by matching technological developments, the social and geographical advantages of its location, and an acute sense of what its buyers want, to provide not only an efficient service, but also one that adds value to both growers and buyers alike. How does it work?

First, blooms from across Europe are sent to VBA to be auctioned. There, they are graded for quality, perfume, color, etc. and are placed in lots onto carts, somewhat similar to the golf carts that are familiar on many US or Japanese golf courses. The carts are guided into the auction rooms before hundreds of buyers sitting in a tiered horseshoe-shaped "theater." Each buyer has a console immediately in front of them, which they activate to make a bid. On the wall in front of all the buyers is a giant clock that is used to "count down" the price of each lot. (Remember that in a Dutch auction – we are in the Netherlands, after all – the price starts at a high point and is counted down.) It is the first bidder who purchases the lot – a very quick decision-making process.

Once the bid has been made, the carts are automatically dispatched to the buyer's loading bay and, while the auction continues, invoices are automatically prepared. In this way, once the auction is over, the buyers can settle their accounts and return to their loading bay to find all of their purchases already loaded for transport. Speed of transaction is of the essence, of course, since the blooms have a very short shelf life. And the Dutch auction system – and the IT employed by VBA – is particularly effective in this regard.

But there is more to the VBA service than mere efficiency. Information is provided to both growers and buyers alike. And it is this additional information that sets VBA's level of service apart from its competition. For example, the growers that supply the VBA are fed back information on demand trends so that they can bring on their blooms faster or slower to meet demand and get the best price. In turn, buyers can rely on getting what they want, when they want it. Moreover, buyers have come to rely on the VBA's provision of information on varying demand the world over and their expertise in grading the blooms has become something of a quality guarantee.

Thus, VBA not only provides an efficient auction service, it also provides added value services to its customers in the form of information – and this is enabled by the IT systems it has employed. While the IT systems can be readily and easily copied by the competition, the expertise and goodwill VBA has built up over the years means that it has been able to sustain its advantage.

1. *Using SWOT analysis, explain why VBA is successful.*
2. *What should VBA consider in thinking about its future strategy?*

Local actions, global response

Nike was founded in 1964 when Phil Knight put an MBA project he'd written into practice with Bill Bowerman, his former track coach at the University of Oregon. At a time when established companies were manufacturing sports shoes in high-wage economies, Knight's project had shown that decreasing transport costs would mean that higher margins could be gained by sourcing shoes from countries with low labor costs. Nike began by importing shoes from Japan. However, one morning Bowerman was standing in his kitchen and had an idea. He made an outsole by pouring a rubber compound into a waffle iron. The waffle trainer was born and Nike became a design company rather than just an importer.

Initially, Nike outsourced almost all of its production to plants in Japan. However, in the early 1970s, as costs there began to rise, it was switched to Taiwan and Korea. By 1982, only Nike's headquarters and design facility (or "campus" as it is called) were located in the USA. In 1999, Nike employed 13,000 people in the USA, while its 350 subcontractors employed nearly 500,000 in plants in China, Vietnam, and Indonesia.

Knight and Bowerman's personalities fired Nike's purpose: a love of athletics, an appreciation of the views of real athletes, and a relentless appetite for competition and striving for *number 1*. "Every time I tour people around [the Nike 'campus']," explains Geoff Hollister, who ran track with Knight at college, "I show them a picture of Phil Knight running behind Jim Grelle. Grelle was a champion and Knight never caught him – but he never stopped pursuing."

Knight's passion for athletic excellence attracted young and confident employees with a similar outlook. According to Nelson Farris, another of Knight's former track teammates: "We like employees who aren't afraid to tee it up." The campus culture was subsequently pervaded with an "athletistocracy" that placed athletic achievement through innovative design above everything else. An article in *The Sunday Times* recently claimed that the words "I work for Nike" seem to have the same appeal as "I work for NASA" did 30 years ago. Those on the Nike campus developed a particular pride in their work. Once part of the fraternity, they are famously devotional. Many have tattoos of Nike's trademark "swoosh" on their bodies.

Nike's values are powerfully expressed in their marketing. The swoosh – which ranks alongside McDonald's golden arches and Coca-Cola's red and white logo as being recognized by 97% of Americans – speaks of a no-nonsense emphasis on speed and performance. The Nike tag-line "Just Do It" (born in 1988 when an advertising executive told Nike staff that: "You Nike guys, you just do it") is the second most recognizable slogan in the US after the Marlboro Man.

In the words of one commentator, this devotion and recognition enabled Nike to "instill its products with a kind of holy superiority." And this "holiness" and the continued growth that ensued saw Nike go from strength to strength. Its share price rose 3,686% in the period from 1980 to 1997. Nike overtook Reebok to become market leader in sports shoes in 1988. In the three years to 1996 Nike more than doubled sales, moving from a 32% share of the market in 1994 to 45% in 1996. In the three years to 1997, the group tripled in size, with worldwide sales up to $9 billion and profits to $800 million.

After achieving number one status in sports footwear Nike pursued an increasing number of new initiatives. In 1992, Knight claimed that he wanted Nike to be not just the world's best athletic shoemaker but "the world's best sports and fitness company." In an interview in the *Harvard Business Review* that same year, Knight described a further transformation in Nike. "For years we thought of ourselves as a production-oriented company, meaning we put all our emphasis on designing and manufacturing the product. But we understand now that the most important thing we do is market the product. We've come around to saying that Nike is a marketing-oriented company." The new emphasis on marketing saw Nike seek to exploit and ram home the rebel image, with "Just Do It" supported with slogans like "You don't win second you lose first."

Nike moved into further pastures – including "redefining retailing" – with the launch of Nike Town stores (described as being "more like theme parks than shops"), and becoming more fashion conscious in its product design. The initial response, from journalists, at publications like *Vogue* at least, was positive. Moreover, Nike set out to "redefine and expand the world of sports entertainment" with a joint venture with a Hollywood talent agency. The aim here was to package up events in which Nike endorsers like Charles Barkley and Michael Jordan were involved and then sell this on to sponsors and media companies. Nike's director of advertising outlined the potential: "Forget the business Nike's in at the moment. This is going to boom across the map, and massive amounts of money can be made." By 1996, Nike was increasingly slapping its swoosh on everything from sunglasses to footballs to batting gloves and hockey sticks, with Nike's VP of corporate communications proclaiming that "We are not a shoe company." Phil Knight's stated objective for Nike in 1996's annual report was the " 'Swooshification' of the world."

However, 1997 saw a decline in Nike's fortunes. Analysts predicted that Nike's share of the world athletic market would drop from 47% in 1997 to 40%; correspondingly, profits had fallen by 69% at the end of 1997. The share price, which stood at $72 at the beginning of 1994, hit $30 in August 1998. Standard & Poors subsequently downgraded its outlook on Nike from "stable" to "negative." The normally gung-ho Knight admitted to *Advertising Age* in 1998 that: "Everything we have tried over the past six months simply has not worked." What happened?

In the ever-fickle fashion stakes, even Nike's own people admitted that "we're just not cool any more." Marketing guru Peter York claims that "Nike [knows that they are] not what matters at the moment," and that this recognition has led to there being: ". . . an air of desperation about them now. They're doing too many special runs and limited editions, trying too hard to keep their cool. They've had brilliant brand marketing, but their brand stretches are unproven."

Even more problematic, however, were the protest groups and media investigations focusing on alleged abuses at Nike's foreign factories. The allegations made included employing children sold to the factories by brokers; poor air quality caused by petroleum-based solvents leading to breathing problems in some factories; paying well under the minimum wage; and the lack of sick pay and compensation, even for industrial injuries. Internet sites with names like www.boycottnike and www.nike-sucks fueled the anti-Nike feeling that these allegations generated.

While Nike was actually doing little that was different from other sportswear companies, Medea Benjamin, director of *Global Watch,* admitted that Nike was targeted because it was "the biggest and it sets the trends. I wish we had the resources to look at Reebok, Adidas, and Converse, but we don't." Indeed, it was not just that Nike had become the biggest; it had also become the loudest. As Thomas Bivins, Professor of Public Relations at the University of Oregon, argued: "When a company goes out of its way to create an image [like Nike's], it is going to be a big target."

Nike responded as if they were mounting a legal defense. They sought to distance themselves from the factories, claiming that what their contractors did was none of their business. After this failed to wash, Nike's PR spokesperson declared that: "In a country where the population is increasing by 2.5 million a year, with 40% unemployment, it is better to work in a shoe factory than not have a job." But the public response just got worse.

In January 1997, Andrew Young, former US ambassador to the UN, visited Nike plants in Vietnam, Indonesia, and China and declared that they were "as clean and modern" as any in the USA. However, the big news story turned out to be the discovery that Nike paid for his trip and that he was shepherded by Nike people and only introduced to appropriately briefed staff. In Britain, the magazine *The Big Issue* begged readers to boycott Nike. Even Nike's move into soccer was subjected to negative scrutiny. After Brazil's defeat by France in the 1998 World Cup, many believed that Nike had bullied Brazil's coach into playing another Nike endorser, Ronaldo, even though he was obviously unfit. Newspaper articles drew links between Nike and Nike endorser Mike Tyson and declared "Nike is one bad dude."

Phil Knight originally refused to comment on the protests, then denied all charges of slave labor, then branded his accusers "activists." However, 1998 marked what *The Financial Times* called "a stunning reversal." Knight came out and personally responded to the criticisms. He explained that: "Basically, our culture, and our style, is to be a rebel, and we sort of enjoy doing that." However, he conceded that "Now that we've reached a certain size, there's a fine line between being a rebel and being a bully, and yeah, we have to walk that line." In May of 1998, Knight unveiled a plan to improve the conditions of 350,000 Nike workers in Asia. Nike would sever ties with contractors because of "unacceptable working conditions"; increase wages by up to 40% for individuals in entry-level footwear manufacturing jobs; improve air quality by switching to water-based rather than petroleum-based adhesives; and increase its minimum working age to 18. And it set up www.nikeworker.com, where people could find information about Nike's production practices. The *Transnational Resource and Action Center*, one of Nike's most vocal critics, subsequently stated that relations with Nike were greatly improved, while the third annual "Protest Nike day" scheduled for the end of 1998 failed to draw any protesters.

However, Nike did not stop there. In 1998 Knight explained that Nike would undergo a total "holistic reorganization." Nike spokespeople admitted that the company had made poor decisions in every area. Tom Clarke, Nike's Chief Operating Officer, confessed "We'd gotten stale on design." Nelson Farris, a Nike employee for 25 years, admitted that "I've been to Chinese-run factories and though we improved upon that, it obviously wasn't good enough. Now we're looking at how we run our company. Are we making the right product? Is our service, our advertising, good enough? Are we good enough people?" The bad publicity had certainly had an impact on the mood of Nike's employees. Farris continued, "It has demoralized a lot of people. We haven't been as on top of things as we'd perhaps have liked. We've got to learn to do business much better." Suddenly, the company whose strength of purpose meant that it seldom stopped to question anything was pondering everything.

One result of this pondering was an attempt to soften Nike's image by watering down "Just Do It" to the new catchphrase "I Can" in the US in 1998. "At a time when cynicism in sports is at an all time high, 'I Can' is an effort to return to a focus on the positive," said Bob Wood, Nike's marketing VP. The *Financial Times* announced that with the "unveiling of the new softer 'I Can' slogan to replace 'Just Do It', Nike may be about to take a [huge] step." However, some industry watchers were not so convinced and many customers seemed confused by the change of tack and what Nike now stood for.

---

1. *How do you account for Nike's tremendous success?*
2. *Using ESTEMPLE, explain why Nike suffered a severe decline in 1997.*
3. *Can Nike repeat its earlier successful strategy?*

Slipping or skidding?

In the 1950s, the Rover Car Company was a highly successful small firm operating in a niche. After World War II, demand had been increasing steadily as disposable incomes and social expectations had risen. It was a time of post-war patriotism, and Rover's conservatively styled cars, built in Britain, had wide appeal. Many cars were also exported.

Rover P4 saloons were conservatively styled and appealed to the professional classes, such as doctors and solicitors. The cars had sumptuous interiors with handmade leather seats and polished wood fascia. The company also led the way in technological developments, such as with the creation of a gas turbine car. Design innovations added to the firm's reputation for quality, with its new models being perceived as cutting edge. The Rover 2000, launched in the 1960s, was a radical new design and a huge hit with customers.

While the car market continued to grow during the 1960s, Rover found itself unable to meet demand, quoting waiting times of up to 3 years. At the same time there was a considerable rise in car imports from the continent so that, by the 1970s, one in seven cars sold in Britain was a continental car. The firm recognized the need for greater scale economies and invested in machinery to improve efficiency and reduce the need for, and costs of, skilled labor. To operate these machines, large numbers of unskilled workers were hired.

While technology was being widely adopted by major car manufacturers, at Rover, skilled workers argued that the machines didn't really replace them. For instance, although a highly sophisticated and very expensive computer controlled paint shop was installed, skilled workers argued that they were still needed to deal with parts of the paintwork not covered adequately by the automated process. Workers were also paid for each task they undertook. Every time a new machine was installed, wages had to be renegotiated.

At this time, trade union power in Rover, and across the UK, was very high. The unions in Rover were very militant and there was real suspicion that this militancy was encouraged by communists attempting to destabilize the capitalist system. The number of strikes reached epidemic proportions with as many as 100 per year. The strikes also seemed to be called over the most inconsequential of issues.

Top management recognized that Rover's profits were not rising as quickly as the cost of developing new cars. The rising costs of new technology were a growing burden and R&D was increasingly expensive. Despite the introduction of greater automation, frequent strikes meant the company was still producing far too few cars. At this time the view became established that Rover was too small to compete worldwide. The Government therefore backed a series of mergers between many of Britain's car companies to form British Leyland (BL).

In 1973, oil prices surged upwards causing a slump in demand for new vehicles. This forced BL into the red. The Government took the view that the UK car industry, predominantly BL, had to be preserved. In 1975, the Government took a stake in its ownership and poured £1.4bn into the company. The most modern car factory in Europe was built to produce 3,000 cars per week, but only managed 1,500 because of outdated working practices. At this time BL was losing £1m per day. At the same time, cars imported from Japan were finding ready buyers in the UK market, where reliability was valued.

To stem the bleeding, Sir Michael Edwardes was appointed to turn BL around. His recommendation was to reduce the size of the company and to get rid of the union activists, Red Robbo (the factory union leader) in particular. Although he knew this would meet with fierce union resistance, Sir Michael believed that the workers were fed up with incessant strikes. He decided to go around the unions and ballot the workers directly about the need for mass redundancies. Although close, Sir Michael won. Red Robbo departed, mass redundancies took place, and union power was reduced substantially. However, despite the cuts, BL still had insufficient funds to invest to produce cars of a similar quality to the Japanese imports.

To address Rover's main weaknesses of poor mass production, poor technology, and a lack of capital for investment, an alliance was formed with Honda. From Honda's perspective, Rover offered good distribution and a design competence for the UK and European markets. The first joint product was the Rover 800, which turned out to be the most successful car since the 1960s. It had Rover styling but contained Honda engines and gearboxes. At the same time, however, there were mass resignations of Rover's engineers who felt that they were now being overlooked. Rover's engineering centre was subsequently put up for sale.

Now that BL had regained profitability, the UK Government tried to sell the company but there were no offers from other car companies. Eventually British Aerospace bought the firm, although it was widely suspected that this was a political deal and not one focused on developing BL for the future. Shortly afterwards, Rover was purchased by BMW who invested huge sums in new product development and the introduction of German practices. Honda immediately withdrew from the alliance and viewed the sale as a breach of trust.

While BMW poured in billions into creating new car designs to complement its own range, such as Land Rover Defender, a new Mini, and new 45 and 75 models, it encountered huge problems at the massive manufacturing facility at Longbridge. Despite sending in hundreds of BMW engineers from Germany, the problems remained. There were also intractable difficulties in dealing with the myriad suppliers who resisted change. BMW's losses were so significant that the parent company was being harmed by "the English Patient" and made strategically vulnerable to takeover itself. There were rumors that Ford was even in talks with BMW's owners. Facing sustained losses of £500m per year, BMW sold Rover to a management buyout team, although they kept the Mini and 4×4 production lines.

---

1. *Why was Rover successful in the 1950s?*
2. *What macro-environmental factors drove change in the car industry post-1950s?*
3. *Why did Rover decline?*
4. *In what ways was the alliance with Honda beneficial to both companies?*
5. *Why did BMW buy Rover?*

Thinking the future . . .

Scenario planning in commercial organizations is usually argued to originate with the work of Shell strategists (under the tutelage of Pierre Wack) who took the then unusual step of looking forward and imagining how things might be very different in the industry in decades to come. The argument is that such a technique enabled Shell to foresee (in the 1960s), and consequently prepare for, the possibility of a severe price increase in crude oil coupled with shortages of supply resulting from the Asian crisis (in the early 1990s). Shell was able to weather this generally unanticipated crisis better than their competitors because they had designed a contingent strategy to deal with such eventualities. The competition had not.

Scenario development is an integral part of scenario planning. Whereas scenario planning focuses on imagining a series of multiple futures to which contingent strategies are then attached, scenario development is more about the process of imagining how different (and in which ways) the future might be.

One way of thinking about this is to view scenario development as addressing degrees of uncertainty that organizations face and grouping different scenarios according to particular degrees of uncertainty. For example, there are uncertainties that are *fairly certain* (within prescribed limits). Demographic trends fall into this category. We can predict with some certainty the number of people in various age bands that will populate the world 20 or more years hence, other factors being equal. Then, there is a second category of uncertainties that are much *more uncertain*. The effects of wars or terrorist activity on trade systems, or the difficulties in assessing the probability of links between variables (such as the relative wealth of countries that adopt the euro) are examples. Thirdly, and for philosophical purposes in the main, there are those uncertainties that take a great leap of thinking to even begin to comprehend. These are *completely new possibilities*, such as social and technological revolutions, that cannot be linked to present realities. For example, Shell's scenarios of price rises and oil shortages fall into the second category, but you should be able to develop other scenarios that might affect the oil industry that would fall into the first or third categories.

In practice, it is useful for companies to sharpen their scenario planning by developing scenarios in all three categories. However, work with managers from all sectors and from a variety of manufacturing and service industries reveals that managers are generally very conservative. The evidence we have collected suggests that they tend to proceed on the basis of first constructing relatively fixed parameters and then working on a number of scenarios. This results in scenarios that fall neatly into the first two categories (and most often into the first). For example, they often assume relative constancy in what their organization does and the structures and processes it has in place to achieve this. They then, typically, will develop a scenario in which existing processes are replaced by more technologically advanced solutions. Communications and interactions via web-based technologies and so-called e-business solutions are often typical of this "fairly certain" incremental change rather than radical thinking. Also typical is a view that strives to increase the efficient exploitation of new inventions, technologies, and organizational environments. Efficiency is defined from the present state of the organization and new technologies (for example) are to be imported as they emerge.

But, asking the same questions of people not already embedded in such organizational contexts and processes elicits quite different responses. For example, after 3 years of developing scenarios with groups of creative and media studies Masters students, it has become clear to us that they come up with much more creative scenarios – if we measure creativity as an ability to see further, deeper, and without an embedded set of values or paradigms, into possibilities that the mainstream could begin to comprehend.

Consistently, these students (who, in the main, run their own businesses in various media activities) began their scenario development by abandoning the notion that their current organization was inherently adaptable to future changes, or was necessary in its current form. Here was a key difference. Managers in traditional organizations relied heavily on *adaptability* – where specific changes in the environment elicit changes in the organization, however inefficiently. The media students rarely pictured the future this way, preferring instead to abandon any fixed points. They talked in terms of temporary, *easily disposable* organizations that, rather like butterflies, shine for a short moment, are successful, and then are gone. There is no set notion here of long-term survival and adaptability.

They were also not as constrained as managers in traditional industries by sticking to the same line of business. A magazine publisher, for example, could become a music distributor and a theater company could dissemble and reform as a consultancy. A key theme in developing scenarios was not just the extent and scale of the projected changes their organizations would likely face, but was also the transferability of knowledge and skills learned in one organization to a totally different set of circumstances. Media students had fewer problems in starting from the idea that total cessation of current activities was a distinct possibility, and subsequently generated much "wilder" scenarios (such as abandoning planet Earth and creating a music business in some other uninhabited space).

There may be a fine line between lunacy and genius but it is nevertheless true that the impact and influence of different ways of thinking about the future will be enormous on current organizational activities and processes. These differences are worth debating and exploring, since the dominance of one over the other will certainly affect the way we live in the future, the values to which we adhere, and the strategy we do or do not follow.

1. *When might scenarios be of use to managers?*
2. *Why were the creative and media students more adept at generating scenarios than other managers?*
3. *Why should the disposability of the firm affect one's views of scenarios?*
4. *Are scenarios a way of "remembering the future"?*

Olympics, SARS, and the Government

For every World Cup football tournament, Expo, or Olympics that can generate millions of new passengers for an airline industry, there is a SARS outbreak or an act of terrorism that can bring it to its knees. These macro-shocks provide massive opportunities as well as threats to companies that have freedom to anticipate and respond.

The domestic airline industry in China had previously been purely reactive to changes in its environment, largely because of the dominating effect of Government influence through CAAC (Civil Aviation Authority of China) regulations. However, huge changes were taking place in Government policy as well as across the country as a whole, with rapid deregulation and increasing engagement with the forces of globalization. Senior executives in the industry realized that if the trend toward deregulation continued, they would need to move from being purely reactive towards anticipating macro-shocks and being prepared to deal with these uncertainties. With China looking forward to hosting the Olympics in 2008 and World Expo in 2020, senior airline executives felt they should appraise their positions in the light of what the future might bring.

In 2001 CAAC controlled three large airlines based in Beijing, Shanghai, and Guangzhou. The eastern part of China is the most prosperous part of the county and accounts for the majority of domestic air routes. These three airlines control 80% of the total market. There are also some 30 registered commercial airlines, some based in the major eastern urban centres and assisted by provincial government aid but the majority are located further inland in new economic zones, providing connections to the coastal areas. The airlines are massively in debt, with estimates around RMB112bn and the gearing of individual businesses being around 80%. Recently two of the three CAAC airlines were listed and the third is set to follow. The Government remains the main shareholder, with 51%, but it is hoped greater foreign involvement will bring increased efficiency and greater fiscal responsibility. It is the perception of competitors that the CAAC hopes its three airlines will drive out or absorb local competition, although this is contrary to the spirit of deregulation and a reduction in Government influence. Earlier attempts at deregulation, by allowing price competition, caused significant damage to the CAAC controlled companies. Today's competitors are restricted to competing on price within a 40% range of the CAAC's published fare, although under-table discounts are known, and also by differentiation through flying to secondary cities.

By 2001, China's airline industry was carrying 60 million passengers and was sixth in the world by volume. It continues to grow at twice the global rate and will become the global leader by 2020.

In 2002, Hu Jin Tao was appointed Chairman and is widely expected to continue to build on the economic foundation laid by former leaders Deng and Jiang. The stated focus is to maintain the prosperity of the east while developing growth of the inland western provinces. This will be achieved by encouraging foreign investments to flow into central and western regions across a wider range of sectors than before, particularly the service sector. This seems to be in recognition that the costs of manufacturing in the eastern area are now higher than in countries such as Indonesia. The last two decades have seen substantial inflows of FDI and, by 2000, 1,330 regions were designated open to FDI. Most investment, however, have been in the eastern region, with Beijing receiving $1.97bn, Shanghai $2.83bn, and Guangdong $1.65bn. By comparison Xinjian, a territory one-sixth the size of the nation, received just $21.6m.

The Government is pushing the "Go West" policy to curb the migration of poor rural workers to the east. Large-scale infrastructure developments, such as the Xinjian natural gas pipeline, will help create many jobs. At the moment, most of China's more than one billion population is just above the poverty line and air travel is an unobtainable luxury. There is also significant social uncertainty, which has led to a series of bombings in the last decade. There were eight bombings in Tibet and in northern China 108 were killed in 2001. However, the Government is reducing air fares on selected routes to increase the number of travelers. Already central and provincial governments are drafting economic incentives to accelerate investments inland, and these include the creation of tourist hotspots. Tourism is recognized as a rapid stimulant to economies and central government has allocated RMB861m towards this end. However, success is dependent upon an adequate and suitable infrastructure. With large distances to be covered, rail is too slow and suitable roads too expensive to build. Under CAAC guidelines and WTO agreements, foreign enterprises are being encouraged to invest in airport construction, airport management, and other supporting industries. This help is needed if the target of 150 new airports all over China, to establish regional hubs, is to be realized. The "Go West" initiative could have far-reaching implications for an airline industry largely based on point-to-point services of the coastal area.

China eagerly awaits the Olympics in Beijing and the Expo in Shanghai and the massive publicity attracting foreign business and tourists will further stimulate the eastern region. However, relationships with Taiwan are a cause for concern. There have been times since 2000 when the pro-independence Democratic Progressive Party came to power. Although its rhetoric has softened somewhat since then, there is no trend in its actions.

Today there are over one million Taiwanese businesspeople in Shanghai and Shenzhen and more would move if Taiwan, fearing a brain-drain, had not imposed restrictions on some segments of its economy. During 2003, Taiwanese planes have been allowed to land in Shanghai via Hong Kong for the first time in 50 years and there are talks that in 2004 Chinese airlines may get a similar favor. Direct cross-strait flights could be major business for airlines serving the main eastern cities. However if political tensions develop, a war would have disastrous regional and international consequences for both countries.

China's GDP has been growing steadily over the last decade and, with it, people's disposable income. The number of domestic travelers has increased from 659 million (1998) to 784 million (2001). However, growth is not homogeneous, with the gap between eastern urban inhabitants and the western rural population widening from 2.2 times in 1990 to 2.71 times in 2001. The most prosperous cities, and largest markets for air travel, are Shanghai, Guangzhou, and Beijing, where residents earn an average of 56% more than the national average. The growth of the cities has been fueled by the real estate market but there is now talk of the kind of property bubble that dragged down Japan's economy. Average rental prices have declined for the last 5 years because of oversupply, and incentives to spend on housing have been reduced by the end of tax rebates and the higher down payments needed. However, restrictions on foreign purchases have been lifted.

A further major international issue is the increasing pressure for China to float its currency in the world market. At the moment, a low RMB makes China's products artificially cheap and competitive. In 2002, China's exports to the US were worth US$61.7bn but it imported just US$27bn. This disparity could lead to a trade war.

Having identified key macro-forces which could exert a powerful effect on the airline industry, senior airline executives wondered what to do next in constructing the future.

---

1. *What are the macro-drivers for change in the Chinese airline industry?*
2. *Carry out a structural analysis of this industry.*
3. *Construct future scenarios for the Chinese airline industry*
4. *What are the implications for: (a) the three main firms and (b) the regional competitors?*
5. *In what ways might the scenarios challenge the prevailing mental models of Chinese airlines?*

[eBay] have got to get their act together and decide what they are – they cannot be black-marketeers of tickets.

Harvey Goldsmith, Live 8 promoter for Bob Geldof

Anything to do with the Lions tour bought over the Internet [from TradeMe] runs a grave risk of being a scam or tickets that have been procured illegally and must be shut down.

Steve Tew, Deputy Chief Executive, New Zealand Rugby Union

In 2005 Bob Geldof, an ageing former rock star and concert promoter, and his Live 8 organization spoke out against eBay selling on Live 8 tickets for people who had successfully taken part in a ticket ballot and then sought to make a quick profit. eBay acted as quickly and as best it could to close down the practice. Just two months earlier, the New Zealand Rugby Union criticized TradeMe, a local eBay equivalent, for re-selling rugby tickets on behalf of people who also successfully took part in a ticket ballot and were also seeking to make a quick profit. TradeMe did little to stop the practice. Why is it that in certain contexts some can shake and move a company's strategy with a few choice words while in other contexts similar words have a negligible effect?

This chapter examines who the influential movers and shakers are. More specifically:

1. Who runs the company and for whom is the company run?
2. What are the constraints on Chief Executive power?
3. Who are the movers and shakers that influence a firm's strategy?
4. How can different stakeholder interests be managed?

1. Who Runs the Company and For Whom Is the Company Run?

In March 2005, Bernie Ebbers, CEO of the telecoms giant WorldCom, was convicted of nine criminal counts for an $11bn (£5.7bn) accounting fraud that led to the largest bankruptcy in US history (*Financial Times*, March 19, 2005). Further high-profile trials of top executives – Jeffrey Skilling and Kenneth Lay (Enron), Dennis Kozlowski (Tyco), and Richard Scrushy (HealthSouth) – are also to take place for alleged corporate wrongdoing. Even the most fêted of US CEOs, the legendary Jack Welch, has come under scrutiny, accused of excessive expenses, with a Manhattan apartment, limousine services, security guards, corporate jet, and best seats at sporting and artistic events, to name but a few. These incidents show an increasing concern for understanding and appraising the role and responsibilities of such "Imperial Chief Executives." To assess the actions of these top

31

executives, fundamental questions concerning the relationship between top management and stakeholders need to be addressed.

In an Anglo-American context, the company should be run for its owners as ultimate beneficiaries. However, as the opening examples show, there is suspicion that Imperial Chief Executives run their firms more for themselves than for shareholders. How has this come about?

Apart from owner-managed firms and small businesses, shareholders do not have the expertise to run the firms in which they have ownership and so require a professional executive to manage the business for them. This means that ownership of the business is separated from control of wealth and results in a principal–agent relationship.[1] The Chief Executive is an agent for the principal (shareholders) and is responsible for maximizing the value of the principal's investment.

The quality of the principal–agent relationship depends on the agent receiving sufficient incentive to work diligently in the principal's best interests. For this reason, Chief Executives are highly incentivized through salary and benefits to maximize company performance. In this light, perhaps the benefits attributed to Jack Welch earlier are justifiable as well as being a small price to pay for winning the services of an outstanding Chief Executive.

Particularly noteworthy in incentivizing top executives is the granting of large numbers of shares and the use of share options to align their interests with those of shareholders. The logic is that if top executives stand to benefit personally and substantially by being able to exercise their options, then they will work to improve the share price to enable this to take place, and, in so doing, benefit shareholders. Of course, this method is not without problems – beneficiaries of these options may be incentivized to maximize short-term profits at the expense of the long-term future of the business.[2]

Where a problem can occur is when agents have the opportunity to benefit at the expense of shareholders. For instance, while some consumption of benefits by Chief Executives is likely to be beneficial to the firm, as it may assist in attracting and retaining good managers, excessive consumption can destroy shareholder value. Former Tyco CEO, Kozlowski, is accused of this by the Securities and Exchange Commission for failing to disclose multimillion-dollar low-interest loans (US SEC, 2002). This divergence of interests is known as an **agency problem**.[3] Evidence can be seen in the enthusiasm for Chief Executives to grow their firms. It is well known that their personal reward and prestige is positively related to the size of their firm and so they have an incentive to increase it beyond the optimal level. When Chief Executives have access to cash flow in excess of that needed to fund all available projects of the firm with positive net present value, the potential for overinvestment is particularly serious. This excess cash should be paid out to investors[4] but is likely to be reinvested at rates well below the corporate cost of capital, particularly in diversifying acquisitions. It is to avoid the worst excesses of the agency problem that various constraints exist on CEO power.

2. What Are the Constraints on CEO power?

The recent surge in court cases against high-profile Chief Executives makes the issue of controls on top management, or corporate governance, a very topical issue.

Corporate governance focuses on whom the firm should serve, the distribution of power and relationships amongst different stakeholders, and the selection and conduct of senior management. It recognizes that the Chief Executive is embedded in a hierarchy of power relationships, consisting of many different groups each with claims and influence upon the firm. The most immediate influence on the Chief Executive is through the chain of ownership.

In small private companies, the owners may be a small number of family members who may or may not have a role in the running of the business itself. While the number of shareholders may be small, the tensions and struggles between family members over the direction of the business can be extraordinary and involve issues far removed from just the maximization of shareholder value. For larger public firms, ownership is far more complex. Just by looking at the share register, one may well find the number of direct share-owners running into thousands of individuals dispersed around the globe. For the majority of these owners, their shares will represent only a fraction of the total issued share capital and so their individual ability to influence the firm will be very low. Individuals may also buy into the firm indirectly (through investment funds, for example) and may not even be aware of the companies in which they have a stake. The same applies for funds placed with pension funds under the management of trustees.

In most share registers of public companies the largest shareholders will be institutions rather than private shareholders. The investment managers of pension funds as well as investment trusts therefore have substantial influence over the firm's management. However other institutions, such as insurance companies, also build sizable stakes. Investment banks, for instance, may have substantial holdings in their own right and in countries such as Germany and Japan, commercial banks are major holders of equity in leading companies.[5] In these countries cross-shareholding is common, unlike the Anglo-American system, and this leads to illiquidity in dealing. It has been argued that this structural difference affects the extent to which shareholders push for shorter or longer term results.

Often, substantial owners of shares may be other companies, either as a pure investment or as competitors keeping informed of activities and using a hedging strategy. It is worth noting that all of these shareholders have their own agendas and time frames. For instance, in the short term, a firm may well have a significant portion of its shares controlled by arbitrageurs whereas pension funds may be committed for the longer term.

One type of ownership is that of the non-equity principal. These are generally banks, which, through the provision of loans and other forms of finance, such as bonds, have ownership rights over the firm's assets. Generally speaking, these non-equity principals become influential when there may be material changes to the nature of the firm, in its ownership, such as when a firm is subject to a takeover bid, or in its financing, when the firm may be trying to raise funds. Debt holders become very significant in influencing CEOs and top management when the firm is in poor financial health. Indeed, there can come a point where the value of the equity is virtually nil and it is the debt holders who control the firm and wield the power.

The parties described above can be thought of as a chain of principal–agent relationships, with the Chief Executive being the agent of the Board of Directors, which in turn is the agent of institutional managers and long-term investors, who

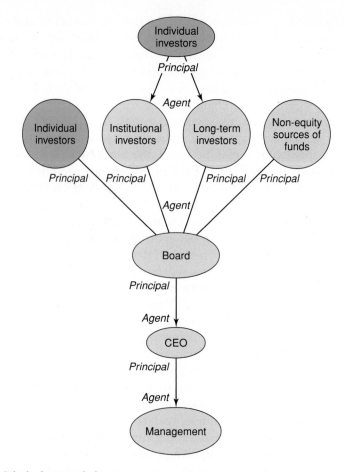

Figure 2.1 Principal–agent chain

are agents for trustees, who are agents for the ultimate principal, the beneficiaries (see figure 2.1).

Between each of these links, information is passed to safeguard the interests of the principal. In the Anglo-American system, the law states that certain information needs to be disclosed to all shareholders. This is done by sending out annual report and accounts together with notification of any material changes to the firm. However, the richness of information obtained, over and above this legally specified minimum, is broadly proportional to the size of the shareholding and the resources available for making this collection. For instance, pension fund managers are likely to meet personally with top management, attend all meetings scheduled by the firm, and speak fairly regularly on the telephone. Individual shareholders, however, may just receive annual report and accounts if direct shareholders, and, if holding shares through an investment fund, may not even receive this information, but a performance report for the fund as a whole.

Mechanisms internal to the firm, to align Chief Executive interests with those of the owners, are financial incentive schemes. The logic is that if the shareholders become rich, then so should the Chief Executive. These schemes may include increasing share ownership and compensation arrangements based on accounts, markets, and contingencies (such as long-term incentive plans, LTIPs). While they reward Chief Executive focus on improving selected performance measures, these techniques can be counterproductive. For instance, if a Chief Executive's remuneration is tied to firm profitability, actions may be taken to boost that profitability by starving the firm of investment for future growth. Other internal mechanisms include improving internal controls and monitoring, through (1) the performance and pay review process and (2) corporate governance (The Cadbury Report 2003). Corporate governance generally insists on the separation of Chairman and Chief Executive roles to avoid undue concentration of executive power (see Disney vs. Disney in case 2-1). The Chairman is primarily responsible for managing external relations while the Chief Executive is responsible for day-to-day operations and relationships within the company. All Executive Directors report to the Chief Executive (but not Non-executive Directors).

Outside of the firm, ownership influence can be achieved by large minority shareholders and activist investors. They have an incentive to collect information and monitor management. A prominent mover and shaker in the UK is Tony Bolton, manager of US fund-managed Fidelity Group. Nicknamed "the quiet assassin," he has been very active recently as an influential institutional investor, bringing about the removal of a number of Chief Executives (see case 2-3, Shareholder revolution).

Poorly performing top executives may also be subject to a hostile takeover as a disciplinary force. The recent bid for Disney by Comcast was interpreted widely as a criticism of the way that Michael Eisner, Disney's Chairman and CEO, managed the company. For Harvard Professor Michael Jensen, hostile bids are evidence of a market for corporate control, where executives compete for the ownership of the firm to manage its resources effectively. Where a bundle of resources, or a firm, is managed badly, better performing managers will act to replace them through a hostile takeover. This threat of takeover, which is prevalent in the US and UK systems, may be seen as a primary external means of ensuring good managerial performance.

3. Who Are the Movers and Shakers that Influence Firm Strategy?

Apart from the movers and shakers of institutional shareholders, there are many other stakeholders who do not have direct ownership rights over the firm but depend on the firm to fulfill their own goals and are able to influence firm strategy. A range of these stakeholders is shown in figure 2.2.

Non-shareholding stakeholders can be divided into three groups: external dependent groups; internal dependent groups; and non-dependent groups.

External dependent groups

Important **external dependent stakeholders** have the following relations: (1) economic (lenders, customers, suppliers, competitors, distributors) where stakeholders can influence the value creation process; (2) advisory (non-executive directors,

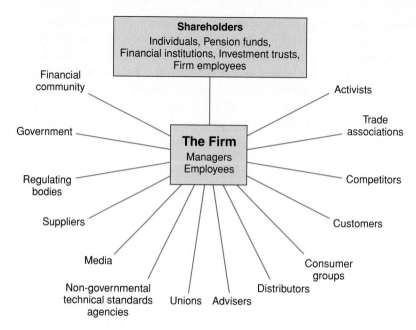

Figure 2.2 A stakeholder map

consultants, gurus, business schools, lawyers, accountants); and (3) socio-political (local authorities, unions).

1. *Economic relations* with the firm can be influenced by lenders, who can withdraw funds if a firm acts in ways that are not approved of. Or it may be that firms are unable to secure loans for strategies that do not fit with the lenders' views. Substantial customers and suppliers can influence the firm through the withdrawal of orders and supplies or the imposition of less attractive terms and conditions, such as payment terms. Competitors can influence the firm through their actions as well as public statements of intent. For instance, Airbus Industries has made public the amount of resources it has been putting into its new super-jumbo aircraft and the contracts it has been awarding for this purpose. This "signaling" is clearly intended to influence its major competitor, Boeing, into reconsidering whether it really wants to compete head on with such a commitment of resources.

2. *Advisory relations* influence the firm by providing ideas and solutions to problems. Non-executive directors perform an important role in having sufficient senior experience to comment on the affairs of the firm but have no management say in the day-to-day running of the organization. Their semi-independent status is an important characteristic to ensure impartiality, and so they should not have a commercial or other interest in the organization beyond drawing a modest remuneration for their time. A key issue, however, is that the company chooses who to appoint.

    Around 90% of Britain's top companies now employ outside consultants to advise them on strategy (a percentage that is typical throughout the western world). These consultants are part of an industry now worth some $40bn worldwide. The executives who pull strings are also increasingly from consulting backgrounds. For instance, the alumni of McKinsey's include the heads of America's IBM, Levi-Strauss, and American Express, France's Bull, and in the UK, Asda, the Confederation of British Industry, and the Deputy Governor of the Bank of England. With their connections, consultants are able to collect impressive data and are well placed to tell firms which companies are doing best. They perform an important role as disseminators of information and, in particular, are associated with communicating "best practice." This message is both pervasive and persuasive, although generally relies on clients fearing being left behind in the competitive race rather than staying ahead. The way that consultants look at strategic problems thus also influences the way their clients see the world. For example, McKinsey's philosophy of "Everything can be measured, and what gets measured gets managed" tends to place the emphasis on certain "hard" generic characteristics and generally leads to less of a focus on the unique "softer," more distinctive, or less tangible, aspects of a firm's competitive advantage, like those discussed in chapters 6 and 7, Living Strategy and Corporate Character.[6]

3. *Socio-political relations* can have influence at the local level through different types of business and planning regulation. Unions can influence the firm through organizing employee action.

Internal dependent groups

Internal dependent stakeholders may not have very much influence on top management and company strategy as individuals unless they are a particularly valued resource. For instance, they may have particular skills or knowledge, such as research scientists, have a substantial reputation that can move markets, or control a vital customer relationship. More frequently, internal stakeholders have greater power where they can group together to achieve collective bargaining power. In France, for example, surgeons grouped together and came en masse to England as a protest to the Government about their terms and conditions of work in France. Internal stakeholders may also align with an external group, such as a union, when internal grouping is insufficient to exert pressure on employers. It is not unusual for external stakeholders to actively seek linkages with internal stakeholders to achieve their aims. For instance, suppliers may link with purchasing officers, or customers with marketing managers, to represent their interests.

Non-dependent groups

Standing above the stakeholders who are dependent on the firm are **non-dependent stakeholders**, stakeholders who can influence the firm but are not themselves dependent on it. These stakeholders include: (1) governmental bodies, which may be at the industry, regional, national, and supranational levels; (2) technical organizations; and (3) opinion influencers.

1. *Governmental bodies* can influence the firm by setting up regulators to protect interests. For instance, within countries such as the UK, "watchdog" bodies have been set up to represent customer interests. Examples include the Office of Fair Trading (OFT) for protecting the consumer and Ofwat to regulate the price of water supply. More recently a new body has been set up to monitor the quality of schools, and has been nicknamed "Off-Toff"![7] More general frameworks have also been used, such as the Citizen's Charter Initiative in UK public services to raise performance standards on "customer service." In the US, Congressional legislation has been bolstered. In the wake

of the collapse of WorldCom, George Bush set up a Corporate Crime Taskforce and gave extra money to the Department of Justice and the Securities and Exchange Commission to pursue corporate wrongdoers. In 2002, Sarbanes-Oxley legislation was rushed into law in response to the Enron scandal. These rules involve an annual assessment of internal controls over financial reporting and certification by the CFO and CEO that the financial statements and accounting practices are accurate. This should remove the "aw, shucks" defense used by lawyers in Bernie Ebber's trial (and being used by former Enron bosses), claiming that, as a former milkman with no formal training in accounting, he was incapable of spotting fraud. Although the amount of detail required to satisfy this legislation is perceived as extremely onerous for US companies, it does force them to "comply or explain" and there is evidence that investors are demanding such explanations.

There are also international bodies that monitor standards, such as Transparency International, which publishes a "perceived corruption index" of countries. This sort of information can influence the decisions of firms to invest abroad and the extent to which they might risk trading in such areas.

It is interesting to note that following the recent wave of mega-mergers, there are now a number of sizable firms which generate such large amounts of tax revenue that the government cannot be seen as a non-dependent stakeholder. In the UK for instance, BP pays billions of pounds in tax and it is inconceivable that this huge contribution to the Treasury does not give this firm some bargaining power.

2. *Technical organizations* can influence the firm where independent credit rating agencies, such as Standard & Poors, can directly affect the ability of the firm to raise funds through the direct costs of borrowing as well as influence on share price. Other standards agencies may determine appropriate technology standards for a market.

3. *Opinion influencers* can have an impact on the firm's strategy by providing the latest ideas and concepts. Here the role of gurus, consultants, and business schools is well documented. The power of ideas such as the Boston Box, best practice, and the S-curve to influence management initiatives is clear to see.[8]

Other groups

Other opinion influencers include campaigners for generic issues, such as fighting poverty in Africa. High-profile media stars like Bob Geldof and Bono have organized events, such as Band Aid and Live 8, which propel issues onto the public stage. At the moment, through tireless campaigning, Geldof among others is attempting to influence the banks of the First World to rescind African debt. Underlying such campaigns is a strong view of what is right and ethical behavior for companies. While it is by no means clear that everyone agrees on what is "right" and "ethical" behavior, as the world consists of very diverse cultural norms and beliefs, there are mounting pressures for socially and environmentally responsible behaviors to be viewed as synonymous with good management and embedded in a firm's strategy. This "corporate social responsibility" (CSR) point of view is gaining ground. There is growing evidence of firms now producing CSR documents and, as we shall see in chapter 10 Sustain Ability, altering their behavior as a consequence of a backlash from, for instance, consumers disapproving of the use of child labor.

CSR focuses on the embeddedness of the organization in a wider set of social conditions and recognizes that business affects society as well as depending on a set of social conditions, such as quality of workforce, government regulation, etc., to be able to operate and compete. Michael Porter suggests that, at the **generic level**, business has little effect on broad social issues. He gives the example that despite a laudable donation from a US software firm in aid of the HIV/AIDs pandemic in Africa, there is little impact either way in this sort of action. However, in terms of focusing on the **value chain** or **operating level** of the firm, he perceives substantial impact in the way that a firm might modify its operations to mitigate harm and improve sustainability. He also perceives overlooked value at the **competitive level**, where the firm's philanthropic efforts can create social change while improving the environment for long-term corporate success. In his view, for firms to be effective and socially responsible, they need to move beyond generalized concepts of good citizenship and set strategic priorities for strategic philanthropy.[9]

4. How Can Different Stakeholder Interests Be Managed?

The expectations and interests of each stakeholder will differ and often be in conflict. The classic conflicts that may exist include:

- short-term results to suit equity markets versus long-term investments to secure the future success of the firm
- improve efficiency versus substantial job loss
- the need for professional managers versus the loss of family control
- reduce costs versus providing a social necessity
- public share ownership versus need for more openness and accountability
- operating locally in one country versus parent ways of operating and expectations located in a different country

Nevertheless top executives need to make decisions. It is useful, therefore, to map these interests to understand political priorities. This can be done using a power/interest grid, which identifies the level of power a stakeholder has to influence the firm and the level of interest they have in supporting or opposing a particular strategy (see figure 2.3).

By categorizing stakeholders on the power/interest matrix, it becomes possible to identify which ones are likely to be key supporters or blockers of a strategy and

Figure 2.3 Stakeholder power/interest matrix (Adapted from Mendelow (1991))

where lobbying efforts ought to be directed. For example, despite seeming a long way removed from eBay's business, Geldof and Live 8 were able, through their ability to generate media attention and public popularity for their cause, to influence eBay's strategy. They had a lot of power to influence the management of eBay, so the firm had to respond to their concerns. If we look at the other example from the beginning of this chapter though, we can say that the NZRU, while keen to influence what TradeMe were doing, lacked either the necessary public sympathy or clout to influence TradeMe's acitivites. Hence, TradeMe issued some lukewarm warnings about checking the terms and conditions of rugby tickets before seeking to sell them on and kept the NZRU informed of what was happening on its sites as a courtesy, but the company felt little further compulsion to act.

Categorizing stakeholders on the power/interest grid raises issues of how to manage those who have power and interest. Through the careful use of information, side payments, or negotiation, objections that these stakeholders may have to a strategy may be removed on the grounds that concessions are given on other fronts. This can raise ethical issues for top managers over whether they are, or should be, weighing the conflicting expectations of stakeholder groups; whether they are answerable to one group, and then work to make those interests acceptable to others; or whether they are really acting in their own interests and managing stakeholders to suit their own purposes.

This returns us to our opening problematic issue of whether CEOs are good agents of shareholders, stewards in looking after the best interests of the firm (and not necessarily prioritizing shareholders) or an agency problem.[10] It is in response to the excesses of some "Imperial CEOs" that there has been a recent rise in legislation and an emboldening of boards of directors and shareholders. They are now beginning to make a difference. Top executives Carly Fiorina (HP), Hank Greenberg (American International Group), and Michael Eisner (Disney) have announced their departures and Sumner Redstone (Viacom) is being forced into an extreme downsizing of his firm. In the eyes of some observers, these events mark a very dramatic shift in the balance of power between CEOs and their firms' stakeholders.

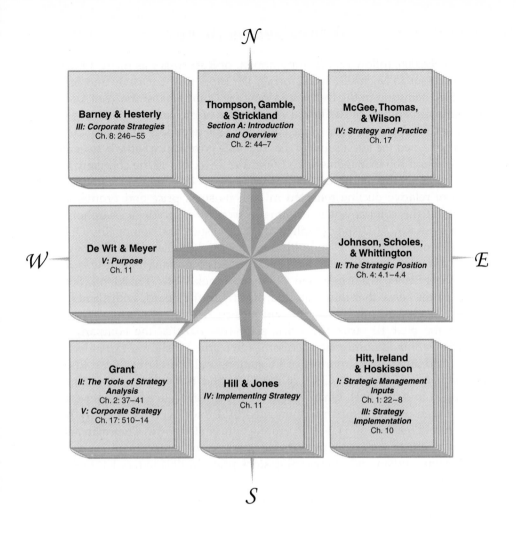

N

Barney & Hesterly
III: Corporate Strategies
Ch. 8: 246–55

Thompson, Gamble, & Strickland
Section A: Introduction and Overview
Ch. 2: 44–7

McGee, Thomas, & Wilson
IV: Strategy and Practice
Ch. 17

W

De Wit & Meyer
V: Purpose
Ch. 11

Johnson, Scholes, & Whittington
II: The Strategic Position
Ch. 4: 4.1–4.4

E

Grant
II: The Tools of Strategy Analysis
Ch. 2: 37–41
V: Corporate Strategy
Ch. 17: 510–14

Hill & Jones
IV: Implementing Strategy
Ch. 11

Hitt, Ireland & Hoskisson
I: Strategic Management Inputs
Ch. 1: 22–8
III: Strategy Implementation
Ch. 10

S

Disney versus Disney

On May 9, 2005, following the appointment of Robert Iger as the CEO designate and successor to Michael Eisner, former Directors Roy E. Disney and Stanley P. Gold filed a lawsuit in the Delaware Chancery Court against the Walt Disney Co. and certain members of the Board of Directors of the company alleging that the Board made false statements to the company's shareholders about its CEO search. This represented the latest salvo in the corporate governance battle between Disney and Gold and the management and Board of Directors of the company.

The roots of this battle can be traced back to 1984 when, following a long period of relative decline reflected in both its stock price and profits, a power struggle at the company was eventually won by a group of shareholders led by Directors Roy E. Disney (nephew of Walt Disney and son of Roy O. Disney, the co-founders of Walt Disney Productions) and Stanley Gold (Disney's close friend, attorney, and financial advisor). The existing management was replaced by Michael Eisner (Chairman and CEO) and Frank Wells (President). Both were equals in the sense that they reported directly to the Board, with Eisner seen as the "creative talent" and Wells the "businessman."

Over the next 10 years the stock price rose 6,000%, the company opened EuroDisney, made numerous successful films and TV shows, expanded Disney World, and purchased a number of TV stations and sports franchises. Eisner was lauded as one of the great CEOs of the 1980s and 1990s. The partnership tragically ended in April 1994, when Frank Wells was killed in a helicopter crash.

From then on the company, dominated by Eisner, who temporarily held the positions of President and Chief Operating Officer along with Chairman and Chief Executive Officer, entered a period characterized by management changes, poor investments, and an underperforming stock price. In 1994 Jeffery Katzenberg, the executive responsible for the most successful animated film ever – *The Lion King* – left after a clash with Eisner, eventually receiving a payoff worth $275m. The following year, Michael Ovitz became Disney President, only to leave 14 months later, with a $140m severance package, once again following a disagreement with Eisner.

In 1996, Disney purchased Capital Cities/ABC for $19bn – the largest media takeover to date and the second largest acquisition of a US firm. When it was acquired, ABC owned the leading television network in the United States but by 2002 it was ranked third among the three leading television networks. Other notable failures included a botched plan to build an American history theme park; the loss of millions of dollars on a new California Adventure attraction at Disneyland; and a $1bn loss attempting to replicate Yahoo!'s internet portal. The acquisition of Fox Family Channel in 2001, for $5.3bn, was widely perceived to be at an exorbitant price.

At this time, Disney's Board of Directors included Eisner's friends Sidney Poitier (the actor), Robert A. M. Stern (the architect who designed many Disney properties), and George Mitchell (the former Senator, who consulted for Disney). The Board's judgment was seen as particularly questionable with regard to the compensation packages it approved for Eisner, who in the 20 years of service following his appointment received total compensation worth almost $1bn. In the eyes of Roy Disney and Stanley Gold, these questionable decisions around remuneration as well as group strategy were enough to prompt them to begin a campaign in 2000 to force the Board to become more independent of Eisner and to develop a plan for his eventual succession.

During November, 2003 Roy E. Disney resigned from the Board because he was not included in the list of Directors for the next election. In his open letter of resignation, in which he claims the company has lost its creative direction, Disney blames Eisner for micro-management and the refusal to establish a clear succession plan. He concludes by saying: ". . . it is my sincere belief that it is you who should be leaving not me. Accordingly, I once again call for your resignation or retirement" (www.savedisney.com/letters/red_resign_letter.asp).

The following month Stanley Gold resigned from the Board and also published his letter of resignation. He criticizes the Board for ". . . not actively engaging in serious discussions regarding the Company's flawed plans and management's unmet projections and unfilled promises" (www.savedisney.com/letters/spg_resign_letter.asp).

Of course, it may be that these negative comments from disposed Directors are sour grapes, but in February 2004, Comcast announced a hostile bid for Disney worth $54bn in stock. The bid was rejected and Comcast did not pursue it further. However, the annual shareholder meeting that followed saw 45.37% of shareholders withhold their vote for Eisner. Later in the day it is announced that Eisner will be replaced as Chairman of the Board by Mitchell.

In September, Eisner announced he will retire when his contract expires in September 2006. This 2-year transition period is heavily criticized for being too long, increasing uncertainty, handicapping the development of corporate strategy, and creating a "lame duck" CEO. Eisner also makes clear that Robert Iger is his personal choice for his successor. Company President and Chief Operating Officer, George Mitchell, who led the search for the new CEO, also announced Robert Iger was the only internal candidate for the post.

Iger was appointed Eisner's successor on March 13, 2005 and, after a 6 month period of working in tandem with Eisner will then assume the post of CEO. Eisner will remain on the Board until September 2006.

According to Roy Disney and Stanley Gold, although the Board promised shareholders that it would conduct the CEO search with "open minds" and with no predeterminations or preconditions, in reality, the Board's CEO selection process precluded serious and effective consideration of external candidates. In particular, they were dissatisfied with Michael Eisner's presence or expected presence at interviews of external candidates and by reports that the Board interviewed only one external candidate, delayed notifying her of any decision, and did little to dissuade her from withdrawing her candidacy. They claimed the Board had failed to properly fulfill its corporate governance responsibilities, including its paramount task, the search for a CEO, and that it was not appropriate for Eisner, who had already decided who his successor should be, to participate in the candidate reviews.

---

1. *What is the evidence that there is a corporate governance issue in Disney?*
2. *What are the problems you see in the case with Eisner holding several offices?*
3. *How should the Board have gone about appointing a new CEO?*
4. *How should an independent Director be defined and how should Directors be appointed to the Board?*

---

1. *What is the evidence that there is a corporate governance issue in Disney?*

Disney vs. Disney raises a number of issues of importance to the ongoing debate about corporate governance. Although the Board should not be involved directly in the management of the business, it is responsible for the company's overall strategy and should approve any major changes in the company's strategic direction and management structure. This case provides a good example of what can happen when a company's Board lacks the independence to effectively separate itself from the company's management.

Although common in the USA, the same individual holding the position of both Chairman and Chief Executive Officer can create problems (see question 3). In addition, many of the Board's members were appointed to the Board by Eisner (see question 4) and/or had a business relationship with the company (e.g. Robert A. M. Stern, architectural work; Sen. George Mitchell, consulting). Directors who were critics of Eisner, Roy E. Disney and Andre Van de Kamp, were forced to leave the Board.

This led to claims by Stanley P. Gold that Disney has ". . . an insular Board of Directors serving as a bulwark to shield management from criticism and accountability." It could be argued the Board had become little more than a rubber stamp, automatically endorsing Eisner's actions. In the 5 years up to August 2002, Disney was the worst performing stock among the 30 companies that make up the Dow Jones Industrial Average. However, the Board did nothing to question Eisner's judgment regarding unsuccessful investments during this period, including the acquisitions of the ABC TV network and the Fox Family Channel, and the loss of more than $1bn invested in the go.com internet portal.

The role of the Board in awarding Eisner a total compensation package worth $737m in the 5 years up to 2001, a period in which company profits fell and the company's stock underperformed the overall market, raises questions about the criteria used to decide his remuneration.

Another key role of the Board of Directors is to ensure that an appropriate succession plan is in place covering the key executive positions in the company. This was not the case at Disney. Potential successors to Eisner, Katzenberg and Ovitz, were both forced out by him at great expense to shareholders. There was an absence of a succession plan should Eisner leave the company and he resisted any attempts to implement one. The Board should have challenged him about this and through the Nominations Committee identified a potential successor.

Finally, it can be argued that Eisner's role in the appointment of Iger as his successor as CEO reduces Iger's credibility, making a difficult job even harder.

2. *What are the problems you see in the case with Eisner holding several offices?*

From his appointment in 1984 until March 2004, Michael Eisner was both Chairman of the Board and Chief Executive Officer of Disney and for a short period following the death of Frank Gates he also held the positions of President and Chief Operating Officer. Although, unlike the UK (where the corporate governance code recommends against it), it is not uncommon in the USA for the same person to be both Chairman and CEO, it does mean that the responsibilities of the head of the company (the Chairman, who leads the Board and looks after shareholders' interests, and the Chief Executive Officer, who leads the executive, who manage the company on a day-to-day basis) are held by the same person. This has the potential for conflict if the Chief Executive's interests differ from those of the company's owners – the shareholders. Many commentators argue that the most important task a company's Chairman will be called upon to perform is to "fire" the Chief Executive Officer. Obviously, if the Chairman and the CEO is the same person, this is unlikely to happen.

As in the case of Eisner, when he held four key positions, the question has to be asked: how is it possible for one person to have sufficient time to undertake the responsibilities of these positions effectively?

3. How should the Board have gone about appointing a new CEO?

The search for a new CEO should be undertaken by the Nominations Committee, which in the UK would normally be headed by an independent director (possibly the Chairman). It should decide on the balance of skills, knowledge, and experience required and prepare a description of the role and capabilities expected of the new CEO. In most cases, the company would then appoint a specialist external search consultant – "headhunter" – to identify and make the initial approach to potential candidates. The next stage would be for all members of the Board to meet, preferably on an individual basis, with a shortlist of candidates determined by the Nomination Committee based on the search consultant's recommendations. After considerable discussion, the Board members would then vote on the appointment, hoping that a split among the members would not become apparent. Should a member of the Board have strong reservations concerning the successful candidate, it would be necessary for him or her to consider whether it was possible to remain as a member of the Board.

4. How should an independent Director be defined and how should Directors be appointed to the Board?

The definition of an independent Director varies internationally. Generally, to be "independent," a Director must have no connection to the company other than a seat on the Board. This excludes full-time employees of the company, family members of employees, and the company's lawyer, banker, and consultants. Some definitions include people with connections to the company, such as suppliers, customers, debtors, and creditors. Others include direct or indirect recipients of corporate charitable donations. The latest version of the UK Combined Code on Corporate Governance (2003) states that a Director is not independent if he or she:

a) has been an employee of the company or group within the last 5 years
b) has, or has had within the last 3 years, a material business relationship with the company either directly, or as a partner, shareholder, Director or senior employee of a body that has such a relationship with the company

c) has received or receives additional remuneration from the company apart from a Director's fee, participates in the company's share option or a performance-related pay scheme, or is a member of the company's pension scheme

d) has close family ties with any of the company's advisors, Directors, or senior employees

e) holds cross-Directorships or has significant links with other Directors through involvement in other companies or bodies

f) represents a significant shareholder

g) has served on the Board for more than 9 years from the date of their first election.

In the USA and the UK, the nomination of individuals for election by the shareholders to the Board of Directors is normally handled by a Nominating Committee. This is largely, if not entirely, made up of independent Directors. They make recommendations concerning potential Directors to the full Board of Directors who, if they agree, then ask the shareholders to approve their nomination. In theory, the Nomination Committee should work independently of the other Board members, including the CEO. However, as this case study shows, this is frequently not the case, with the CEO and/or Chairman often making "recommendations" to the Nominations Committee.

In the UK, a separate section of the annual report should describe the work of the Nomination Committee, including the process used in relation to Board appointments. An explanation should be given if neither an external search consultancy nor open advertising has been used in the appointment of a Chairman or a Non-executive Director.

Changing the face of industry

On January 9, 2003, Wm Morrison, the UK's fourth largest food retailer, announced a £2.9bn offer for its larger rival, Safeway PLC. Morrisons was concentrated in the north of England while Safeway's chain of stores was located mainly in the Midlands and the south of England.

UK consumers buy 80% of their food, 75% of fresh vegetables and fruit, 65% of fish and meat, and 50% of their milk from the five largest supermarkets. The supermarket industry as a whole is worth some £100bn a year. However, overall growth rates had slowed to 2.9%, which was equal to the growth of the economy as a whole. In the last few years, overseas supermarket giants had entered the industry, with Wal-Mart of the US (the world's largest retailer) purchasing Asda in June 1999 and discount operators Aldi, Netto and Lidl setting up their own operations. To compete in this more difficult market and with these global players, the UK supermarkets had to become more powerful and larger.

It may not be surprising, then, that just 1 week after the Morrison bid, J. Sainsbury confirmed its interest in Safeway, followed by Asda registering its interest and delivering details of its bid, except the price, to the Office of Fair Trading. Meanwhile, rumors that Kohlberg Kravis Roberts, the American buyout giant, was interested were also confirmed just as Safeway's broker of 10 years, CSFB, swapped sides to help the bid. It was also rumored that the entrepreneur Michael Green was looking closely at the opportunity. The retail giant Tesco, however, was thought unlikely to bid because it would then have 35% of the UK market and this would undoubtedly be blocked by the regulator on the grounds of it being anti-competitive.

With potential overconcentration in the supermarket industry about to occur, the Office of Fair Trading (OFT) referred the takeover bid (Morrisons) to the Competition Commission, whose role it is to protect the public interest and ensure that excessive concentration in an industry will not result from a merger and potentially damage consumer interests. Rivalry between companies is viewed as a healthy virtue by the regulator as it encourages competition and innovation and allows the possibility of new entrants into the industry. In looking at the overall concentration of the supermarket industry, the Commission realized that while the overall market share of the supermarkets was 69.2% for all stores, for stores over 2,300 m^2 it was 95.2%. Calculating the weighted Herfindahl-Hirschman Index (HHI) for industry concentration gave a figure of 2,672, which is very high given that scores above 1,800 are considered indicative of concentrated markets.

Crucial to whether an industry is concentrated is the definition of the industry itself. In 2000 there had been an enquiry into the concentration of the supermarket industry and the distance the consumer had to travel for choice between competitors was a critical issue. A 15 minutes driving time rule had been developed as a test and now this was used again to assess shopper choice in their immediate neighbourhood.

To assess the likelihood that a further acquisition in the sector might damage the public interest, the Competition Commission requested submissions from interested parties at the Haberdasher's Hall in London. In this grand City setting, packed with chief executives, directors, bankers, and lawyers, with combined personal wealth of tens of millions of pounds, the hearing took place.

Morrisons: "We need the merger to enable us to compete effectively with the larger players. We would 'leap-frog' to third place in the sector, running a close race with Sainsbury's. Combining with Safeway will increase our market share to 16%, which is below the threshold of 25% at which the OFT would normally investigate. Combining with Safeway would have the least effect of potential supermarket bidders on the HHI. There are very few geographic areas where we overlap with Safeway. Unfortunately, since the bid, our share price has plummeted, wiping 15% off the value of our bid."

Sainsbury's: "Amalgamating with Safeway will confirm our position as number two and help us resist global players. It would result in significant industry concentration. Our sales proposition is different to Safeway's low price strategy. However, we do realize that a successful bid would heavily indebt the group and since announcement our share price has already fallen 11%."

Asda: The bookies' favourite, Asda argued the deal would make it number two in the UK. "With a combined market share of 26%, together with Tesco, we would control over 50% of the market which the Competition

Commission would see as against the public interest." A substantial sale of many Safeway's stores in the North and Scotland, where both groups were strong, would be likely. There would also likely be a ferocious price war with Tesco post-deal.

Philip Green: "I have a lot of experience in clothes retailing through my ownership of clothing retailers BHS and Arcadia. Owning Safeway will allow me to sell clothing through those outlets which currently have few non-food items. My bid does not trigger market concentration issues."

KKR: "Safeway is underperforming. We could run it for 5 to 7 years to improve operations and then sell it off. We do not trigger market concentration issues."

Consumers' Association: "The reduction in the number of major supermarkets will reduce the overall level of competition in the industry. There will be a reduction in product offering and that may lead to price increases. Consumer interests will be damaged."

Smaller supermarkets: "Most supermarkets now offer a wide range of items, including newspapers, dry-cleaning, pharmacies, post-office outlets, petrol, and a huge range of 'non-grocery' items such as clothes and electronics. The overall effect has been to decrease the number of smaller and independent operators."

Small and convenience stores: "Further amalgamation will damage our businesses even more. Already many convenience stores have closed, unable to compete with the scale economies of supermarkets. Further amalgamation would drive them out of business. During the last 10 years, 425 superstores have opened and 25,000 corner shops have closed."

Paul Rhodes: The pig farmer of the year and Chairman of United Pig Marketing told Sir Derek Morris's panel of competition experts that the supermarket slogan of "every day low prices really stands for every day less pigs." In 1997, pig farmers received 50% of the value of the pig. This has gone down to 38% and more than 35% of the pig industry has gone out of business. Since 1998, the production of pigs in the UK has halved but consumers have not reduced the amount they eat, so the gap is filled from abroad. The industry is in intensive care.

Somerset cheese farmers: "The increasing scale of purchase by supermarkets has given them enormous bargaining power. This has greatly depressed our margins to the point of driving some of us out of business. If this trend continues, further exits are inevitable and to attempt to avoid this situation, the prices charged to convenience businesses will have to rise to compensate."

Makers of branded goods: "The Competition Commission enquiry in 2000 recommended that sharp practices be curbed – where supermarkets force a supplier to cut the price of one of its best-selling lines in order to win shelf space for a new product. There have been no complaints since then, because who would complain against their biggest customer?"

Friends of the Earth: "The 2000 report's Supermarket Code is not working and suppliers are being leaned on. No mergers should be allowed."

In considering these submissions, the Competition Commission also considered that it would probably have to formulate a remedies statement requiring the

Table 2-2.1 Supermarket industry (April 2003)

	Market share (%)	T/O (£bn)	PTP (£m)	EPS (p)	Employees	Stores (UK)
Tesco	25.8	26.33	1,401	13.98	296,000	730
Sainsbury's	17.4	18.20	571	21.5	173,000	463
Safeway	10.0	9.40	335	24.4	92,000	480
Asda*	15.9	n/a	810 (est)	n/a	117,000	258
Morrisons**	5.9	3.92	243	10.0	46,000	119

* Owned by Wal-Mart (US), T/O £150bn, PTP £7.6bn
** Only in North England

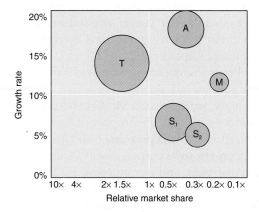

Key: T = Tesco, A = Asda,
S₁ = Sainsbury's, S₂ = Safeway,
M = Morrissons
Size of circle = profitability

Figure 2-2.1 Growth share matrix

successful bidder to take certain actions to avoid problems they identified. For Sainsbury's, such a remedies statement would probably require the disposal of some 90 to 130 Safeway stores to avoid prejudicing customers. A potentially awkward consideration was that Lord Sainsbury is a major shareholder and a Minister within the Department of Trade and Industry, which has overall responsibility for the bid. For Morrisons, around 30 stores would probably need to be divested and for Asda, assuming that the bid could succeed, the number would be very substantial. Another important consideration was whether the merger would make it more difficult for other new players to enter the industry.

1. *What, or who, were the drivers for this takeover battle and how are they moving or shaking Morrisons' strategy? Why did the battle come about at this time?*
2. *Using the stakeholder power/interest matrix, discuss the main issues the regulator should consider. How might they be resolved?*
3. *Which bidders do you think the regulator should recommend to proceed and which should be prevented from continuing?*
4. *If you were CEO of Safeway, what would you have looked for in a deal?*
5. *If you were CEO of one of the bidding companies, and you thought that you wouldn't win the battle, what would you have done next?*

Shareholder revolution

As Carlton and ITV rival Granada pursued a $7.5bn merger, an extraordinary battle of wills blew up between institutional shareholders and top management, threatening to undermine the deal. A group of institutional shareholders wanted the removal of Michael Green (Executive Chairman and founder of Carlton TV) while Non-executive Directors insisted that they would not be forced to jettison him without detailed negotiations.

Sir George Russell, the Deputy Chairman of Granada and its Senior Non-executive Director, chaired an emergency meeting of the Granada Board that lasted for 3 hours and focused on Mr. Green stepping down as chairman of the merged companies of Carlton Communications and Granada Group. Sir George was reported to have never seen such shareholder power massed against a single executive and, in the words of Will Hutton writing for *The Observer* newspaper, "it was, in truth, the loudest attack on a company chairman I have ever witnessed." Granada's Board's backing of rebellious shareholders, who held 33% of Granada's and 36% of Carlton's shares, calling for an independent non-exec to be appointed as Chairman of the enlarged company, extinguished Mr. Green's ambitions. The Board said it wanted to go forward "with the full support of its shareholders." Although Mr. Green, founder of Carlton TV, had presided over the firm's growth, through multiple acquisitions and mergers, to its current size of £4.6bn, many investors perceived him to be arrogant, overpaid, and incompetent. He was reportedly capable of incandescent rage like few other people and he was often at odds with shareholders, which earned him a reputation for indifference to the wishes of the company's shareholders. In terms of overpayment, he latterly received a salary of £843,000, an annual bonus of £670,000, benefits of £47,000, had taken £100m out of the company by selling shares, and currently held 10.2 million Carlton shares worth £22.5m (October 2003). Mr. Green also owned five types of share options with those in the money being worth £4.3m, was entitled to a pension of £134,000 from age 60, could be awarded severance pay, and had the right to a cash bonus of £707,000. His supposed incompetence related to the loss of $2bn in the ill-fated attempt to give ITV a digital broadcasting platform, On Digital. He was also blamed for the loss of advertising revenue and pre-tax losses of previous years.

Once the Competition Commission cleared the way for Granada to take over Carlton and deliver ITV as one integrated television contractor, the big shareholders were able to call for new leadership. The "quiet assassin," Tony Bolton, manager of US fund-managed Fidelity Group in £2.6bn Special Situations Fund and leader of the shareholder campaign, issued an ultimatum for Mr. Green to step down, saying it would call an extraordinary general meeting of shareholders if its demands were not met on Tuesday, October 28, 2003. Michael Green was removed unwillingly from his post.

In an attempt to appease Fidelity and other disaffected shareholders, Carlton offered a three-point plan to avert a shareholder revolt. This included making Mr. Green Non-executive Chairman in May 2005; the appointment of an independent Deputy Chairman and to seek two other Non-execs for the ITV Board. Mr. Bolton found this proposal counterproductive and disappointing and felt there was a window of opportunity for change.

The implications of such shareholder activeness are that the success in removing Mr. Green may give investors the appetite for outright confrontation with other management Boards in the future rather than behind the scenes negotiations. These fears may be justified in the light of a number of controversial decisions. Investors are reported to be unhappy with: Matt Barratt, CEO of Barclays, aiming to become Chairman after a disastrous performance in front of the Treasury Select Committee; the elevation of James Murdoch, 30, to the Board of BSkyB, where he may be more interested in representing the interests of the 35.4% holder, The News Corporation, rather than other investors; and the intention of Sir Peter Davis to step up to Chairmanship of Sainsbury's after the Group's poor performance.

---

1. Why did a group of institutional shareholders want the removal of Michael Green?
2. How did the shareholders bring about Green's demise?
3. Why does Tony Bolton have such power?
4. What can other CEOs do to avoid a similar fate to Michael Green?

Fiorina's folly

In 1998, Ms. Carly Fiorina was named "The most powerful woman in American business" by *Fortune Magazine* following the spin-off of Lucent Technologies from AT&T, her philosophy of "reinvention" and image as pioneer of a communications revolution, and sparkling marketing performances. In July 1999, she was appointed CEO at Hewlett Packard (HP) to reverse its decline and inject new dynamism. She was the first woman to become CEO in one of the 30 companies in the Dow Jones Industrial Average, and also the first outsider and first non-engineer to run HP. Even her strongest critics, though, applauded her bringing an important marketing approach to an engineering-led high-technology firm. The slogan "HP Invent" was symbolic of HP's reinvention.

As part of reinventing HP, Ms. Fiorina shook the technology world in September 2001 by announcing a bid for Compaq Computer worth $19bn. The intended merger was part of her quest to reinvent HP, which was in clear need of a new strategic direction. While strong in the Unix server market, HP lacked scale in less expensive "industry standard" servers built around the Intel chip. Its personal computing business was struggling to make money in the face of fierce competition from Dell, the market leader. Through acquiring Compaq, these issues could be addressed. Compaq's industry standard server business was strong and would improve HP's position in the fast-growing server segment. By combining the PC businesses, there would be sufficient scale to give Dell a run for its money.

Analysts were quick to point out, however, that the Compaq acquisition was a huge investment in businesses that were low margin. Would it not be better to gradually withdraw from PCs, as IBM had done, and invest in higher margin areas such as software? Indeed, it was clear that, despite HP's scale in PCs, Dell's low-cost model was beating them as they chalked up losses through aggressive price competition while losing market share. For these reasons, the analysts dubbed the HP/Compaq merger as "Fiorina's folly."

In November 2001, a bitter war broke out between Ms. Fiorina and the heirs of HP's founders, incensed at the idea of the merger. Led by Walter Hewlett, a Board member and son of Bill Hewlett, they waged a proxy battle for control of the company. Walter Hewlett also took Ms. Fiorina to court, accusing her of improper conduct during the campaign to win shareholder support. These allegations were subsequently dismissed. Ultimately Ms. Fiorina won by the narrowest of margins, with 51.4% in favor against 48.6%.

Some of the objectives of the merger were successful, with cost savings of $2.5bn per year achieved. However, Michael Capellas, the Compaq boss who had been named President of HP, left soon after the deal having been deprived of any influential role at the company. The executives directly responsible for the biggest success of the deal, the integration of HP and Compaq, were let go.

Profits stayed flat despite a doubling in sales ($42.4bn in 1999 to $79.9bn in 2004). Performance was erratic, with expectations being missed twice in the past 2 years. The higher margin businesses, although growing, were doing so from a low base. The analysts generally agreed that the merger was really just putting together two business models that were inferior to Dell's. Instead of Ms. Fiorina's four-word summary "high tech low cost," HP appeared to remain high cost with declining margins on its technology.

Ms. Fiorina's supporters on the Board included Dick Hackborn, HP's elder statesman, director and executive responsible for creating the company's hugely successful printing business. Hackborn had close personal ties with the company's management and founding families and had been instrumental in the departure of the previous Chief Executive, Lew Platt, who had been pushed aside to make room for Ms. Fiorina. It was Hackborn's sounding out of opinions that cemented the Board's decision in 1999 to find new leadership. Other staunch supporters included Larry Babbio, Vice-Chairman of Verizon, Sam Ginn, who had led the search committee when Fiorina was hired, and Phil Condit, the former Boeing chairman. Both Ginn and Condit steered the Board's Nominating and Governance Committee, a key inner group with influence over the composition and workings of the Board.

However, the balance of power in the Board changed. Patricia Dunn, Vice-Chairman of Barclays Global Investors, was said to be against Ms. Fiorina. Sandy Litvack, a former general counsel of Walt Disney, who had publicly supported embattled CEOs, left unexpectedly, Sam Ginn and Phil Condit had left a year ago, and Tom Perkins, an eminent venture capitalist, rejoined the Board a year after retiring, allegedly for age reasons.

Dick Hackborn was aware from soundings of the senior management team that the Board was becoming increasingly concerned about HP's mishaps. Close observers believe he played a key role in the behind the scenes maneuvering that led to Ms. Fiorina's removal in February 2005.

1. *Why was Ms. Fiorina appointed to HP?*
2. *Why did the merger with Compaq take place?*
3. *Why was Ms. Fiorina ousted from HP?*
4. *How was she ousted?*
5. *What can we say about the distribution of power in the Board of a large firm such as HP?*

Repel borders

On January 21, 2000, the giant French buildings materials group, Lafarge, launched an all-cash hostile bid for Blue Circle PLC, the sixth largest cement producer in the world. At 430 pence per share, the offer valued the target at £3.4bn and represented a premium of just 1.4% over Blue Circle's closing middle market price. At the time, the dot.com bubble was in full swing and fund managers were desperate to release money tied up in unfashionable "old economy" stocks, which appeared overvalued. Lafarge was the only real bidder for Blue Circle and was confident after an earlier acquisition. The slim premium offered seemed a shrewd move. If the takeover bid succeeded, Lafarge would become the largest cement company in the world.

Lafarge attacked Blue Circle for mistakes made in the past, including the diversification strategy of the 1980s and early 1990s which resulted in a number of subsequent losses on disposal. Blue Circle had then not expanded internationally through cement acquisitions to the same extent as its competitors and was now heavily dependent on too few countries, which meant its profitability was inherently volatile. Its new CEO, Rick Haythornthwaite, appointed in July 1999, argued that Blue Circle's recent expansion into Asia was an enviable achievement, but he was also conscious that just after taking office he had had to announce a profits warning, which had affected Blue Circle's share price.

For Blue Circle the first critical issue was what value to put on the firm. The valuations prepared by City analysts were generally around 500 pence. Blue Circle's advisor's valuation was in line with this and seemed reasonable provided profit forecasts in the business plan were achievable. Haythornthwaite recognized, however, that the firm tended to achieve actual results lower than plan, and instructed them to reduce their profit forecasts, which led to a revised valuation of the business at a relatively conservative 486 pence.

Blue Circle's first formal response to Lafarge's offer document was to assert that the offer undervalued the company and to claim that the bid was a "quest for our Asian assets, which justifies our investment strategy." The final dividend for the year was raised to 10.95 pence per share, which was now in line with the industry. Assets were revalued and a profit forecast issued for the Asian businesses to convince shareholders that those investments would pay off in the short term.

On April 6, Blue Circle announced its operational improvements program (OIP). The document announced details of the projected benefits arising from such cost savings and included forecasts of £116m of benefits per annum to be achieved by 2002.

The final salvo in Blue Circle's defence was on April 11, 2000. Blue Circle announced it would return £800m to shareholders in advance. The first tranche of £400m was to take place by way of a tender offer for Blue Circle's shares. This return of capital was in effect a down payment to shareholders demonstrating the confidence of management in delivering the promises they had made. Blue Circle's gearing increased significantly (17.2% in 1999 to 107.7% in 2000) and free cash flow available for future projects was reduced dramatically.

At the same time Haythornthwaite reviewed a number of other options. "Many were dismissed because they did not give cash to shareholders, and because of the reluctance of other parties to get involved." The pressure from shareholders for cash was palpable: "The only consideration of shareholders was cash. They were not interested in any wider responsibilities to the company and there was a total lack of engagement," said an Executive Committee member.

Options considered but rejected were a management buy-out, a large acquisition, a white squire defence (where another firm would invest in new Blue Circle equity), and a white knight (where a friendly company would take them over). For various reasons, no other companies wished to be involved in this way.

On April 19, day 46 of the bid, Lafarge launched a dawn raid and picked up 19.9% of Blue Circle directly and a further 9.6% through its bankers. Lafarge then increased its offer to £4.50 per share and was confident of victory.

During the last 10 days of the offer period, Haythornthwaite and his Finance Director held a number of meetings with institutional investors to persuade them to back management and reject the bid. As day 60 approached, the lobbying of shareholders paid off when Schroeder's Bank publicly backed the incumbent management and other shareholders followed. On May 3, the bid lapsed as Lafarge's acceptances and holdings totaled 44.5% of Blue Circle shares. This was the first all-cash bid for a FTSE 100 company to fail for 15 years.

Collomb, the Lafarge CEO, was severely shaken with the failure and the defeat was seen by many as a personal failure. It is highly unlikely that he would have launched another hostile bid for Blue Circle in 2001 as he would not have been prepared to risk failure again.

Haythornthwaite was widely fêted by commentators for his successful defence of Blue Circle. "The smile on Rick Haythornthwaite's face says it all. . . . His success in beating off a cash bid in a market where cash was clearly king has propelled a little known executive into prominence. With the target having seemed doomed at the outset, the escape was seen to be a considerable personal victory for Rick Haythornthwaite" (*Financial Times*, May 6, 2000).

Blue Circle was left with a major competitor effectively owning 32.2% of the firm. To remain independent, a major acquisition was needed but, with such a large minority shareholder, potential partners were not interested. The group also had to deliver on defense promises, which analysts suspected might have been too ambitious. Haythornthwaite also realized that forecast operating profits were significantly below analysts' estimates and earnings quality appeared to be deteriorating.

Haythornthwaite presented three strategy options to the Board to deal with Blue Circle's relative short-term strength but medium-term weakness: (1) achieve an early deal with Lafarge; (2) make an acquisition to move out of Lafarge's reach; (3) execute a merger with another party. Considerable time and resources had been devoted to evaluating acquisitions of or mergers with various parties but the Board decided that negotiations should begin with Lafarge. Lafarge offered £4.70 with no dividend but Haythornthwaite needed to present the deal as being worth over £5.00 per share in order to recommend it to shareholders. The advisors to both sides worked in the period up to and over Christmas, finally agreeing a deal at £4.95 per share plus a final dividend. A Board meeting on Sunday January 7, 2001 recommended the offer to shareholders.

The vast majority of Blue Circle's shareholders were institutions and readily agreed to the bid, which was regarded by analysts as being "a sensibly priced deal." However, many individual shareholders, who were mainly ex-employees with an emotional attachment to the firm, voted against the takeover, as they saw Blue Circle as a "British Institution." Nevertheless, the deal was completed and Lafarge's shares responded favorably. As for Haythornthwaite, he left Blue Circle on July 11, 2001 and on July 24, 2001, it was announced he would become CEO of Invensys PLC.

1. *Why was Blue Circle bid for?*
2. *Was it in the interests of Blue Circle's shareholders for the hostile bid to fail?*
3. *Were the defense strategies adopted by Blue Circle consistent with reducing the chance of takeover but not prejudicial towards its shareholders?*
4. *Did Haythornthwaite act in his own best interests or his shareholders'?*

Merry men and virgins

As a means of demonstrating how students of strategy, like management consultants, or anyone else for that matter, can bring assumptions based on their own experience to bear on problems that may require a different mindset, we often use a little exercise based on Robin Hood and his merry men. Robin has a problem, which is described below. The question we pose to students is: Robin has hired you as a management consultant; what would you advise him to do?

Robin Hood's revolt against the Sheriff of Nottingham began as a personal dispute. But Robin knew that he could do little to exact his revenge without the help of others. So, he set out to find allies – men with similar grievances that he could unite under a common cause. He did not have to look very hard, and as he looked back on the first year of his operation he was still surprised at how quickly he had gathered around him able men who shared his personal hatred of the Sheriff and his overlord – the brutal Prince John, who ruled, unjustly in Robin's eyes, in the absence of Richard the Lionheart.

There had been little structure or routine to the establishment of the band of merry men that had emerged. Robin asked few questions of his charges and their motives and only required that they trusted his ultimate decision-making authority and gave their all in pursuit of what had become their motto: "rob from the rich and give to the poor." Under Robin's rule, a simple structure had evolved with particular tasks delegated to those who Robin saw as his most able lieutenants, such as Will Scarlett, Little John, and Friar Tuck.

But, as the legend of the merry men spread, so the number of recruits from further afield increased. Some came with a taste for adventure; others with a desire, or need, to live outside of the law. As the band grew larger, what was once but a few tents was turning into an established camp with an increased range of ancillary services attached. More and more men spent more and more time sitting around waiting to be organized and waiting for adventure. The cost of maintaining this organization was on the rise.

In the meantime, revenue was declining. The rich were becoming more adept at avoiding capture by Robin's less than nimble organization and the Sheriff and Prince John were becoming more skillful in anticipating and combating Robin's raids. Moreover, in response to Robin's opposition and stirring up of the region's common folk against them, they had worked hard to shore up their own defenses and political alliances, so as to make their overthrow – which had, at one point, been Robin's driving ambition – increasingly difficult.

As he moved into the second year of his campaign, Robin was confronted with some difficult problems. Was his strategy effective? How should he organize his forces? What did he need to change and what should he seek to retain? One thing was clear, however: he did not know the answers to these problems himself. He would need to consult with others. "Perhaps," he mused, "I could benefit from hearing more about the latest thinking in these domains."

Students don't tend to begin by imagining the particular "macro context" within which Robin operates before thinking of solutions that would fit with this. Hence, they tend to unthinkingly provide modern answers to Robin's problems. For example, from a modern management consultant's perspective, what Robin should do is decentralize, devolve responsibility, empower those beneath him, or franchise. However, in Robin's cultural setting – where his forceful, charismatic, almost divine leadership is the core that holds everything together – such solutions would likely be seen as a sign of weakness, that Robin is losing his "mojo," or that he is no longer committed to the cause. They would likely leave the organization in a greater state of malaise then when the consultants came in.

Many believe that a similar overlaying of generic solutions that did not take account of the particular operational context occurred when consultants from the Virgin Group, famous for revamping maturing consumer product and service markets like air and rail travel, cola, vodka, and banking, were called in by Government ministers to write a report on Britain's hospitals at the beginning of the year 2000. In an article in *The Sunday Times,* the Secretary for Health, Alan Milburn, described Britain's publicly funded NHS (National Health Service) as "a 1948 system operating in a 21st century world. That is why," he explained, "I have now asked Sir Richard Branson's award-winning Virgin Group to advise us on how hospitals can be made consumer friendly . . . It is about transforming the very culture of the NHS to make it a modern consumer service." Press releases claimed that the Prime Minister, Tony Blair, would use the report to follow up on accusations made by his Health Secretary of the dire "forces of conservatism" within the NHS and "the gross inefficiencies built into the system."

The consultants visited nine hospitals and several GPs' surgeries over a 26-day period and composed a damning report. They wrote of "over-centralization," "too much red-tape," "chaotic booking-arrangements," and "poor management." They concluded that "the patient is required to fit into the system, rather than the other way around," and that the "dead hand of bureaucracy seems to stifle imagination and flair." However, on the up side, they claimed that "most [staff] are probably decent people who just need a little leadership and direction." The actions they believed should be taken to remedy the situation included the sort of ideas that have become commonplace in many organizations: "empowering workers to be more innovative," making hospitals more "consumer friendly," and increasing transparency and accountability. (One recommended means of doing this was to allow patient representatives to go behind the scenes and carry out "snap inspections.") There was also talk of snack trolleys and making hospitals "more fun."

However, NHS employees were critical of the Virgin report and the Government's handling of it. Doctors felt they were being blamed for poor public perception of the NHS, which, they argued, was caused by lack of funding. Stephen Thornton, the Chief Executive of the NHS Confederation, accepted that declining standards needed to be addressed but challenged "the Virgin team to show me what they describe as a suffocating bureaucracy . . . Where on earth do they get ridiculous figures that imply there is one administrator to every two clinical staff?" Of all NHS staff, only 3% were managers/administrators, compared with 44% nurses, 8% doctors and 17% clerical, he said, asking "I wonder how many backup staff it takes Virgin to get one pilot into the air." In any case, he continued, "many administrative and clerical staff undertake critical patient-related tasks. It is disingenuous to suggest these people hinder rather than help the treatment of patients." Peter Hawker, Chairman of the British Medical Association's Consultants' Committee, similarly suggested that he was "all for improving the services to patients but we need real resources, not an exercise in spin [doctoring]."

These criticisms sparked a wider debate about the Blair Government's use of consultants. A survey by the *Independent on Sunday* showed that it had spent almost a billion pounds hiring private consulting firms in its first three years in office. It was revealed that The Department for Education and its agencies spent almost £10m between 1997 and 1999. In response, Nigel de Gruchy, General Secretary of a prominent teaching union, claimed that: "The money could be much better spent. The Government paid Hey McBer consultancies £3m to come up with criteria for what makes a good teacher. We could have told them that for nothing."

The Department of Health's spending on consultants in the same period was two and a half times that of Education. According to one source, this could have paid for 2,327 heart bypass operations, 4,421 hip replacements, 737 full cancer treatments, and the wages of 1,133 junior doctors. A spokeswoman for the Unison health union said: "It's an awful amount of money to spend on consultants, particularly if those consultants are at the expense of money going into front-line care. We generally know what the problems are, the difficulty is getting the Government to listen to the people who are on the ground."

---

1. *Why were consultants from Virgin used to advise the NHS?*
2. *What are the advantages and disadvantages of hiring management consultants to move or shake a company's strategy?*
3. *Having read this case, how would you now approach the situation if you were asked to act as a consultant advising Robin Hood about the best way to deal with the predicament outlined in the first part of this case?*

Fad power

Business process reengineering (the 1990s' most pervasive strategic management mantra) and the Mozart effect (the idea, which also became popular in the 1990s, that babies who are exposed to classical music grow up to be more intelligent) might seem worlds apart but, according to Michael Skapinker, management columnist for the *Financial Times*, the similarities between both phenomena are many.

Where did the classical music and babies theory come from? In 1993, the science journal *Nature* published a study that showed that college students (i.e., not babies) who listened to a Mozart sonata for 10 minutes increased their performance on a subsequent spatial intelligence test. This became known as the "Mozart effect."

Subsequent studies produced mixed results, at best. In 1999, an analysis of 16 such studies, also published in *Nature*, concluded that the overall effect of playing music on spatial intelligence was in fact negligible. In another article entitled "The Mozart Effect: Tracking the Evolution of a Scientific Legend," Adrian Bangerter and Chip Heath of Stanford University analyzed both why people projected what had originally been a study of students on to infants, and why the story achieved such wide currency (in US surveys, 80% of respondents had heard of the Mozart effect).

Bangerter and Heath concluded that the reason the nature of the original study shifted from students to babies was because infants are the focus of so much uncertainty and anxiety. All parents worry about whether they can do more for their children and this seemed to give them something to do that would temporarily assuage their anxiety. They also noted that media references to the Mozart effect had now tailed off. This was partly because of the subsequent scientific studies questioning the link between music and intelligence, but also because it had lost its novelty. Parents' attention switched to newer fads.

Skapinker claimed that reading about the rise and fall of the Mozart effect reminded him of several other frenzies, involving companies rather than children: business process reengineering (BPR), the dash to go online, and, now, locating the organization's core competence and outsourcing everything else. As he explained in his *FT* column: "Reengineering is particularly apposite because, like the Mozart effect, it began with a founding text. When Michael Hammer and James Champy's *Reengineering the Corporation* was published in 1993, it caught US and Western business at a low ebb, very scared of what appeared to be frighteningly efficient Japanese companies selling high-quality goods at low prices."

In an uncertain business environment most companies were desperate to cut their costs (just as parents are desperate not to deny their infants any advantage). BPR seemed to show them how. Most never read Hammer and Champy's book, or understood what it was based on, or whether it was founded on solid science, but "the idea" of it, they believed, told them what to do: reexamine every business process as if they were setting it up from scratch; ask whether they really needed all those employees; slash their workforces. Subsequently, and at great long-term cost, middle managers, deemed worthless and superfluous because what they did (communicate, for example) could not be easily quantified, were dispatched with particular vigor.

Reengineering the Corporation was not as simple-minded as that, Skapinker pointed out. It actually advocated looking at each encounter from the customers' point of view and designing processes to ensure those particular customers were best served. This could have involved merging departments that were previously separate, but it required taking employees' abilities more, rather than less, seriously. But, all that was drowned out in the stampede to follow the simple mantra of "downsizing." And when the rush was over, companies were left to rue the experience and expertise they had lost. Indeed, all the factors that lay behind the Mozart effect were there, too: anxiety, weakness, and misinterpretation of the original writing.

Skapinker also saw Mozart effect parallels with what he terms "dotcom madness," where so many companies were panicked into believing that they would be overtaken unless they made the internet the core of their future development – whether it suited their particular competitive advantage and business environment or not.

Perhaps the current craze to outsource to and get established in developing countries will play out the same way? As Skapinker's column concludes: "Of course there is an Indian and Chinese challenge – and opportunity [in this respect]. These are potentially huge markets that are just beginning to open up. In the same way the internet was extremely important – it was just [in reality] not very clear why that was. But there is more than one method to deal with any new situation. When everybody believes they have found the way to do it, there is a good chance that everyone is wrong."

---

1. *Why might a company's strategies be so easily moved or shaken by fads and the management gurus that issue them?*
2. *What are the dangers of following fads or trends like BPR?*
3. *What could you as a manager do to help your company resist following the latest fads blindly?*

Show me the margin!

Title in a 2005 brokerage report from Bear Stearns & Co. A play on words based on Tom Cruise's "Show me the money!" line from the movie Jerry Maguire

When an industry with a reputation for difficult economics meets a manager with a reputation for excellence, it is usually the industry that keeps its reputation intact.

Warren Buffett, CEO of Berkshire Hathaway

You must have received marketing letters from financial institutions showing graphs of how much better off you would be if you invested your money in their funds rather than putting it in a bank account or under a mattress. Underlying this sort of promotional material, however, is a perennial question for investors. If you had $1,000, in which industry[1] would you invest? Why is it that some *industries* seem to be more profitable year in and year out than others?

Table 3.1 shows the annual compound percentage returns gained through reinvested dividends and capital appreciation through investing in particular US industry segments or US Treasury Bonds for the 10 years 1993–2003. $1,000 in Treasury Bonds would have grown to $1,524 over that period compared with the $1,105 you would have finished up with by taking a chance on the airline industry. It could have been worse, however, as $1,000 in the "building materials" sector would have shrunk to $599. On the other hand, it could have been much

Table 3.1 Investment returns 1993–2003, selected industry segments

Industry segment	Returns (%)
Computer software	22
Home builders	19
Beverages	15
Pharmaceuticals	14
Healthcare	9
Mining, crude oil production	9
Motors	6
Hotels/casinos/resorts	5
US Treasury Bonds	4.3
Airlines	1
Building materials	(5)

(Source: Fortune.com)

better; had you chosen the "computer software" industry as the vehicle for your $1,000, you would be smiling at the $7,305 you had after 10 years of 22% compound returns.

The returns to investors in these industries are a proxy for the profitability or "attractiveness" of those industries. Clearly, some industries are better places to be in than others for both the firms in those industries and investors in general. The reasons as to why this is so lie in an understanding of each industry's characteristics, its dominant structure, evolutionary phase, and the competitive/cooperative forces underpinning all of these.

Strategic Hell – Perfect Competition

For strategists, "hell" is a set of (industry) circumstances that combine to remove any options other than to do what everyone else is doing. This culminates in being forced to take the industry price (be a "price taker") rather than having discretion to set a different price (be a "price maker") through innovative products and services or through having proprietary ways of reducing costs. The epitome of such hell is perfect competition.[2]

In perfect competition (figure 3.1) there are many sellers and hence no scope for coordination of market pricing. The businesses are too small to achieve any firm-specific advantages through economies of scale and, as they all use the same technology and production techniques, no cost advantages are available at the process level. They all sell products that, in the eyes of their buyers, are the same and those buyers can easily switch from one supplier to another. On both the demand and supply side, there is informational transparency and hence swift dissemination of any innovation in product or process.

In such an industry a business is forced to take the prevailing market price. If the firm increases prices above the market it sells nothing and there is little point in setting a lower price as it is already selling all it can. In these industries, the long-term profits will equal the cost of capital (what economists call "normal" profits) because if profits move above this level, new firms enter the industry to

Figure 3.1 Perfect competition

Figure 3.2 Imperfections

grab their share and, if profits fall, then the most disenchanted exit and overall profitability returns to the normal level.

To achieve returns greater than the cost of capital (what economist call "rents") industry *imperfections* must exist. These imperfections (summarized in figure 3.2) are the opposite of the factors driving perfect markets and include product differentiation, entry barriers, switching costs, and so on. If a firm can develop and exploit such imperfections better than its rivals then it will outperform the average of its industry returns and have competitive advantage. This advantage will be sustained as long as those imperfections, and the firm's unique ability to exploit them, last. One view of *strategy*, then, is that it is the ongoing quest for returns (greater than the cost of capital) through the establishment and exploitation of firm-specific imperfections. While some industries are born (nearly) perfect, some become that way over time because of the underlying evolutionary forces. It is to these industry-shaping forces that we now turn our attention.

The Industry Life Cycle[3]

Industries are born; they grow; they mature; and in some cases they eventually die (figure 3.3). At each stage of this cycle each industry has its own critical success factors (CSFs) that all firms must address to be successful (figure 3.4). Those attributes that give a competitive edge initially ("win-the-game") become a standard requirement ("in-the-game") as competitors imitate and improve on the original. Japanese manufactures stole a march on their international rivals in the 1980s with the quality and reliability of their products but these features are standard for durable consumer goods like cars, washing machines, and televisions in the 21st century.

The life cycle is a description of the past and not a predictor of the future and there is no straitjacket forcing specific dynamics to emerge at each stage. For example, industries can be de-matured by innovation or new thinking, as in the airline industry, which has been de-matured in terms of passenger growth by the development of the low-cost operator. However, what the life cycle does tell us is that what firms need to do to be successful varies with the stage of the industry.

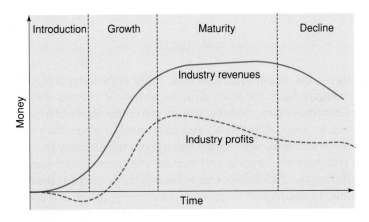

Figure 3.3 The industry life cycle

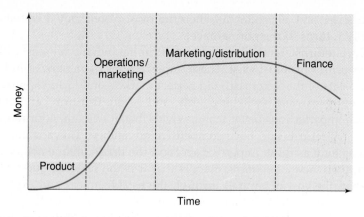

Figure 3.4   Generic critical success factors across the industry life cycle

Introduction

In the early, innovative phases of the life cycle, profitability and cash flow are sacrificed to gain a foothold for the future (figure 3.3). At this stage of industry development the features, benefits, and functions of the *product* are the CSFs. Most product-industries go from birth to death rapidly because the new product fails to generate sufficient customers. Those that do find sufficient acceptance grow rapidly once a critical mass of consumers develops.

Growth

As the industry grows, there tends to be a convergence to a dominant set of product features. These become standard "in-the-game" requirements (e.g. all VCRs, mobile phones, personal computers, financial products, etc. offer essentially the same set of features and benefits). From then onwards, the foundations of ongoing success rest on superior *marketing* (distribution channels, brand, reputation) and *operating processes* (production, logistics, service).

Maturity

As growth slows, consumers have become more knowledgeable, and processes as well as products have become common across all players. Product/process development continues and products around the common standards proliferate as companies seek to cover all the bases and gain an edge where they can. However, any improvements disseminate rapidly throughout the industry and parity is soon restored as competitors emulate and imitate the innovators.[4] Increasingly it is superior *marketing and distribution* that separates the successful from the average. Cost reduction, to counteract increased price competition, is now an essential in-the-game factor for long-term survivors. Most industries in the industrialized world are mature, with growth rates in the home countries at about the same level as GDP. Accelerating sales in less-developed countries becomes the prime source of real industry growth. Hence, industry consolidation through merger and acquisition, a fanatical focus on brand and marketing, and relentless cost-cutting (e.g. through outsourcing call centers or manufacturing to cheaper locations) become essential to ensure profitability. Industries can be "de-matured" and grow to new levels through innovation (e.g., as previously mentioned, the low-cost airlines have markedly increased the number of people flying in Europe and America) or sometimes through a macro-shock or a change in key movers and shakers (e.g. an unforeseen war or the election of a more hawkish government can revitalize certain sectors of the armaments industry).

Decline

In this phase, the skills of the financial undertaker come to the fore. Consolidation of (now-cheap) businesses and, hence, management of overcapacity, minimal investment, and a controlled milking of the product until its final demise or niche existence are the basis of success. Whether the declining industry is profitable (e.g. cigars, quality fountain pens) or not (e.g. prepared baby foods) depends on how well surplus capacity is adjusted to fit the prevailing environment and also the extent to which resilient niches of price-insensitive demand remain among the general decline.[5]

Industry Structure

Mature industries are characterized by an overall structure that dictates to a large extent the nature and scope of the competitive advantages (imperfections) theoretically available for companies to exploit. Economists have suggested the following four generic structures, each of which carries different implications for the firms comprising the industry.

1. **Perfect competition** has been discussed above and by definition there are no sources of competitive advantage. One of the most important strategic implications in such markets is that companies are forced to *take the market price*. Regardless of other factors, commodity producers (e.g. steel, wheat, oil) take the market price, whether that price is high, low, or medium, and so at the *product* level these are examples of perfect competition.
2. **Monopolistic competition** exists when there are many sellers but they are selling slightly differentiated products (i.e. each seller has a monopoly in its own products). Sellers can charge different prices because individual price differences are not noticed by the many other sellers who do not respond because they have differentiated products and hence (relatively) loyal customers. Restaurants, doctors, and hairdressers are all examples of such structures. An important characteristic of such industries is that economies of size (e.g. economies of scale, scope, experience, and distribution channels) are not important. In such industries, firms do not have carte blanche over pricing discretion but can *price to what their market (segment) will bear*.

65

3. **Oligopoly** occurs when there are significant economies of size available to bigger companies and where there are many opportunities to differentiate. The industry coalesces to a few companies that become big enough to leverage the economies of size and have differentiation options. Pharmaceutical, soap powder, supermarket, and aircraft industries are examples. It is in such industries that pricing is truly strategic in that *the potential response of the other players is a critical input to the pricing decision.*[6]

4. **Monopolies** are firms that have no (or at least very limited) competitors for their products and hence *can raise or lower prices without taking into account the responses of other firms.* Market-based monopolies (as contrasted with government legislated ones) can form where there are substantial economies of size and limited options for differentiation. The cost of getting big enough to compete with the entrenched incumbent is too high for potential rivals. So-called "natural" monopolies are industries where economies of size are large and where the firm size to gain optimal effect from these (the minimum efficient size or MES[7]) is greater than 50% of the market – hence the first one to get to 50% market share wipes out the others and goes on to gain the other 50%.[8] Power and water utilities and railways are examples of (regional) monopolies in most countries.

Industry Forces

Driving the final industry structure as it evolves are underlying industry forces. Of course it is more than a "simple" structure that eventuates. Pankaj Ghemawat[9] uses the intuitively appealing metaphor of the "business landscape" to capture the complex multidimensional hills, valleys, and plateaus that result from the interaction of industry forces with particular business models. These forces are stylized in figure 3.5, which is Michael Porter's encapsulation of decades of industrial organization economics research and thinking into a framework that captures the resultant theories and findings for non-economist managers. The model tells us that three broad dynamics, **power**, **entry**, and **rivalry**, interact to contribute to the "attractiveness" of an industry to firms trying to earn more than their cost of capital. These dynamics all influence the degree to which firms have control over pricing, particularly in terms of being able to increase prices to lift margins or even just to compensate for increased costs.

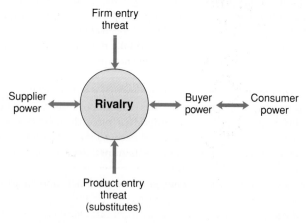

Figure 3.5 The Five Forces of industry structure (Source: adapted from Porter (1985) p. 6)

Power – the horizontal axis

Despite pious talk of "partnerships" the buyer–supplier relationships are power-based struggles focused on capturing as much long-term value for the firm as possible while giving enough to the other buyer or supplier firm to keep it in business. There are many characteristics that interact to determine which party is the more powerful. These include relative size (which does matter), relative difficulty in finding a new partner/product (switching costs), and whether either party could do things for themselves (backward/forward integration).

The balance of power varies over time. For example, in the relatively recent past the major brand name suppliers such as Coca-Cola, Unilever, Procter & Gamble, etc. held pricing power over their supermarket customers. They were bigger (i.e. were more concentrated than their customers) and had more pull-through power over the brand-sensitive end consumers. Now, with the growing credibility of the supermarkets' own-label products (e.g. Tesco in the UK) and the increasing consolidation of the worldwide supermarket industry, the power has shifted. The "pain" that a Wal-Mart might feel from not stocking Coca-Cola is now (probably) less than the pain that the Coca-Cola Corporation would feel from being de-listed. Power is related to the degree of switching costs/pain that is incurred in changing from one supplier or product to another. Hence, while it is easy for any super-market to not stock Coca-Cola, the costs of this action would be high if substantial numbers of potential customers wanted Coke and chose to shop for it in a rival store rather than accepting the alternative cola offered.

Power is one thing but the inclination to use that power is another. This inclination is referred to as **price sensitivity** and indicates that customers are more sensitive to changes in prices of some products or services than others. The factors that contribute to price sensitivity are mainly components of the extent to which a price rise from one firm takes value away from the other. Rich buyers who can easily pass on cost increases to their own customers tend to be relatively insensitive to price increases, particularly for a product/service that, while a low part of their overall costs, is important to their own product/service in terms of function or quality. However, buyers who are struggling to make money, and/or whose own customers will not accept price rises, tend to be much more sensitive to the impact of price, particularly for products/services that are a relatively large component of their total costs.

Entry/substitution – the vertical axis

The vertical axis covers two areas: the entry of other firms trying to get some of the industry value for themselves and the potential substitution by other products meeting the same needs. These both act to keep a cap on *industry* pricing. With no possibility of entry (because of cost, fear of retaliation, lack of distribution, etc.) and a lack of credible substitute products, then industry pricing is only restricted by power battles (above) and rivalry (below). Hence, the cost of widely available substitute forms of entertainment (e.g. bowling, football, television) acts as a cap on cinema ticket prices even if rivalry did not exist between cinema chains. On the other hand it is virtually impossible to set up a new water utility in the UK (entry by acquisition does not change industry structure) and there is no viable substitute for water for most of its uses. This means that the Government must regulate pricing because the consumer is powerless in the face of price increases. Entire industries can emerge as substitutes for existing products. For example, the main driver of the growth of the plastics industry was its value-adding **substitution** for other packaging (paper, cardboard, glass, metal etc.) and structural (metals, timber) materials. What might the mobile handset substitute for over the next 10 years?

Rivalry

This middle force of the five, which is also engaged in both the horizontal power play and the vertical entry play, captures the impact of the ongoing direct competition between industry participants. The more that the industry reassembles perfect competition, the fiercer becomes the price competition and the more "unattractive" (i.e. unprofitable) it becomes. Rivalry is driven by more than industry structure, however, as managers with different personalities and from different local and international cultures have different goals and different ways of dealing with competition. Some prefer an ongoing knock-down, drag-out fight while others favor a more genteel way of doing business. Hence, some oligopolies engage in marketing wars (e.g. pharmaceuticals) while other oligopolies engage in price wars (e.g. French hypermarkets) where the attractive returns of some are gained at the expense of others.

Industries are not necessarily homogeneous with respect to competition. In some cases there are clear demarcations between sets of competitors adopting similar strategies aimed at similar customer segments. These **strategic groups** can have high "mobility barriers" that prevent companies moving in the same way that entry barriers deter movement into an industry. Department stores, for example, compete more directly with other department stores than they do with supermarkets, although both are in the retailing industry. Mobility barriers, however, erode or can be overcome, and so French hypermarkets now sell luxury goods and the formerly down-at-heel, "pile it high and sell it cheap" Tesco of post-war Britain firstly admired, then emulated, and now dominates Sainsbury's, formerly its up-market rival. Tesco overcame the substantial mobility barriers between the "deep discount" strategic group and the "value for money" (middle-class customers) group previously dominated by Sainsbury's.

Other Forces: Cooperation

The overriding goal of business strategy is to *create value* for the firm's stakeholders. With this in mind, we can see that, while **competition** over your share of the value "pie" might be an inevitable consequence of being in business, there is also much to be gained by **cooperation** with other firms in increasing the overall size of that value pie. Figure 3.6 captures this idea by explicitly identifying the role of complementors.[10]

Complementors are companies from which customers buy or to which suppliers sell products that are *complementary* to the company's products. A complementary

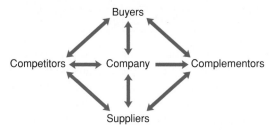

Figure 3.6 The value net (Source: Brandenburger and Nalebuff (1996))

product is one that makes customers more willing to buy your product or suppliers more willing to supply. Hence, manufacturers of games consoles and designers of games are in a complementary relationship in that increased success of X-box, for example, is of value to the designer of X-box games. Similarly, Microsoft (X-box) would cooperate readily with a games designer who promised a "killer" X-box game.

Functional necessities, such as games and consoles, CDs/DVDs and players, pens and paper, etc. are obvious examples of complementary products/relationships. But so too is the relationship between roads and cars, yet initially the major car companies in the US had to build "seedling roads" to encourage public pressure on the Government to develop highways – a lack of roads would have discouraged many from buying a car.[11] The Michelin restaurant guide, by encouraging gastronomically inclined car owners to drive to distant restaurants, also encouraged tire wear and purchase – hence, restaurants become complementors of tire companies.

Competitors can also be complementors by increasing the market size for the product. Hence, although the low-cost airlines in the Western world have certainly caused major problems for the large incumbent airlines, they have also generated a significant increase in the number of people who are flying. In the long term this may prove to be very valuable to the major airlines once they have reduced their operating costs in line with the low-price industry in which they now operate.

The fact that competitors can be complementors illustrates the ambivalence of the complementary relationship captured by the term *co-opetition* coined by Adam Brandenburger and Barry Nalebuff (1996). As well as helping to increase the size of the value pie, complementors become increasingly able to grab more of it:

- if they become bigger than competitors
- if they have a greater influence on pull-through of customers
- if they have more credible threats of integration into competitor functions
- if it becomes more costly for the customer to switch from the complementor than from the competitor.

As IBM learned from its relationship with Microsoft, value from complementarity is based on eternal vigilance. Heightened vigilance about complementors has been a factor in mergers between content and channel providers, such as Sony/Columbia Pictures and AOL/Time Warner. In these examples the complementarity was seemingly obvious but subsequent value was not – for example, Sony wrote off US$3.2bn at the end of its complement-driven acquisition.

Conclusions

So, to understand why some industries are more profitable, for companies and investors, than others, we can see that some reasons lie in the interacting forces of the industry and the different stages of industry evolution. While some industries have product–process–buyer interrelationships that lend themselves to multiple opportunities for advantage over other firms, others have dynamics that constrain the ability of firms to outpace their rivals. The strategic "hells" of perfect competition and overcapacity in capital-intensive industry can be contrasted with the strategic "heavens" of differentiated oligopolies or brute monopoly power.

For the investor or corporate portfolio manager the implication is clear – choose your industry carefully. However, for the practicing manager, already running a business within an industry, that advice may be too late; akin to wise suggestions such as "choose your parents carefully," or the Irish answer when asked travel directions, "I wouldn't start from here." To what extent, then, is such a manager locked into the deterministic ebb and flow of the industry tide? Can management initiated strategy make a difference or is it nothing more than a rain dance performed ever more elaborately but with little chance of influencing the inevitable? We shall examine the scope for management driven strategy later.

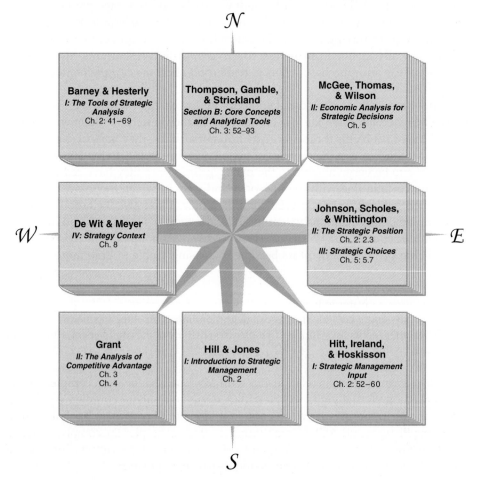

Power is money

In the 1960s, a change took place in the sporting apparel and footwear markets. Until then, by far the most important consumer had been the amateur and professional athlete who wore the shorts, tops, tracksuits, specialist shoes, and other paraphernalia necessary for his/her particular sport. Of this group, the largest segment comprised the millions of amateur sports enthusiasts throughout the world. Direct promotions to these consumers and promotion via endorsement by top athletes made a performance enhancing proposition (i.e. "wear our kit and be a winner"). Then, in the "swinging sixties," pop groups like The Rolling Stones began to wear "trainers" (i.e. running shoes) as a counter-cultural symbol of youthful rebellion. And so sports apparel by firms such as Reebok, Nike, and Adidas became fashion as well as sports brands.

The wholesale global sportswear industry is worth more than US$60bn per year and nearly US$150bn at retail. The top three brand companies, Nike, Adidas and Reebok, share 40% of the branded market (29% of the total). While these firms retain the core competitive functions of marketing and design, manufacturing is outsourced to the lowest cost sources in a long global supply chain (figure 3-1.1). For instance, Nike (market leader, with 20% of the branded market) has over 700 suppliers worldwide.

The targeted sportswear consumer, particularly the teenage and young adult segment, is fashion sensitive and relatively price insensitive. Wearing what is "in"

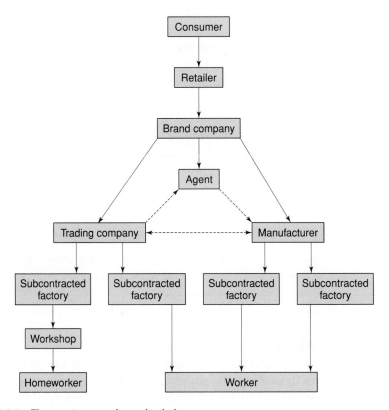

Figure 3-1.1 The sports apparel supply chain

is more important than wearing what you have until it is worn out. High-profile sports teams are aware of this dynamic and regularly change the design of their (branded) playing shirts (their "strip") to profit from loyal fans who "must have" the latest shirt with the name and number of their favorite player added at extra cost. Sporting teams, however, pale into retailing insignificance compared with giant consumer distributors like US-based Wal-Mart or France's Carrefour. While 80% of athletic footwear sales and 75% of sportswear are sold under brands, retailers understand that even fashion-conscious, price insensitive customers will, if given the choice, pay the lower of two prices for their chosen branded item. So being able to offer that lower price is a key competitive weapon. As they thrust and parry with price reductions, the retailers constantly put pressure on their suppliers for compensating cost reductions so that retail margins are maintained.

While retailers set the consumer price, the brand company infuses the product with its *value*. Creating image-based value means that marketing is *the* major cost as both saturation media coverage and celebrity endorsements are expensive. In making over US$1bn profit in 2004, Nike expensed nearly as much on marketing. Yet, while nothing is spared on value-creation in design and marketing, things are entirely different at the production end. Here the watchwords are "efficiency" and "cost reduction." These watchwords are passwords for the agents, trading companies, and manufacturers seeking access to "manufacture and supply" orders.

Some of these intermediaries themselves are large multinationals but, like the myriad smaller companies and the even smaller subcontractors that supply them, are dependent for their corporate lives on winning the orders of Reebok, Adidas, etc. As well as pressures on product cost, this level of the supply chain must manage complex forecasting, inventory, and logistics algorithms as retailers respond to variable consumer demand by giving shorter lead times for more frequent but smaller orders. Hence, these suppliers bear most of the risk and costs of inventory management as well as the challenge of continuous cost reduction.

Flexible low-cost manufacture in a labor-intensive product demands flexible, low-cost workers. Hence, the supply chain ends in countries like China, Cambodia, or Indonesia, the comparative advantage of which lies in an abundant supply of low-cost (i.e. poor) workers. On July 1, 2005 the official minimum wage for full-time workers in Shanghai, one of China's most dynamic and modern cities, rose for the thirteenth time since 1993 to 690 yuan (US$83) per month (*Shanghai Daily*, June 4, 2005).

---

1. *Explain the power relationships in this supply chain and how they might predict the winners and losers in terms of ongoing profitability.*

◄◄◄ Power is Money: Some Ideas . . .

Price is the final manifestation of the ongoing power struggle for value between suppliers and buyers throughout the supply chain. In the supply chain (i.e. the horizontal dimension of the Five Forces diagram as it is represented in the text), it is **price sensitivity** that determines how keenly price gains and reductions will be sought and **relative power** that determines which "partner" bears more of the ensuing cost. "Winners and losers" in the power struggle are those "winning and losing" at the downstream (i.e. more towards the consumer) end of this industry. This is because there tends to be an ebb and flow of who is on top as the big guys (large manufacturers, brand companies, and retailers) arm wrestle each other. But, like all power hierarchies, the less power you have, the more dependent you are on the largesse of others and the final upstream supplier. In this particular industry the upstream supplier has little power, but this varies industry by industry. In general the firm captures value consistent with its low power.

Consumers – winners
The individual sportswear consumer is powerless to change the price set by the retailer, no matter how price sensitive he or she might be. Even if many consumers are price sensitive they lack power because they cannot effectively coordinate with other like-minded consumers to act together to threaten to shift their custom if price reductions are not forthcoming. However, **transparent pricing** (transparent through advertising and word-of-mouth) effectively acts as a **coordinating mechanism** and forces retailers to deal with consumers as if they were a coordinated group rather than a bunch of separate individuals. While a consumer lacks power, the consumer is powerful in the context of retailer price rivalry. Big retailers know that if one of them decides to price a particular pair of Nike trainers at $42.50 against a prevailing price of $50.00 then the consumer will tend to take this offer and hence it must be matched.

Sportswear retailers – winners
The sportswear retail industry is increasingly **concentrated** and hence has enormous power as the major distribution outlet (and point-of-sale promoter) for the brand companies. Given the consumer traffic through Wal-Mart in the US, for example, it would be a brave marketing manager who would risk being de-listed by this giant retailer. The retailer is price sensitive to the extent it cannot pass on price increases to the consumer but the force that most deters retail price increases is **rivalry** between the retailers themselves. Hence, retailers are always seeking "exclusive product" arrangements with major brand suppliers (although such arrangements flirt with illegality in several countries). Despite their power the retailers cannot push the brand companies too far. They are dependent on the heavily promoted brands to generate traffic through their stores and so it would be an equally brave Wal-Mart buyer that chose to de-list Nike, for example: Nike spends a lot of money creating brand loyalty and these brand loyal Nike buyers would buy the "swoosh" and perhaps other products at the same time at a Wal-Mart rival. Not stocking the major brands would result in lower sales for Wal-Mart even if it also hurt the brand.

Brand companies – winners
The reciprocal power relationship between the retailers and the brand companies has been mentioned above. Unlike their retailers, these firms do not want to compete with each other on price. They are all in need of high margins (supported by high price) to support the marketing/promotion that goes into creating their value proposition that in turn drives the high price that consumers

are prepared to pay. This is a battle of marketing where **barriers to entry** (need for a brand and guaranteed distribution) are high and **substitutes** few. Hence, with relatively price-insensitive final consumers and equality of power with retailers, there is no need for price wars and the inevitable erosion of profits that results. However, the other side of the margin equation is cost and here the brand companies are ruthless.

Trading companies, manufacturers, agents – win some, lose some

This sector is **less concentrated** than its buyers, cannot **forward integrate**, and lacks **unique assets or capabilities**. **Barriers to entry** are low in that there are many trading companies/agents with the necessary skills/infrastructure than can enter the industry and develop contacts, or already have the necessary connections. Even large manufacturers that supply multiple brands can be bypassed by an agent/trading company willing to coordinate subcontractors. These firms are under constant pressure for cost reduction, quality improvement, and increased inventory efficiency, with the (implicit) threat from the buyer that "if you can't do it, I'll find someone who can." As these intermediaries get bigger, they are, paradoxically, under more pressure, as the loss of a big order can result in ongoing losses and potential bankruptcy. Most are locked in to their customers but the converse does not apply.

Subcontracted companies – win some, lose more

By now you can see the picture. At this lowly level, power is limited. These are the last structured parts of the system. The financial penalties imposed for late deliveries or poor quality often end up here, passed down from above, as do the consequences of delay and obsolescence should the retailer not want the stock after all. And if these organizations don't want the business, **new entrants** from underdeveloped countries around the globe, as well as myriad rivals in their own backyard, are queuing up to fill the gap. With no power to make a price these companies exert the only power they have to make a profit – on their controllable "costs," namely labor.

The manufacturing workers – losers

These "suppliers" face numerous **competitors** (replacement workers) in their own neighborhood and numerous potential **entrants** in other countries. They tend to have a relatively **low skill base**, to act as individuals rather than collectively, and to have no alternative "customers" to whom they can tender. While the price (wages) might be low and constantly subject to being lowered (through non-payment of holiday pay, increased piecework rates, etc.), the options that exist tend to be at the level of "take the 'price' reduction (and be hungry) or leave it (and starve)."

As the title of the case suggests, power is money in the supply chain: where you find power, you find money; where you find no power . . .

The price of entry

As the takeover battle for Safeway PLC, Britain's third largest supermarket chain, was being waged in 2003, there was widespread speculation that the French superstore giant, Carrefour, might enter the fray. For them the question was whether the UK supermarket industry was sufficiently attractive to enter.

The UK supermarket industry as a whole was worth some £100bn a year. The main activity of these supermarkets was food and drink retail, although most had also added petrol stations to their outlets and had also begun to branch into clothing retail with significant success. The primary activity, however, remained food and drink retail and UK consumers bought 80% of their food, 75% of fresh vegetables and fruit, 65% of fish and meat, and 50% of milk from the five largest supermarkets. These supermarkets, in order of market share in 2003, were Tesco (25.8%), Sainsbury's (17.4%), Asda (15.9%), Safeway (10.0%), and Wm Morrison (5.9%). Pre-tax profits for these companies mirrored their size, with Tesco generating £1.4bn, Sainsbury's £0.57bn, Safeway £0.36bn, and Morrisons £0.24bn. Asda's figures are not known because it had been acquired in 1999 by the world's largest grocer, Wal-Mart of the US. Despite this profitability, the overall growth rate for the industry had slowed in recent years to 2.9%, which was equal to the growth of the economy as a whole.

The main suppliers to the industry were farmers and fast-moving consumer goods (FMCG) companies. Located around the world and supplying thousands of products, the number of farmers involved was huge. Colossal improvements in transportation in terms of both lower costs and refrigeration had opened massive sourcing opportunities for the supermarkets. With increasing levels of competition, farmers attempted to work together through cooperatives to improve their negotiating position vis-à-vis the supermarkets. However, unless the product was particularly valued by the supermarkets, these organizations had little effect on the terms of trade achieved by the farmers. The FMCG companies, however, such as Kelloggs and Heinz, operated on much larger scales than the farmers, but still faced a challenge in finding opportunities for large volume sales in the UK. While their brands protected their margins, the supermarkets had been investing in their own brands with mixed results. Some FMCG companies were willing to supply stores' own brands alongside their own, despite some cannibalization of their products, whereas others, such as Kelloggs, refused to manufacture anything other than their own branded product. At the time of writing, a very large merger was announced between Procter & Gamble and Gillette – two large FMCG companies.

The main customers of the supermarkets are ordinary people in the UK. Everyone is within around 15 minutes' driving time from one or more supermarkets. Many people use the supermarkets for large volumes of shopping and may go once a week or less frequently, but spend well over £100 each time. Most supermarkets operate a reward scheme so that consumers gain points on their store card relative to the amount spent. This can be redeemed against later in-store or petrol purchases. Most regard the supermarkets as an efficient way to buy a wide range of foods and essential household products. In an increasingly time-poor society, this efficiency is attractive to many shoppers. However, there are also good café facilities for those with more time to spend, such as older people or those with children. The supermarkets have also launched home shopping, where customers set up their order preferences on the internet and then are able to order whatever they want for a specific delivery time. Although it is time consuming to set up the initial order, home shopping is proving increasingly popular. Despite the heavy use of supermarkets, both in-store and home delivery, supermarket shopping is not really much of a topic for conversation amongst shoppers and it is fairly rare for them to compare these sorts of shopping experiences.

The prime competition for supermarkets is the corner shop, which has fared very badly in recent years. However, trade magazines suggest that the local shop is fighting back by focusing on more speciality products. Delicatessens, wine shops, butchers, and cafés are all beginning to flourish again as consumers enjoy taking time choosing amongst high-quality produce. Another source of competition is from farmers' markets. Mindful of the huge profit margin that supermarkets are making on products sourced from the UK, English farmers are setting up their own farm shops and also attending farmers' markets where they can sell fresh produce at prices significantly below those of the supermarket. Interestingly, Sainsbury's recently announced the opening of its own farmers' market shop in central London, to much disapproval from consumer groups.

For Carrefour, the UK supermarket industry would be a significantly different environment from France. There are strict planning regulations for the building of large out-of-town supermarkets, and very few stores of this appropriate size are now allowed anywhere. The best sites are also taken. Carrefour also does not have a reputation in the UK and it was also mindful that the French are not always well regarded in the UK. Carrefour was also aware of the frustrating tactics that the UK supermarkets used in their attempts to prevent discount operators Aldi, Netto, and Lidl from setting up their own operations. Through lobbying Parliament, these low-cost retailers had to operate initially as clubs, requiring a membership fee from new customers. With all of these factors to consider, Carrefour needed to decide whether to try to enter the UK supermarket industry and whether a bid for Safeway was an appropriate step to take.

---

1. *Using the Five Forces model, determine whether the UK supermarket industry is attractive in general in 2003.*
2. *Should Carrefour seek to enter this industry by taking over Safeway?*
3. *Using a supply chain analysis, give evidence to show how the main groups of players are continuously wrestling for greater bargaining power.*
4. *How might the supermarket industry evolve after 2003?*

The golden arches

Twoallbeefpattiesspecialsaucelettucecheesepicklesoniononasesameseedbun

McDonald's advertising slogan, first used in 1975

INDUSTRY TERRAIN

White Castle, started in 1916 by J. Walter Anderson of Wichita Kansas, was the first US hamburger chain. Selling hamburgers at 5 cents each, along with French fries and cola, it, and other similar operations grew rapidly. On May 15, 1940 Richard "Dick" and Maurice "Mac" McDonald opened their first hamburger stand. In 1948 they sketched out a new, octagonal-shaped layout on a tennis court and opened a restaurant of that design in San Bernardino, California. This new outlet incorporated their "Speedee Service System" – an assembly line approach based on a restricted product range of hamburgers, cheeseburgers, French fries, and drinks only. It encouraged customers to place their orders at a window and eat in their cars as the restaurant had no tables. It also made use of innovative preparation techniques such as "Multimixers" (machines that mixed six milkshakes simultaneously) to enable a faster throughput of customers.

The mass-production system proved a winner. Dick redesigned the restaurant with the now famous "golden arches" going through the roof and sloping to the front and in 1953 the brothers began to franchise their operations. They commanded an upfront fee and an ongoing percentage of sales from new operations in Phoenix (Arizona) and Downey (California), both built on the San Bernardino model. Intrigued to find out why the brothers were ordering so many Multimixers from him, Ray Kroc visited San Bernardino. He was so impressed that he became a McDonald's franchise seller before opening his own store in Des Plaines, Illinois, on April 15, 1955.

People flooding into Kroc's restaurant to buy the 15 cent burgers and 10 cent fries were often amused to see the cleanliness-obsessed owner scraping chewing gum off the surrounding footpaths with a putty knife. He introduced further streamlining and other initiatives to ensure a total focus on timely, efficient, and clean service, and "Q.S.C. & V" (Quality, Service, Cleanliness and Value) became the company motto in 1957. The hundredth McDonald's opened in Chicago in 1959. In 1960 the company was renamed "McDonald's Corporation" and 1 year later Kroc bought out the brothers for US$2.7m. Then, insisting on the same look, food, and attention to cleanliness in all outlets, and backed by a huge marketing and branding campaign based on the friendly clown Ronald McDonald, he set out to grow by opening new restaurants. The first non-US franchises opened in Canada and Puerto Rico in 1967. By the 1990s the company was opening a new store every 18 hours somewhere in the world. Today over 30,000 McDonald's restaurants serve over 47 million people in 122 countries every day.

Ray Kroc, when asked why McDonald's was so successful, replied: "We take the hamburger business more seriously than anyone else." So seriously that in 1961 the McDonald's "Hamburger University" was opened in Elk Grove, near Chicago. Here, each year, hand-picked "undergraduates" from the thousands of McDonald's stores worldwide go to learn and to compete for honors in the "Hot Hamburger" competitions. Despite such commitment, McDonald's was not alone in growing rapidly in the fast food industry. Kentucky Fried Chicken opened in 1939 and licensed its first franchise in 1952. In hamburgers, Burger King opened in Florida in 1954 and Wendy's in Columbus, Ohio in 1969. By the start of the 1990s, there were 12,000 McDonald's, 6,300 Burger Kings and 3,700 Wendy's in the US, along with a host of other hamburger chains and other fast-food outlets selling everything from chicken, pizza, tacos, and sandwiches to sushi and noodles. More lately Subway, boasting sandwiches with fresh, healthy ingredients and an ever-changing menu, has entered to challenge the dominance of the Big Mac.

After its public flotation in 1965, McDonald's enjoyed 35 years of perpetual profit growth. However, between 1997 and 2003 it lost 3% of its US market share and in December 2002 declared its first loss as a public company. The interacting dynamics seen to contribute to the decline had been evolving for some time. Increased rivalry was an obvious feature, with McDonald's entering a price war in the US and UK markets with the 99 cent (99 pence) burger. Environmentalists (e.g. Greenpeace) had targeted the fast-food industry, and particularly McDonald's, in terms of animal welfare, environmental integrity, advertising, censorship, etc. Nutritionists had also taken aim through filmmakers (Morgan Spurlock's *Super Size Me*), authors (Eric Schlosser and *Fast Food Nation*), and US lawyers mounting lawsuits on behalf of obese "junk-food addicts." Added to this was the expensive loss of a lawsuit mounted by the owner of several franchises for damages done by other stores being opened in close proximity.

In response to its first ever loss, the Board dispensed with the existing CEO and recalled retired veteran Jim Cantalupo. His first instinct was to continue with the 2,000-store annual building rate. However, figures showing that more than 100% of the McDonald's sales growth came from new stores convinced him that the major problems lay with current store performance and he focused strategy at this level. Store grading had fallen into disuse and was reestablished; menus were revamped with an increase in non-burger items, such as salads and sandwiches; nutritional and environmental information was placed on tray mats; and a host of other incremental improvements, such as stronger forks, thicker straws, and competitive tendering for marketing funds was complemented by McDonald's first global marketing campaign, "I'm lovin' it."

These "back to basics" actions reversed the downward trend. The focus on getting more customers into existing stores, continued by the company after the untimely deaths of both Cantalupo and his successor, Charlie Bell, drove the company's same-store sales, profits, and share price upwards. By 2004, McDonald's was back at the forefront of the global fast-food industry as an operator and investment vehicle.

The McDonald's history is a good example of different phases of industry evolution. What wins the game today might not even be good enough to keep you in the game tomorrow.

---

1. *How does the case link with the theoretical models in the chapter?*
2. *How might the managers of McDonald's have been able to predict the potential problems if they had applied the theory?*

High-tech hell

Many of the technology giants of Silicon Valley are under threat. The rise of low-cost computing has caught out Sun Systems, HP, and IBM. Technology standardization and overcapacity are acting together to drive prices down. The standardization of information technology, exemplified by the emergence of low-cost computers running the open source Linux operating system on mass-produced hardware, is a problem for big technology companies with huge R&D spend and massively expensive sales forces.

There is also massive change in the software industry, with open source software programs produced by worldwide communities of volunteers bringing low-cost alternatives to branded products. There are also cheaper ways to produce and distribute software, from web-based delivery to techniques for building applications from reusable software "components."

The choice for the technology giants is whether they should strive to produce high-technology products that command high profit margins or compete on lower priced products from a lower cost base. The most competitive player in this market is Dell, with sales of $50bn and a growth rate of nearly 20% per year. It has little R&D to support, and it sells direct to consumers rather than distributors. Its overheads are less than 10% of sales compared with 18% at HP and 47% at Sun.

What are the giants to do? IBM is seeking an optimal business mix. Its recent attempt to sell its personal computer business to Lenovo of China is a further move in redefining Big Blue. HP and Sun have abandoned parts of their high-tech business to compete more directly with Dell. This has put their earnings under pressure and their market share has fallen. Standardization and commoditization are leaching profits out of the businesses. The problem of standardization is that it makes it harder for companies to differentiate their products and demand premium prices. It also makes it easier for customers to shop around and frees them from "lock-in."

Overcapacity is giving customers the power to influence manufacturers into giving them interchangeable products. IBM, HP, and Sun have responded by offering cheaper and more flexible products. By purchasing Compaq, HP hoped to take the lead in low-cost servers, even though this cannibalizes their existing business in corporate computers. Although HP has seen its sales rise strongly, its profits and revenue have failed to follow. Part of the reason is that HP has been selling this new low-price technology using its traditional expensive sales techniques. Although there were efforts by Ms. Fiorina, HP's CEO, to adjust salespeople's compensation, this is widely perceived as too little, too late. Is HP doomed to play Dell's game or can it energize its innovation engine? With a $3.5bn spend on R&D, 200 products were launched last year. However, none caught the consumer's imagination.

---

1. *Why do large parts of the technology industry appear to be turning into waste-lands of low profit margins?*
2. *Why are some technology giants struggling and others succeeding?*
3. *What can the struggling giants do to position themselves effectively to anticipate and respond to future industry dynamics?*
4. *Is "strategic hell" inevitable for the high-tech industry?*

Bouncing back

Condoms have been produced for thousands of years, so the beginnings of the industry's life cycle are lost in the mists of time. However, analysts could be forgiven for thinking they had seen the maturity and decline of the condom industry in the last century. While the substitution of synthetic materials for organic animal casings, industrialization and mass production enabled revenues, profits, and margins to increase across the early parts of the 20th century, maturity followed, before a marked decline occurred in the 1970s following the invention and spread of new forms of contraception.

But condoms defied the life cycle to bounce back in the late 1980s. Since then, the industry has been thriving with whole new distribution channels opening up. For example, walk through any Western supermarket now and you will likely find a large section devoted to a dozen or more different brands of condom competing for attention, something that would have been unthinkable in the 1970s and 1980s.

---

1. *What macro-shocks in the global environment or changes in attitude among key movers and shakers may have contributed to the de-maturation of the condom industry?*
2. *What strategies might companies producing condoms, or the industry as a whole, take to further advance this de-maturation?*
3. *Can you think of any other products or services that have defied maturity? Describe the circumstances that enable their de-maturation.*

The "lows" of "highs"

Following their recent promotions, Sam and Mary had just joined the drugs squad. Their new boss called them in on their first day and said, "I am puzzled. We are seizing more and more drugs and yet the street prices keep going down [figure 3-6.1]. I suspect the answers lie in the business of drugs and not the policing . . . and as you each have an MBA please take this folder of information and come up with some answers for me . . . by 9.00 AM tomorrow please."

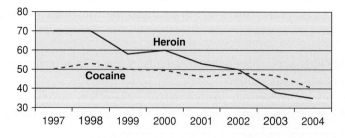

Figure 3-6.1 Street prices UK drugs (£ per gram) (Adapted from www.idmu.co.uk)

Foregoing their lunch break the two young detectives began to systematically sort through the information gathered from a variety of sources. Heroin (street names: "smack," "junk," "skag," and "H") is manufactured by processing morphine, a natural extract of the Asian poppy plant. Cocaine ("coke," "rock," and "crack") also has agricultural beginnings as cocoa leaves. While grown in different parts of the world – the cocoa plant in the Andean regions of South America and the poppy in Asia – they both tend to be harvested by subsistence farmers for whom the growing of legal crops (coffee beans in South America and wheat in Asia) does not sustain their lives. According to the United Nations Office of Drug Control (UNODC), antigrowth efforts had caused falls in the global cocoa leaf production each year since 1999 (353,000 tonnes) to a 2004 total of 236,000 tonnes.

It was different for poppies in Afghanistan. At the end of the Taliban's reign in 2001, poppy growing had been virtually wiped out (although not the Taliban's own drug dealing). However, by the end of 2004, poppies flowered over 324,000 acres, itself a 60% increase over 2003. The sale of the 2003/4 crop, the source of nearly 90% of the world's heroin, pumped an estimated US$2.8bn into the Afghan economy, equal to half that country's GDP. The 365,000 farmers tending the crop earned some 20 times more per acre than they could by growing wheat. The 2004/5 scenario looked brighter for antidrugs agencies as a combination of Government action and payments to farmers seemed to have reduced poppy cultivation, with 6% of farmers' arable land being sown with poppy as opposed to 34% the year before. However, the agility of Afghan opium dealers is legendary and what happens this year is no guide to next.

In the early days of illegal drug distribution, closely linked intermediaries manufactured and traded almost exclusively with each other. This close integration reduced the risks of police infiltration, non-payment, non-delivery, and being betrayed by non-loyal associates bargaining for a lighter sentence. However, these family-style alliances were also unwieldy, well known (and hence easy for law enforcement agencies to target), and needed reasonable margins at each level to keep everyone in the gang happy and to compensate for the high levels of risk. Price competition, initially in cocaine, a perishable product, has forced these margins down and, along with police focus, forced the disintegration of these family units. (Price depends on quality but an average price for bulk supply from a Columbian producer in 2004 was £23,000 per kilo – not much different from the £25,000 for buying just 1 kilo. As more middle layers took payment, the final street price reached £40,000 per kilo.)

Columbian importers now trade happily with UK entrepreneurs. The producers in Columbia also deal with British middlemen who live outside of the UK and who in turn may sell on to other distributors, Columbian or not, in Britain. Cocaine users are also likely to use other "recreational" drugs like ecstasy ("E") or amphetamines ("speed") and so distributors often carry a variety of drug options. Paradoxically, police success in attacking major importation routes from Jamaica and Spain has added to the variety of supply options as new supply lines opened up from other parts of the Caribbean and Africa and new players joined in. Notes from an interview with Lefty, a veteran drug criminal, detailed his complaints that, "with enough Spanish to say 'hello,' 'how much,' and 'when can you deliver?' any small-time dip [pickpocket] can get into selling 'smack' these days."

The heroin trade was different in that the distribution chain had tended to stay exclusively with the one product and had retained traditional linkages for longer. Heroin has more lifestyle and less recreational usage and hence buyers, particularly the end consumers, are more concerned with quality of product and supply, and not with shopping for the lowest price or the latest drug fad. Landing the drug at £19,000 per kilo the (predominantly) Turkish importer would cut it (i.e. dilute it with some inert substance) and sell on at £33,000 to retailers who would cut it again, finally getting end prices of £60,000. Lefty's gang had never been part of this trade as, according to his testimony, "You had to speak Turkish, Italian, Urdu, you name it, just to get a price list! No one spoke English and they looked after their own – different firms in the 'H' business would help each other out; lend each other goods if a shipment got lost – but they wouldn't give us outsiders the time of day."

But since the mid-1990s, things had been changing. Increased migration across Europe had already seen a penetration of the heroin trade by Kurdish and Albanian distributors. Dealers in cocaine had begun to broaden their range further to include the more profitable heroin and prices had fallen to levels below cocaine in a short time. A more business-like orientation had also taken root, with titles such as Marketing Director, Finance Director, and so on, being used within the gangs.

"Well," said Mary, "if we combine the macro and industry issues, it is quite clear what's happening and it's bad news for the drugs squad but 'good' news for drug users."

---

1. *Apply industry analysis to past, present, and future heroin and cocaine distribution to support Mary's conclusions.*

Barbershop harmonies

If you were a company operating in the sportswear or music industry and you needed to expand your marketing and distribution, what new channels might you investigate? The Internet, perhaps? Maybe supermarkets or gas stations? A less obvious route might be barbershops, but it is one now being taken very seriously by major shoe manufacturers and record companies.

Reebok was perhaps the first to take barbershops to heart in this respect. The company's market share had been slipping through most of the 1990s. In response, Reebok formed a team of what they called "aggressive grassroots marketers" named the DROP squad (which stands for Deprogramming off Nike, Reprogramming on Our Product). The squad researched innovative ways to lure young men, particularly those from inner-city neighborhoods, away from Nike merchandise.

One of their more interesting initiatives involved identifying "influential" barbershops in a few major cities and outfitting employees with Reebok shoes and smocks and supplying the stores with combs and displaying cases containing Reebok shoes and sports memorabilia.

What was the logic behind such an approach? First, after a couple of lean decades for American barbers, when more flamboyant unisex styles encouraged men to patronize the same salons as women, barbershops are making a comeback – especially among urban black men, a key market for the likes of Reebok. They have done so partly by upping their own skills and range of cuts, partly by feeding nostalgia for simpler times, and partly by providing a neighborhood focal point and a sense of community. A new wave of barbershops, often organized around sports themes with sports memorabilia and big-screen TVs hanging from the walls, is subsequently sprouting up all over America's cities and towns.

Second, "If you are black, you are at [your barbershop] at least once a week to keep your hair right, but you end up going every other day just to catch up on the news," says Henry Gaskins, the Reebok executive who headed the DROP squad. "It's a very receptive audience."

According to Tim Story, the director of the movie *Barbershop*, one of the surprise hits of 2002, "Word of mouth from your barber is a deep thing – your barber is the one person you're going to trust, who's going to be uncensored with you." Hence, people like Shannon Jones, a dapper and dreadlocked young barber who recently opened his own basketball-themed barbershop "Timeout at Shannon's" in Chicago, are key influencers. Subsequently, Jones is well known and regularly courted by designers, marketers, and promoters from record and sportswear labels. Says Jones: "Barbers are like priests, we're influential, and if I'm dressed head to toe in Adidas, that's a powerful thing."

Such channels are difficult to manage, though. Because they are based on the integrity of the barber–customer relationship, the word-of-mouth influence that companies like Reebok and Adidas are trying to accomplish cannot be bought and sold, or tied down by legal contracts.

Eric Patton, a former Marketing Director at Nike's Air Jordan division, claims that he had the same idea as Reebok's DROP squad, but before he could get it off the ground he was dismayed to find that Reebok had already outfitted the stores he had targeted. But he wasn't put off. Because the DROP squad did not draw up contracts with its barbers, Patton outfitted the same barbers with Nike shoes anyway. "I'm pretty sure they wore them," he said. It is also worth noting that when the Adidas marketing representative who outfitted Timeout at Shannon's moved to AND1 (a rival manufacturer), Jones and his staff moved with him, promptly switching their allegiances to AND1.

Despite these difficulties, the capacities of the new barbershop channels continue to be explored. Timeout at Shannon's has hosted customer focus group discussions, and other similar stores now host record launches and fashion shows. Alex Calderwood, owner of the Seattle-based chain of Rudy's barbershops, explains that his stores have hosted a film festival and several concerts. Now record labels hoping to earn a spot on Rudy's exclusive in-house music playlist regularly visit his door. "We keep the rotation to no more than 20 CDs and sell them all in store, so it's intimate, like a good friend recommending a CD," he explains. "When you're in line for an hour and a half waiting for a cut, you get exposed to a lot of music." Soon to be seen alongside the CDs, and exclusively available at Rudy's stores, will be the "Rudy's Shoe" – developed by Calderwood and his staff in association with Nike.

1. *Why are barbershops being seen as "complementary" to the sports shoe and music industries?*
2. *Would this be the case in every market or only in the US markets described here?*
3. *What advantages would there be for certain record labels or shoe manu-facturers to integrate barbershops into their "horizontal axis" or distribution chain?*

Crumbling palaces

We have often found that students are good at extracting data from cases and filling in models. However, in many cases, far less ability is found in interpreting these analyses and synthesizing results. The following case about Royal Air Maroc, a North-African airline, therefore consists of the following tools and frameworks already deployed and largely completed:

1. An industry analysis using Porter's Five Forces framework (figure 3-8.1)
2. A competitor analysis looking at service quality and scope or coverage (figure 3-8.2)
3. A macro-environmental analysis using the PESTLE framework (figure 3-8.3)

The exercise is for you to interpret them and to construct an argument toward answering the questions posed at the end.

1. Industry analysis (2004)

Note that free access in Morocco to low-cost airlines (easyJet, RyanAir) has recently been agreed.

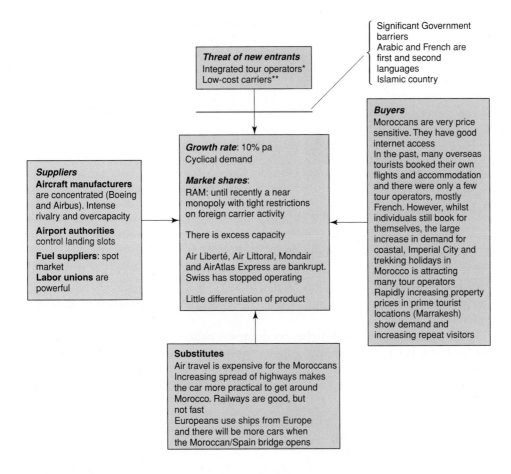

Threat of new entrants
Integrated tour operators*
Low-cost carriers**

Significant Government barriers
Arabic and French are first and second languages
Islamic country

Growth rate: 10% pa
Cyclical demand

Market shares:
RAM: until recently a near monopoly with tight restrictions on foreign carrier activity

There is excess capacity

Air Liberté, Air Littoral, Mondair and AirAtlas Express are bankrupt. Swiss has stopped operating

Little differentiation of product

Suppliers
Aircraft manufacturers are concentrated (Boeing and Airbus). Intense rivalry and overcapacity
Airport authorities control landing slots
Fuel suppliers: spot market
Labor unions are powerful

Buyers
Moroccans are very price sensitive. They have good internet access
In the past, many overseas tourists booked their own flights and accommodation and there were only a few tour operators, mostly French. However, whilst individuals still book for themselves, the large increase in demand for coastal, Imperial City and trekking holidays in Morocco is attracting many tour operators
Rapidly increasing property prices in prime tourist locations (Marrakesh) show demand and increasing repeat visitors

Substitutes
Air travel is expensive for the Moroccans
Increasing spread of highways makes the car more practical to get around Morocco. Railways are good, but not fast
Europeans use ships from Europe and there will be more cars when the Moroccan/Spain bridge opens

*Threat of new entrants	**Low-cost carriers
UK: FirstChoice	Corsair
Germany: TUI	AirEurope
Belgium: Jetair	Air Horizon
Spain: Globalia	easyJet
France: TUI France	Virgin Express
Italy: Alpitour	GB airways
	Hapag Lloyd and Air Berlin
	Neos
	RyanAir

Figure 3-8.1 Industry analysis (2004)

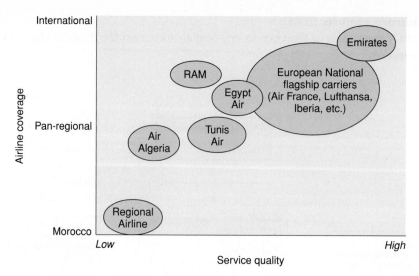

Figure 3-8.2 Competitor analysis (January 2004)

2. Competitor analysis (January 2004)

RAM (Royal Air Maroc) is the flagship carrier for Morocco. Created in 1957, it now has a capital of some 1.5bn MAD (16 MAD = £1). The main shareholder is the Moroccan Government with 94.39%. The remaining shareholders include Air France and Iberia.

RAM operates scheduled flights on domestic routes and over 40 international destinations. It has a fast-growing fleet consisting of Airbus A321-220s and new Boeing 737s. RAM conveys 3.7 million passengers per year and runs 150 flights per day. It operates out of Casablanca, which is the main hub for international flights in Morocco.

RAM has a partnership with Regional Airlines, in which it leases them the aircraft and decides on networks, products, and markets. RAM deals with distribution and operational costs.

RAM has obtained the first international certificates in Africa for technical skills, including ISO 9002, ISO 9001.

3. Macro-environmental analysis

Political	Moroccan Government's priority is the growth of the tourist industry through '2010 Vision'; to reach 10 million tourists p.a. This involves the investment of 3bn euros in hotels and the opening of five new sea resorts The Government is also encouraging foreign tour operators to come to Morocco In 2001 Morocco approved an open sky agreement with the USA as well as other European countries Morocco is requesting integration into the EU sky. EU regulations and technical controls are being applied increasingly The Government has signed the liberalization programme between Arab countries. Complete liberalization is intended for November 2006 9/11 raises need for increased security through pre-flight identification Iraq war Terrorist bomb in Casablanca
Economic	The currency is tightly controlled and stable against major world currencies Rising petrol costs Iraq war
Sociocultural	The Moroccan communities in Europe are important and make regular trips to Morocco for holidays Religious events, such as pilgrimage to Mecca and "Omra" generate significant traffic from Morocco to MEA While Arabic and French are the first two languages in Morocco, English is spreading rapidly in major tourist areas Morocco has realized that the hospitality of shop owners insisting on inviting tourists into their shops is often perceived in a negative way by foreigners and this "pestering" is now more tightly controlled
Technological	New channels of distribution are evolving rapidly with internet technology Although statistics show relatively low per-head use of the internet in Morocco, each terminal has a large number of users The growth in worldwide demand has led to the development of high-capacity aircraft
Legal	The air transport sector is being liberalized at the national and pan-national levels – scheduled and chartered activities are effective February 2004

Figure 3-8.3   Macro-environmental analysis

> **1.** *Looking at the frameworks above, discuss the challenges facing the Moroccan airline industry.*
> **2.** *What actions should RAM take resulting from your conclusions?*

NB: you can develop the issues discussed in this case further and compare what you would do against more recent events by reading the "Red, green, and blue" case (4-6) in the next chapter, The Big Picture.

The Big Picture

4:00

Diversification is a corporate minefield. In no other area of corporate strategy have so many companies made such disastrous investments.

Robert Grant (1991) **Contemporary Strategy Analysis**

Large firm diversification activity has frequently been followed by a process of ignominious sell-offs and retrenchment.

Michael E. Porter (1987) **Harvard Business Review**

During 1991 in the UK, Hanson plc acquired 3% of ICI (Imperial Chemical Industries) plc, with an apparent intent to make a full bid for the firm. There was outrage in the media that a major pillar of British industry should be subject to such a bid. Hanson had made a reputation as a corporate raider, taking over under-performing businesses and restructuring them by selling off surplus assets and sweating the retained assets for greater profitability. The implication of the bid from this break-up specialist was that ICI was badly run and could be worth more broken up. The level of feeling was such that the UK Prime Minister herself, Margaret Thatcher, intervened and prevented one of the UK's industrial icons becoming part of the Hanson empire.

Although the takeover bid failed, ICI was spurred into action. Shortly after-wards, in 1993, it floated off its pharmaceutical arm as a separate business named Zeneca. To observers at the time, this de-merger was proof that the corporate entity ICI, containing its industrial chemical companies and its pharmaceutical arm, was worth far less on the stock market than the combined value of the two separate bodies.

This raises fundamental questions about the strategy of large multibusiness firms:

1. Why do multibusiness firms exist?
2. What businesses should they be in?
3. How can the corporate center add value?

These questions are the core concerns of the role of the corporate center and corporate strategy.

Why Does the Multibusiness (M-form) Exist?[1]

Historically, companies in the US were configured as a "Unitary" whole, divided into functional responsibilities. The CEO's major strategic role in managing this U-form was to coordinate the efforts of the various functions of the business (see

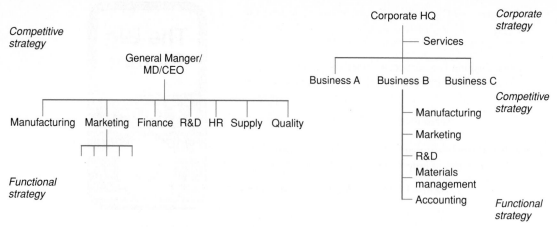

Figure 4.1   The U-form (left) and the M-form (right)

figure 4.1). However, the weakness of the U-form became apparent as firms grew in size and complexity and attempted to adjust to environmental changes. CEOs became overly involved in routine matters and neglected their longer term strategic role. Functional managers saw their function as an end in itself. Coordination between increasingly stand-alone "functional silos" became more demanding and less fruitful.

Facing such problems, the large US companies Sears Roebuck, Dupont, General Motors, and Jersey Standard moved to the "Multidivisional" (M-form) structure in the early 1920s. They were divided into semi-autonomous profit centers, later known as "strategic business units" (SBUs), responsible for a stand-alone segment of the firm's operations, such as a particular product, brand, or national/regional market. In this structure (see figure 4.1) the new business managers were able to specialize in the operations of their particular competitive arena and engage in **"competitive" strategy** – managing the customer/competitor dynamic as the ultimate source of profit. This freed corporate managers at the center of the firm to focus on the over-all strategic direction of the company, or **"corporate" strategy**. Here the concerns are the **scope** of the product markets, industries, and geographies addressed by the firm and how value may be added above the sum of the component parts.

By the late 1960s over 80% of the Fortune 500 companies were structured in this way with similar trends in other industrialized countries. Now the M-form company is the most prevalent structure among large businesses. It has established a new layer of management, the corporate office, and with it, *corporate strategy*.

What Businesses Should They Be In?

The original M-form adopters had a relatively narrow product-market focus. Their component businesses had similarities in terms of products, processes, markets, underlying capabilities, or some other important attribute. These businesses can be described as **related**. However, companies faced limits to growth in their original product markets and, over the past 80 years, other factors encouraged further increases in product market diversity:

- Many firms had significant levels of free cash and managers tend to reinvest rather than return money to shareholders – this is linked to the fact that managerial salary and perks are often positively related to the size of their business empire.[2]
- The concept of the company as a portfolio of risky assets became popular in the 1970s and the risk of the bundle could be reduced by diversifying into different assets.
- The M-structure made the acquisition and divestment of business units easier than before as the messy tie-ups with other products/regions had been cut.

These factors encouraged expansion through **related diversification**, which is typically manifested as **vertical** and/or **horizontal integration** beyond the original narrow product-market focus.

Firms **vertically integrate** by buying other businesses upstream in their value chain (i.e. they buy into their supplier base) or downstream (i.e. they buy into the customer end). The original Ford Motor Company was integrated from the forests supplying the wood for the dashboard facia to the dealers selling the final, black, product. Essentially vertical integration can be characterized as the "make" side of the **"make or buy" decision**. The benefits of vertical integration lie in the reduction of **transaction costs**. In particular, where businesses are dependent on one supplier or customer, then they are vulnerable to being held to ransom and hence might be better off buying that supplier or customer.[3]

Horizontal integration means buying businesses with products, processes, or services that are **complementary** to those of other businesses in the portfolio. Typical manifestations are when firms buy other businesses selling the "same" products in the same industry (e.g. Daimler buying Chrysler in the automobile industry) or buy other businesses with complementary skills (e.g. Procter & Gamble buying Gillette on the basis of complementary consumer branding capabilities). The value from horizontal integration lies in optimizing **economies of scale and scope**. These kinds of gains are what managers often mean when they justify an acquisition on the grounds of "**synergy**" (more on synergy later). A firm might also gain through an increase in **market power** through being able to exert increased pressure on suppliers or customers or by simply reducing competitive rivalry by acquiring rivals or complementary firms.

Where businesses are brought into the corporate portfolio and have no common characteristic, they can be described as **unrelated diversifications**. *In extremis* these are conglomerate companies of which GE (of Jack Welch fame) is a classic example. Unrelated diversification initially emerged as a means for corporate growth when anti-monopoly legislation prevented related diversification. It was also encouraged by developments in the practices and theory of corporate strategy, particularly those emphasizing the value of general management and the risk reduction of diversified portfolios. The value logic of unrelated diversification relies on the corporate center acting as a better-informed and powerful "shareholder." In stand-alone businesses, managers can maximize their "on-the-job consumption" by, for example, taking "business trips" to exotic locations with their wives. They can also disguise or hide poor performance. As part of a corporation the business is subject to the frequent reporting and the use of auditing functions to maintain the integrity of information. Managers are paid at market rates but are compelled to perform to high standards to maintain their position and the corporate level can intervene at an early stage to correct poor performance.

As the number of multidivisional firms grew, so too did the interest in their financial performance, with the debate generally centering on the differences between related and unrelated diversifiers. In an early study, Richard Rumelt[4] came up with the intuitively appealing conclusion that, in terms of value creation, related diversifiers outperformed unrelated diversifiers – "intuitively appealing" because "synergy" seems more logical among related businesses. Subsequent research has not unanimously supported this finding and it seems that the characteristics of the business and its industry, the skills and imagination of management, and the corporate strategy being implemented all have impacts on performance.

With these strategic options available to corporate centers, there was a need to make decisions about which direction of development was most desirable. This corporate strategy question of "where should we expand/invest?" gave rise to portfolio management tools, the most famous of which was the growth-share matrix or, more colloquially, the "Boston Box" (from its origins with the Boston Consulting Group). Beginning life in the early 1970s, as a doodled framework for the Mead Paper Corporation, the Boston Box evolved into the now-famous **cash cows**, **dogs** (initially "pets"), **question marks**, and **stars** (figure 4.2). It combined insights about the cost-reducing effects of the **experience curve** (and hence the importance of relative market share) with the notion of **sustainable growth** and fostered the orientation that cash-generating cows provided funds for cash-needy question marks so that they might become cash rich and growing stars. This virtuous cycle is illustrated in the figure. Dogs were either run down for cash or sold off.[5]

Other more complex matrices followed.[6] McKinsey, through its association with GE, developed the GE/McKinsey Business screen – a well-known, nine-cell portfolio planning matrix with an "industry attractiveness" axis in place of the "market growth rate" and the business unit's "competitive strength" instead of "relative market share" (figure 4.3). The **industry attractiveness** axis combines an aggregate weighting[7] of factors deemed important in the organization's industry (e.g. market size, projected growth, structure, profitability) while the **competitive strength** axis aggregates such factors as market share, advertising effectiveness, experience curve effects, and others deemed relevant.

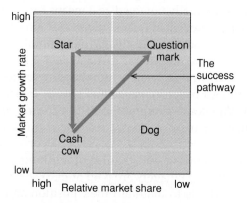

Figure 4.2 The growth–share matrix

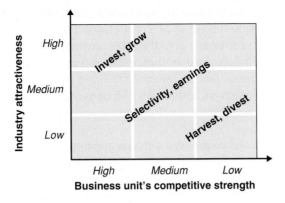

Figure 4.3 The GE/McKinsey Business Screen

Both matrices generated strategic imperatives (such as "invest," "divest," "harvest," and "manage for cash") that depended on a business unit's position in the matrix. Through these matrices the corporate direction of the firm could be established.

By the end of the 1970s, nearly half of the Fortune 500 companies were using portfolio planning as a driver of their corporate strategy. What had begun as an analytic aid to one corporation had become a strategic model for all multibusiness companies. Corporate strategists believed in the need for "balance" in their portfolio of companies, where balance extended to risk,[8] cash generation, geographical spread, etc. This logic legitimated the acquisition of businesses outside of the parent's core activity and gave rise to a huge wave of diversifying mergers and acquisitions during the 1970s and 1980s. Share markets responded positively and "rewarded" diversification moves through increased stock prices. Businesses were treated as financial instruments to be bought and sold in the context of an existing portfolio of assets rather than to be *managed*. The stand-alone dynamics of the M-form structure facilitated this orientation, as did the movement towards controlling business units through financial outputs rather than managing them through behavioral inputs.

Unfortunately the search for cash and risk balance brought more and more unconnected businesses together under one corporate umbrella, and the complexity of managing these different businesses became too much for even the most capable corporate office. As a result the share market began to devalue conglomerates and the stock value of the firm became lower than the sum of the market capitalization of the separate businesses – the so-called **conglomerate discount**. The corporate raiders of the 1980s benefited from this by recognizing that the sum of the parts of these conglomerates greatly exceeded the value of the whole. They borrowed huge amounts to buy these conglomerates and then "un-bundled" the component businesses, paid back their borrowings, and became even richer on the proceeds.

By the end of the 1980s, the academic, business, and investment worlds had largely turned away from portfolio management as a viable corporate strategy, despite the odd exception like GE. Even here it is worth noting that Jack Welch vigorously attacked anyone who described GE as a conglomerate, and, in the UK, anyone using the "C" word in a takeover contest was reprimanded by the Monopolies and Mergers Commission because the term had a deleterious effect on share prices (c.f. Granada plc's hostile takeover of Trust House Forte plc).

Even though debate continues as to the relative merits of *related* versus *unrelated* acquisitions, the overall picture is that most corporate acquisitions destroyed rather than created value (see Angwin 2000 for a review of performance). As Goold et al. (1994) pointed out, companies had to overcome the "beating the odds" paradox, in that the probability of value-adding success through acquisition was empirically low.

While the portfolio technique was a major approach to determine which businesses to own, it became clear that the corporate center had to provide inputs to add value to these businesses. Without group-based value, shareholders should invest in the separate businesses themselves without the imposition of expensive corporate overhead. This raises the questions, then, of how to achieve synergistic value between the businesses in excess of their value as individual units and how the corporate center can bring about such added value.

Corporate Strategy in Practice

The beginning of the chapter described the problem that ICI was forced to consider as a consequence of Hanson's hostile bid – how can the firm justify not breaking itself up into separate stand-alone businesses in which shareholders can invest as they see fit?

There are two important, interrelated questions here for those managing a multibusiness firm (and for those planning to invest in multidivisional firms):

1. *What is the added value created by having a set of businesses in one "business"?* To make sense from an economics/financial perspective, any multidivisional business must have a greater ongoing value (V_c) than the sum of its component, stand-alone businesses (A_s, B_s, etc.): i.e. $V_c > A_s + B_s + C_s$. This is the age-old corporate dynamic of **synergy**. In non-economic terms, authors have expressed the quest for synergy in terms of a **dominant logic**[9] (the concept that a unifying idea links the unit) and/or in shared **core competences**[10] (a unifying set of resources or capabilities that underpin the value-generating processes or product of all business units).
2. *How should this grouping be managed to develop and maintain this added value?* The answers to this question lie in the organizational processes of corporate strategy, with a particular focus on the role and activities of the corporate center.

In addressing these questions, Michael Porter[11] suggested four mechanisms of value-creation. Michael Goold and his colleagues also identified four routes to **parenting advantage**,[12] which, although named differently, are congruent with Porter's classification. These mechanisms (Goold et al.'s version in brackets) are as follows:

- Portfolio management ("Corporate development")
- Restructuring ("Stand-alone influence")
- Sharing activities ("Central functions and services")
- Transferring skills ("Linkage influence")

These four styles can be represented diagrammatically as shown in figure 4.4.

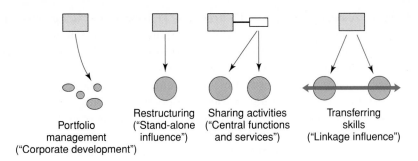

Figure 4.4 Valuing adding approaches of the center

Portfolio management (corporate development)

Despite the negative view of the portfolio-based conglomerate, this does not mean that it no longer exists as a business technique, or that those that use it inevitably perform badly. GE, even post Jack Welch, remains a formidable corporation that provided 30.9% returns to shareholders in its 2003 financial year and has averaged a 15.8% annual return from 1993–2003. These impressive returns are despite the fact that the company is a classic conglomerate, with a portfolio of four slow growth "cash generators" in insurance, consumer and industrial products, advanced materials, and equipment services supporting seven "growth businesses" in commercial finance, consumer finance, energy, transportation, healthcare, media, and infrastructure. The smallest of these 11 businesses (infrastructure), with a 2003 turnover of US$3.5bn, would be comfortably placed in the Fortune 500 in its own right were it not in the GE stable. GE divests poorly performing businesses and acquires others that have more potential for value generation – a classic portfolio orientation but one that seems to work well for this company.

Restructuring (stand-alone influence)

In its purest sense, "restructuring" relies for its value adding potential on (1) the insight of the corporate office in spotting and buying an underperforming business at a low price and (2) its capability to then address the weaknesses of the business and bring it to its full potential (and then re-sell it at a higher price commensurate with its new value). The sale rarely happens in practice and this form of corporate strategy more generally entails the corporate layer (including the CEO) exerting *ongoing* and direct *stand-alone influence* on the actions and decisions of otherwise autonomous business units.

Business units may still be fully autonomous with respect to other business units but they are subject to strategic and operational direction and control from above. Influence occurs through a variety of mechanisms, ranging from direct commands ("do this!") to indirect control through policy manuals, pronouncements, or a set of prescribed targets ("achieve this!"). The frequency, intensity, and focus of interaction depends on the culture of the corporation and the personality of the CEO, and varies from the "light touch" of strategic reviews to the "blowtorch" inquisition of every negative variance.

The classic **restructurer** was ICI's predator, Hanson PLC. Along with its arm in the US (Hanson Industries), this company made a practice of acquiring companies in mature, asset-based industries providing essential goods and services. To meet the Hanson criteria for purchase, the businesses needed to have a leading position (and, hence, a good cash flow) and well-known name in its market and, most importantly, be performing at a level below its capability. Having acquired the business, a Hanson team immediately came in to lift operating efficiency, reduce waste and excess overhead, cull non-profitable products and customers, divest non-core assets, and identify strategic focus and new management. The local management then ran the business in a completely decentralized way, although heavily incentivized through substantial bonus payments or the threat of dismissal, to meet fiercely demanding operating and growth targets "agreed" with the parent body.

In this category of corporate strategy, the center is an *active* manager of its businesses rather than the passive investor of the portfolio management approach. However, it is still difficult for the center, having completed any restructuring, to add value on an ongoing basis over that of a motivated, informed set of business managers. Goold et al. refer to the "10 percent verses 100 percent" paradox, wherein it defies logic that "part-time" corporate managers can, by spending only 10% of their time in the business, do better in terms of business performance than the dedicated business managers spending 100% of their time on the same issues. If this were to be the case it would suggest a chronic incapability in the business managers and the solution to that problem is obvious.

Sharing activities (central functions and services)

Parenting advantage, or core competence, from this category of corporate strategy arises from functional or process experts at the corporate level. These individual or departmental experts either **augment** the existing expertise in the business or **substitute** for it.

In an *augmenting* structure, the central resources have the time and resources to develop world-class capability in their functional expertise whereas the business function, through time and resource restriction, must focus on the day-to-day operations. One corporation in the automotive components industry in the UK has a "*Kaizen*" (continuous improvement) team in each of its businesses but also has a corporate team that brings best practice *Kaizen processes* to the businesses. In a corporation with an augmenting orientation, the business units may still have autonomous capability but be subject to compulsory oversight by the corporate function (an influencing relationship) or may have a voluntary consultancy or customer–supplier relationship. A classic example of a mix of compulsory/voluntary inputs is the corporate manufacturing services function of the American company Cooper Industries. New businesses acquired by Cooper underwent a compulsory process of "Cooperization" by the Manufacturing Services group, who worked with the operations staff of the acquired business to transfer Cooper's processes and know-how. Once businesses had become fully fledged members, however, the Manufacturing Services group intervened only on invitation from the Division Manager.[13]

Substitution means that particular functions or facilities are taken out of the businesses and centralized at corporate level. As well as the standard "service" functions, such as taxation and legal offices, more strategic functions, including distribution, branding, quality, R&D, finance, manufacturing, and others, have been centralized by various M-form companies around the world. Synergistic value is added through economies of scale, benefits of functional specialization, and increased focus on a smaller number of key processes at operational level. Businesses are no longer completely autonomous in their overall day-to-day functioning but rely on "sharing activities" with the corporate function to function as a business. A typical example of substitution took place at a UK multi-business automotive company that, since 2002, has centralized the purchasing of steel. The corporate center realized that autonomous purchasing by the businesses was not exploiting the potential supplier power that concentrating the buying might bring. Annual savings of over £3m were achieved by this consolidation.

To truly add value at the level of sharing activities, Goold and his colleagues emphasize that the corporate center has to overcome the "beating the specialists" paradox. Stand-alone businesses are free to outsource any function or process to outside specialists who have greater capability and/or higher efficiency in that arena. This is happening on a worldwide scale, as companies outsource call centers, software writing, manufacturing, and other functions to Eastern Europe, Mexico, India, China or any other country with comparative advantage. To justify its place as the "external" provider of a business function/process, the corporate center needs to show that it has a sustainable competitive advantage over other external providers. The fact that the corporate center can provide a central service *better than the businesses can do separately* is only one part of the corporate strategy question. An increasingly important second part is: can the corporate center provide that service better than a world-class specialist?

Transferring skills (linkage influence)

Corporate strategy in this category is based on interactions *between* the businesses. The primary source of parenting advantage lies in the transfer of knowledge-based best practice and competitive capabilities and occurs in practice through such mechanisms as staff transfer, cross-business work teams, and shared objectives. Economists describe this as facilitating economies of scope wherein related business units share specialized physical capital, learning and knowledge, management expertise, and so on. Of all of the categories of corporate strategy, this is the level that seems to have most theoretical support as having the potential for adding value beyond the individual businesses through the development of *core competences* that transcend business boundaries.

Canon's capabilities in optics, mechanics, and electronics transcend its product–business boundaries in printers, cameras, copiers, faxes, etc., as does Sony's focus on miniaturization and Wal-Mart's complex capability in logistics. Honda's complex matrix structure in Europe aims to exploit a core competence in engine design as well as economies of scale across all its country-based businesses and its product groupings of motorcycles, lawn mowers, and cars. Similarly 3M's obsession with innovation is primary whereas the product groups resulting from this obsession are the secondary consequence of this competence. Large corporate staffs often manage these pan-corporate competences; they require ongoing effort, commitment, and expense. Another requirement is to do battle with business/country/product managers, who rarely relinquish their autonomy without a fight – a fight they continue to engage in even when the benefits of sharing seem well established.[14]

Goold et al. (1994) suggest that the paradox to overcome here is one of "enlightened self-interest," wherein the managers of stand-alone businesses could link with other businesses equally well outside of a corporate framework. While such sharing is theoretically possible for stand-alone businesses, it is unlikely because these (related) businesses would normally be competitors and the risk of opportunistic exploitation is difficult to eliminate. The risks are particularly acute where the sharing involves knowledge-based competencies. Once the knowledge is transferred from one party there is little incentive for the other party to reciprocate or to maintain the relationship unless there are significant ongoing and/or future gains that are contingent on continuous dealing. Many well-intentioned alliances flounder when one or other party begins to feel that their outcomes from the engagement are minor compared with those of their partner. Once businesses are part of the same corporation, however, these issues of exploitation theoretically disappear because all parties are on the same team and therefore have a mutual interest in the *overall value* of the interactions.

Hence, corporate strategy at this level offers the potential for substantial value creation, but the *force* of a corporate hierarchy is generally needed to ensure the development and maintenance of pan-business capabilities, as business units cease to be autonomous in the conventional sense of stand-alone operation. While not necessarily dependent on other units or functions for day-to-day operating, they become strategically interdependent on one another or on a corporate function or activity they all share. The businesses are participants in or users of important strategic resources that they cannot unilaterally direct or control. Their delegated, stand-alone activities are fewer and narrower and performance measurement is more ambiguous. Rarely do the managers in the businesses become completely comfortable with these constraints and rarely do they totally cease struggling against them.

Corporate Strategy and the Role of the Center

The unwelcome bid by Hanson for ICI, which opened the chapter, asked a pertinent question of a multibusiness firm: is the value of the whole greater than the sum of the parts? Directly this questions whether the corporate center is adding value beyond the intrinsic components of the firm.

If we viewed ICI as an unrelated group of businesses, then corporate managers should be better-informed shareholders who have access to their businesses in a way that outside shareholders do not and they can intervene earlier if there are signs of underperformance. Being closer to the businesses, they can ask more relevant questions of local managers and replace those who are unable to achieve. The corporate center is also able to allocate resources and capital more efficiently than external markets. Clearly Hanson did not perceive the corporate center to be adding any value through these mechanisms that couldn't be achieved by the businesses standing alone.

If we viewed ICI as a set of related businesses, then we would expect to find value added from the sharing of activities and linkages between the businesses. The corporate center would provide centralized facilities – **coaching** at both general and functional management level and **coordinating and driving** the inter-business relationships. Hanson, however, believed that the corporate center was not better than an outsourced specialist supplier at providing facilities or better at developing business value through developing linkages than motivated, competent, self-interested business managers.

Hanson's bid poses a generic question for all multibusinesses: why should their portfolios not be floated and become truly autonomous without the encumbrance of an additional layer of expensive management? Although ultimately unsuccessful in its bid for ICI, the de-merger of Zeneca shortly afterwards suggests Hanson's question was a good one.

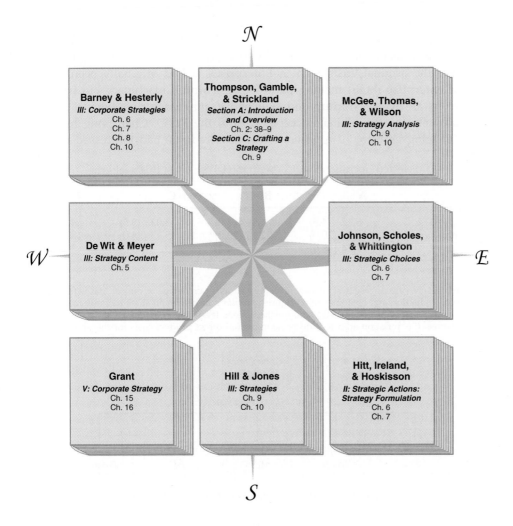

Parenting problems

Chen Song, the CEO of Z Enterprises, had a dilemma. Although Z was profitable and growing, it had failed to achieve a number of operating targets for the most recent financial year. The key among these were *quality*, *inventory* control, and product *cost* reduction (see table 4-1.1). The US-based Board, on which Chen Song sat, had expressed its disappointment with these shortfalls and had asked him to prepare a report detailing how he planned to get these measures back on track for the following year.

Z is a corporation made of three businesses (A, B, and C) that design and manufacture parts for the domestic and export automotive industry. They all use capital-intensive processes in value added manufacture and have to meet the same quality, cost, and delivery standards. Seventy percent of the original equipment manufacturer (OEM) customer base is common to all three, with over 90% being common to at least two. The managers and technical staff and many of the senior shop-floor personnel have expertise in a variety of the processes that contribute to increasing productivity and quality through total quality management (TQM), business process reengineering (BPR), and just-in-time (JIT) inventory control. The Managing Directors, along with the Corporate Finance Office and a small Human Resources department, report to Chen Song as part of the Corporate Management Board (CMB), which meets monthly, hosted by each business in turn. (See figure 4-1.1.)

A was the original business of Z Enterprises. It had originally been a state-owned enterprise (SOE) making parts for agricultural machinery but had been bought by an overseas group and switched to manufacturing exhaust systems for automobiles after China's acceptance into the WTO. Chen Song had been the Managing Director of A when it was acquired. He had impressed the new

Table 4-1.1 Selected operational outcomes (targets) for latest financial year[1]

	A	B	C	Z
Quality (%)	6.12 (4.5)	4.54 (4.0)	**3.03 (3.5)**	4.51 (4.0)
Inventory (turns)	16.34 (20.0)	**22.18 (20.0)**	15.17 (24.0)	18.23 (22.0)
Cost (%)	**−7.24 (−5.0)**	−2.1 (−4.0)	0 (−6.0)	−3.5 (−5.0)

Best in **bold**

[1] These measures are aggregates: i.e. *quality*, expressed as a percentage of output that is faulty, combines production and customer reject figures; *inventory* measures all stock (i.e. raw material, components, work in progress (WIP), and finished goods (FG)) and is expressed as stock turns; and *cost* is the real (i.e. inflation adjusted) decrease in overall direct product costs for the year.

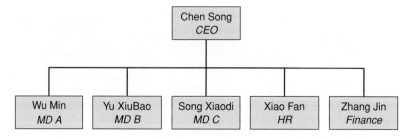

Figure 4-1.1 Organizational structure of Z's Corporate Management Board

owners with his energy and dedication and the way in which he had transformed the culture and operations of A from an inefficient, bloated, run-down SOE to a productive, lean, state-of-the-art company.

A, a Shanghai-based operation, now employs 530 people (down from over 2,000). The MD, Wu Min, who had risen through the engineering function to become Chen Song's understudy, is regarded as a tough but fair manager who engenders a shared passion (and expertise) for cost reduction in all employees. B and C were acquired in the past 3 years. They had both been start-up companies aimed at cashing in on the growing automotive industry. B, located near Guangzhou, has 370 employees engaged in the manufacture of various pressed metal components. MD Yu XiuBao, part of the original start-up syndicate, is an aggressive, entrepreneurial woman who believes that inventory is the basis of all (manufacturing) evil. C, close to Beijing, employs 250 people in generating the highest margins in the corporation from its high-technology components for sophisticated "vision systems" ("mirrors"). MD Song Xiaodi is well-liked but has a reputation for sometimes favoring analysis over action except when it comes to his obsession with quality. The managers of C feel superior to their counterparts in A and B. This sense of superiority is well known by the others and strongly resented.

As well as a salary each MD earns a significant bonus based on a percentage of his/her business's profit. Business (and, hence, corporate) profits had initially grown rapidly but the industry was maturing, sales growth had plateaued, and there was increasing pressure on price. It was therefore clear to Chen Song that more returns needed to be squeezed from internal processes. The businesses currently operate as stand-alone, autonomous units, with the only structured contact being between the MDs at the monthly CMB meeting. As well as direct instruction to the MDs at these meetings (and individually), Chen Song had often pointed out to the group that each of the businesses was excellent at some things but poor at others (table 4-1.1) and that it would benefit everyone if this "best practice" were shared. "We have islands of excellence – we need bridges!" he exhorted. The MDs insisted that they did share knowledge but in reality interbusiness relationships were highly competitive and there had been too many examples where managers had "forgotten" to pass on necessary knowledge to their counterparts outside of their own businesses. Even Chen Song's practice of rotating the CMB meetings between businesses was to avoid charges of a Shanghai bias that would arise from meeting in his office in Pudong (Shanghai).

Chen Song pondered his dilemma. When he was a business MD he had vehemently defended business autonomy and the right to manage "his" business without corporate interference. "Let me run it, and if you're not happy, sack me" was one of his typical responses. He knew his own MDs would be just as aggressive. Despite this he could see clearly that without some corporate intervention the business improvement in their areas of weakness would take far too long. Having thought about it for some time he could see a variety of options, each with its own benefits and challenges.

> 1. *What are the options, their strengths and weaknesses, and what would you recommend?*

◄ ◄ ◄ Parenting Problems: Some Ideas . . .

Chen Song faces a dilemma that confronts many who are in charge of multi-divisional companies. The businesses and their MDs are fiercely autonomous and want to stay that way but this desire for separateness – what Prahalad and Hamel (1990) refer to as the "tyranny of the SBU [strategic business unit]" – prevents the development of pan-corporate competences and/or the sharing of best practice. From table 4-1.1 in the case we can see, for example, that business A is the best at cost reduction. Hence, the corporation can benefit from A sharing its expertise with B and C while at the same time benefiting from their knowledge of inventory control techniques and quality management respectively. Similarly B and C will improve by sharing with each other and A. Note that although each business is meeting its target on one of the measures, the corporation as a whole is not meeting its targets on any measure. Chen Song has the following three major options (and any mixture of the three, of course), each of which has advantages and disadvantages.

(1) Use direct influence on stand-alone units

In this corporate style, Chen Song would be a "guru." He would work directly with each MD to improve the areas of shortfall. So, for example, he would work with Wu Min to improve A's quality and inventory management. This might involve such things as changing the bonus structure to incorporate more measures than just profit (i.e. an internal "balanced scorecard"), insisting that A hired more experts or used outside consultants to focus on those areas, or merely threatening to replace Wu Min if improvements are not forthcoming.

The advantages of this approach are that it maintains the focus of the businesses on their particular product/market/customers and their particular problems (what the economists would call "optimizing economies of specialization"). Also it does not add to corporate overheads and keeps the MDs happy in that they are running autonomous businesses. The disadvantages are that it does not promote any pan-corporate competences but maintains the "islands of (different) excellence." It also puts Chen Song in a supervisory role and will take up all his time. It is unlikely that he is an expert in all three processes and so the potential for conflict between him and his subordinates is high, particularly if business priorities change and he is forced to change focus.

(2) Develop corporate centers of excellence

In this option, the corporate center develops competence in a process or function. For example, Chen Song could hire a Corporate Quality Manager who would put together a team of experts to form the Corporate Quality Department. There are three general mechanisms by which such corporate services operate:

1. As advisory experts to the business function, to be called on when needed by the business or to be imposed if targets are not met.
2. As a centralized function, wherein the responsibility is at corporate and not at business level. Functional employees, although perhaps located in the business, are controlled and administered from the corporate level.
3. As a matrix-like amalgam of 1 and 2, whereby the business function reports to both the MD of the business and the corporate department. This is a very common structure for the finance function, for example, which often reports to both the local business manager and the corporate finance function.

With arrangements of this sort, the corporate center becomes a facilities manager. The advantages are such that Chen Song can be more confident that business functions will be directly focused on corporate-level targets without him having to try and influence this through the MDs and spending a lot of time on it. The corporate-level functions, free from the grind of day-to-day operations, can maintain a world-class capability by visiting and benchmarking world leaders and attending training events. They can then pass this expertise on to the business level through normal interactions (tacit knowledge is shared by interaction). The disadvantages lie in the added costs at corporate level (and the MDs are always very sensitive to allocated overhead costs) and the fact that it may engender an "us (business) versus them (corporate)" dynamic. Mr. Chen would need to be sure that the benefits would outweigh the added cost (including the costs of the turmoil of start-up) because he can be sure that the MDs and his corporate bosses will notice if they don't.

(3) Broaden the responsibility of the businesses
With this approach, Chen Song changes the roles of the MDs. Currently they "own" "their" business and are rewarded in both monetary and psychological terms for championing their own causes. It is the sense of what they "own" that needs to change under this approach. The MDs need to see themselves as "stewards" of the businesses and (part) "owners" of the corporation. Some mechanisms for moving to this approach include:

1. Changing the bonuses of the MDs from being based on business results to being based on corporate results or a combination of both (e.g. the bonus is based on business results but is only triggered if the corporation achieves its targets).
2. Making the MDs accountable for overall operating processes (i.e. corporate level) rather than just the business processes. So, Song Xiaodi might become the Corporate Quality Manager, for example, as well as the MD of C. In this way he has a vested interest in sharing his experts around the other businesses because his quality responsibilities have been broadened. In a similar way the MDs of the other businesses can be given corporate responsibilities.
3. Ensuring that robust interbusiness processes – such as regular meetings, exchange of employees, co-located functions (i.e. multisite), shared databases, joint presentation to customers etc. – are established and maintained.

In this approach, the corporate center (Chen Song) acts as a "boundary rider" ensuring that fences are being knocked down and not rebuilt. It has the advantages of developing truly pan-corporate best practice across a number of dimensions and getting the MDs (and eventually all employees) to have a broader perspective. Its disadvantages lie in the additional costs, including those of complexity and hassle and the strong possibility that by getting managers to focus on both the business and the corporation they will not focus sufficiently on either. As somebody once said: "more than one objective is no objective."

So, now what would you do?

A conglomerate by any other name?

In 1879, Thomas Edison invented the electric light bulb and by 1890 had organized his various businesses into the Edison General Electric Company – now the General Electric Company (GE). GE is the sole survivor of the Dow Jones Index of 1896 and number 5 in the 2005 Fortune 500. It delivered a handsome 20.7% total return to shareholders in its 2004 financial year and averaged 18.0% annually for the 10 years before that. Jeff Immelt was appointed GE's ninth CEO in 2001. His predecessor, the legendary Jack Welch, had passed on the advice he himself had been given by his predecessor when he gained the top position – "blow it up." On June 23, 2005, Immelt announced his most recent "explosion" – a restructuring of the company.

GE comprised 11 divisions, seven of them designated as "growth" businesses (table 4-2.1) and the other four as "cash generators" (table 4-2.2). As the revenue and profit figures show, these are large businesses. On the basis of 2004 sales revenue, only one of them (Infrastructure) would not be a 2005 Fortune 500 company in its own right. The largest (Commercial Finance) would be ranked at number 81 for revenues and 28 for profits. Jeff Immelt, however, denies that GE is a conglomerate: "A conglomerate generates returns by trading in and out of businesses; it's basically a gigantic mutual fund. By contrast, GE generates returns by undertaking projects that only it has the wherewithal to undertake: the biggest, the most difficult, the longest term. Scale is one of GE's traditional strengths" (*Fortune*, 05/04/04).

Table 4-2.1 GE's growth portfolio

Division	Products/businesses
Commercial Finance	Loans, leases; other financial services to corporate customers for real estate, aircraft, and equipment financing, etc. 2004: Revenues: $23,489m Profits: $4,465m
Consumer Finance	Private label credit cards, personal loans, leases and inventory financing, residential mortgages, home equity loans, etc. 2004: Revenues: $15,734m Profits: $2,520m
Energy	Gas, steam, hydro, nuclear, renewable energy power plant products/services, including design, installation and maintenance 2004: Revenues: $17,348m Profits: $2,845m
Healthcare	Medical technologies, including imaging systems, monitoring equipment, diagnostic systems, information management etc. 2004: Revenues: $13,456m Profits: $2,286m
Infrastructure	Water treatment; security; temperature, flow rates, pressure sensors, etc. for commercial and industrial users 2004: Revenues: $3,447m Profits: $563m
NBC Universal	Films; television programs; theme parks; global cable/satellite broadcasting; multimedia; etc. 2004: Revenues: $12,886m Profits: $2,588m
Transportation	Jet engines and replacement/repair and maintenance for all categories of commercial and military aircraft 2004: Revenues: $15,562m Profits: $3,213m

Table 4-2.2 GE's cash generators

Division	Products/businesses
Advanced Materials	High performance engineered plastics used in automotive parts, computer enclosures, telecommunication equipment etc. 2004: Revenues: $8,290m Profits $710m
Consumer and Industrial	Major appliances and related services for refrigerators, freezers, ovens, stoves, and cooktops, dishwashers, driers, etc. 2004: Revenues: $13,767m Profits $716m
Equipment and Other Services	Rentals, leases, sales, asset management services, and loans for portfolios of commercial and transportation equipment 2004: Revenues: $8,986m Profits $833m
Insurance	US and international reinsurance, investment, and retirement services, mortgage insurance, etc. 2004: Revenues: $23,070m Profits $569m

Table 4-2.3 GE's new structure

New division	In terms of the former divisions (tables 4-2.1 and 4-2.2)
Infrastructure	Transportation + Energy + Infrastructure (minus security and sensors)
Industrial	Advanced Materials + Consumer and Industrial + Equipment and Other Services (as well as security and sensors from the former "Infrastructure" division)
Commercial Financial Services	Commercial Finance and Insurance
Consumer Finance	Consumer Finance
Healthcare	Healthcare
NBC Universal	NBC Universal

The new structure (table 4-2.3), effective from July 5, 2005, moved to industry-focused groups, with the stated aims of accelerating the company's progress in developing markets such as China and India, and speeding decision making while saving up to $300 million per year. It also retained senior management talent by creating bigger jobs.

While some praised "[a] turning point for GE in which GE's younger generation of business leaders . . . will now take over the job of leading GE as well as overseeing all its key businesses" (Nicholas Heymann of Prudential), others were ". . . unclear how consolidating across GE's diverse business units will allow the company to streamline decision making, since each has different demand drivers and business economics" (S&P Equity Research) (both cited on Reuters, 23/06/05).

> 1. *What do you think?*
> 2. *How does having such a disparate collection of businesses make value adding sense?*
> 3. *Does the reorganization change anything?*
> 4. *Should it be broken up and, if so, why; if not, why not?*

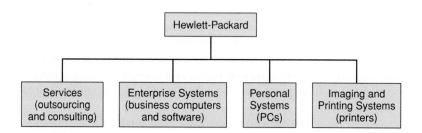

Follow the Hurd?

On March 29, 2005, Mark Hurd, a 25 year veteran of NCR and its CEO since 2003, was appointed CEO of Hewlett-Packard (HP). He replaced Carleton "Carly" Fiorina, who had been sacked some 6 weeks earlier, having joined HP as CEO in July 1999 and been named Chairman in September, 2000. Hurd inherited an underperforming diversified corporation (figure 4-3.1) racked with strategic dilemmas and beset by contradictory advice from all quarters.

On Hurd's ascension, HP's share price was hovering around $23, having hit a 5-year high of $68.09 on July 14, 2000 and a low of $10.75 on July 26 just 2 years later. The price had been falling well before the May 2002 merger with Compaq. The decline reflected the tougher conditions in the marketplace and, perhaps more significantly, the fact that HP kept missing its forecast earnings targets and had lost the trust of the share market. For example, in August 2004 the company announced that earnings per share (EPS) for that July's quarter would be 23% below analysts' expectations – expectations that had been fanned by an upbeat conference speech by "Carly" a short time earlier. According to stock analysts, the $23 reflected mainly the value of the (very profitable) printer business. The remainder of the company, representing $55bn (two-thirds) of HP's revenue, was being significantly discounted. Merrill Lynch analyst Steven Miluvovich, a long-time HP watcher, calculated the break-up share value of HP to be $28 (table 4-3.1) (*Fortune*, 13/06/05: 75). Several hedge funds shared the view that HP was undervalued and had been aggressive purchasers of stock at $23 and below on the basis that *any* improvement in the non-printer businesses would lift the price.

When Hurd took over at NCR, its share price was $10. Over the following 2 years he cut $250m of costs, and the share price was $37 when he left for the HP job. In

```
                        ┌─────────────────┐
                        │ Hewlett-Packard │
                        └─────────────────┘
```

| Services (outsourcing and consulting) | Enterprise Systems (business computers and software) | Personal Systems (PCs) | Imaging and Printing Systems (printers) |

Figure 4-3.1 HP's business structure

Table 4-3.1 HP's "break-up" share price

Cash	$4
Services	$1
Enterprise Systems	$6
Personal Systems	$2
Imaging & Printing Systems	$15
Total	$28

this new role, he has already indicated that significant cost reductions, involving laying off thousands of employees, would again be an integral part of his attempts to revive his new company. He has also committed to lifting the standards against which HP benchmarks itself and to ensuring that announcements made to shareholders and analysts about earnings would be accurate and promises would be kept. What he has yet to unveil, however, is how HP will regain its competitive edge and what shape the future company will take.

Competitively, HP had attempted to reinvent itself with its merger with Compaq. Despite its lack of experience with big mergers, and the fact that Compaq was struggling to digest a large acquisition of its own (DEC), even Carly's most vehement critics acknowledged that the post-merger integration was managed successfully and ahead of schedule. The acquisition created the second largest global technology provider (behind IBM) with the potential for competitive advantage through a full suite of linked solutions from servers, via access devices to storage and printing. On the negative side HP became even more exposed to the highly competitive, increasingly commoditized PC sector, where razor thin margins are the norm and from which even IBM has now exited through its sale to Chinese company Lenovo. However, other than the notable markets of PCs, where Dell took over leadership in 2004, and IT services and consultancy, headed by IBM, HP is today a market leader in many other aspects of computer-based consumer and business technology. It remains overly dependent on its original printer business, which still provides over two-thirds of total profits from its one-third share of total revenues. Even in the printer business, margins are dropping and, ominously, Dell has entered the segment and has expressed surprise at the high margins in consumables (i.e. print cartridges).

The future structure of the company is another issue that the new CEO will need to resolve. One school of thought (predicated on the break-up value) is that the company should split itself up. In particular, it has been argued that the imaging and printing systems division should be spun off to become a stand-alone business. It dominates its market and whatever synergies are gained by linking computer and imaging technologies/markets in the same corporation are insignificant compared with the losses from a lack of total focus on defending market share and growing the entire category of printing/imaging. Another break-up orientation would separate the company into corporate and consumer focused divisions.

Not all market observers agree with the idea of a break-up. PCs and printers share common distribution/marketing channels and much core technology, and the fact that Dell is entering the printing market is offered as evidence of such synergies. The company would also lose the benefits of economies of scale in R&D and global branding (60% of sales are outside the US) as well as forfeiting the benefits of cross-selling and being a broad solution provider.

All in all there is much to be decided and much to be done . . . and soon.

---

1. What do you think Mr. Hurd should do now and why?

easyEmpire

In 1995, Stelios Haji-Iannou, just 27 years old and with a loan from his family, launched easyJet. Started with just six hired planes working one route, by 2003 it had 74 aircraft flying 105 routes to 38 airports and carrying over 20 million passengers per year. easyJet by then had a dense point-to-point network, linking major airports with large catchments with very frequent flights. The fleet of aircraft is now large, modern, and relatively environmentally friendly. The brand is very strong, with a high degree of consumer awareness of the company's orange color and logo.

easyJet aims to be the lowest fare on a route and a low-cost philosophy permeates throughout the business. Tickets are not issued to passengers and around 90% are purchased online. Because 100% of sales are direct to consumers, easyJet does not pay intermediaries. The fare system is dynamic: "the earlier you book, the less you pay." There are no free in-flight refreshments, although they can be purchased. Travelers are expected to clear up after themselves and this helps to reduce the amount of time aircraft need to remain on the ground. There is no distinction between economy or business class.

While easyJet goes from strength to strength, Stelios has also been starting up other new ventures. This dynamic, serial entrepreneur, as he describes himself, is a highly energized presence, a terrific talker, and full of ideas and reasons. His mission is to "paint the world orange." easyCar resulted from his observation that the cost of renting cars from airports that easyJet served was a "rip-off." With easyCar, a Mercedes A-class, in the trademark orange of the group, can be rented for a very competitive price. Other ventures include easyInternet café, easyCruise, easyBus, easyHotel, easyMobile, and easyCinema.

easyCinema follows the familiar Stelios mission of identifying industries where a new venture can compete on low cost, innovation, and fun. In cinema, Stelios observed asset underutilization, with only one in five seats on average being sold, inflated prices, which also did not reflect that films become less valuable over time, and overpriced popcorn and coke for sale. Stelios felt that an "easy" makeover was called for. He searched for a location to offer a cinema based on easyGroup values. Eventually, he found an aging multiplex in Milton Keynes, a large conurbation some 40 miles north of London.

The interior of the once lavish multiplex was ripped out and the whole complex painted a bright orange, much to the annoyance of passers by. Gone were the popcorn, drink, and ticketing facilities. In the words of his posters, "If you really want to eat popcorn, bring your own, but don't make a mess!" Tickets are purchasable over the internet. Through payment by credit or debit card, the customer can print out a bar code for use at the entry scanners in the multiplex. Prices start at 20p per ticket, compared with around £4.60 per ticket at neighboring cinemas.

With just 2 weeks to go before opening, Stelios did not have films to show at his new cinema. The only major blockbuster to open near this time was *The Matrix Reloaded*. However, none of the four major film distributors was interested in supplying Stelios with their films when they heard that he would be selling tickets for just 20p per person. He received many criticisms over the lack of staff at his facility, concerns over public order and health and safety, and whether piracy could be avoided. Stelios interpreted these as stalling tactics as the film distributors were not happy with his intention to have low prices. To remove the potential loss distributors might incur through low box-office takings, Stelios decided to offer them a £2,000 cash lump sum for a week for a film three weeks post-opening, which he had calculated to be the entire box-office takings for such a film at this stage in the US. He did not receive acceptance and so still had to find films for his cinema. Fortunately, he was able to procure films from a leading independent producer, Pathé. While Stelios was unsure that *The Little Polar Bear* would really provide competition for *The Matrix Reloaded*, which would be showing across the street at the same time, it was, at least, a new release.

With film distributors controlling 90% of the market, Stelios had to find a way to deal with these large players. On their part, they could not be seen to collude against him because that would be anticompetitive and illegal. However, Stelios' lawyers suggested that their uniform action to date could be deemed to be evidence of tacit collusion. When this observation was sent to the distributors in a formal letter, the net result was that they then provided Stelios with some films. Although not the blockbusters he had hoped for, they were, nonetheless, new releases.

Just days before launching the new cinema, easyGroup and Stelios launched a public relations offensive, with widespread advertising on radio, internet, and television, as well as the prominent display of provocative orange posters on buses, taxis, and billboards. Stelios himself walked around Milton Keynes with a billboard proclaiming: "The end of rip-off cinema is nigh!" Followed by television cameras, he entered shopping malls and the foyers of competitor cinemas where he was forcibly ejected. There is little doubt that the people of Milton Keynes were aware of Stelios' enterprise and many would have met him or at least heard his evangelical tirade.

Despite a few technical difficulties on the opening night, customer volumes during the first week were good, despite only having a "little polar bear" rather than a "matrix." Even when customers were in their seats, the Stelios offensive continued. Although they had entered for as little as 20p per ticket, Stelios explained that the film distributors were forcing him to pay £1.30 per person. Could they put a further contribution into the bucket he was passing around? The goodwill of the customers was evident as people did contribute. Stelios then announced that these funds would in fact be donated to a local hospice. The point, however, had been made: Stelios was trying to protect his customers by providing entertainment at a reasonable cost.

Despite a slackening in demand at easyCinema in the ensuing weeks, there is evidence of an underlying level of support. However, Stelios realizes that for the project to really take off, he needs to be able to show the new blockbusters. To gain leverage over the distributors, Stelios has engaged US competition lawyers (for in the US, if you lose litigation, you do not pay the other side's costs). The lawyers have found a 1950s legal precedent in favor of a cinema exhibiter who faced producers ganging up against him. Stelios is now considering opening further cinemas in London to extend the concept.

However, observers are beginning to wonder if Stelios is struggling. easyJet was floated in 2000, with the easyGroup, although still the largest shareholder, taking more of a back seat. Stelios stepped down as chairman in 2005. easyCinema can't seem to get the films it needs; the internet cafés at one point were losing £3m per month; and the easyCar business is still losing money. And yet the group continues to expand. The year 2005 saw the launch of easyMusic.com, where users can download tracks for as little as 25p, and easyMobile, which offers voice calls for a flat rate of 15p per minute and SMS text messages for 5p each (rates that were due to fall by June 2005). The group plans to keep costs low by only selling over the internet and by not subsidizing sales of handsets. The mobile giant Orange has now sued the group over the use of the color orange, but Stelios's response was: "I have been using this color for ten years and I will not stop using it now for anyone. Let the battle commence."

1. *Why has easyJet been a corporate success?*
2. *Why have the national flagship airline operators struggled to imitate easyJet's model?*
3. *Is the cinema industry a good addition to the easyGroup portfolio? Where would you place it in the BCG matrix?*
4. *Does the easyGroup parent company add value to its subsidiaries?*
5. *What would you recommend to Stelios for the future of his group?*

Pendulum swings . . .

Like many organizations over the past two decades, public and private, Telco bought into the decentralization revolution. In 1988, its annual report described the way in which it had "adopted a new business philosophy." It explained: "With the centralized demands of a centralized head office, the company was slow and unresponsive. [However], a decentralized organization structure is now being adopted to improve Telco's operating performance."

In 1989's report, it reiterated that: "A bureaucratic organization with centralized control could never function effectively in a competitive marketplace. The new organization structure is now in place." Although 1990's annual report stuck to the same script, it was less gung-ho about the task having been completed: "The former system of centralized and bureaucratic controls added to overall costs and inhibited the development of a market-reactive business. However, the company is now capable of functioning efficiently in a competitive environment. The restructuring of Telco is largely completed."

Three years later, Telco representatives announced that the Company was "reverting back to centralized control." With hindsight, it was claimed that the rationale for decentralization was that it was simply "a phase in the Company's development, designed to achieve what the head of a prominent union involved in the process called the 'creation of a new culture'."

Whether or not this was in fact the plan, many practicing managers will find the story of a company seemingly on a pendulum, swinging back and forth from centralization to decentralization, very familiar. Interviewing many of the Telco's senior managers in 1991 and 1992 – the period between the wholehearted embrace of decentralization and moving back to centralized control – revealed some interesting insights into the process.

The then Marketing Director explained the logic behind the move in 1988 as follows: "Essentially we used to be a very bureaucratic organization, with everything centrally controlled and directed, and the restructuring concept was to create a much flatter organization with decision making much closer to the customer base and a substantial degree of autonomy in each of the operating companies."

The Director of New Ventures was more to the point: "We had a very big problem with what was called Head Office. You couldn't order a rubber [eraser] out of Auckland unless you actually got a bit of paper from Head Office. So, we went through a very deliberate breaking up of Head Office."

Telco's corporate office was scaled back, or "emasculated" in the CFO's words. As the GM of Accounting explained, "we had to move very quickly, so the way to do that is to break up the bureaucracy into autonomous responsible divisions."

The head of one of the newly autonomous operating companies summed up his own philosophy, and that of the other new power-brokers that had been brought in to shake up the organization, thus: "Any holding company or any corporate office or any central group should be minimized as much as possible." However, later on this manager would admit that: "There is not the same degree of performance across the operating companies that we would like . . . I guess a lot of this is because we have taken an organization that was totally centralized and said 'we have to be decentralized – quickly'."

Other managers spoke of the impact of the move to decentralization going too fast, and too far:

CFO: "They wanted to concentrate on getting stuff down close to the customer. But in the process they all started inventing things that actually ended up with entirely different approaches . . . I mean it's swung too far . . . the operating companies were getting the feeling that they had autonomy in a number of areas, and of course they ran off in a number of different directions . . . There is this tendency for people to run off and invent their own bloody systems because they have got their own agendas one way or the other."

Head of Corporate Strategy: "The problem with that kind of responsiveness is the anarchy. And I'll give you a piece of day-to-day responsiveness. You know when someone has a rush of blood to the head, decides to change the numbering plan in the Hill region, so Countytown vanishes from the toll network. OK. You need that coordinated thing, because we are in a network business."

Director of New Ventures: "As is often the case we went too far in practical terms by devolving to the regional operating companies too much autonomy. What tended to happen was we saw a breaking up of direction. We heard of some, who were a division of arseholes, going in that direction; another going in this . . ."

GM of Accounting: "In fact, you ended up with a whole series of different strategies . . . you had one regional unit that believed they were in the customer premises equipment market. Another believed they weren't.

111

And another one that wasn't but believed we should be because of what they perceived to be our corporate image. It all depended on individuals . . . you didn't have a common policy."

Head of Technology Strategy: "I think there needs to be a lot more standardization of processes. The example I use at the moment, which I really find quite frustrating, is the fact that information systems are purchased and the project managed in a totally different way to other technology contracts."

The Head of Corporate Strategy summed up the views of most in explaining what went wrong and prefacing why Telco would now seek to recentralize: "We went from extreme centralization to extreme decentralization very rapidly and because we are a network business, by taking the heart out of the organization like that, a lot of the coordinating mechanisms were broken."

In 1991, new committees were formed to cut across the regional operating companies and were empowered to develop common policies in functional areas like human resources, marketing, and technology. This was rationalized in the following ways:

- GM of Accounting: "We had to bring back the control aspect that was missing."
- CFO: "There clearly needed to be brought back a common approach throughout the organization."
- Director of Marketing: "I think we had to reduce some of the devolved responsibility."

The committees grew quickly.

By the time the company formally announced it was reverting back to full-blown centralized control there were murmurings that the early recentralization initiatives were already showing signs of being taken too far. One senior manager was resigned: "There is a danger that the pendulum will swing back too far as a reaction. Yes. It will happen." In the CFO's words: "You just hope that the pendulum doesn't swing too far, [but,] well, it's inevitable; the pendulum swings and then we are up the creek." He expanded on this with an example: "Telco is becoming strikingly similar to the old organization – run by committees. I mean when the first schedule of the meeting came out, 25% of the nominal working year was taken up with bloody committee meetings. They are pretty much a waste of time anyway – I tend not to go now."

"I don't think we have solved the central versus decentral item yet," said another manager in conclusion. "We have swung the pendulum from one extreme to the other. We are now on the way back, and we haven't got to a stable end point yet."

Despite the swings and roundabouts, many, perhaps most, of the managers interviewed did reflect that perhaps the notions of centralization and decentralization did not really constitute an either/or choice. The CFO mused that, "it's a paradoxical situation – you provide much more computer ability now to the individual than was ever possible before, but you have to do that within a common framework or else there will be no meaning." One regional operating company head offered that: "In actual fact, to some degree, all of the tasks we have, have a central element and a decentral element in them." The GM of Accounting concluded by saying: "I have been one of the biggest catalysts in making decentralization happen. But at the end of the day a decentralized environment really didn't make any sense to me, so I began to talk about 'centralized decentralization' – that's my phrase word – and it's not stupid because I can't afford to have, as we have had, 14 computer sites and 14 different configurations, and heaven knows how many sets of accounts."

1. *Why did Telco move away from centralization towards decentralization?*
2. *Why did Telco move back towards centralization?*
3. *Why do firms often get confused about how the center can best add value and swing from one approach to another?*
4. *How would you go about thinking through how Telco's center could best add value in this case?*
5. *Does the concept of centralized decentralization make sense to you? How would you make it work?*

Red, green, and blue

Compagnie Royal Air Maroc was founded in 1957. It had 443 employees, a fleet of three DC3s, and was able to draw on the facilities and expertise of Air Atlas, which was developed after World War II primarily to ship freight on Junkers JU52s between Morocco, Algeria, Spain, and France. Royal Air Maroc now flies over 44,000 flights per year to 60 destinations in 30 countries in Europe, Africa, North America, and the Middle East. The Moroccan Government holds about a two-thirds stake of the company's capital.

The company is extremely proud of its "Royal" status, not surprisingly in a country that reveres and has great respect for its royal family. The proudest moments listed in its corporate history often involve the opening of facilities, or blessings of events, by members of Morocco's Royal family. It also takes its status as the "national flag carrier" (hence the colors of Royal Air Maroc: red and green) very seriously.

Royal Air Maroc's strategy is thus closely tied to the Moroccan Government's national strategy. In November 2001, Royal Air Maroc initiated a strategic vision with the objective of turning the company into a national multiple service entity and driving force tied to Morocco's economic development. Its website (www.royalairmaroc.com) proudly states that it is "fully aware of the citizen role [we] should play, Royal Air Maroc actively contributes to the economic development of Morocco and its international image" and that Royal Air Maroc's strategy is "intimately linked to the economic and industrial dynamism of our country." Furthermore, Royal Air Maroc sponsors almost all of the major Moroccan cultural and artistic events, such as the Fez Sacred Music Festival, the Rabat Festival, Essaouira Festival, and the International Film Festival at Marrakesh.

The Royal Air Maroc Group is organized around six "principal growth activities" that relate to its core expertise in air transport and allied activities. There are three "basic areas," as the company describes them (Regularly Scheduled Transport, Tourist Transport, and Air Cargo), and three "allied areas" (Hospitality, Industrial Activities, and Service and Innovation).

Over the past few years, Royal Air Maroc has been growing nicely, with the "basic" divisions performing especially well, despite a business environment that has been difficult for airlines. The restructuring of these divisions' activities around Casablanca's airport (named after King Mohammed V) toward establishing "Casa" as the international airline hub linking Europe, Asia, and the Americas into Africa has been particularly successful. This development has seen a great expansion in the number of services offered in and out of Morocco, through strategic partnerships formed with airlines such as Air France, Spain's Iberia, Delta Airlines from the US, Saudi's Gulf Air, Tunisair, and Emirates, and through growing Royal Air Maroc's own services (the company opened up 11 new routes in 2004 and had added a further 15 by October 2005). Africa has been the biggest growth area, and Royal Air Maroc is seeking to play a leading role in developing further growth in the region. Toward this end, it recently created Air Sénégal International, a subsidiary based at Dakar, with 51% of the stock held by Royal Air Maroc and 49% by the Government of Senegal. This growth has seen Royal Air Maroc recently top four million passengers per year, 7bn dirhams in turnover, and acquire four new Airbus jets towards a planned fleet of 45 aircraft by 2010.

Royal Air Maroc's latest advertising campaign subsequently promotes a strong message of confidence in the company's future. It claims that: "in a turbulent marketplace, Royal Air Maroc affirms its assets and consolidates its strong position: this is an airline company passionately Moroccan, eager to participate in solving the big challenges facing the Kingdom, [and] modern and effective in its goals of developing tourism and industry in Morocco." In the words of Royal Air Maroc's own press statements: "this is an airline company perfectly armed to battle the economic 'war of the skies'."

However, despite this claim to be "perfectly armed," in 2004 Royal Air Maroc announced the creation of a new subsidiary called Atlas Blue that would compete with Royal Air Maroc in the passenger air transport arena. Royal Air Maroc management explained that: "The creation of [Atlas Blue as] the low-cost air carrier of Royal Air Maroc fits into the Governmental vision of initiating in our country a strong national tool geared to the development of tourist transport. This national tool will make it possible to strengthen the competitiveness of the air transport industry in our country and to turn it into a major vector for the growth of tourism in the framework of the Vision 2010 program."

Perhaps the African continent's first purpose-built, low-cost airline, Atlas Blue, was established with the expressed purpose of "flying certain routes from Moroccan provinces [at present Marrakesh and Agadir are the two airports served] and to and from tourist issuing markets [initially France, Belgium, Italy, Holland, England, and Germany – with research currently being done into developing Russian services] with point-to-point service."

Atlas Blue would draw on Royal Air Maroc knowledge, facilities, capital, maintenance and other services, as well as Royal Air Maroc's HR training facilities. But many other aspects of Atlas Blue would be separate:

- The primary distribution channel for Atlas Blue's reservations and sales operations would be direct selling through stand-alone websites and call centers.
- Marketing: its advertising slogan is "Atlas Blue ... Morocco at unbeatable prices." Atlas Blue's "corporate colors" are sky blue with ochre, to represent the sea and the distinctive mountains of Morocco's inland districts (testing had shown these to be enduring images for tourists to Morocco).
- Atlas Blue's head office would not be in Casablanca but in Marrakesh, Morocco's premier tourist destination.

Atlas Blue's initial fleet comprises six B737-400s with the company planning to add two further aircraft each year until 2012.

1. *Would you describe Royal Air Maroc as a corporation in its own right, or is it better thought of as a business unit of "Morocco Inc."?*
2. *What are the corporate advantages and disadvantages of such a close relationship with the Moroccan Government?*
3. *Royal Air Maroc seems to be doing well, so why create Atlas Blue? Why could they not have simply expanded Royal Air Maroc's own services rather than incurring all the cost associated with establishing a new identity?*
4. *How can Royal Air Maroc – or the "corporate center" – best add value to Atlas Blue?*
5. *Given that Royal Air Maroc sponsors Moroccan cultural events, what should Atlas Blue sponsor?*

Perfect Positioning

Any corporate policy and plan which is typical of the industry is doomed to mediocrity.

Bruce Henderson, former Managing Partner of Boston Consulting Group

If a man write a better book, preach a better sermon, or make a better mouse-trap than his neighbor, tho' he build his house in the woods, the world will make a beaten path to his door.

Attributed to Ralph Waldo Emerson (1803–82) US poet and essayist

While we have seen that different levels of return can be obtained by investing in different industries, why is it that, in the same industry, some firms always seem to do better than others? If one, for instance, had invested selectively *within* the motor industry, in which the median 10-year return from 1993–2003 was 6% (marginally above US Treasury Bonds at 4.3%), why might a "stock picker" do better or worse than that median figure?

Table 5.1 shows that an investor lucky or smart enough to have invested solely in Oskosh Truck would have turned his/her US$1,000 into $21,647 – some 12 times the final amount from investing in GM. At the other end of the scale, those who had chosen Exide Technologies would not be ordering a new yacht on the basis of their returns. Why is it that Oskosh Trucks has continuously outperformed its rivals?

Table 5.1   1993–2003 median returns of selected companies in the US "motor" industry

Company	Returns (%)
Oskosh Truck	36
Paccar	23
Johnson Controls	18
Ford Motor	7
General Motors	6
Median	*6*
Federal Signal	1
Fleetwood Enterprises	(6)
Tenneco Automotive	(11)
Federal Mogul	(38)
Exide Technologies	(50)

(Source: Fortune.com)

Answers to why some firms, *in the same industry*, consistently perform better or worse than others can be found in an understanding of competitive **advantage** and competitive **strategy** and the links between the two. In particular, as Henderson points out above, and went on to say, "the essential element of successful strategy is that it derives its success from the differences between competitors with a consequent difference in their behavior." In other words, uniqueness is valuable in earning above average returns.[1] Correspondingly it is important that those acting out this advantage and strategy clearly understand it. If it can't be simply expressed, understood, and internalized then it probably won't work. Seth Godin outlines the positioning challenge thus: "If you can't explain your strategic position in eight words or less, then you don't have one." This chapter provides a range of approaches that can help you determine and simply express a company's position relative to its competition.

Competitive Advantage and Competitive Strategy

Industry rivalry (competition) benefits consumers/buyers but harms industry profitability because marketing or development costs go up and/or industry prices come down. Most firms have to compete (monopolists being the exception) to survive. However, some do so with a **sustainable competitive advantage** that enables them to maintain prices and/or win new customers and increase profitability compared with their rivals. Competitive advantage is the *unique* set of assets, capabilities, positions, and environmental circumstances that enable an organization to consistently out-perform its competitors in its chosen strategic outcomes. In industry terms, competitive advantage means that a firm exploits industry imperfections better than its rivals or reaps the benefits of firm-specific imperfection(s).

Although exceptions may exist, it is generally true that:

- Firms with competitive advantage are more profitable than their rivals (unless incompetent, greedy, and/or dishonest managers dissipate the extra gains).
- Firms that consistently demonstrate higher profitability than rivals have competitive advantage(s).
- *Most firms do not have competitive advantage* – this is a logical consequence of the relativity of "advantage." Firms may be very good but may not be better than the others.
- The degree to which a firm can achieve competitive advantage is constrained by the dynamics of its industry (see chapter 3 Industry Terrain).

There are two generic forms of competitive advantage:

1. **Cost advantage**: a firm can do the same things as its rivals but do so at a lower *delivered cost* (i.e. total costs – not just product/service costs). Such firms exploit economies of scale, scope, and learning (experience) effects and are obsessed with efficiency and cost control.
2. **Differentiation advantage**: a firm offers something of value that is unique or sufficiently better than its rivals' offerings to be seen as unique. These businesses create a form of monopoly in that no other firm can deliver the same product/service-based value to the target market. Their obsessions center on protecting and improving their uniqueness in brand, product, or process for instance.

Competitive advantage is a *measure* of the relative superiority of a few companies over others, whereas competitive strategy comprises the ongoing actions/decisions that each company undertakes to achieve its goals, a major one of which is competitive advantage. Definitions of strategy are legion and rather than attempt to reinvent the already reinvented we will stick with the non-controversial and classic definition by Alfred Chandler (1962) that strategy is:

> "... the determination of the long-run goals and objectives of an enterprise, and the adoption of courses of action and the allocation of resources necessary for carrying out these goals."

Strategies manifest themselves in three ways:

1. the **position** a company adopts in terms of its stance against competitors and its choice of buyer segments as it attempts to **fit** with the industry's critical success factors
2. the source of value that is the primary driver of the company's offering and
3. the resources and capabilities underpinning that value and the position of the firm

Strategy as Positioning (or "Fit")

As industries grow and evolve, the requirements for strategic success, or the critical success factors (CSFs), also change. All firms in the industry, in order to survive, must first ensure a **fit** between their strategy and the CSFs of the industry and, second, strive for competitive advantage over rivals[2] who are doing the same thing. In this sense, all businesses have a "strategy" – it matters little whether this is a formally designed set of goals and plans or an unspoken consistency in a stream of decisions/actions. However, as indicated above, only a few businesses have **competitive advantage(s)**.

Unfortunately the traditional use of the same generic terminology, such as "cost" and "differentiation," to describe both advantage *and* strategy (figure 5.1), can lead to confusion.[3] This confusion is potentially damaging to your wealth because the differences between cost or differentiation *advantages* and cost (price)

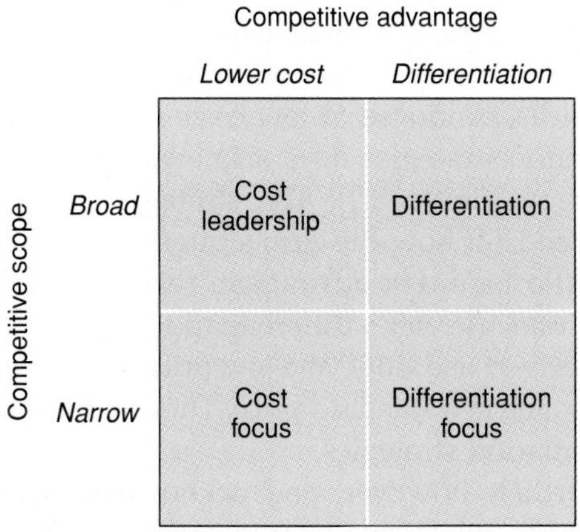

Competitive advantage

	Lower cost	Differentiation
Broad	Cost leadership	Differentiation
Narrow	Cost focus	Differentiation focus

(Competitive scope)

Figure 5.1   Generic competitive strategies (Source: Porter (1985))

or differentiation *strategies* are critical. Cost and differentiation *advantages* protect the firm against rivals and reduce the power of buyers/suppliers and the threat of entry and substitution – cost and differentiation *strategies* per se do not.

As figure 5.1 also illustrates, the firm's choice of advantage/strategy is accompanied by its choices about the market segments it will address. Hence it can pursue a cost or differentiation strategy and, given this choice, it can attack on a wide front across the industry or focus its firepower on a particular segment or niche.

In a more detailed description of strategic **scope**, Henry Mintzberg[4] suggests that there are four generic approaches:

1. **Unsegmentation**: the firm offers the same products across a broad range of market segments (e.g. Coca-Cola, Wal-Mart, Google)
2. **Segmentation**: the firm still addresses a broad range of market segments but designs different products for those segments (e.g. Honda, Dell, British Airways)
3. **Niche**: the firm focuses on one segment of the market (e.g. Ryanair, Cray Computers, Morgan Cars)
4. **Customization**: the firm focuses on individual customers and shapes their offering to the unique requirements of that buyer (e.g. upmarket homes, event organization, golf course design)

One way to think about how an industry might be composed of different pools of competition is to use strategic group analysis. By looking broadly at the characteristics of firms (rather than just market characteristics), maps can be created showing how firms in the same industry compete more or less intensively with other competitors – for instance, one would not suggest that, in the watch industry, Swatch should compete head to head with Rolex. In constructing these maps, using criteria distinctive to firms (rather than generic terms such as price and quality), it is possible to identify "white spaces" that could be untapped areas of opportunity. (Of course, for the analysis to work effectively, it is important to identify axes that are not correlated.)

In his original work, Michael Porter (1980) suggested that it is a major problem for any firm to be "stuck in the middle" with neither sufficient differentiation advantage to claim a price premium or guarantee customer loyalty, nor sufficient cost advantage to underpin superior margins at prevailing prices. However, other authors are not so sure that this is such an either/or choice and point to the success of Japanese car companies such as Toyota in offering high quality, highly and flexibly featured vehicles produced at low costs with substantial brand equity.

Another set of generic strategies does acknowledge the possibility of a high-value/low-cost strategy (figure 5.2). The **strategic clock** suggests that viable strategy options depend on how the firm's offering is perceived by the market in terms of its *price* (Porter's cost advantage) relative to other offerings and its relative *perceived use value* (Porter's differentiation). Whereas a *low-price* strategy offers a standard perceived use value at a low price, a *differentiation* strategy offers a high perceived use value at a standard price. These options correspond to Porter's low-cost and differentiation strategies.

The clock goes further, however, and acknowledges the viability of high-value/low-price "hybrid" (the Japanese car manufacturers?), high-value/high-price "focused differentiator" (luxury goods?), and low-value/low-price "no frills"

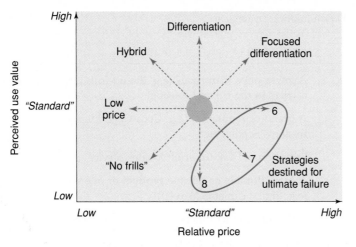

Figure 5.2 The strategic clock (Source: Bowman (1988))

(low-cost airlines?) strategic options. The strategies that are doomed to ultimate failure are those where the offering ends up being perceived to have low relative use value but standard or higher relative price. Marlboro (cigarettes) and Compaq (computers) were able to maintain high relative prices over a long period. However, as their perceived relative use value declined, they ended up in the lower right-hand quadrant and sales declined accordingly. Significant price decreases were needed to save them from a niche existence.

You will have noticed that Bowman with his strategic clock has made a subtle but significant reorientation to *price* as an advantage rather than cost. Henry Mintzberg is another who endorses this stance in suggesting that all strategy and advantage is based on some form of differentiation, *of which price is one variant.* He suggests six basic forms of differentiation strategy (table 5.2). Any of these may or may not lead to sustainable competitive advantage, depending on (1) the value the customer places on the chosen option and (2) how much better the firm is than its rivals in delivering this option.

One last useful set of generic positioning categories is Nigel Slack's five advantage categories from his book *Manufacturing Advantage.* Slack looks at strategy from an operational perspective to outline the following options:

1. **quality advantage** (or "doing it right")
2. **speed advantage** (or "doing things fast")
3. **dependability advantage** (or "doing things on time")
4. **flexibility advantage** (or "being able to adapt what you do")
5. **cost advantage** (or "doing things cheap")

An interesting aspect of these generic strategy options is the fact that many firms will belong to the same category – *they are undifferentiated.* They offer similar products at similar prices with similar service etc. and still make enough money to earn an acceptable return on the capital invested – just how differentiated is one financial services institution from another, for example? Note that whether a strategy is undifferentiated or not will depend on who you ask – most (all?) firms are *trying* to be different.

Table 5.2 Differentiation strategies

Strategy	Description
Price (low cost)	A lower price than rivals (e.g. the no-frills airlines verses the big carriers in the US and Europe)
Image	A brand or reputation (e.g. Coca-Cola, Mercedes, Gucci, Harvard Business School, etc.)
Support	Provision of back-up or after-sales service (e.g. Dell)
Quality	A more durable or reliable product or one with higher performance (e.g. digital cameras (pixels))
Design	Different product functions (e.g. pharmaceuticals, mobile phones)
Undifferentiation	Same as the others (e.g. car rental firms, financial service firms, petrol stations, steel companies, etc.)

(Source: Mintzberg (1998))

Jockeying For Position – Game Theory

While the underlying dynamic of all competitive strategy, and particularly the positioning school, is one of dealing with competition, when there are very few competitors (as, for example, in an oligopolistic industry – see chapter 3, Industry Terrain), strategic moves must explicitly take into account the potential (and likely) responses of rivals. Game theory is that branch of economics/strategy that analyzes decision processes and outcomes when each actor makes decisions – for example, pricing, capacity, product introduction – based on the anticipated actions and reactions of its rivals. Delving into the full intricacies (and mathematics) of game theory is beyond the scope of this text but the following example gives a flavor of the sort of reasoning in a game theoretic decision.

Suppose that a capital-intensive industry, dominated by two main and equal-size companies called Caesar and Brutus, has demand that exceeds current supply. The CEOs of Caesar and Brutus are contemplating expanding capacity but the nature of the manufacturing process is such that capacity can only be expanded in relatively large and expensive lumps. The CEO of Brutus has a financial model that shows her the following profit figures for her company depending on the expansion outcomes:

1. No expansion by either – Brutus profit: US$360 million per year (i.e. current profits).
2. Brutus expands and Caesar does not – Brutus profit: US$400 million per year.
3. Brutus does not expand but Caesar does – Brutus profit: US$300 million per year.
4. Both expand – Brutus profit: US$320 million per year.

But she knows that the CEO of Caesar has exactly the same set of figures for his company. So what to do?

John Nash, made popularly famous through the film *A Beautiful Mind*, won a Nobel Prize in economics for his analysis of such situations (which include such things as the arms race). His insights demonstrated why the most likely outcome in such cases, known as the Nash equilibrium, is that both companies expand (i.e. outcome 4 above) despite the fact that the best outcome for both is to stay as they are. One way to understand why this is so is to put yourself in the place of either CEO and answer this question: "Given you do not know what the other firm will do, what is the decision you can make that you will never (financially) regret *whatever* your opposite number does?" You might also further understand why tacit or even explicit (illegal) collusion is so tempting in oligopolistic competition.

Case 5–6 "Customers – those bastards!" illustrates how game theory can be used by buyers to get price reductions.

Value-Creating Activities

Industrial organizational theorists like Porter stress the importance of establishing a close fit between the strategy of the firm and the critical success factors of the environment. This emphasis has tended to deflect attention away from the fact that establishing an advantageous position depends on performing competitively valuable activities better than rivals. Porter discusses this through the value chain (figure 5.3).

Whether an activity is merely a (necessary) cost or a source of strategic value (advantage) varies between different firms across different industries. Marketing (via branding and distribution) is the key value differentiator for Coca-Cola, and so is a focus on investment and development, whereas operations and outbound logistics, making and delivering the cola, are operations to be made as efficient and cost effective as possible. On the other hand, for Federal Express, distribution is its core strategic offering.

Efficiency-based activities may be outsourced to more focused suppliers or lower cost locations whereas strategically vital activities are kept in house. Hence many Western firms are locating call centres in India and China to take advantage of lower costs in these regions. The prime source of value may not be clear cut to those in the firm. A former CEO of Ford, for example, believed that the company's key strategic advantage lay in designing and marketing its vehicles. He forecast that eventually the firm would outsource all of its manufacturing – the fact that he is a *former* CEO suggests that the Ford family were not in agreement with this view.

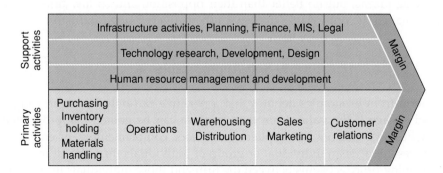

Figure 5.3 The generic value chain (Source: Porter (1985))

What the value chain does make us do is to focus on the underlying activities and capabilities that are the prime source of developing and maintaining an advantageous position, as the next section explores.

Resources and Capabilities – The Resource-Based View (RBV)

A reaction to the dominance of the "strategy as positioning" school, but in fact a logical complement of it, emerged in the 1980s and developed rapidly to become a major influence on strategic thinking. Building on insights first developed in the 1950s,[5] RBV proponents emphasize that competitive advantage stems from the **uniqueness** of a firm's resources. "Resources" in this sense include the usual tangible (e.g. plant and equipment) and intangible (e.g. brand) assets but also include learning-based capabilities and competences.[6] This approach links with the positioning school because the cost advantage of a business stems from its capabilities/competences[7] in cost reduction or success from a brand depends on capabilities in brand development and management etc. Even if luck[8] plays a part in getting a firm to an initial position of advantage, the constant erosion of that advantage by competitors can only be held at bay by superior learning competences embedded in the social fabric of the firm.

For a resource to have competitive advantage for a firm, it must have certain characteristics. Our acronym for these characteristics is **CASIS**, which stands for Congruence, non-Appropriable, non-Substitutable, non-Imitable, Supported. An alternative acronym is **VRIO**.[9] In more detail, resources must be:

1. Congruent with the critical success factors of the industry

In this sense a resource must, through the products/services it underpins, fulfill customer needs in ways that are *competitively superior* to rivals. This is critical: a common mistake that managers make is to identify a resource (often "management"!) as a "strength" without assessing it against that of rivals. To be competitively superior a resource must increase value through higher prices or volumes or through lower costs – anything else might be good (and necessary) but it is not competitively superior. For instance, Domino were good at making/ delivering pizzas, but no better than their opposition and so low price became (and remains) the only viable strategy in the delivered pizza industry.

2. Non-Appropriable

This term from economics denotes that a resource can only underpin competitive advantage if the value from that resource can be gained ("appropriated") by the business and not by suppliers, customers, complementors, or employees. If the "resource" is an individual or group of individuals then almost invariably a bargaining process begins between the firm and those individuals for the value created. The ongoing threat to the firm is that their "resources" can be tempted away by other firms or can set up in opposition themselves. This dynamic is most obvious in professional sports teams, financial firms, consultancies, etc., where the "star" players gather more and more of the income for themselves. However, the increasing size of remuneration packages for CEOs of large corporations across the Western world suggests that more and more value is being appropriated by the "stars(?)" of the boardroom, who can leave to manage the competition if their wants are not met. Note that the size of the package is bearing less and less relationship to company performance – shareholders pay for the "star" and not necessarily his or her best game.

3. Non-Substitutable

Resources can diminish in value as substitute capabilities emerge. For example, the big broking houses found that their in-house capability for research and analysis in stock investment became less valuable as low price, broking-only services on the internet encouraged investors to do the research themselves. Buyers developing the expertise and doing it themselves is an ongoing substitution threat to in-house capabilities in any expertise-based industry like education, consultancy, brokering, house repairs, restaurants, etc. The important point with substitution is that the resource is not copied (see below), but is threatened by an alternative.

4. Non-Imitable

Once rivals learn of a competitor's superior and valuable capability they begin the quest to copy it and rapid imitation erodes the *durability* of any advantage. This is most obvious at the product level, where eventually all DVD players, mobile phones, washing machines, life insurance polices, supermarkets, etc. offer the same set of benefits and features. However, imitation also takes place at the resource level. The US car companies eventually overcame their pride and overtly imitated the lean production processes of their Japanese rivals. Similarly, consumer goods firms around the world became as expert in quality management capabilities as Sony, Matsushita, and Canon through blatant, consultant-assisted copying. If legal blockages cannot be established through patents or copyrights, then imitation can only be prevented/slowed if:

1. the resource is **physically unique** (e.g. the Saudi oil fields) and/or
2. it is **expensive to develop** (e.g. Intel's processor factories) and/or
3. it will take a long time and involve a lot of prior learning to develop (so-called **path-dependency**) (e.g. Coca-Cola's branding expertise) and/or
4. there is little understanding of the processes underlying the capability, even in the business with the capability (so-called **causal ambiguity**) (e.g. Southwest Airlines' low-cost capability: everyone knows the parts – the internet booking system, the fast plane turnaround, the lack of onboard services, etc. have all been extensively examined, written about, and imitated – but the implicit, cultural "glue" that makes up the whole, and which is much more the key to financial success, has proven much more difficult for its US rivals to copy)

5. Supported organizationally

While a firm may have resources and capabilities that are valuable, rare, and inimitable, they do need to be supported by management structures, organizational structure, and controls. These complementary resources and capabilities may not generate much value in themselves, but are critical to enabling the firm to realize its full competitive advantage. Xerox, for instance, invested heavily in a series of innovative technologies, including the PC, the mouse, windows software, the paperless office, etc. The market potential was enormous and, of course, this was realized by Bill Gates. The reason Xerox did not benefit was that it lacked appropriate organizational supports. There was no structure to allow senior managers to be fully aware of the products that were being developed, managers were compensated based on maximizing current revenue and so had no incentive to develop future markets, and the highly bureaucratic product development process meant most products didn't survive. As a consequence, Xerox's rare and valuable technologies were not exploited.[10]

At the beginning of the chapter we asked the question: why has Oskosh Truck been able to remain a star performer over a sustained period of time, with 36% annual returns to investors over a 10-year period? We can now see that such long-term superior profitability depends on how much better a firm's strategy fits with its industry forces *relative to its rivals* and its greater skill in developing and marshaling *unique* resources to maintain and improve that position. We also know that others in the industry are attempting to wrest away Oskosh's advantage, because that's what happens in mature industries. On rare occasions, macro-shocks in the form of significant technological advance (e.g. electricity, the telephone, the internet) batter down the existing advantages of incumbents but, in the main, advantages are slowly eroded by the prevailing winds of *imitation* and *substitution*.

In line with Bruce Henderson's quote at the beginning of the chapter, the driving quest of all business strategy must be for the development and maintenance of *unique* valuable positions and/or capabilities that cannot be imitated. Being better than others at the same thing is highly unlikely to remain unique (advantageous) in the long term.

Strategists must be paranoid – they *are* out to catch you and you must stay apart from the crowd!

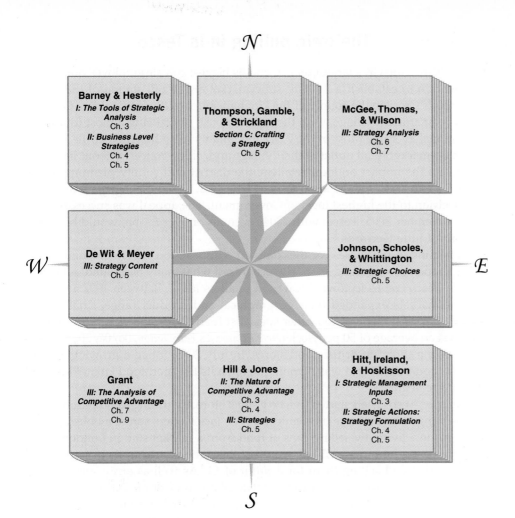

N

Barney & Hesterly
I: The Tools of Strategic Analysis
Ch. 3
II: Business Level Strategies
Ch. 4
Ch. 5

Thompson, Gamble, & Strickland
Section C: Crafting a Strategy
Ch. 5

McGee, Thomas, & Wilson
III: Strategy Analysis
Ch. 6
Ch. 7

W

De Wit & Meyer
III: Strategy Content
Ch. 5

Johnson, Scholes, & Whittington
III: Strategic Choices
Ch. 5

E

Grant
III: The Analysis of Competitive Advantage
Ch. 7
Ch. 9

Hill & Jones
II: The Nature of Competitive Advantage
Ch. 3
Ch. 4
III: Strategies
Ch. 5

Hitt, Ireland, & Hoskisson
I: Strategic Management Inputs
Ch. 3
II: Strategic Actions: Strategy Formulation
Ch. 4
Ch. 5

S

PERFECT POSITIONING

The train pulling in is Tesco

In 1997, Tesco, the UK's largest retailer and its biggest private employer, announced its intention to establish a 2,508m^2 supermarket at the rail station of the village of Gerrards Cross in the county of Buckinghamshire, southeast England. Gerrards Cross is an affluent village, with the typical house price being almost four times the national average. Most of the 7,342 inhabitants were horrified at the thought of a mass-market retail outlet in their village and, citing concerns about increased traffic and the impact on local retailers, the district and county planning offices refused permission for the store to be established. Tesco management appealed that decision to the highest level of Government. The appeal was successful and, from November 2005, Tesco, with 2004 revenues of over £31bn, would become a big part of little Gerrards Cross.

On hearing of the success of the company's appeal, the village greengrocer re-let his property to a betting shop. He recognized what many had found out before – when Tesco comes to town, local food retailers leave. Between 1997 and 2002, as supermarkets expanded their geographical and product range, small greengrocers, bakers, butchers, and other specialist food shops had closed throughout Britain at an average of 50 per week (*New Economics Foundation*, 06/06/2005). Tesco is not only a threat to British food stores. In July 2005, it had a growing 6.5% of the non-food market and was planning to open its first non-food HomePlus store later in the year.

Ironically, Tesco itself started as a *very* small store. Returning to his family home after serving as an air force mechanic in WWI, Jack Cohen, son of a Polish-Jewish tailor, made a living by selling cans of food from a market stall in London's East End. He began by buying £30 of army surplus rations, taking them to the Well Street market and selling them for a profit of £1. As well as army surplus food stocks, Cohen's low-cost purchases included unlabeled tins from salvage merchants who had themselves bought the products as reject batches from large manufacturers. Cohen would relabel the dented cans and sell them on at very low prices to grateful customers living on tight post-war budgets; customers who could not afford the prices charged by the established high street retailers like J. Sainsbury and Marks & Spencer.

By 1930, Jack Cohen was operating a string of stalls across markets all over London and, such was his increased purchasing power and acumen, had become a wholesaler to other stall holders. The dubious sourcing strategies of some of their supply channels meant that he and his nephew still had to rebadge cans with new labels to disguise their brand origins. One day, needing a new label for a batch of tea, Cohen combined the first three letters of the supplier's name with the first two letters of his surname and "Tesco" was born. He opened his first store in 1931. By taking advantage of the post-war housing boom outside London, and paying low rents to grateful developers, he had 100 stores by 1939. Tesco's profits came from high volume sales driven by low prices ("pile it high, sell it cheap") based on Cohen's obsession for low-cost inputs that included low employee wages. On a 1946 visit to America he found a mechanism that both increased throughput and reduced (employee) costs – self-service. Tesco stores became self-service "supermarkets."

By the early 1960s, as J. Sainsbury opened lavish new premises that focused on offering well-presented, quality products (at higher prices) to its middle-class customers, Tesco had expanded to over 400 outlets through the acquisition of cheap stores. In 1961, it opened a new-look store in Leicester, combining food and non-food items and providing undercover parking for 1,000 cars. Its new format caused further clashes with the brand-name manufacturers. They had often taken the company to court for setting its own retail prices in defiance of the "resale price maintenance" laws, under which the supplier set the retail prices. Tesco fought these laws and eventually, by one vote, the British Parliament struck them down; price wars were now legal between competing chains. Over the next decade, Tesco grew rapidly as thousands of small stores, stripped of price protection, closed throughout the country.

In the mid-1960s Tesco increased sales further when it introduced Green Shield Stamps. Customers collected these based on the value of their purchases and traded them in for goods when they had collected the stipulated amount. Its upmarket rival J. Sainsbury was disdainful of such inducements and campaigned unsuccessfully for their removal. In the 1970s, with Britain in the grip of national union action and the working week reduced to 3 days, Tesco's sales and profits declined. In response the company dispensed with stamps and slashed prices to reflect the £20 million annual cost savings. The shoppers returned and sales surged ahead once more.

Throughout the next two decades, Tesco extended its product range, expanded its store size, and polished a new image as it wooed consumers, employees, and local authorities. It introduced share incentive programs for workers. Its small, crowded, untidy, "pile it high" stores were closed to make way for spacious, tidy supermarkets, hypermarkets, and speciality shops catering for the increased affluence and mobility of its customer base. High-end brands shared shelf space with (cheaper) Tesco branded goods across an increased range of products. This enabled the brand-conscious consumers to shop alongside their more price-sensitive companions. In 1995, Tesco overtook J. Sainsbury to become the largest retailer in Britain.

Tesco remains price competitive. In the first half of 2005, it slashed prices by £147m to attract new custom. It has an aggressive reputation with suppliers and has been accused of sustaining its own profitability at the expense of the growers and manufacturers who provide the products. Suppliers are asked to contribute to promotional costs and support retail price reductions by taking price cuts themselves based on the expectation of additional volume. These "overrider" clauses are costly if the promised volume increase is not forthcoming. The UK's Office of Fair Trading (OFT) instigated an enquiry into such practices but, in its report of March 2005, found them to be legitimate.

Today, of every £8 spent on food and non-food items by the British consumer, £1 is spent in a store owned by Tesco. While nearly half of Tesco's total 2005 shopping area is in the UK, it now operates in 12 other countries, including China, Japan, and South Korea. It is market leader in six of these countries.

Tesco is a classic "rags to riches" story.

---

1. *Account for the rise of Tesco.*
2. *Explain Tesco's strategic strength today.*
3. *What strategies might J. Sainsbury have pursued to combat Tesco's success?*

◀◀◀The train pulling in is Tesco: Some Ideas . . .

1. Account for the rise of Tesco

Beginning in an era when many people suffered great financial hardship, Jack Cohen's market stall sold damaged cans of food at very cheap prices. This is the ultimate in a **no-frills** (strategic clock), **cost-focus** (Porter), or **low-price** (Mintzberg) strategy. Cohen's **competitive advantage** was based in **low costs** derived from his buying acumen (a **capability**) and his willingness to use (legally) dubious sources. In contrast, the more traditional high street retailers such as J. Sainsbury and Marks & Spencer were firmly in the category of broad-based **differentiators** offering **quality** of goods to underpin their higher prices. Even after the stall became "Tesco," Cohen continued to focus on price rather than quality or product range as his main profit generating approach. His stores were small, untidy, and crowded with goods. In a sense they were mini-warehouses staffed by few people, who were largely there to take customers' money, and finally by even fewer people following the move to self-service.

The move to Green Shield Stamps was both a form of **price discount** (added value for the same price) and a mechanism for **locking in** customers who were tempted to add more and more points to gain higher value "rewards." While this value adding ploy was in effect, Tesco still offered low prices and no-frills products/services. Dumping the stamps and slashing prices was Tesco's last major initiative as a "no-frills" retailer.

Throughout the 1970s and 80s, Tesco's consumers became increasingly affluent and less in need of lowest prices. They began to move upmarket in their food and drink tastes and, while perhaps shopping for basics at the cheaper Tesco, began selectively purchasing higher value items at J. Sainsbury and Marks & Spencer. Although strongly resisted by Cohen (see note below), Tesco began to follow its customers upmarket as it moved from a **no-frills** to a **low-cost** (strategic clock) strategy (more broadly targeted **cost leadership** in Porter's terms). Its stores became bigger, cleaner, and brighter and offered a more pleasant shopping environment, yet the prices were still keen.

Gradually Tesco crossed the major **mobility barriers** between its **strategic group** (the "pile it high and sell it cheap" retailers) and the "quality and service" strategic group made up of the likes of J. Sainsbury and Marks & Spencer. It did so by adding a perception of value without sacrificing the inducement of price. Its "strategy" **emerged** so gradually that its competitors did not notice the gradual erosion of the mobility barriers.

Notes

It is doubtful that Tesco's management ever articulated a **formal (design) plan** to "take on" J. Sainsbury – they just followed their customers. The danger of an **emergent strategy** is that if even the company does not "know" that this "strategy" is in place, the competitors may also remain ignorant and not respond until it is too late.

What the case does not reveal is the extent to which Jack Cohen persevered with a no-frills philosophy throughout his tenure firstly as owner, then as Chairman/CEO, and finally as Honorary Life President but non-Chairman.

He could never resist buying cheap goods or cheap, run-down premises from which to sell these cheap goods. On one occasion, a consignment of tins of "Gambos" arrived that he had purchased on holiday in South America. Nobody at Tesco knew what they were, but guessed from the label that they were plums and so stocked them in the canned fruit section. They turned out to be seeded (and hot!) peppers. In 1968, he unilaterally bought the 200 run-down stores of former rival Victor Value. It took 18 months for Tesco management to refurbish these premises one at a time. Tesco financed this deal with a rights issue that diluted Cohen's ownership to 16%. In 1973, Cohen again made a deal for a set of run-down premises, this time offering to buy the Square Meals chain from Brooke Bonds. These stores were so dilapidated (some even lacked appropriate planning permission to be in existence) that the Tesco Board defied their founder and persuaded Brooke Bonds to buy them back. This, plus being on the losing side of the decision to discontinue Green Shield Stamps (the vote was lost by one and was taken several times at the one Board meeting), signaled the end of Cohen's unchallenged rule.

2. Explain Tesco's strategic strength today

Today Tesco's strategic strength emanates from its **hybrid** position on the strategic clock. On the one hand it offers a wide range of branded and own-brand products in modern, clean, efficient supermarkets with parking, facilities for children, and other on-site specialist services. Its **competitive advantage** is still based in its **low costs**, which it enjoys because of its unparalled **buying power**. With many suppliers, Tesco enjoys **monopsony** power in that it takes most (if not all) of the supplier's product. (Readers are probably more familiar with the term **monopoly**, which is where the supplier dominates the market.)

UK retailers like J. Sainsbury and Marks & Spencer are struggling in the 21st century to find a way to fight back. Tesco continues to grow into various other segments of consumer goods and as it grows so too does its **relative buying power**. Price is the key competitive weapon for broad-based retailers stocking the same goods. Any retailer with a structural cost advantage that offers the same (or better) perceived value as its competitors is a formidable competitor. The Tesco train will take some stopping.

Living with the Amazons

The most talked about new company at the end of the 20th century was almost certainly Amazon.com. It was attributed with having changed the way that we think about shopping. Some say it has challenged traditional notions of economics and strategy. All of a sudden, retailers can broaden their scope and increase sales quickly and dramatically without the traditional costs associated with employing a bigger sales force and setting up new branches, depots, or dealerships. All sales can be processed at a central depot and mailed out from one huge warehouse, with the saving made from not having to maintain a chain of real-world stores passed on to happy customers. Amazon's ubiquitous website (www.amazon.com) and its clean, efficient "white space" style is increasingly familiar to book-buyers, and increasingly copied by retailers moving into internet sales. In order to overcome the one barrier that Amazon has to increasing international sales, the high cost of international postage and customs duties added to the selling price of their books making them less attractive to those overseas, it is now looking at setting up bases in other countries. Recently, Amazon has established an arm in the UK. The formula is the same (compare www.amazon.com with www.amazon.co.uk) but sales are processed and the books dispatched from a center in the UK.

The big question now being asked in book retailing circles is: "How can any company compete with Amazon?" More generally, people are asking whether any form of traditional retailing can survive in the face of their market share being eroded by online providers unencumbered by traditional cost structures.

Ottakar's is a UK chain of bookshops that has built a reputation for strongly individual high street shops staffed by book enthusiasts. It is described by one recent newspaper report as "rather traditional and vaguely quirky." Ottakar's came into being in 1987, when its current Managing Director, James Heneage, saw an opportunity to establish a chain of bookshops offering high levels of service in English market towns – those places bigger than villages but smaller than cities. At the time, the idea of a national chain of bookshops was relatively new. Waterstone's and Dillons were opening branches within Britain's major cities, but otherwise the competition consisted of regional chains, like WH Smith, and the independent booksellers that existed in every town.

Ottakar's started life as three branches in southern England. It acquired a small chain of West Country shops in 1990 on the back of the success of the original three. In 1992, Heneage was able to point to enough evidence of a successful formula to persuade backers to refinance the company so as to enable a more rapid expansion. Over the next 8 years Ottakar's grew to encompass 72 branches employing over 800 staff throughout the UK. In 1998 the company was successfully floated on the London Stock Exchange.

"The secret of great bookselling," according to Heneage, "lies in the recruitment of people who enjoy a passion for books and are able to articulate that passion to their customers." Subsequently, he claims, "we recruit on love and knowledge of books above all else." And, contrary to a lot of recent management thinking advocating bringing in people who have been successful in one field to shake up an organization operating in another, Ottakar's has a policy of not recruiting from outside the book trade at the management level.

Heneage describes Ottakar's today as: "A paradox. On the one hand it is a national book chain striving to offer uniform excellence in range and service over 70 branches. On the other hand it is a collection of intensely individual bookshops, run with great autonomy by staff whose commitment to books is matched only by their commitment to provide a bookselling service tailor-made for the communities they serve."

Ottakar's results through to the end of 1999 have been impressive, with sales of £13.2m in 1996 and a before-tax profit of £0.7m in 1996, increasing to sales of £57.3m and a before-tax profit of £3.1m. According to Heneage, this success "has been founded on allowing . . . individuals [the] freedom to create very original and individual shops." However, for Ottakar's, as for any bookseller, the main threat looming on the horizon is the market share being gobbled up by Amazon. In response, Ottakar's has recently developed its own "net strategy."

Jim McClellan, who writes on e-commerce for *The Guardian* newspaper, claims that the assumption in e-commerce "seems to be that successful first movers have probably got things right so all competitors can do is copy their approach, perhaps tweaking it slightly." He expands on this view using the example of online book retailing: "Amazon showed how to do it and all subsequent sites, from net-only concerns like BOL and Alphabet Street to real-world chains like WH Smith and Waterstone's, have imitated their basic model. So much for the net as a hotbed of innovation and experiment."

Lacking the size or market-clout of the chains mentioned by McClellan, and saddled with the fixed costs of real-world stores, unlike the net-only operators, Ottakar's has been forced to come up with something different. Heneage claims that Ottakar's internet strategy is to "faithfully reproduce local branch individualism and expertise." As opposed to Amazon's clean lines and universal sites, Ottakar's has attempted to get every one of its branches to create its own website, one that reflects their own characteristics and passions. "Our shops are locally oriented," explains Heneage, "We want to portray that online." When one logs on to www.ottakars.co.uk one is immediately taken to a page listing local sites divided by region, each of which can be "walked into" at a click. Each site has its own low-tech "homely homepage" look, with pictures of local staff, inside and outside views of the store, details of particular in-store events featured prominently, and maps of where the store is highlighting local traditions and landmarks drawn by the staff themselves.

Heneage's hope is that these attempts to localize the website will bring Ottakar's staff in behind the initiative, and in this way their quirky passion will bring home to people the things lacking from net-only bookstores. "The main idea behind the site is to bring the enthusiasm and knowledge in our real-world shops on to the net. Our staff know a great deal about books. That's why people come back to us."

Staff expertise is available through a number of features. "Ask the Expert" enables people to post enquiries that can be answered by a local staff member or referred on by local staff to somebody else they know within the organization better qualified to answer. People can read reviews of books recently read by staff at their local store and tap into a network of reviews posted by Ottakar's staff from around the country. Other innovations include a daily quiz (recently copied by Waterstone's), a book gossip column, and links to Ottakar's microsites devoted to specific areas or genres, like science fiction.

One aspect of Ottakar's new strategy that has proved surprisingly popular is the option for the customers to collect books purchased on the website from their nearest store. It seems that many prefer this more tactile approach rather than waiting for books to be posted, wondering when they are going to arrive, worrying that they will not be at home to meet the mailman when they do, and incurring the extra cost associated with mail delivery. Once these customers come in to collect their books they are likely to browse around and converse with Ottakar's staff. Unlike the Amazons of this world, whose approach is to cut out the middleman (i.e. the bookstores) and pull customers away from the high street, Ottakar's is taking an opposite view. It sees the internet as a way of enabling customers to develop a stronger relationship with local stores and, subsequently, pulling them in. One could counter that once customers get more comfortable about purchasing online they will care less and less about local identity and relationships and more and more about getting books as cheaply as possible. But, at this point, this seems to be a gamble that Ottakar's is prepared to take. While lower and lower prices on books seem to be the way that companies are seeking to build up traffic and sales through their sites, Ottakar's says that it will only match the discounts offered on the lead titles and new books (prices that it will replicate in the real-world stores). It will not discount backlist titles in the way that Amazon and others do.

While the interest, customer reception (most surveyed really liked the different, local feel of the sites), and net-sales achieved in the first few weeks after the launch were very encouraging, the first financial results following the initiative raised some eyebrows. Ottakar's saw turnover rise by 27% but pre-tax profits tumble in the financial year 1999/2000. Subsequently, the yearly dividend to shareholders was reduced to 1.5 pence per share from 2.25 pence the year previous. Heneage blamed internet set-up costs and Ottakar's store expansion program, but admitted that "new store sales performance was disappointing." However, he described the results as an "aberration" and a "savage hiccup." Shareholders, however, were understandably nervous.

Moreover, most website experts seemed unimpressed by www.ottakars.co.uk. An analysis carried out by James Wallis in the *Sunday Times* assessed the UK's nine major booksellers' sites according to three criteria: "prices," "service," and "usability." He placed Amazon first and Ottakar's last. Of the two companies, Wallis wrote:

> "Amazon is coming under increasing pressure, but the site is still a joy to use: well designed and easy to navigate. Its loading times, although not nippy, are fast enough. More important, it was one of only two sites that found all four titles that we requested in this survey (a UK bestseller, a biography, an American title, and one from a small UK press). Amazon's site is the best of all surveyed. Four stars."

"Ottakar's website is confusingly over-designed, which distracts you from what you are looking for, and it scores low for usability, even though the search and delivery options were good (including free shipping to your local branch of the chain). Prices were disappointing – all books are at the recommended price. Needs a thorough rethink. One star."

1. *How could you define Ottakar's competitive position on the back of a business card?*
2. *Ottakar's had generally taken an evolutionary approach to change in order to build on its existing resources and capabilities. However, the shock caused by players like Amazon entering its industry appears to have led to a more revolutionary response. Ottakar's is now selling books online although at the moment its online image is "vaguely quirky; things appear a little confused." To quell this confusion over Ottakar's online image, would you: (a) make the sites more like Amazon's? (b) keep them as they are but discontinue the selling of books online? (c) pull the sites off the internet altogether? (d) do something different?*
3. *While Ottakar's new websites may have only constituted a change to operational facilities, how might its operations and performance ripple through the organization and its strategic positioning?*
4. *If you were James Heneage, how would you have responded to the* Sunday Times' *review?*

Can hybrids fly?

On November 12, 2001 the *Birmingham Post* ran a story entitled "Restructuring will target cutting costs and airfares." It reported on how Britain's second largest airline BMI (British Midland International) was set to undergo a major strategic shift and restructure itself into a low-cost airline. A BMI spokeswoman said: "We are restructuring the airline into a low-cost business. We know our costs are too high and we are looking to see how they can be reduced." She said the move was part of a restructuring program that had actually begun earlier, and stressed that, while the group was cutting costs, it had no plans to relaunch itself as a no-frills airline, such as rivals Go, easyJet, or Ryanair, that kept costs low by operating out of regional airports, flying limited routes, focusing on internet sales, and offering minimal pre-flight and in-flight services.

Other national papers followed up the story. *The Guardian* reported Austin Reed, Chief Executive of BMI, saying that airlines needed to reinvent themselves and cut costs if they were to survive in the current market. Hence, BMI would follow a new strategy of adopting low-cost principles and building alliances with other airlines. Mr. Reed's statements followed the remarks of British Airways' Chief Executive, Rod Eddington, who said that BA might have to examine some of the methods of the low-cost airlines. Mr. Reed warned that if BMI was to survive, it would have to consider the cost of its entire operation. However, he also stressed that BMI had no plans to become a low-cost carrier.

The Independent also described BMI's "radical plans to transform itself into a 'low-cost, full-frills' carrier." Here Mr. Reed was reported as claiming that BMI was likely to make a loss next year and a re-think of the way it operated was necessary if it was to return to profitability. "BMI remains and will continue to remain a full-service airline and we have no intention of becoming a budget carrier," he said. "However, it is vital that if we are to survive in the current climate we have to continually examine the cost of the operation as a whole. If we are still going to be profitable we have to adjust our cost base and if we are going to compete our prices will have to be lower and more transparent." Mr. Reed concluded that BMI would remain a full-service airline but one which operated on "low-cost principles" offering cheaper fares: a hybrid, in other words.

However, an editorial in the same paper sounded a note of caution. It claimed that the post-September 11 environment had spelled bad news for the bigger full-service scheduled carriers but not necessarily for the low-cost operators such as easyJet and Ryanair. BMI, it claimed, "fits, uncomfortably, in between the two ends of the spectrum – neither a flag-carrier for all its transatlantic ambitions, nor a budget airline for all the low fares it offers in comparison with the likes of British Airways." In response to this, the editorial continued: "BMI has now decided to move closer to the low-cost model, while still retaining its full-service status. Pilots will work more hours and planes will stay in the air for longer. The airline will fly to fewer destinations but more often and the fleet will eventually consist of a single aircraft type. The money saved will be used to offer cheaper fares. At the same time there will still be a curtain half-way down the cabin separating business class from the 'plebs', an executive lounge to call into and a frequent flyer programme . . . It will be fascinating to see whether BMI can pull off this hybrid concept of a low-cost, full-frills airline. The last time it was tried, with [a British airline called] Debonair, it ended in disaster."

It was not long before BMI appeared to change course again in terms of its strategic positioning. In January 2002, it announced the impending launch of a new low-cost, no-frills airline: BMIbaby. The company's own press releases explained its thinking: "BMI British Midland announces the launch of a major initiative: a new no-frills airline based at East Midlands Airport. The new airline will have a dedicated fleet of Boeing 737-300 aircraft and serve key leisure destinations, including high-frequency services to Barcelona, Nice, Palma, Malaga, Faro, and Alicante. The airline will have a strong focus on giving passengers value for money. Fares will be highly competitive with additional savings for tickets booked via the Internet. The new airline will have a separate name and corporate identity from BMI British Midland, which will continue to operate and develop as a full-service international scheduled carrier . . . and continue to develop services in Europe and to the USA, particularly from our main operating hubs at Heathrow and Manchester."

Nigel Turner, BMI's Director responsible for the new airline, said: "BMI is launching a new airline in response to a clear market opportunity and consumer demand. We have been operating from East Midlands Airport for over 35 years and we are delighted to increase our commitment to the airport and the region through the creation of this new no-frills carrier. The new airline is an independent and valuable addition to the BMI family and we believe it will have a long and successful future. BMI will have a strong presence in both the no-frills and full-service airline sectors." (You can view the different identities that BMI is trying to project for its two airlines by going to www.flybmi.com and www.bmibaby.com.)

Tony Davis, appointed as BMIbaby's Managing Director, added that its birth marked the coming to fruition of BMI's "long held ambition to launch a no-frills airline." However, the extent to which this had always been the long-term positioning plan for BMI, or whether BMIbaby had emerged as an opportunistic response to changing market forces in the light of BMI's past successes and failures, was unclear.

---

1. *Do you think that BMI's "low-cost, full-frills" position could have provided them with a competitive advantage?*
2. *Will the advent of BMIbaby help or hinder BMI's attempts to position itself effectively?*
3. *How would you seek to position BMI and BMIbaby? Can you express each of these positions in eight words or less?*

Anticipation*

PA: "Mr. John Frobisher of Universal on the line for you, Bob. Will you take the call now?"

John Frobisher was CEO of one of the largest branded foods retailers in the USA. Bob's consultancy in the UK had recently carried out a substantial project for them, investigating a potential acquisition target in Canada.

Bob: "Yes, that's great. Put him straight through."
John: "Hey Bob, how are you doing?"
Bob: "I'm doing fine John – how are you?"
John: "Well, thank you Bob – things are going great. That last presentation you gave to the Board was right on the button. They were very pleased – good clear points, strong conclusion and recommendation; none of this 'sitting on the fence' type analysis we've had before, which leads me to the reason for the call. You know our branded business has been booming here in the US – demand has been strong and consistent for our high-end products. Now we have sorted out our cost structure, so it's the lowest amongst our direct competitors, and beginning to close in on the non-branded producers, we believe we can sustain our profitability in the US for some time to come. However, we must not be complacent. The Board has been wondering why not replicate this success in the UK. There is likely to be demand for products of our quality and our brand

---

* This is a real case but has been disguised to protect the identity of the individuals and firms involved.

may well transfer across border. They wondered who we could ask to look into this for us, as we don't have the resources at Head Office for this task, and I mentioned you and your team. You did a great job on the last project and your credibility here is high. Would you be willing to take this on?"

Bob: "Well John it's great you are pleased with our last project. We'd be delighted to investigate this opportunity for you. As you know, contrary to many big name consulting practices, we do not have templates for projects so we'll have to think over the main issues and get back to you with our thoughts on how we would structure our investigation, the sort of data we would aim to get, and what the deliverables would be."

John: "Sure, Bob – no problem. We like your approach. I have some contacts here at Universal who can help on the data front and when you're ready we can fix up a meeting. Speak soon. Bye."

Bob smiled as he replaced the phone. The best of all worlds, he thought – a large satisfied customer coming back with more assignments. However, as his firm's policy was not to have standard solutions to problems, or a bank of questions, as this led to lazy thinking, his team would have to come up with the key questions for this opportunity and work out what data would be needed as well as how it would be acquired. Somehow they had to decide whether the idea of Universal launching in the UK was sound or fanciful.

---

1.   *Draw up a list of the key questions that are critical to understanding whether Universal should enter the UK market.*
2.   *What data would you need to acquire (and how would you get it) to be able to answer your questions?*

Note: Students are used to getting cases with questions that steer them towards certain techniques and tools to be applied to a carefully crafted set of "perfect" data. However, this situation is rare in the real world. More often the questions are not clear, the data patchy (unreliable, unavailable) at best, and the results not clear cut. This case, *Anticipation*, is much closer to reality – a 15 minute phone call from a client requesting an investigation, with few clues about how such an investigation might be carried out, what data are available (and whether they are available at all), and what deliverables are expected, beyond a definitive recommendation. The exercise then is about shaping research to address a strategic problem. This is a much more open-ended approach than traditional cases and forces readers to create their own structures to shape and address the issue. It shows the value of being able to frame problems, construct analytical enquiry, consider what data might be useful and to think about where they may come from. There is also an important role for being creative in this process.

Two brews

Two decades ago, the Browerij Huyghe was in trouble. The brewery was founded in 1906 by Leon Huyghe, a brewery worker married to a brewer's daughter. It grew steadily by producing pils and basic "table beers." By the 1960s, it was supplying its own chain of 300 pubs in addition to filling several big Government contracts, most notably to provide beer for hospital restaurants and railway workers. However, things went against Huyghe in the 1970s and 80s. There had been as many breweries as there were villages in Belgium, but consolidation now meant that Huyghe did not have the relative economies of scale necessary to compete on cost in the pils and table beer segments. Advances in distribution networks made competition less regionalized and subsequently fiercer. Government organizations like hospitals and railways began to question whether supplying their workers with beer, the traditional Belgian drink, was necessarily a good thing. In fact, it is doubtful that the brewery would have survived if it were not for the discovery of *Delirium Tremens*.

According to brewery manager Alain De Laet, the creation of Delirium Tremens was "coincidental." De Laet explains how in 1988 a distributor asked for a strong blond beer for the Italian market. Brew engineer Patrick De Wael made a first experimental batch on December 26, 1988. "It was dead on target," claims De Laet. "The process hasn't been changed a bit ever since."

The distinctive features of Delirium's packaging also emerged serendipitously. The grey speckled bottle was the remnant of a failed campaign. Painted by a German company and three times more expensive than normal bottles (too pricey to fill with pils or table beer, where the margins are far lower), these had been intended for a "Grand Cru" for a German customer. After this deal fell through, they sat in storage and were due to be destroyed – until a bottle was used for the trial batches of Delirium.

Another part of the eclectic but distinctive packaging mix is the label with its pink elephants, and brightly coloured monsters and birds. The formulation of this is the subject of folklore. The story goes that De Wael, excited by his creation, immediately brought it to a small meeting of Huyghe staff and family members. After tasting it and agreeing it was good they sat down to drink more. After four bottles, one of the group said, "if I drink much more of this I'll start to see pink elephants." After seven, eight, nine, somebody else said, "if I drink any more of this I'll be seeing monsters." After eleven, somebody said they'd start to see those birds from Alfred Hitchcock's movie *The Birds*. (It is worth pointing out that the beer contains a hefty 9% alcohol.)

Jean De Laet, Alain's father, who was running things at the time, remembers it slightly differently: "Initially, the label showed a skull, to clarify the link with the disease." (Delirium tremens is an acute disorder following withdrawal from alcoholic intoxication and, because seizures can last up to six days and involve terrifying hallucinations and violent tremors, it can be fatal.) "But a student working with us once drew the now well-known Pink Elephant, and bingo!"

The name Delirium Tremens (born when an inspector from the Excise Office tasted the new beer and said, "If I drink too much of this, I'll get a delirium") is unlikely to have been approved by a multinational corporation, but it works for Huyghe. In the company's view: "The most important thing is that people really remember the beer." In a market where there are hundreds of alternatives, this is crucial.

Delirium has subsequently been "remembered" by some very influential people. In 1997, beer guru Stuart Kallen surprised aficionados by declaring Delirium Tremens the world's best beer, despite the fact that it would make his life more difficult – "If I simply mentioned a beer everyone had heard of, without the name of a drinker's disease, I would get more peace," he wrote. In 1998, it won at the World Beer Championships. Subsequently, sales are booming. About two-thirds of the Huyghe's output is now Delirium. The vast majority of this is sold outside of Belgium, where it attracts a premium price.

Despite the prospects for small breweries being seen as bleak by many commentators (their cost structure makes it extremely difficult for them to compete against increasingly large conglomerates), Huyghe's management is upbeat, claiming that the company has certain advantages. "What we can do is when a buyer comes to us from Guadeloupe – or wherever – he comes and visits us and talks to us. It's a nice trip for him. Then if he only has a small shop we can make up a mixed pallet, half a crate of this and that, whatever he wants. So, he walks away with a ready-made shop of specialty beers. Big companies like Interbrew can't do that," explains Wim Van Mannem, Huyghe's accountant.

More than just tailor-making pallets, Huyghe will also tailor-make beers to suit particular clients' needs – a claim proved by a quick look around the warehouse piled high with surplus labels for different niche-fillers. Alain De Laet sums up Huyghe's philosophy as "meeting the demand of the customer as good as possible, and as it were, providing 'made to measure'. Important customers asking us for a new beer must be able to get it. We are open to all possibilities."

Interbrew's is an altogether different Belgian brewery. Interbrew's operation is state of the art. The factory, only a few years old, all polished steel vats and piping, produces around 10 million units of Stella Artois, Interbrew's flagship brand, each day. There are very few people to be seen, apart from the computer operators in the control room. Across the road, the old plant is now producing smaller runs of specialist brands, like the famous abbey beer Leffe, which are now an integral part of the Interbrew "family."

Interbrew has grown very big and very global very fast, having made 24 acquisitions in 14 countries in the 10 years to 2003. According to CEO Hugo Powell, Interbrew's seemingly paradoxical aim is to become "the world's local brewer. Our global approach is based on strong regional platforms and supported by our great ability to adapt to local markets and cultures."

Ludo Degelin, director of operations and manager of international technical support, explains the approach in greater detail. He begins by reviewing some of the approaches favored by Interbrew's competitors. Anheuser-Busch (AB), the world's largest brewing group, tends to buy up local production facilities (important given the high distribution costs associated with beer) that can then be converted and standardized to produce their global brand – Budweiser. "It's a good strategy that has worked well for them, but it works because they started from such a large base and they have a huge global brand. We start from a different position and in any case I don't think their approach suits us," Ludo explains. Guinness attempts to match local tastes (and take advantage of different licensing laws) by varying their recipe. Hence, the Belgian Guinness is stronger than in Britain, where the excise regime is a lot stiffer, and the African brew is both stronger and sweeter than the Irish. A lot of mileage can be got out of one brand in this way. However, Ludo believes this strategy is becoming problematic as drinkers increasingly move across national boundaries and are confused by the variation in what they assume to be the same product.

Interbrew, by contrast, looks to acquire breweries with brands that have a strong local identity and are market leaders, and, unlike AB, they look to develop these brands. "It is difficult to recreate the emotional attachment that local people already have for these beers," claims Johan Robbrecht, who works with Ludo on aspects of packaging development, "they are deeply rooted in the community, linked to particular sports and so on." However, Interbrew does change some things. In Ludo's words, while they do not alter the taste of a local brew too radically, they do seek to "clean up the production, using our technical experience and expertise, and then effectively re-launch it. Once this is done we offer the local management the opportunity to brew Stella, which we are building as our global flagship brand. However, [unlike Guinness] they must be able to produce it using the Belgian recipe so that it tastes as close as possible to the Stella brewed in Leuven." And, importantly, Ludo adds, "it must come into the local market at a premium price in keeping with a premium brand."

Over time, Interbrew aims to operate high-volume local brands that generally tap into that area's traditional masculine sporting culture in tandem with Stella as the premium more refined brand "over and above these," to use Ludo's words. In this way, Ludo believes that Interbrew avoids pitfalls such as those encountered by its competitor Heineken as it attempted to penetrate Eastern Europe. In one country in particular, its approach was to discontinue local brands and replace their production with Heineken. This caused local resentment, with Heineken seen as a foreign intruder even though local people produced the beer. Then, because of Heineken's global branding, it had to be sold at a price that very few drinkers in the East could afford (any lower would diminish the value of the product in neighboring countries).

Ludo sees the way that Heineken now follows the same approach to international development as Interbrew as a vindication of Interbrew's strategy. However, he stresses that tolerance for local difference must have its limits. Just adding more and more brands to the portfolio creates logistical and organizational problems, and the cost savings that can be made by discontinuing brands that are not performing must be realized in a company of Interbrew's size. Plus, it has to be admitted that some of the local brews are not, in Ludo's diplomatic words, "as good as they could be." Indeed, Corporate Marketing Director Johan Peeters points out that there are some global constants in beer. "For example, if a beer is colder people will drink more of it: physiologically this is true, and this is why Guinness is brewing colder now. And all people appreciate a beer that is more consistent and technically better brewed." However, Ludo and Johan agree that beer is also connected to human emotions and traditions. So, if you are going to change production approaches, recipes, or temperatures, it must be done gradually. That local people do not like to see their traditional tastes trashed appears to be another "global constant."

Despite the challenges associated with its rapid internationalization, Interbrew has little option but to grow quickly given the nature of developments in the brewing industry. Analysts predict that five or six players will dominate the world market by the mid-2000s (Interbrew is currently about the sixth largest). Stefan Descheemaeker explains the situation with a simple diagram, with *profitability* on the vertical axis and *size* on the horizontal. Between the axes he draws a "U" shape. "In the future, only the smallest micro-breweries and the largest groups will exist. You cannot survive in the middle."

---

1. *Define Hugyhe's strategic advantage.*
2. *Define Interbrew's strategic advantage.*
3. *If you were a fund manager, which firm would you choose to invest in? Give reasons for your answer.*
4. *What advice would you give Huyghe and Interbrew for the future?*

5:6

"Customers – those bastards!"

You are the managing director of Mother's Preference, a manufacturer of baby furniture, prams, and child restraints. The Target chain of discount stores is your largest customer, taking 30% of your sales, worth about A\$19m in contribution to your total margin per annum. Louis is Target's new 23-year-old Nursery Buyer and he is determined to make his mark and progress quickly up through the company. You are about to go into session to draw up the contract for next year's order from Target.

In a stagnant market, you hold about 25% total market share. Your closest competitor, Mother's Hope, holds a similar share. Two or three other smaller competitors have around 10–12% each. Both you and Mother's Hope have well-established brand names and similar product ranges that are sold exclusively through retail outlets. Although you have active advertising programs, the most important influences on the buying decision are point-of-sale and word-of-mouth. Because of the "top-of-mind" nature of the two major brands, the large chain and department stores tend to use one or other of you as a loss-leading traffic generator on the front of their catalogs (i.e. to lure customers into the store in the hope that they buy other, higher margin items while picking up their "cheap" pushchair or child-seat).

After each major promotion your phone always runs hot as other buyers ring to demand to know: "How the hell can those bastards at Target/Big W/Baby Co./ K-Mart/etc. afford to offer those prices? You must have given them a sweet discount. So you better give it to us or else."

Despite your generally truthful assertions to the contrary, you are rarely believed and never sympathized with, and all of your customers continue to demand preferential discounts in a downward spiral as they claim that "there's no bloody margin in your product!"

A couple of years ago you were the clear market leader, but Mother's Hope has recently gained ground by taking share from the lesser brands. Your "moles" suggest that this has been achieved by significant discounting cleverly disguised as either *contribution to advertising, consignment stock, volume rebates,* and *early payment discounts* or *payments for buyers to visit supply factories in Taiwan* (via Hong Kong for shopping and/or hours of pleasure, depending on the buyer). But when you had the opportunity to confront the MD of Mother's Hope about this, he vehemently denied any such underhand behavior.

"So, here's the deal," says Louis. "For the supply contract next year I need a 15% reduction in your delivered price across each of the three major product groupings. Oh, and by the way, my assistant is outlining the exact same proposal to your chief competitor across the hall."

At this point you start to wail about the effects this will have on your children and the children of the employees you will be compelled to "retrench" with one day's pay, but Louis is unrepentant. He offers three possibilities:

1. "If one of you gives me the reduction and the other doesn't then the one who does gets all the business" (which you currently split with Mother's Hope 50:50 in all the product categories).
2. "If you both give me the discount, I'll leave the share split as it is for next year."
3. "If neither of you gives me the discount, I am forced to leave it as it is for next year, but I will begin to look for some other suppliers who we can work with."

You are pretty sure that this last point is a bluff. He could not afford to de-list both of you. Or could he? However, he can easily afford to de-list one of you (although, if he was honest, he would probably prefer not to).

"I will not negotiate any other price, and here, in writing, is my contractual commitment to go by the decisions that you and your competitor make. Decide what you will do with furniture first, prams and pushchairs second, and child restraints last. I will send my assistant for your first decision [on furniture] in 15 minutes. He will let you know what your competitor has decided on this category. Then we will do the same thing for the second and then the third categories."

You had been expecting something like this from Target and had roughly worked out the losses/gains based on various combinations of price reduction and percentage loss of share of the Target account. Table 5-6.1 shows your best-shot quick calculation for the alternatives that Louis has laid down. The figure in the last column, relating to the position where you offer the discount and Mother's Hope does not (thus leaving you to fulfill all of Target's needs), includes the advantages to be gained through greater economies of scale.

Table 5-6.1 Implications of reductions

Category	Current contribution to margins	15% reduction with half Target account	15% reduction with all Target account
Furniture	5	3	8
Prams/pushchairs	5	3	8
Child restraints	9	5	14
Totals	19	11	30

Although it is technically illegal, it is not unknown for you to discuss issues of pricing and the like with competitors. After all, you do sit on standards committees together in an attempt to protect the Australian mother from "unscrupulous operators," and an "orderly" market can only be a good thing for mothers. There may (or may not) be an opportunity for one of your number to be in the toilets at the same time as one of theirs . . .

1. *Assuming you can get no further information, what would be your overall intention for this decision-making process?*
2. *Assuming you can get no further information, what would be your first decision on furniture?*
3. *What then would your strategy be as the rest of the decision-making process unfolds?*
4. *What do this case and the application of game theory teach us about strategy?*

Mirage?

In August 2004, the Financial Services Authority granted a banking license allowing the Islamic Bank of Britain (IBB) to open its first retail branch in London, promoting *sharia*-compliant products. Islamic law (the *sharia*) bans the payment and acceptance of interest – fundamental concepts in Western banking. In early 2005, IBB opened a branch and head office opened in Birmingham, a lower cost location than London, and one where a substantial proportion of the country's Muslim population resides. Other branches followed in London and Leicester, with further branches planned for other areas of high Muslim concentration (www.islamic-bank.com). However, start-up costs on branches and direct banking widened losses to £3.1m in the first 5 months to December 2004. IBB is imprisoned by its fixed costs and has to grow to escape its constraints and compete with the huge cost-reducing scale economies of its giant conventional competitors. Is this quest to become the first fully fledged Islamic bank in the UK and Europe really chasing a mirage?

Muslims are the second largest religious group in Britain and, with 2 million followers, there is clearly a potential market for an Islamic bank. However, there are two problems facing IBB: (1) Muslims avoid banks if they want to retain their beliefs and (2) the Islamic banking model may not be competitive in the mature UK banking market.

Islamic Beliefs

In Islam, human beings are God's co-managers on earth and the well-being of the community must be considered when it comes to economic actions. Wealth should be neither hoarded nor wasted on unproductive ventures. Money should not be created from money, but through investment in useful activities. Interest is opposed on several grounds, but from a social perspective, it is the poor and needy who are forced to borrow whereas the rich have money to save. Interest therefore penalizes the poor and rewards the rich. The accumulation of wealth through interest is deemed a reward without productive effort and is therefore selfish. On this basis, conventional banking is not appropriate for Muslims.

Islamic Banking

The essential feature of Islamic finance is that it is interest-free. *Sharia* explicitly prohibits interest (*riba*) and excessive risk or uncertainty (*gharar*). The prohibition of interest does not mean that money may not be lent under Islamic law, it simply rules out what might be considered unearned profit. Indeed, the provider of capital should be allowed an adequate return by having a stake in the undertaking, but is not permitted to fix a predetermined rate of interest. Money is not considered a commodity in Islamic economics, but rather a bearer of risk. There should be a price for time, but not fixed in advance. Owners of capital can share the profits made by the entrepreneur based on a profit-sharing ratio rather than a pre-determined rate of return. This means the borrower and lender share risk and work more closely together to ensure the business's success, which is more productive for society and provides cohesion between social classes because finance is available equally to anyone with a productive idea.

Two of the most popular types of "compliant" business in Islamic banking are: (1) *murabaha*, a contract for purchase and resale that allows customers to make purchases without having to take out loans and pay interest and (2) *mudarabah*, an investment on your behalf by a more skilled person who shares part of the profits in return for time and effort (see case note for further details).

IBB offers the following products to both Muslim and non-Muslim customers and stresses the fact that it tries to make all transactions with the bank simple for customers in terms of delivery and understanding.

1. *Current account:* includes the same facilities as conventional current accounts but no interest is paid or charged and a credit balance preferred.
2. *Saving account:* offers term structures and operates on a *mudarabah* basis, with the clients sharing in the bank's profits, the rate being reviewed monthly.
3. *Treasury deposit account:* for high net worth clients. The minimum deposit is £100,000, with fixed periods. Structured on a *murabahah* basis, the depositor obtains the profit from the purchase and sale of commodities.
4. *Masjid (mosque) proposition:* a free overdraft of £1,000 to mosques for a maximum of 30 days. This is very successful because mosques are major influences on local communities. When Muslims see their mosques dealing with IBB, this boosts their confidence in the bank and its Islamic nature.
5. *Sweeping facility:* transfers money automatically from the customers' saving accounts to their current accounts to avoid the latter getting overdrawn.
6. *Other products:* home finance, Islamic credit cards, internet banking in 2006. In the horizon of 3 to 5 years, the bank plans to introduce mobile banking, to offer investment and insurance products – possibly through the establishment of a UK subsidiary – and to establish physical continental European branches.

The banking market in the UK is highly consolidated, with the top six players accounting for 83% of the total market for financial retail services. The market grew at 10% (2002–3) and the banks have been posting record profits, aided by aggressive reduction in costs through the use of technology. At the same time there has been a reduction in customer satisfaction in the level of service received.

Within the UK market of 65 million, there are over 2 million Muslims. Of these, 62% are drawn from the Indian subcontinent and 21% from the Middle East and Africa. There are high concentrations in urban areas, with half living in London, and this promotes strong social cohesion. Unemployment among Muslims is almost three times the national average and the quality of their housing is amongst the lowest in the country. The young and old show strong religious devotion, with 250,000 attending mosques regularly. Although strongly influenced by British society and culture, the majority of the young are proud of their Muslim identity. Many Muslims have small businesses and an increasing proportion of young Muslims are joining the professional classes. The estimated pool of savings of Muslims in the UK was £1bn in 2003.

The recent spate of terrorist attacks has raised anti-Muslim sentiment in Britain. However, no Islamic bank has been linked in any way to these activities. Interestingly, the effect upon Muslims has been to cause them to turn more to their religion, and Islamic banks in general have witnessed a huge surge in business when their links to terrorism were shown to be unfounded.

Competition for Muslims worldwide has been rising rapidly. Many of the key players in conventional banks, such as HSBC, now provide Islamic offerings targeted at institutional clients and overseas high net worth individuals, rather than Muslims in Britain. Other competition comes from the providers of ethical banking such as the Co-operative Bank and Islamic institutions operating in the UK as subsidiaries owned by offshore operators such as Pakistani and Bangladeshi banks. These latter banks also provide reliable and trustworthy communications channels for British Muslims with families in the Indian subcontinent. However, this service may be more valuable to first generation immigrants rather than younger generations with weaker overseas ties. Also these banks are limited in their product range, such as money transfer.

IBB feels the increasing competition may make customers more aware of this type of banking practice and help to sell the concept and "grow the cake." However, they think these Islamic offerings are not really Islamic in either manner or essence of operations. For instance, HSBC Amanah in raising money can borrow this informally from the parent, which is a non-Islamic channel. From a conservative Islamic point of view, this money is tainted.

There is no doubt that IBB differs significantly from conventional banks:

1. Although there are similar types of risk, they are run at higher levels because of extensive trade and investment activities. However there is no interest-rate risk.
2. Liquidity management is a problem owing to the lack of *sharia*-compliant liquid assets and no "lender of last resort facility" with the central bank. Conventional banks' treasuries place the excess funds overnight in money markets, lend the surplus in the interbank network, or invest in Government securities. IBB cannot utilize these options, and is obliged to hold relatively large amounts of non-income-generating cash (www.islamicbankingnetwork.com).

3. Islamic banks' focus of financial accounting information is on asset allocation and return from investments and trade rather than interest rate spread, provision of loan portfolios, and maturities of liabilities.

4. In theory, Islamic banks should guarantee neither the capital value nor the return on investments; these banks basically pool depositors' funds to provide professional investment management. This is similar to the operations of investment companies in the West. However, for investment companies the public are entitled to voting rights and can monitor the company's performance. In IBB, depositors are only entitled to share the bank's net profit (or loss) according to the profit/loss sharing ratio stipulated in their contracts, and they cannot influence IBB's policies. However, under English law, IBB is required to provide guarantes to depositors' capital.

5. In cases of default, there is no ambiguity about control of the assets under Islamic mark-up contracts because the financial institution retains title to the asset until the agent makes all payments.

Being an Islamic bank poses internal challenges. Firstly the bank has had to establish an Islamic *Sharia* Committee to assess whether its activities are in accordance with Islamic law. This is time-consuming, costly, leads to confusion about what Islamic banking really encompasses, and hinders its widespread acceptance. It also makes it difficult for Western regulators to understand the idea of Islamic banking. This lack of understanding, coupled with lack of regulation, causes tension between Islamic banks and British regulators, and affects the regulators' willingness to support such organizations. Indeed, the collapse of BCCI in 1991, a conventional bank but with many Muslims on its Board, prompted significant tightening of banking regulations in the UK, which caused Al-Baraka International Bank, IBB's predecessor, to close down. Today, Western regulators require Islamic banks to maintain higher liquidity requirements because their operations are riskier than those of conventional banks. Until recently, the British tax system was unfair to Islamic banks because interest is tax-deductible, whereas profit is taxed. However, IBB has recently claimed a major victory in the battle with the authorities since changes in legislation have been announced.

There are few professional courses and training tailored for Islamic banking and this has resulted in a lack of qualified staff for IBB and it has to resort to recruiting staff from conventional banks. However, such staff find adjusting difficult. In addition the lack of trained staff slows innovation in Islamic products and means unqualified management.

Against a very competitive background, and the lack of awareness of what Islamic banking is, IBB was pleasantly surprised at the launch of its Whitechapel Branch in London, when 60 accounts were opened within the first 4 hours.

---

1. *Has IBB identified imperfections in the market, or is this really a mirage?*
2. *How can IBB compete with the large well-resourced incumbents?*
3. *Should IBB focus on increasing its product range (scope) or open new branches?*
4. *Would the creation of an online banking facility help? Why?*

Note: The *sharia*-compliant products are:

(1) *Murabaha* – a contract for purchase and resale, which allows customers to make purchases without having to take out loans and pay interest. The financial institution purchases the goods for the customer, and re-sells them to the customer on a deferred basis, adding an agreed profit margin. The customer then pays the sale price for the goods over installments, effectively obtaining credit without paying interest.

(2) *Mudarabah* – refers to an investment on your behalf by a more skilled person. It takes the form of a contract between two parties, one who provides the funds and the other who provides the expertise. They agree to the division of any profits made in advance. In other words, Islamic Bank of Britain would make *sharia*-compliant investments and share the profits with the customer, in effect charging for its time and effort. If no profit is made, the loss is borne by the customer and Islamic Bank of Britain takes no fee.

Out of the frying pan . . .

Tayto's Crisps have dominated the Irish savory snack market for 40 years. Every week the Tayto Group produces and sells 8 million packets of potato crisps (chips) and snacks in a country with a population of fewer than 4 million people. This means that, on average, every Irish person consumes almost 100 packets a year.

However, Tayto's position is now under threat. British company Walkers, backed by the muscle of its parent company Frito Lay and Frito Lay's owner, the giant Pepsico Corporation, launched the UK's most popular brand of crisps in the Republic of Ireland on March 17, 2000 (St. Patrick's Day). According to Andrew Hartshorn, Walkers Brand Manager for Ireland, Walkers intends to capture a "substantial share of the [Irish] market quickly." Indeed, Walkers appears to not only want to eat up market share, but to change the way Irish consumers see potato chips. While Tayto's generally come in dinky 25 gram bags, replete with the skin shavings and blemishes of the potatoes they once were, Walkers is a crisp without blemish. They come with a minimal trace of vegetable oil in bigger servings with a modern foil bag decorated in the global Frito Lay format.

While Walkers is now backed by an American parent, Tayto has recently gone the other way, returning to Irish ownership after US firm TLC Beatrice sold it to the Irish drinks company Cantrell & Cochrane.

All of Ireland's crisps were imported from the UK until Mr. Joe Murphy from Donabate, County Dublin founded the Tayto Company in 1954. Murphy's biggest claim to fame was his invention of cheese and onion flavored crisps (prior to this the only "flavoring" option was salt). Cheese and onion is now the top selling flavor in Ireland and in the UK, where Murphy's innovation was quickly copied. Originally, Tayto's were produced by hand using two sets of deep-fat fryers, but the company grew quickly, aided by the financial association with Beatrice, who first acquired a stake in the Company in 1965. Factories were built in Rathmines, Harold's Cross, and Coolock, all in the Dublin area. Tayto now employs over 250 people and boasts a low staff turnover as testimony to the family atmosphere of the company.

Tayto's supply and distribution chains go deep into the Irish fabric. It only uses Irish potatoes grown under contract by farmers with whom Tayto has been associated for many years, and it has developed an intricate distribution network. Tayto's distributes its crisps through one of the largest direct van sales operations in the country, with ten regional depots located through the country supporting a roving fleet of 35 Tayto's vans. This provides a 99% domestic distribution level – a quite remarkable feat given the still rural nature of large parts of Ireland.

To further consolidate these channels a central distribution center was created in 1996 in Ballymount, Dublin. The center is fully automated and contains ten automated loading bays, with the capacity to hold in excess of 150,000 cartons of crisps. All types of outlets are serviced by this system: supermarket chains, pubs, newsagents, garage forecourts, off-licenses, and independent owner-operator stores, and Tayto guarantees that each customer receives fresh product through weekly service calls.

The result: almost every shop in Ireland – from the biggest supermarket to the smallest independent corner grocer and the most remote petrol station – prominently displays Tayto crisps, a big factor in a market where it is estimated that approximately half of all sales are impulse purchases. Finding an Irish person, or anybody with a connection to Ireland, who is unaware of the brand is a difficult task. Indeed, the way in which some Irish speak of Tayto crisps seems to indicate a kind of spiritual attachment. In a recent survey of brands, Tayto was rated the third biggest Irish brand and first in the grocery sector.

While Tayto holds a domestic market position enjoyed by few indigenous consumer brands (in 1999, it held 60% of Ireland's crisp market, and the second highest selling brand, King Crisps, is also owned by Tayto), it has no official export business in an increasingly global savory snack market. However, there are what could be called "independent initiatives" that bring Tayto crisps to the world. It is often claimed that there are more Irish living outside of Ireland than within, and packets of Tayto are regularly dispatched to Irish emigrants from friends and family at home. Martin McElroy, an Irishman now living in Philadelphia, has developed an agency that now orders over 100,000 bags of Tayto a week which he sells through local wholesalers. "It's wonderful to see the reaction of all the Irish people here when they walk into a shop and there is a box of Tayto Cheese & Onion," claims McElroy. "But the Americans are really developing a taste for them too. In fact I can see that Tayto will be regarded as the luxury import in the same way that many American products such as nachos are regarded at home [Ireland]." The crisps are retailing for $1 a pack, twice what they sell for in Irish stores.

Walkers can also trace its history back 50 years. As a local pork butcher's in Leicester in the English midlands, Walkers began producing crisps as a way of utilizing staff and facilities in its small factory while meat was heavily rationed after World War II. It began to expand into other British regions around 20 years ago. In recent years, with the backing of its new parents and the help of a big marketing budget wisely spent, particularly on television advertisements featuring British soccer stars, it has become the UK's second most powerful grocery brand after Coca-Cola. Walkers now boasts annual sales of well over £300m and a 65% share of the UK potato chip sector.

Walkers/Frito-Lay/Pepsico is taking the Irish launch of its products very seriously. It has given away more than a million free packets of crisps and made an Irish variation on its theme of soccer-star television advertisements starring Roy Keane, an Irish midfielder who plays for Manchester United and is one of the highest paid players in the English football league. Andrew Hartshorn explains that the huge marketing budget that Walkers is currently using to push its crisps in Ireland is a "long term investment" – a strategy that is part of a bigger global picture. Success in Ireland, Europe's fastest growing economy and Walkers' first overseas target, will help the company develop the knowledge, experience, and confidence necessary to launch into other European countries.

Evidence from Northern Ireland does not bode well for Tayto. While the Tayto brand (owned by a different company in the North) is still well regarded, Walkers replaced it as the best-selling crisp in just 3 years. However, there are many cultural and business factors that make the Republic a different market – not least of which is the clout of the myriad smaller independent stores which still contribute a much higher percentage of sales than in Britain or America and with whom Tayto's has long-standing relationships. Tayto's Managing Director, Vincent O'Sullivan, subsequently believes that Tayto can compete against the might of the multinational threat: "We're not going to give away market share to anyone," insists O'Sullivan. "What [Walkers] are going to find out is that it's a very competitive market with strong local brands."

1. *What resources and capabilities might Tayto's have that will be difficult for Walkers to replicate?*
2. *If you were CEO of Tayto's, what strategies would you employ to protect the company's advantage?*
3. *If you were CEO of Walkers Ireland, what strategies would you employ to build the company's advantage?*

Get Cata

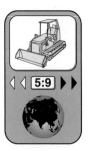

The Japanese industrial and construction machinery company Komatsu was lauded for the simplicity of its strategic positioning in the 1980s and 1990s. This was simply articulated as "Encircle Catapillar." Throughout this period, this created a clear picture of the company's strategy in the mind of employees. Catapillar was the big global producer of earth-moving machinery, which succeeded through the economies of scale achieved by producing a small range of models in each product or strategy category. Komatsu would succeed by producing a more varied and tailored range that "encircled" Catapillar's products and then "get Cata" by collective nibbling away at the corners of Catapillar's markets from all directions.

---

1. *Can you broadly draw Komatsu's strategic position (or positions) relative to Catapillar on the generic strategy matrix?*
2. *What advantages might this simple drawing provide to Komatsu employees, suppliers, and distributors?*
3. *How might Catapillar position itself in response to Komatsu's encircling strategy, should Komatsu's strategy prove to be successful?*

Cereality

The idea, explains David Roth, co-founder of Cereality Cereal Bar and Café, "is to become the Starbucks of cereal." Cereality simply provides bowls of common branded cereals such Cheerios, Lucky Charms, and Quaker Oats to which customers can add toppings and milk, but some commentators believe that Roth and co-founder Rick Bacher may actually be on to something.

The pair began testing a prototype store at the end of 2003 at Arizona State University (the store took just 2 months to turn a profit as students flocked to it), and by the end of 2004 new outlets had been opened in Philadelphia and Chicago, with 15 more stores to open in 2005. Thinking further ahead, Roth and Bacher are currently also negotiating for space at train stations, arenas, airports, and hotels.

The founders claim they created Cereality "to celebrate the very personal nature of enjoying a good bowl of cereal, anywhere and at any time. It's a life-long staple, and yet nobody had ever figured out a way to make it work in fast food." At Cereality, customers can get a 32 oz bowl of branded cereal, or combine brands as they wish, and select from toppings like fruit, nuts, and candy and different kinds of milk for about $3. Or they can choose ready-made mixes selected by Cereality staff (called "Cereologists"). Cereality also does Smoothies made with cereal (Slurrealities™) and goods baked with cereals (Cereality Bars™ and Cereality Bites™). Bacher seems to be serious when he boasts that: "Cereality is so unique, it has a patent pending."

Customers are greeted by waiting staff wearing pyjamas in surroundings that are comfortably homely. "I wanted to create a totally cool experienced where all of those (cereal) rituals and habits can be celebrated out of the home," explains Roth. In so doing, Cereality is hoping to cash in on the comfort and nostalgia that people attach to breakfast cereal. *USA Today* wrote that this: "latest fast-food concept is so absurdly simple, self-indulgent and reflective on one's inner child that; well, how can it fail?"

Cereal makers, who have been trying to find an outlet for their products beyond the breakfast table for decades and have been battling the current trend toward toward "low-carbs" that has contributed to an 8% decline in cereal sales in the 5 years to 2004, have been keen to get behind Roth and Bacher's venture. Quaker has invested an undisclosed amount in Cereality, and General Mills and Kellogg have offered business advice. In return, the big cereal companies not only get another distribution channel, but valuable information as well. Cereality kiosks gather interesting data on who's buying what and what combinations of cereals and toppings are popular. The pilot store has already yielded some surprises, such as a strong yearning among collegians for *Cinnamon Toast Crunch* and that Quaker's old-fashioned *Life* brand is the number one seller.

Roth claims to have been inspired by the cereal-loving characters on the TV show *Seinfeld*: the show which boldly claimed to be "about nothing" but was greatly loved and tremendously successful. There are some that might say that serving bowls of cereal commonly available in any supermarket is similarly a "nothing" strategy. But could Cereality become as successful as its role models Starbucks and *Seinfeld*?

---

1. *Do you think Cereality has a sustainable competitive advantage? If not, why not? If so, how would you articulate it?*

> There is no such thing as society. There are individual men and women, and there are families.
>
> *Margaret Thatcher (1987)*

> [The myth of individualism] gets in the way of understanding how the world actually works. And in doing so it lowers our chances of success, depresses our pay, limits our promotions, decreases the value we create, reduces our ability to get things done, and even jeopardizes our health, happiness, and welfare. And it closes off all the great possibilities of life.
>
> *Wayne Baker (2000)* Achieving Success Through Social Capital

Having learnt much from the previous decade (where conservative right-wing political parties held sway), Bill Clinton's wily advisor James Carville focused his boss's 1992 presidential campaign around a simple slogan: "It's the economy, stupid." It became one of the most remembered catchphrases of the early 90s. By the later 90s, however, the slogan and the idea that people's most important concern was their individual economic well-being, had fallen out of favor. While most leading management thinkers up until the late 20th century would have supported Carville's words, at the beginning of the 21st century, management guru Tom Peters was winning plaudits for turning it on its head – "It's relationships, stupid", claimed Peters.

Peters' phrase spoke to a growing recognition that while economic considerations were important for living beings, they were no more primary than the social. Living beings rely on, are sustained by, and are fulfilled by relationships. In this light, Thatcher's notion that there is no such thing as society now seems rather odd. If anything, it seems to make more sense nowadays to speak of their being no such thing as an individual: "no man is an island," to borrow a popular saying.

This chapter on living strategy looks at how business strategy too is shaped by the relationships that are so much a part of everyday life and the social capital that can grow out of them. Managed well, they can make strategic progress seem effortless; managed poorly, they can place insurmountable barriers in the way of success.

Four recognitions have led the shift from a focus on economics and mechanical individuals to seeing organizations as living beings and relationships:

1. Organizations, like living organisms, need to learn. Machines can't learn.
2. Organizations, like living organisms, live in the world and they are subject to multiple layers of influence from which they cannot be separated (e.g., the individual is part of a team, which is part of a division, which is part of a company, which is part of an industry, which is part of a society).
3. An organism's past, present, and future are closely interwoven. The same is true for organizations. They are "thrown" by their pasts in particular directions that shape their future aspirations and possibilities.[1] Points 2 and 3 mean that the being of an individual living organism (and thus an organization if we think of it as a living organism)

153

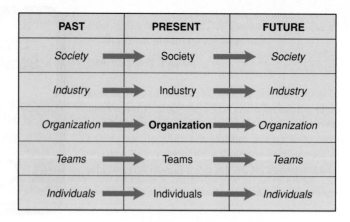

Figure 6.1 The matrix within which an individual organization lives

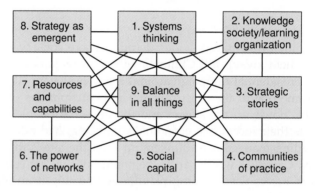

Figure 6.2 Living strategy: strategy development through living relationships

exists within a complex and multilayered system, or matrix, of relationships, as depicted in figure 6.1.

4. Finally, the points above mean that living organisms are greater than the sum of their parts: they are not just discrete independent individuals. In other words, they have a metaphysical as well as physical dimension. The problem, according to Jesper Kunde, is that: "Most executives have no idea how to add value to a market in the metaphysical world. But that is what the market will cry out for in the future. There is no lack of 'physical' products to choose between."[2]

These recognitions have led to the development of new interrelated themes for exploring how to add value in organizations as living beings through focusing on metaphysical living relationships (figure 6.2). These are outlined in the sections below.

Systems Thinking

Perhaps the most influential systems-thinker to affect how we look at strategy is Peter Senge, author of *The Fifth Discipline*.[3] Senge identified five interrelated "disciplines" required to build a learning organization: (1) personal visions; (2) surfacing the often implicit models currently used for decision making; (3) developing a shared vision; (4) team learning; and finally, (5) the fifth discipline: **systems thinking** to understand how the relationships and interactions between the elements of the organization and the environment affect the whole. This systems thinking should entail:

1. seeing interrelationships and processes rather than things and snapshots
2. recognizing that individual "cogs" are not to blame for poor performance – they can only do what the system allows them to do
3. distinguishing which parts of the system have high impact on strategy and which are only minor details
4. paying attention to 3 and focusing on areas of "high leverage" – the 20% of things that will make 80% of difference
5. looking beyond solving *symptoms* and *outcomes* through popular quick fixes or applying generic buzzwords – poorly performing systems require **systematic solutions**

The Knowledge Society and the Learning Organization

Senge credits much of his development as a systems and a strategic thinker to Arie de Geus, author of *The Living Company*.[4] De Geus's thesis is quite simple: "We are living in a new *knowledge society*. This requires that companies must learn and adapt quickly to remain successful. But, we tend to see companies as machines. Machines can't learn. Only living beings can. We must change the way we perceive companies."

De Geus describes the historical development of the knowledge society as follows. Basic economic theory suggests that there have always been three sources of wealth: land and natural resources, capital, and labor. Up until the late Middle Ages, the critical factor was land. Those who possessed and controlled land controlled the accumulation of wealth. But a shift began in the Middle Ages. Nation states became concerned with expansion, and the capital to finance endeavors became the most valuable commodity of production. During this time, the modern company was developed, as capital was made available for the wealth-creating processes of the medieval tradesperson. At the same time, the break up of old craft guilds and their evolution into competing companies gave the speculative owners of capital great control over human resources. In the language of economics, capital was far more scarce and worth far more than labor.

Over the past 50 years, however, the world of business has shifted from one dominated by capital to one based on knowledge. Capital has become less scarce. After the Second World War, a huge capital accumulation began and individuals, banks, and companies sought to be more skilful and forthright in maintaining and building their investment portfolios. Technological advances made capital easier to move around, share, and invest. And, with capital more easily available, labor (or, more correctly, the knowledge held in the heads of labor) became the most valuable component. Increasing cross-border competition and the subsequent complexity of work fed a need for people to be a source of inventiveness. With globalization making capital easier to obtain and the possession of land less of an issue, those who had knowledge and knew how to apply it would henceforth be the wealthiest. The shift has become visible in the rise, since the 1950s, of traditional asset-poor but knowledge-rich companies such as international auditing firms, management consultancies, advertising and media businesses, and IT providers.

This changing nature of the economics of the firm, combined with globalization and the growth in information technology, has meant that organizational knowledge is now not only the most valuable commodity, it also moves more quickly than ever. Hence, an organization cannot survive for long unless it continually adapts and reshapes its knowledge and thus itself. And, adaptation to a changing environment requires **learning**: the ability to manage change by changing oneself. A simple model of the elements of the learning process is mapped out in figure 6.3 below.

De Geus then suggests that there are two ways in which this learning process can happen: (1) **Learning by assimilation**: perceiving changes for which the learner already has structures in place to recognize what is being taught (e.g. skilled bank strategists are well set up to recognize and respond to a change in interest rates); (2) **Learning by accommodation**: changing one's learning process to remain in harmony with a changed environment (e.g. only a few banks have picked up on a shift in customer preferences for a bank that seems more like a retail environment and reconfigured accordingly (see micro-case 6-3)). Whereas learning by assimilation is generally a mechanical process, with change constrained by predetermined parameters, learning by accommodation becomes a living attitude and the possibilities for change here are infinite. Given the increasingly fast-paced and unpredictable nature of the knowledge society, there is no doubt that learning by accommodation is the more important of the two types of learning for organizations to master.

In summary, de Geus defines the successful living company as having four aspects:

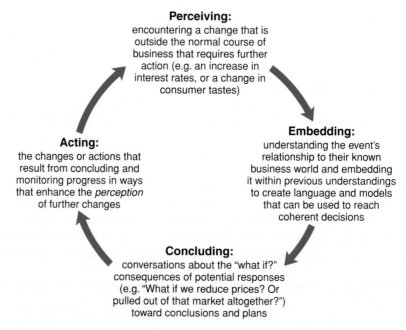

Perceiving:
encountering a change that is outside the normal course of business that requires further action (e.g. an increase in interest rates, or a change in consumer tastes)

Embedding:
understanding the event's relationship to their known business world and embedding it within previous understandings to create language and models that can be used to reach coherent decisions

Acting:
the changes or actions that result from concluding and monitoring progress in ways that enhance the *perception* of further changes

Concluding:
conversations about the "what if?" consequences of potential responses (e.g. "What if we reduce prices? Or pulled out of that market altogether?") toward conclusions and plans

Figure 6.3   A learning process cycle (Adapted from de Geus (2000))

1. *Sensitivity to the environment* – an ability to learn and adapt.
2. *Cohesion and identity* – an ability to build a personality and a community for itself.
3. *Tolerance and decentralization* – awareness of its ecology, its ability to build constructive relationships with other entities, within and outside itself.
4. *Conservative financing* – an ability to govern its own life and evolution effectively.

James Collins and Jerry Porras' book *Built to Last* came to similar conclusions.[5] It claimed that the most admired companies combined a powerful drive for progress that enabled them to change and adapt without compromising their core ideals, a strong sense of identity, and sensitivity to their ecology. And, they found that while financial gain was also a secondary objective for these companies, financial gain tends to follow from focusing on long-term survival.

Many others have also looked at the importance of knowledge and learning to strategy. A particularly influential stream of research is that developed by Ikujiro Nonaka. This looks at the importance of turning tacit knowledge into explicit knowledge through a cycle of **socialization** (sharing of tacit knowledge between individuals); **externalization** (articulation of systemization of this into explicit knowledge); **combination** (putting this knowledge together with existing knowledge in useful ways); and **internalization** (converting this knowledge into new organizational and individual routines).[6]

The Power of Strategic Stories

Living beings can learn by accommodation through two practical means: by being changed by personal experience, or through encountering other people who communicate stories encapsulating other experiences. Given the inherent limitations of personal experience, stories are invaluable for the learning organization. In the words of Annette Simmons, "When you tell a compelling story, you connect people to you or what you are trying to achieve." While stories have for some time played a role in conveying complex marketing messages to customers (e.g. the identities of Unilever's main ice cream brands have been organized around the following storylines for many years: Solero – stories of refreshment; Magnum – self-indulgence; Carte d'Or – sharing), they are now playing a part in the way that many companies think about leading strategic development.

In 1998, "Strategic Stories: How 3M is Rewriting Business Planning" was published in the *Harvard Business Review*.[7] It clearly struck a chord, becoming one of the *HBR*'s best-selling offprints. In the article, 3M ascribed much of its success to the company's "story-intensive culture" and how this has changed the way it "does strategy." 3M attributes its new approach to two things. First, a recognition that traditional bullet points and list-making approaches to communicating strategic plans are too generic, leave critical relationships unspecified, and subsequently do not inspire thinking or commitment. Second, a recognition that communicating and developing the same ideas through stories enables people to see themselves and their business operations in complex, multidimensional ways, helping them explore opportunities for strategic change and form ideas about future success. "When people locate themselves in these strategic stories," the authors concluded, "their sense of commitment and involvement is enhanced."

There are more scientific reasons why stories, or conversations about stories, are important for strategy. Psychologists have established that lists are much harder to remember than stories because of "recency" and "primacy" effects. People mainly remember the first and the last items on a list but not the rest of it. Also, lists enable "selective memory" as people tend to select the individual points that they like and focus on those, forgetting about the whole and the many integrated parts that make this up. Language researchers have found that when they translated history textbooks into the story-based style of *Time* or *The Economist*, students could recall up to three times more information. Cognitive scientists have examined how the stories we hear in childhood enable us to imagine a course of action, imagine its effects on others, decide whether or not a particular direction should be taken, and plan accordingly.

If a picture paints a thousand words, then a story or an anecdote about a company can connect up a thousand threads and give a corporation a flexible focus that can launch a thousand initiatives that build from core values. In the words of Gardner and Laskin, authors of *Leading Minds: An Anatomy of Leadership*: "Stories of identity – narratives that help individuals think about and feel who they are, where they come from, and where they are headed – constitute the single most powerful weapon in the leader's arsenal."[8] Tom Peters even has a term for a management style based on this type of thinking: MBSA – management by storying around. It is interesting that living beings can communicate and learn an incredibly complex system of meaning through a whole series of convoluted stories, yet be unable to remember a vision statement, code of ethics, or list of policy objectives. In a knowledge society, where learning organizations are imperative, strategists must take stories seriously.

Communities of Practice

Communities of practice are informal networks bound together by shared expertise or experiences and a passion for a particular joint enterprise. They tend to be self-selecting, self-organizing, self-reinforcing, and self-renewing, attracting new members through the strong sense of self-identity that they convey. They are held together by strong relationships and have a shared value system, memory, and knowledge base.[9] According to proponents of the view, it is these communities of practice, rather than senior planners and consultants, that really drive strategy. They can spread knowledge, develop professional skills, retain and recruit talent, and generate new lines of business. And, what they do is more likely to stick because they are organic beings, not manufactured policies. It is little wonder, therefore, that strategists should be aware of and get onside with the key communities of practice within their organization and the external communities that might either help or hinder the achievement of the company's strategic goals.

Social Capital

Social capital refers to the resources available in and through personal and business networks. The word *social* is used to emphasize that key personal and business resources (e.g. ideas, opportunities, promising leads, access to financial capital, power and influence, emotional support, good-will, trust, and cooperation) are not owned by any single person, but reside in interdependent networks of relationships. The word *capital* emphasizes that resources like these can, and increasingly must, be used to create value and achieve business goals. The main insight offered to strategists by social capital theory is that most organizations and individuals within organizations need to build more entrepreneurial networks (i.e. larger, more diverse, and outwardly focused). Some strategies for achieving this include: encouraging rising managers to partake in external education programs (such as a high-quality MBA); sending delegations to interesting conferences; arranging staff exchanges with allied companies; allying with key influencers in other related industries; or arranging business forums and meetings for companies and other key stakeholders in an industry.[10]

The Power of Networks

These ideas about the power of communities of individuals and networks in shaping effective strategic directions are not that new. In 1982, Peters and Waterman's *In Search of Excellence* saw the advantages of "simultaneously loose-tight properties" or organizations as coalitions of individuals and belief systems, rather than machine bureaucracies, as a key to business success.[11] In 1993, two articles in the same issue of the *Harvard Business Review* looked at ways of rethinking business processes in terms of networks. Normann and Ramirez's "From Value Chain to Value Constellation: Designing Interactive Strategy" argued that a constellation of relationships was a better metaphor for understanding how firms really add value than the traditional linear value chain. Krackhardt and Hanson's "Informal Networks: The Company Behind the Chart" claimed that one needs to see behind the formal hierarchies outlined in an organization's official chart to find the networks or communities of practice that really influence strategic direction setting.[12] In 1997, Evans and Wurster's "Strategy and the New Economics of Information" demonstrated how this new thinking about the loose-tight nature of interdependent relationships and communities, combined with advances in information technology, was changing the economics of the firm. The future, they argued would be one of "hyperarchies": fluid networks and temporary coalitions of different, but like-minded, bodies rather than clearly stratified hierarchies.[13]

While articles like these have demonstrated the importance of looking at strategy as influenced by a wider network of internal and external influences than was traditionally thought to be the case, they often present an overly rosy view of the effects of these influences. Networks, and tightly knit communities of practice, are not always good for sponsoring effective strategies. Just like strong cultures, strong networks can become conservative, unquestioning, and resistant to outsiders and changing by learning through accommodation.

This is not a new idea outside of the management literature. Philosopher Michel Foucault developed the term **power/knowledge** to express the inescapable link between the two. Those who have power also to a very large extent determine what is knowledge, or at least what is valuable knowledge. Foucault also challenged preconceptions about power and networks by arguing that power does not exist in "bodies of authority" (e.g. government, the police, the media, the education system), but in the relationships (tangible or otherwise) between these bodies. Hence, protesting through directly confronting such bodies may cause the network to organize knowledge against the protest and make traditional conservative bonds stronger.[14] The best form of resistance is therefore to organize alternative networks of like-minded individuals who can help a cause behind the scenes. In similar vein, William Foote Whyte's 1943 study, *Street Corner Society*, diagrammed interactions between individuals to understand relationships between group structure and individual performance. Whyte found that the most successful and influential people were those with the most key "connections."[15]

Resources and Capabilities

This brings us back into contact with the "resource-based view" of the firm, which was introduced in the previous chapter.[16] The RBV argues that each organization is made up of a constellation of tangible and intangible resources: *physical* resources like land, offices, and machinery; *financial* resources like access to capital; *human* resources like experience and expertise; and *organizational* resources like reputation, culture, and traditional relationships. (The ideas of Kunde and de Geus expressed earlier in this chapter would suggest that the human and metaphysical resources are key. This indicates why HR has come to be seen as such a strategic issue. No amount of cutting-edge technology or state-of-the-art business processes can compensate for a lack of human skill and teamwork. Hence, top-performing companies are up to four times more likely than the rest to pay what it takes to prevent losing top performers.[17]) When these **resources** are networked together in ways that enable the effective performance of a task or activity, they become **capabilities**. And, when these capabilities are superior to those of a firm's competitors they become a **competitive advantage**. In fact, the RBV approach suggests that an analysis of the firm's network of resources, rather than the external environment, is a better place from which to begin to understand a company's strategic potential.

The constellation of relationships between resources, and the knowledge embedded within them, suggests that the whole will always be greater than the sum of the parts, and indicates such constellations cannot be engineered – they have to grow organically. Because a system of relationships is an organic living being, it is reflective of a particular geography, history, and emergent relations between employees within the firm, and then between them and suppliers and customers and so forth. Therefore, each organization's RBV constellation will likely be **rare** and **difficult to imitate**. This is important to recognize, because in an age when firms have become very good at copying what they can copy through best practice benchmarking and reverse engineering, it may be claimed that tacit resource and knowledge webs will become the key to an organization's sustainable competitive advantage.

Strategy As Emerging From Processes and Practice

The living strategy view described above reinforces the importance of the emergence view of strategy championed by Henry Mintzberg and a new breed of strategic thinkers. We may believe that strategy is a rational and analytical activity resulting in plans and predetermined objectives that are then acted upon and achieved, but the emergence view suggests that strategy is in reality more about being adaptive enough to bend to follow opportunities and possibilities as they crop up. Here strategy is as much about the patterns that emerge as life unfolds as it is about planning.

Mintzberg's views are supported by Andrew Pettigrew's research, which suggests that the content or outcomes of a company's strategy (e.g. its plans, vision, or positions) is more a function of the particular processual patterns by which strategy emerges than by rational design. Hence, to understand a strategy's content, one should first consider the organizational context and processes. This *process* view of strategy has been developed further in recent times by the strategy as *practice* perspective.[18] The practice perspective builds on the strategy as process view, but looks at the particular behaviors and activities of individuals and groups who may influence strategy rather than organizational processes. For instance, what managers say or don't say, their choice of language, how they communicate through "technology" (such as Lotus Notes or Microsoft software), how meetings are conducted, the use of flip charts to control and steer discussion for instance, and the role of away days are all of great interest as "micro-practices" in how strategy may be formed. Valuable insight can be gained looking at strategy in this way. For example, we can recognize how middle managers are key gatekeepers of strategy: their communications can undermine or translate and promote the strategies espoused by those at the top of an organization or disrupt or facilitate the ideas of those below. Individuals within the organization who impact upon strategy are also likely to be connected across the organizational boundary both vertically and horizontally, perhaps with links to key suppliers and customers, or to institutional bodies. This raises interesting questions of how external parties can influence the internal workings of the firm and also how these strategy workers may shape external opinions. Strategy as practice allows us to focus on how managers, in practice, actually work with, adapt, and work around the "clean lines" and tidy categorizations of the classical frameworks depicted in the previous chapter.

The focus on strategy as emerging organically in an organization has taken on increasing importance as it is realized that such strategies are more difficult to replicate than conventional approaches, which saw strategy as about explicit plans and positions issued from the top of the bureaucracy. As figure 6.4 shows, generally speaking, the further down the diagonal line a firm goes in terms of an organic structural approach and an emergent strategy, the more difficult it is for competitors to replicate that strategy and the firm's competitive advantage thus becomes more sustainable.

This focus on the RBV and strategies emerging organically out of particular processes and practices should not imply that strategists are powerless to plan and design and position and lead change. Indeed, as opportunities emerge in the life of an organization, it is up to strategists to seize on them and get the corporation in behind them. Just as a human being must face two directions at once (both taking stock and moving forward; carrying on traditions yet taking up new directions), the living strategy perspective requires the strategist to be agile in facing both back and forwards at once. The metaphor sometimes used to express this attitude

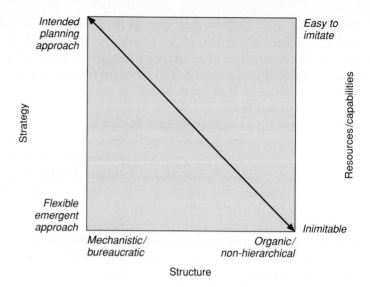

Figure 6.4 The strategic approaches and structures that tend to produce non-replicable sources of sustainable competitive advantage (Source: Sorenson (2005))

is surfing. Because strategists cannot engineer waves or relationships, they must instead surf or work on the most favorable ones that already exist and be open to harnessing new waves, or promising practices, as they emerge.[19]

Balance In All Things

As the paragraph above indicates, living strategy, like life itself, is about balancing competing desires. Just as people must balance acknowledging past relationships, enjoying the present, and planning for future well-being, organizations too must achieve a similar balance in determining their strategies. One approach that has become an extremely popular means of helping an organization to achieve a balance between financial performance in the past, customer satisfaction in

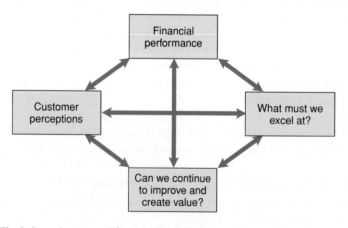

Figure 6.5 The balanced scorecard (Adapted from Kaplan and Norton (1992))

the present, and developing organizational capabilities for the future is Kaplan and Norton's **balanced scorecard approach**. This encourages the use of multiple criteria beyond the financial measures that have generally been used for assessing performance.

Thus, by using a balanced scorecard, firms must consider and match assessments about "How do our customers see us?" with "What must we excel at?" and "How good is our present financial performance?" with "How can we continue to improve and create value?" These measures of performance are developed with a view to assessing future potential as well as assessing current performance. Hence, each of these measures should be subdivided into two component parts. These are **outcomes**, which measure the results of actions in the past, and **performance drivers** (or **goals**) that predict future success. Measures for assessing outcomes can be metrics, such as return on capital employed or return on net assets, or factors like employee attitudes, extent of customer satisfaction, or further developing knowledge within the organization to help drive innovation and new product development. Goals are desired states that would indicate that success is being achieved.

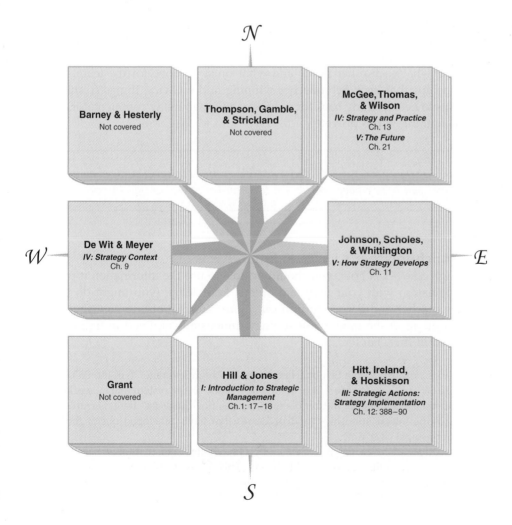

Schumacher's success

Perhaps the most popular story used to illustrate the power of relationships is that of Michael Schumacher's move to Ferrari. In 1996, Schumacher left the Benetton Formula 1 racing team, which he had helped lead to unprecedented successes, to join Ferrari, the world's most powerful team. Many thought the world's best driver combined with the richest team would be invincible, but it was not to be. In 1996 Schumacher only recorded three wins and the team finished second behind Williams.

The next year, Ferrari's 50th anniversary, the story was much the same: Williams first, Ferrari second. But something very important happened at the end of that season. Ferrari lured Technical Director Ross Brawn and Chief Designer Rory Byrne from Benetton. The old Benetton team was reunited. Apparently it took some time for the Brawn–Byrne–Schumacher team to bed in to the Ferrari community, and while 1998 was encouraging, Ferrari still finished second, this time to McLaren. But in 1999 everything clicked. At the time of writing this, Ferrari had won every Formula 1 championship since 1999, and by increasingly grand margins.

For Schumacher, winning races has seemed to get easier and easier. But he is not stupid. Listen to him being interviewed and he will always credit the team, the relationships, the innate combinations, the camaraderie, the instinctive knowing what each other needs and what must be done for the team. It is the relationships that keep Schumacher winning and enjoying things so much that he wants to keep coming back for more, even though many commentators believe he has nothing left to prove.

> *1. Using figure 6.2 as a guiding framework, outline the living strategy dimensions that you believe have contributed to Team Ferrari's eventual success.*

◀◀◀ Schumacher's success: Some Ideas . . .

Although case 6-1 is brief, you should be able to use the information it provides, in combination with your own and others' knowledge (you might do a search on Schumacher and Ferrari to find out more information), to contribute something from all of the nine living strategy dimensions outlined in figure 6.2 and described in this chapter.

1. *Systems thinking*: While Schumacher might be "high leverage" (i.e. the 20% that can make 80% of the difference), he can only be as good as the system that he works within. Schumacher is integral, but on his own he was no "quick fix" here. Ferrari's success lies in the interrelationships (and processes that have developed out of those interrelationships) over time.

2. *Knowledge society/learning organization*: In a knowledge society, human capital is more valuable than other more tangible assets. This seems to be true in motor racing at the highest levels. All of the top teams have access to capital and technology – it's the human factors, like the knowledge that exists in Schumacher and his associates'

heads, that make the difference. Recognizing this, Ferrari showed willingness to learn from and adapt to their previous poor performance and the success of others.

3. *Strategic stories*: While there are no explicit examples of this mentioned in the case, a lot of the power surrounding the Ferrari brand, and its ability to attract the likes of Schumacher and Brawn, is provided by the stories and myths of characters like Enzo Ferrari and the "tifosi" (Ferrari's ultra-loyal fans).

4. *Communities of practice*: Schumacher, Brawn, and Byrne form a community of practice. They are bound by similar passions and values and know each other so well that they can learn, act, and effectively adapt in unison, without the need for time-consuming deliberation. It is they who drive Ferrari's success more than the company's strategic planners.

5. *Social capital*: As this community of practice began to embed into Ferrari's broader network of alliances, these relationships began to produce social capital – a form of capital that is very difficult for Ferrari's competitors to replicate.

6. *Networks*: The old Italian Ferrari network seemed resistant to change. For many years the idea that a German would lead Ferrari would have been resisted. However, the new Ferrari is a more open network in which information flows quickly across the organization to where it is needed without having to follow the old hierarchies and power structures. This makes the organization more adaptive, while it still holds true to Ferrari's core ideals.

7. *Resources and capabilities*: Ferrari now comprises a network of physical resources, financial resources, and organizational resources like reputation, culture, and brand (which it has had for some time) with the best human resources. Networked together, this has led to the development of capabilities that contribute to its competitive advantage.

8. *Strategy as emergent*: While some, in hindsight, might put Ferrari's recent success down to good planning, the team's success has emerged gradually over time through Ferrari becoming open to adapting to emergent opportunities as they have presented themselves, and then letting Schumacher, Brawn, Byrne, and others get on with things, developing processes and practices that would shape effective strategic plans.

9. *Balanced scorecard*: For an F1 racing team it should be obvious that financial success is only one measure of performance. It must be balanced against keeping fans or customers happy, maintaining the capabilities that will enable new developments and future success, and keeping a clear sense of how the team identity is distinct from others.

And finally, returning to systems thinking helps us understand that Ferrari's real strength lies in the interrelationships between all of these nine dimensions.

The band

As well as a decision analyst, I am a guitarist and I play music in a band (an organization). The latter is often more enjoyable than the former! The band's decision-making processes with regard to what material we play is heavily influenced by what might be called *inter-subjectivity*. "We" only play particular material and, by definition, not other sorts of material. "We" articulate this to audiences who might ask for a tune that does not fit our repertoire – "we" say "we" don't play that song. However, this is completely different from saying "we" *can't* play that song.

As individual players, we are quite capable of playing a wide variety of music and styles. Yet, as an organization that is constantly evolving by adding new material, "we" play only selected material and in a style that conforms to (and is created by) the shared meaning and interpretation of the band's members. Change the band, of course, and you will also change the shared collective consciousness. But it too will evolve into a new shared inter-subjectivity that will, consciously and unconsciously, take the organization's decision making down a particular lane of things that the organization will, and will not, do.

> 1. *Apply Senge's five disciplines, and any other frameworks you think appropriate, to analyze what makes a group of musicians, like the one described above, successful.*
> 2. *Why does a group produce music that is different from, and often superior to, that produced by the individuals who make up the group? (The Beatles are a good case in point.)*
> 3. *Can you relate your answers in questions 1 and 2 to how you might want to develop strategy in an organization?*

Bringing back the branch

A recent survey on international banking by *The Economist* began with the headline that "Banks have rediscovered the virtue of knowing their customers." Smaller banks probably never lost sight of this fact, but now even the biggest banks are rediscovering the value of the personal touch.

Until recently, the trend was to cut costs through automation. Branches fell out of fashion because the accountants deemed buildings to be too expensive and people too expensive and too unreliable. Banks found numerous ways of discouraging customers from bothering their tellers (such an antiquated term now), from charging them for the privilege, to removing staff or branches altogether, to incentivizing the use of web-based banking through discounts or prizes.

In addition, a bank's call-center might put an inquiry from Wolverhampton through to Mumbai. With the decline in the cost of telephone calls, increases in English language capabilities, and weaker union agreements making it easier to have people work odd shifts that correspond to business hours in countries many time zones away, it's certainly now much cheaper to operate in this way. And the customers probably wouldn't even be able to tell the difference; and, if they could, they probably wouldn't care. Or so the banks thought.

While telephones and computers are fine for checking bank balances or making fund transfers, they are much less good at selling products of any complexity. According to *The Economist*'s review: "Most people prefer to discuss mortgages, mutual funds, and so forth face-to-face. Moreover, banks these days want potential customers to do more than open a new current account. They aim, in the industry jargon, to maximize their 'share of wallet' by selling a whole portfolio of services . . . People are much better at that than machines are."

According to Charles H. Green, author of *Streetwise Financing for the Small Business* and Vice President of Atlanta's Sunrise Bank: "As big became bigger, the fate of smaller banks was written off many years ago. But the fact is that [the mega-banks] never really threatened community banks. More often than not, they have been outgunned by smaller, more focused banks that have chosen to stay true to their primary business of meeting customers' real needs."

Take banks like the Seattle-based Washington Mutual or New Jersey's Commerce Bank who have adapted their practices to suit customers' needs and wants rather than trying to funnel them into using less labor-intensive channels such as the internet.

At Washington Mutual (or WaMu as it is widely known) branches sell coffee and chocolates and piggy banks shaped like footballs, and there are play areas for young children. Some branches have given away the (somewhat tongue-in-cheek) "Action teller" dolls dressed as WaMu staff. There are no counters and no ropes to funnel people toward glass bound tellers. It looks more like a shop than a bank, which isn't surprising when you learn that WaMu managers are seeking to model themselves on leading retailers such as Wal-Mart and Home Depot rather than other banks.

Its marketing is similarly innovative. When they launched in Chicago employees handed out WaMu wallets containing $1.50 to advertise that they would not impose the usual surcharge on other banks' customers to use its ATMs. To announce their arrival in New York, WaMu bought out Broadway theatres for a day and gave the seats to the City's teachers. Both gestures won customers.

WaMu's assets have doubled in the past 7 years and now stand at US$275bn, making it America's seventh-biggest bank. In mortgage lending it now jockeys with Wells Fargo for the No. 1 spot in the US market.

Vernon Hill, who founded Commerce Bank in 1973, claims to "love it when other banks merge." The growth in deposits at Commerce surged after the last two big mergers on his patch. Acquisition, says Hill, "is a good way to lose customers. It dilutes your model, dilutes your culture, distracts your firm, and dilutes your brand. No great retailer ever grew by acquisition."

Hill insists on calling himself a retailer, not a banker, and also extolls the likes of Wal-Mart and McDonald's. Indeed, Commerce's business hours are much more like those of a retail store than a bank. Branches are open from 7.30 AM to 8.00 PM on weekdays and from 11.00 to 4.00 PM on Sundays. Somebody greets you as you enter a branch and Commerce's interiors are designed to be more homely than the austere surroundings one encounters at traditional banks. There are no screens to separate customers from tellers (a rarity in the New York area) and there are "penny arcades" where you can convert your loose change and maybe win a small prize.

Commerce has been growing at a furious pace. The increase in like-for-like sales (or deposits to use banking terms) has been close to 30% for the last few years. At the end of 1998, it had 96 outlets and US$4.9bn in deposits. It has now spread from New Jersey into Philadelphia and Manhattan and has 275 branches and US$20.7bn in deposits. By 2009, Commerce plans to have 700 branches.

But it's now not only smaller banks that are trying to play the relationships and communities cards. Bigger banks are seeking to configure themselves in ways that are far less impersonal. The HSBC's attempts to configure itself as "The World's Local Bank" and Barclays Bank's retraction of its advertising campaign that told people that what they really wanted was a "Big Bank," of Robbie Coltrane proportions, are good examples (see case 8-7). Moreover, in the US the number of bank branches has been on the rise for several years (up from around 69,000 in 1992 to 80,000 in 2003) and much of this rise is now coming from big banks re-opening branches. "In 1999 and 2000," says Todd Thompson, CFO of Citigroup, "conventional wisdom was that branches were bad. What we understand [now] is that stores are good. People like to go to a real physical presence. It feels safe. It feels solid." Bank of America currently has plans to open 350 new branches and Bank One is adding new branches for the first time in over 5 years. It is also building in "teller towers" and waiting areas for customers' children.

In other countries, overall branch growth may be stagnant or declining, but banks all over the world are beginning to re-think how branches could be used. Given the increased recognition of the importance of long-lasting relationships that engender trust, for example, they are certainly less inclined now to whisk promising managers off to head office and more willing to leave them in the field.

"The wake up call for the mega-banks may be this," explains Charles H. Green: "As long as there are people who want to deal with people rather than an 800 number, a website, or a standard computer scoring program, there will be a demand for community bankers. It's relationships, stupid."

> 1. *Why might branches staffed with living beings (as opposed to other, technological banking interfaces) become more important in a "knowledge society"?*
> 2. *What learning and social capital might accrue from these local branches? How could you feed this learning and social capital into strategy development?*

Helping old people eat

Like all big companies, Prudential has a formal statement of purpose:

> Prudential plc provides retail financial products and services and fund management to many millions of customers worldwide. Our commitment to the shareholders who own Prudential is to maximize the value over time of their investment. We do this by investing for the long term to develop and bring out the best in our people and our businesses to produce superior products and services, and hence superior financial returns. Our aim is to deliver top quartile performance among our international peer group in terms of total shareholder returns. At Prudential our aim is lasting relationships with our customers and policyholders, through products and services that offer value for money and security. We also seek to enhance our company's reputation, built over 150 years, for integrity and for acting responsibly within society.

While CEO Mark Wood recognizes the necessity of such a statement, recently he has been trying to bring what it means to life through the sharing of stories about the company. Below are some extracts from his "Prudential Story" which he presented to a conference of Pru managers in 2003. Wood's story has two key chords.

First, is the attempt to take the best of the company's history into the future. The Prudential was founded 150 years ago in London with a purpose to offer life assurance and loans to the middle and working classes. It took its name and corporate symbol from the form of Prudence, one of the four cardinal virtues, and developed a new system for providing insurance based on door-to-door agents supported by actuarial tables to enable them to provide personalized advice and simple explanations of its products. The Prudential – affectionately known as "the Pru" (probably the only nickname of a multinational company to have become an official part of the English language) – and its calling salesmen, affectionately referred to as "The Men From the Pru," became a part of the fabric of everyday life in the UK. By the 1900s, the Pru's values of security, plain-speaking honesty, value for money, integrity, and the ensuing emphasis on sound and solid investments and innovations that made things simple for ordinary people had led to Prudential insuring one-third of the UK population. However, by the 1990s shifts in the way in which financial services could be sold had made the Pru's door-to-door distribution channel unworkable. The company's strategic response: to update the Man From the Pru to "Plan From the Pru."

Second, Wood has a keen ear for the stories shared between employees that characterize what the Pru aims to be about. For example, a story was told of a young telephone operator in Scotland who made a regular follow-up call to a lapsed customer. He turned out to be an elderly man who told her that he always meant to fill in the forms that were sent to him to renew and update his Pru policy, but he found them to be too long and confusing and so never completed them. He said that when the Man From the Pru used to call at his door, they would fill out the forms together over a cup of tea. So, the telephone operator said to the gentleman that she was going to take a tea break in ten minutes. If he liked he could go and make himself a cup of tea and by the time that was done she would have hers and she would call him back and they would fill out the forms together. He liked the idea very much. They filled out the forms and a satisfied member of the Pru was back in the fold. You will see the influence of this story in Wood's.

"I want to tell you a story – a story about our business, the place where we work, where we are each investing our time, where we are building our careers. My purpose in telling this story is to describe my ambition for our part of the Pru over the next 1,000 days and indeed into the next century.

"What has shaped our future success? Cost reduction? No, but it played a big part in getting us to where we need to be; it has been the price to be paid to enable our business to prosper but it is only a first step. We have become a low-cost operator. By knocking out all the obvious areas of duplication while simultaneously making more significant moves, including the transformation of our customer service operation and the development of our Indian service center, we have shifted from the old high-cost model to low-cost, fast-delivery, and enhanced service. We have combined this with working hard to maximize the return on our customers' savings, and to providing the best possible service and incentives to our distributors. Our long-term future is dependent on the profit we accrue day by day, week by week, month by month. This determined approach has resulted in the achievement of our doubling of intrinsic value.

"However, the preservation and increase of our reputation – our *brand* – have been much more important . . . Underpinning the financial strength I've just described is the way we do things – *our values*. We are a friendly place, approachable, concerned to correct mistakes, but generally known by our customers for being careful, caring, and conscientious. The Pru is a place for consistent good value over the long term rather than the best rate for a short period of time. The Pru is prudent rather than expedient. We believe that if it seems too good to be true, it probably is. We would rather be criticized for cutting bonuses and maturity values than risk our financial strength. Our speed of service, while prompt, is not unsustainably or flashily fast. We are a place where you talk to real people at the end of the telephone rather than one of those computer thingies; if you are a bit muddled in your thinking about your finances at the Pru, you will find somebody, using words you understand who will take you through what you need to do and in a straightforward way. You will not find us talking in jargon. We are a place where, whatever the purpose of your call, you'll get a professional and sympathetic ear – someone concerned to ensure that your confidence in the Pru grows with every contact . . .

"To double our intrinsic value we knew that we had to have the right priorities. We made some tough decisions. We stopped some big projects. We have placed increasing importance on return on capital. This meant that we decided not to pursue some profitable opportunities. They required too much capital. We disappointed, irritated, and confused people. Some decided to leave us because they did not enjoy our disciplined pursuit of return on capital. But we knew we were focusing in the right place, on our brand, our product strengths, on our distribution channels, and on our costs and our financial strength. We focused on our product strengths in Group Pensions, Bulk Annuities, and our capability within the With Profits and Annuities markets. Our clear view and a particular focus on managing our scarce capital and long-term financial strengths dictated our priorities. Nonetheless, on several occasions we acted tactically. Without notice we changed tack, spotting an opportunity, moving swiftly and decisively, often against competitors, following rapid analysis and assessment to pounce and to profit. We have ceased to be a thinking organization enjoying debate for its own sake, insisting on perfection rather than delivery. We have become prone to action, valuing 'sooner rather than perfect,' earning the right to exist by charting a pragmatic course and having something to show for it.

"So at the end of these 1,000 days what has changed? Well in 1,000 days we, each of us individually, will be here because we want to be. The pulse rate of the organization has quickened. The acceptable standard of performance has risen. The error rate has dropped. Decisions result from analysis not opinion. Effectiveness counts more than seniority. We like the people we work with. We can depend on each other as we work to a common set of clear, defined, stretching – but achievable – 90-day deliverables. We trust each other based on our experience of working with each other.

"But there is something else beyond all this. We have shown each other what happens when we pull together. We have realized that one plus one can equal three. We understand that we are interdependent. This has made our teamwork more effective – we are listening to each other, analyzing what we hear, checking, and then taking action. We are developing a sense of balance between working for today and learning for tomorrow. We are recognizing that what we put into the organization will be reflected in what the organization achieves and in how we are rewarded. When something is being developed, changed, and implemented, we run as a project. When we are chasing new business, somehow, we are all aware of it, and we hunt as a pack. We now have a head office that feels more like a college library than a corporate bureaucracy; we have meetings standing up, we informally gather around open-plan tables, we pop round to see each other rather than sending an e-mail. We are on the move. We are constructive. We are optimistic.

"But smooth interfaces, effective products, excellent investment performance, fast decisions, competitive pricing and commissions, even financial strength, are just 'hygiene factors.' Our key differentiated product and service is The Plan From the Pru. The Plan From the Pru has transformed the way in which people think about their savings. Now they understand what they are doing. With the Plan From the Pru as their guide, they have set themselves financial objectives. We work relentlessly to simplify our products to ensure that our customers understand what they are buying, how the product works, what the promise is, what they can expect, and what they are risking.

"We have disregarded unnecessary processes, duplicate activities, restrictive bureaucracy, valueless overheads, pretentious practices; these will never have a place in our business. Grand offices, layers of management, ponderous meetings, lengthy decision making, hesitant procrastination, ineffective delegation, and the avoiding of individual responsibility have no place with us. But there is more to it than that, something more fundamental. Above all else we have worked, first and foremost, to ensure that our customers, in their old age, can afford to eat, to heat their homes, to take the style of holiday they are used to, to replace worn-out clothes, and continue to tend the garden they love and live in the home in which they are comfortable.

"Thus, the job we have chosen to do is among the most valuable in society. Doctors and priests, depending on your outlook, have more worthy roles in our community – they deal with our physical and spiritual well-being. We are the custodians of people's material well-being. We provide the foundation for a civilized society. Civilization, a society that can afford leisure, depends on a secure store for savings protected for the future. We provide that secure place. We have an obligation to perform at the highest possible level in every aspect of what we do. People trust us; we must be worthy of that trust. Prudential is a mighty business."

The second last paragraph already has a good deal of folklore around it. Wood has become well known throughout the company for touting "Helping Old People Eat" as the Pru's true calling or mission. While the conventional vision outlined at the head of this case remains, the far more unlikely sounding Helping Old People Eat (and the ensuing acronym HOPE) is striking a chord with an ever-increasing number of employees.

---

1. *What is the strategic value of Mark Wood and Prudential's story-telling approach outlined in this case?*
2. *What does the HOPE mission provide that the conventional Pru vision described at the beginning of the case does not?*

The power of the WEB

When Heinz Fischer arrived as head of human resources at Deutsche Bank he found that women accounted for fewer than one in six at the managerial level despite making up half the bank's workforce. Experience had shown him that companies that pursue diversity enjoy better performance, largely because their strategies subsequently reflect a cross-section of society rather than just one particular category and because putting different types of people together in teams often sparks creative solutions to business problems. So, Fischer invited 30 women employees to a workshop to discuss the obstacles they faced. The most critical barrier the women identified was the lack of informal networks of the type used by men, such as the golf course or the drink after work.

Pilar Conde, a Managing Director at JP Morgan, claims that networking is a key in any individual or group achieving their goals. He says that people often mis-understand networking: "They ask: 'Why do I need a network to be successful? If I do my job well, my manager will recognize me.' But everyone in a position of power has used a network." Women, or any under-represented group, will thus find it difficult to influence agendas as they emerge from the lower levels of an organization, or steer strategies as they are handed down from the top, because they lack the "common-interest" networks drawn upon by others in corporations to grease the wheels. Directly confronting these networks can often create counter-productive "underground" forms of resistance. So, perhaps the best solution is to form alternative networks.

In response to the problems outlined by Heinz Fischer above, Deutsche Bank encouraged the establishment of a "women's network" within the European arm of the company. This network then decided to extend its web beyond the organization. A group of the bank's female executives organized and hosted, and Deutsche Bank funded, the first Women in European Business (WEB) Conference in Frankfurt in March 2000. Four hundred delegates were anticipated; more than 1,000 women attended. The success of this conference led to it becoming estab-lished as an annual event sponsored by Deutsche Bank.

Deutsche Bank now links WEB to a collection of other women's networks. Within the firm, operating across the three main centers of London, Frankfurt, and New York, is the Global Partnership Network for Women (GPNW). This network actually began life in 1991 when it was established by a group of women at the American organization Bankers Trust prior to it becoming part of the Deutsche Bank group. GPNW sponsors an American equivalent of the WEB conference: Women on Wall Street (WOWS), something that Deutsche Bank was very keen to continue. WOWS is now attended by over 2,000 men and women annually, from across the Deutsche Bank group and beyond, from all parts of the wider business community.

Speaking about a recent WOWS conference, Karen Meyer, Head of Global Diversity at Deutsche Bank, claimed that it "demonstrated the company's commit-ment to providing forums which foster the personal and professional development of women, where they can have access to role models, learn from peers, and con-tinue to build their professional networks."

Deutsche Bank sees these developments as being very good for business. Annette Fraser, the Chair of the Executive Committee organizing the 2003 WEB conference and an executive with Deutsche Asset Management, noted that while the growth of these networks is important to women with the bank "it is also good for Deutsche Bank itself, which is now seen as a leading promoter of diversity in the workplace." And the bank seems to be able to back this promotion up: Deutsche Bank was named one of the top 100 companies for working mothers by *Working Mother Magazine* in 2002, and received a score of 100% in the Human Rights Campaign (HRC) Corporate Equality Index 2003 report.

1. *What strategic benefits might accrue to the members of this network?*
2. *What strategic benefits might accrue to Deutsche Bank through its involvement in developing and helping to maintain this network?*
3. *Can you foresee any negative effects that might emerge as WEB becomes more established? How would you manage these?*

Breathing fresh air into business

With 4 years' experience as a "coolhunter" (young people picked out by companies to tell them what will be "cool" next year), Matt Hardisty was looking for a new challenge, one that would allow him to explore his interest in the creativity beginning to be showcased over the internet. He took a year out to do a MA in Creative and Media Enterprises, during which time folkdevil.com was born. Matt was awarded a distinction for his Masters and, while continuing to guide folkdevil's organic growth, he joined Naked Communications as a strategist. Quick to spot Naked and folkdevil's rapid development, *Campaign* magazine listed Matt as one of its key "faces to watch" in 2001. Matt explains the symbiotic relationship between the styles of thinking that Naked and folkdevil promote:

"Configuring yourself to sell things used to be about defining a demographic or target segment, developing something that provided the general function that that group wanted, then using economies of scale to reduce costs, and then pushing the product on to those people through one or two static channels. But Britain's cities have actually been awash with a new mode of marketing in the creative industries for quite some time. The division between the traditional creative disciplines of music, clothing, and art are dissolving for branded *association*. Age is no longer considered to be such a big measure, as the word *youth* becomes blurred as we progress to targeting by *lifestyle*. Brands have become *cultures*, creating immersive environments through which consumers can experience a brand's values. There has been an explosion in new, innovative types of channels. And this diminishing of traditional boundaries has led to a new creative fusion. Beyond bland "sponsorship" and "promotional activities," new processes of *promotional symbiosis* have evolved whereby particular relationships are developed by networking together a blend of micro and macro channels to convey a particular set of values or *mythology* about a brand. An example of this new phenomenon can be seen in the fashion brand, skim.com. The label's clothing featured a unique e-mail address on each garment facilitating passers-by to contact the wearer in an attempt to traverse the on- and the off-line realms and this helps build a particular sense of what skim is about."

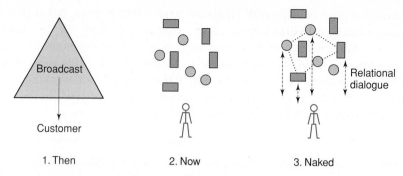

Figure 6-6.1 Pictorial representation of Naked's concept

"It's all about how hard you push the boundaries," Matt explains. "And what we try and do at Naked is to help our clients think of themselves as not contained within traditional boundaries or channels. We network a web of channels into a dynamic family that helps develop a complex relationship with customers to convey a sense of something truly different in order to capture people's attention." Figure 6-6.1 shows how Matt draws pictures to convey the concept.

One of Matt's latest projects for Naked involved connecting Reebok, local radio stations, skateboarding and bmx communities, various DJs, and people who wanted to have a laugh playing football, for "The Sofa Games." Inspired by Reebok's recent ads featuring underactive people being eaten by sofas, this involved temporarily transforming an urban area of Dublin into a playground featuring old sofas as goals for five-a-side football and "urban furniture" for skateboarders and bmx-ers, surrounded by "chill-out lounges" serving drinks and food, all "cushioned by an Irish backdrop of progressive nu-skool beats" – according to the website.

This way of "connecting" and building links or a "relational dialogue" is very similar to that which inspires Matt's work with folkdevil. Here, partners are helped to think of their organizations differently: not as isolated fragments or separated stand-alone monoliths, but independent local units that are at the same time interconnected across traditional boundaries with other like-minded customers and organizations. Indeed, Matt claims that the distinction between "customer" and "company" and "competitor" is becoming increasingly irrelevant as things fragment:

"The internet is enabling a new entrepreneurial spirit to emerge. No longer marginalized to the classifieds, fly-posting, or word-of-mouth communication, new local start-ups can now focus on particular niche characteristics and personal identities and then extend beyond their immediate geography and embrace a 'global' audience. But, for all the cries of an emerging egalitarian environment (coupled with IBM's visions of 'Mom and Pop' stores selling olive oil from remote parts of Italy to 'cash rich, time poor' consumers in urban areas), the reality is that while these 'Folkdevils' [Matt's word for these new little 'global' players] are good at producing innovative content, they are bad at consolidating this into a viable ongoing organization. These independent enterprises behave like a quasi-cottage industry – 'folksy' – which is good, but also introverted and detached. A cross-cutting collaborative network promoting independent talent is needed. To allow 'folkdevils' to progress beyond 'contacts' and facilitate business on a global basis, a new empathetic resource is needed to enable their dreams to become a reality – a 'virtual cultural intermediary' – to

174

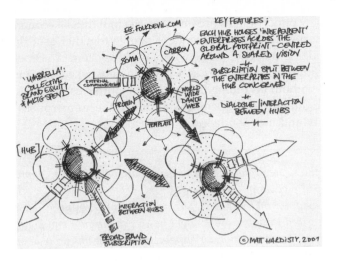

Figure 6-6.2

compensate for the increasing fragmentation in the workplace, and a means through which productive exchange can take place. That's where folkdevil.com comes in."

One way that folkdevil.com "comes in" is through an individualized mapping technique. Matt explains this while free-handing a configuration of identities that he has been working on recently (see figure 6-6.2):

"Here you've got a radio station, a ticket seller, a record label, an info-website and a couple of clothing labels. They share what we call the same *tribal frequency*, so they benefit by linking their marketing spends and subsequently developing a collective brand equity. But they all stay independent, which is what they're into it for. Collectively they hook into other internet sites and channels that help convey their *tribal freq.*, while these sites and channels also gain by association while staying independent and creative. Drawing things in this way helps them see how they can change with the new environment, keeping what they like about their histories – their independence and creativity – and growing for the future."

The recently launched "Reading Room Media Network" provides an example of the independent/co-joined model that Matt and folkdevil help develop. The Reading Room Media Network's organic sites are a showcase for independent British talent – from record labels to filmmakers – while also providing credible content for the astute cultural consumer. Not only do the sites provide independent lifestyle brands (with little budget) with the ability to reach larger audiences, they also allow a marketer wishing to target a "fiber-optic" audience the chance to communicate in a credible fashion across a previously elusive network of channels.

Matt believes that these united folkdevils are breathing a breath of fresh air into business: "They are stamping out the earlier apathy of Generation X and the British condition of it being a crime to take anything too seriously." Moreover, more traditional businesses must similarly rethink the way they perceive themselves as being configured. "There is now a real need for many organizations to fragment and focus on particular vibes while sharing information and ideas about their often-common customers, and begin to collaborate and co-evolve in order to exploit the new opportunities presented by the multimedia economy," says Matt. "With central 'sites' holding independent people together as a fluid entity," he explains, "the idea is that enterprises within the ecosystem can benefit from shared traffic across different ecosystems in a globally networked environment. So that they can grow without becoming the sort of monolithic corporations that, by their nature, dull the things that the people who started these enterprises are passionate about: creativity and independence."

1. *Outline the strategic advantages of the "relational dialogue" approach outlined in the third picture in figure 6-6.1.*
2. *Draw a diagram that shows the greater range of **resources** that the organizations described in figure 6-6.2 might be able to tap into and how they are networked together. What superior **capabilities** might this provide that could give little "folkdevil" networks like this a **competitive advantage** over bigger more established companies?*
3. *How might bigger companies also seek to learn from what Matt and Naked and folkdevil.com are advocating in this case?*

Practice above content

While we often tend to focus on the explicit outcomes or content of strategy, much of the value in developing strategy comes as people engage in the process of strategy making, articulating, challenging, and adjusting our views as we communicate with others. The three examples below may seem disappointing in terms of the outcomes or impure in terms of the application of theoretical frameworks, but from a practice perspective they can be seen as interesting success stories.

* * *

In March 2001, a spokesperson for the American Association for the Advancement of Science's (AAAS) campaign for an oath to set global ethical standards for scientists announced that they were "dropping the future pursuit of it." It wasn't so much a lack of interest in its pursuit or failing to see it as an important issue that had brought things to a halt, as the inability of the many bodies concerned to agree the wording of a common code. Having collected 101 different proposed or existing codes of ethics from science groups worldwide, Vivian Weil, director of the Center for Study of Ethics in the Professions at the Illinois Institute of Technology, told AAAS members at a recent meeting in San Francisco that agreeing a common oath that could be practically applied was proving to be a problem.

Interest in a common pledge, seen as the scientist's equivalent of the Hippocratic oath, was kindled by Sir Joseph Rotblat advocating such an oath during his Nobel peace prize acceptance speech in 1995. He suggests that "[such] a pledge is becoming more important because the impact of science, with the cloning of humans and genetic modification of food, is becoming so much more direct."

Subsequently, Rotblat has admitted that the ongoing disagreement over such an oath or common code was a big blow.

However, the cloud hanging over the scientists' common code may contain silver linings. Rotblat is heartened by the grass-roots support for the oath that had emerged from young scientists keen to embrace such a standard. And, as one executive director of a leading scientific research society reasoned: "While I'm skeptical about the practicality of an oath that can be widely applied, the spirit of the discussions that led toward an oath may be more important than the oath itself."

* * *

The young lieutenant of a Hungarian detachment in the Alps sent a reconnaissance unit into the icy wilderness. It began to snow immediately, and unexpectedly continued to snow for two days. The unit did not return. The lieutenant feared that he had dispatched his own people to their death. However, on the third day the unit came back. Where had they been? How had they made their way? "Yes," they said: "We considered ourselves lost and waited for the end. We did not have any maps, compasses or other equipment with which to ascertain our position or a probable route out. But then one of us found an old tattered map in a seldom-used pocket. That calmed us down. The map did not seem to quite fit the terrain but eventually we discovered our bearings. We followed the map down the mountain and after a few wrong turns eventually found our way."

The lieutenant borrowed the map and had a good look at it. "This isn't a map of the Alps," he said. "It's a map of the Pyrenees."

* * *

Power's, a pub/restaurant group, has grown fast through successful acquisitions. It now owns many big-name brands, including Mr. Beef, M.J.'s, and Pizza Court. To aid the company's coordination as it grows, managers need to think through how the various elements of the growing company relate to one another. The diagram in figure 6-7.1 and dialogue below came about as the result of encouraging them

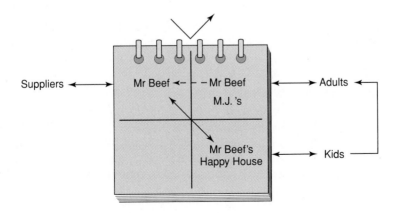

Figure 6-7.1 Analysis of Mr. Beef

to use Michael Porter's classic strategy frameworks to express their own ideas about where the company was going. The diagram, a conglomeration of Porter's Generic Strategy Matrix, Five-Forces of Industry, and Value Chain, is one group's analysis of Mr. Beef and the presentation and debate that followed.

Manager 1: "Basically we saw Mr. Beef as being a family pub/restaurant, but a bit better than the competition – differentiated. However, over time this has been kind of forgotten. It's been easier to focus on cost reduction and it's drifted back into the broad-cost segment. The interesting progression is the development of Mr. Beef's Happy House [Mr. Beef's Happy House is a children's restaurant/playground that had been established within a number of Mr. Beef pubs]. These have proved really popular and are differentiated and focused on kids, obviously. So, what do we do? Perhaps we need to revamp Mr. Beef and move it into the differentiated end again?"

Manager 2: "Maybe, but there it's almost directly competing against M.J.'s."

Manager 1: "And surely Mr. Beef is such a big chain now that we should be in the broad-cost segment. If you add in that part of Porter's Five-Forces of Industry, that's where we can really exercise power over suppliers by using our size as a buying strength."

Manager 2: "But what about the disparity between Mr. Beef and Mr. Beef Happy House? If we continue with your bringing in the Five-Forces and look at the other side of things, buyer power, we all know that for family pub/restaurants it's kids who often make the buying decision. We can't afford to damage that link by letting Big Steak Wacky Warehouse slide the way of Mr. Beef."

Manager 3: "Sure, but if we realize the difference and the relationship between the two then surely we can benefit at both ends of the value chain – a strong link into key suppliers and a key hook into a special type of buyers."

Manager 4: "Yeah, in a way, if we could do this, and get the best of both sides, then this could be a source of competitive advantage hard to replicate. It would create a real barrier to new entrants up at the top of the box there."

1. *Although the scientists did not arrive at an official "all-purpose" oath, what learning and social capital might have accrued from the process of seeking one?*
2. *Despite this seemingly negative outcome, can you develop a strategic story based on these events that provides a positive message about the value of what members of the AAAS do?*
3. *How did the change in the strategy-making process help the soldiers get down the mountain even though their map was flawed?*
4. *Even though they did not apply Porter's frameworks in the manner that they are generally presented, why might Power's managers have benefited from the practice they engaged in as described above?*

Emergence

In the 1970s, senior executives of the Japanese manufacturer Honda decided to investigate the possibility of entering into the US market for motorcycles. Their detailed strategic analysis and research extrapolations of the US market led Honda to leave behind the little bikes it produced and sold in Japan (American motorcycle riders rode much bigger bikes) and develop bigger American-style bikes for the US market. But Honda's big bikes flopped. American motorcyclists could already buy big bikes: American companies like Harley-Davidson, that enjoyed great customer loyalty, produced them. Honda was about to pull out of the US but then people who had never thought about riding a motorcycle before started asking Honda's couriers where they could get one of the little 50cc bikes that they were riding around US cities to make deliveries. (Honda had shipped out a small number of these Japanese-style bikes for its employees but had no intention of selling them in the US.) After this news filtered up the company, however, Honda decided to take a final crack at the market with its small bikes. People who were not traditional motorbike riders could see themselves using this much smaller, more fuel-efficient, and less intimidating mode of transport. Once these new riders were introduced to motorbike riding by Honda, and gained confidence with them, opportunities began to emerge to sell them bigger bikes. And, over time, Honda established itself as the leading motorcycle brand in the world's biggest market.

3M's most famous product – Post-It Notes – did not come about through the senior management team and its advisors doing an industry analysis or finding out what the gaps in the market were. It emerged in the mind of a research scientist who took advantage of the long-standing 3M policy of allowing research staff to spend 15% of their time on developing their own ideas and projects. In this time, the researcher in question had been experimenting with glues, unsuccessfully (they didn't stick very well). However, a bit of lateral thinking turned the failed glues into Post-It Note prototypes – and the rest, as they say, is history.

---

1. *Where did Honda and 3M's winning strategies described above come from? How is this different from the classical view of strategic planning?*

2. *What skills do managers need to enable winning strategies to **emerge** in organizations?*

3. *In reality, do you think that the best strategies emerge from the bottom of an organization, are instilled from the top down, or both?*

4. *Briefly describe how Honda's or 3M's approaches could be evaluated according to each of the four dimensions of Kaplan and Norton's balanced scorecard.*

5. *Although they were not explicitly following a balanced scorecard approach when developing the strategies described here, do you think their implicit balancing of short-term financial performance with other aspects had an influence on their development of the approaches outlined above?*

These days, building the best server isn't enough. That's the price of entry.

Ann Livermore, CFO Hewlett-Packard

This land is me
rock, water, animal, tree,
they are my song.

Aboriginal tracker in the 2002 Australian film One Night the Moon
by Kev Carmody

In the late 1990s, many companies, like Hewlett-Packard, embarked on extensive campaigns to promote their distinctive corporate character as a reflection of the "land" or geographical setting from which the company emerged. HP put considerable effort into understanding and promoting the values of its founders, Bill Hewlett and Dave Packard, their individualistic pioneering spirit, and the company's subsequent history of significant innovation. HP articulated what it termed "the rules of the garage" – part an expression of the beliefs shared by Bill and Dave as they toiled away in their little inventor's shed in Palo Alto, California, and part a devotional rallying call to today's stakeholders in the company's fortunes. These "rules" were boiled down to one underlying characteristic – "Invention." Subsequently, the company has ensured that wherever one sees the HP symbol, it stands upon the word "Invent."

Why would a company that essentially makes and sells technology put so much effort into celebrating its mythology? The answer, to a large extent at least, lies in the quotation from HP's CFO above. Thanks to the increasing speed with which knowledge flows, the increasing ease with which the technical aspects of a company can be reverse engineered and copied, and the increasing homogeneity of the processes of corporations and their consultants, everybody's technology is good: a "first-rate server" just gets you into the game. So, what else can a company utilize to make it stand out as an entity that people choose to do business with over its competitors? Not only is HP's character a key point of differentiation (in that it is unique to it), this character also is inimitable (in that it, unlike technology, cannot be copied by its competitors). For this reason corporate character has become a key element in the development of a sustainable competitive strategy for many corporations in the 21st century.

There are many definitions of character in the *Oxford English Dictionary*, but the following two best describe this chapter's focus. The first stems from natural science: "character is the aggregate of the distinctive features of any thing; its *essential peculiarity*." The second connects with the peculiarly human aspects of character: "the sum of the moral and mental *qualities* which *distinguish* an individual or a race; the *individuality* impressed by nature and habit on man or nation."

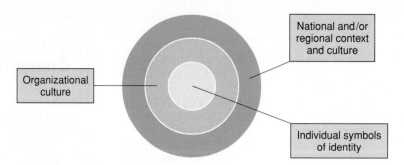

Figure 7.1 Layers that contribute to corporate character

The character, of an individual or an organization, is deeply rooted and multi-layered. Figure 7.1 separates out some of the layers that create a distinguishing corporate character. We can apply this simple model to better understand why the HP character described above works. Moving from the outer layer in, we can say that HP's character draws on the national context of the USA. This is the **country** in which the **context** that led to the computer industry, as we know it, emerged. HP's character draws on US cultural traits, such as individualism and entrepreneurial spirit. It also connects to California's **regional culture**, something that one might characterize as a combination of a pioneering spirit, a hard-work ethic, and a free-thinking nature. HP has an **organizational culture** built around the fact that it is a long-established player in the industry, with a history of being an innovator. And, it seeks to enact an **identity** personified by the spirit of Bill and Dave, in a garage, working hard, challenging conventions, and doing things that people thought couldn't be done. The sum of these essential qualities is something truly peculiar to HP and hence should distinguish the company and its strategic decisions from others.

This chapter examines the importance of national culture and context before looking deeper at the elements that constitute an organization's culture. It then reviews how thinking of corporations as if they were individuals with unique characters can also add value to any strategy-making process.

National Culture and Context

Perhaps the best-known framework for analyzing how a nation's context, and the character that stems from it, can influence a region's natural competitive advantage is The Porter Diamond.[1] Michael Porter developed the Diamond in the late 1980s as a means of better understanding why, for example, the best watches seem to come from Switzerland, the biggest computer companies are American, or the best equipment for racing yachts might be made in New Zealand. He claimed that the answer lay in distinctive background provided by the interrelationships between the following four contextual elements. The Diamond examines (1) the context for firm strategy and rivalry (vigorousness of competition), (2) the demand conditions (whether customers are sophisticated and demanding), (3) the factor conditions (quality and cost of factors such as labor, natural resources, capital, and physical infrastructure), and (4) the presence of supporting industries (is there a critical mass of capable suppliers?). These made up the four points of the Diamond, to which Porter added the outlying, but important, elements of (1) government strategy (government can influence all four of the major factors listed above through subsidies, education policies, regulation of markets and product standards, taxes, and antitrust laws) and (2) chance (which can nullify advantages and bring about shifts in competitive position through new inventions, wars, shifts in world markets, and political decisions).

Using Porter's framework, table 7.1 offers an explanation of why many of the world's great beers come from Belgium. The constellation of these elements, which have emerged over time to provide the context within which Belgian brewers operate, is unique and inimitable. No other region's contextual background provides quite the same positive environment for making great beer.

Table 7.1   The context underpinning Belgium's competitive advantage in brewing

Factor conditions	Belgium's breweries lie close to some of the best natural ingredients for beer, while long established apprenticeships and training programmes, combined with the traditional high status afforded brewers in Belgium, ensures a good supply of quality human resources.
Demand conditions	Beer is Belgium's national drink and consumers are consequently knowledgeable and discerning. They will not tolerate bad beer.
Related and supporting industries	As mentioned above, Belgium's breweries benefit through close proximity to quality hop farmers. Moreover, with the major cost involved in selling a bottle of beer being distribution, it helps that Belgium is a hub for many major distribution networks and companies.
Firm strategy, structure and rivalry	There are perhaps more breweries per capita in Belgium than in any other country. While they are all fiercely competitive, they also have a history of collaborating when in the collective best interests.
Government strategy	The Belgian Government has supported the beer industry throughout many centuries. It has supported the industry's training programs and its low-excise regime for beer makes it very inexpensive in Belgium relative to other parts of the world. More recently, the Belgian Government has actively sought to become the center of the European Union.
Chance	Belgium happens to be well placed as a lynchpin between major powers such as France and Germany (see above) and at the center of the world's greatest beer-consuming bloc – Europe.

While the elements that make up the Porter Diamond reflect the harder side of corporate character, we might gather the softer, but no less influential, aspects of character under the heading of *culture*. There have been innumerable attempts to define culture. These range from Geert Hofstede's austere "culture is the collective programming that distinguishes one group of people from another" to Linda Smircich's plainly put "culture is the specific collection of values and norms that are shared by people in a corporation that control the way they interact with each other and with stakeholders outside of the corporate body."[2] However, it is unlikely that any definition has approached the clarity of the colloquial expression that culture is "the way things are done around here."

The focus on how culture can differentiate what a corporation does entered the mainstream strategy literature in the late 1970s, as people began to question what had enabled Japanese companies to emerge as such a potent force. Books appeared urging Western managers to embrace Japanese management practices such as *kaizen* (continuous improvement) and quality circles (and, subsequently, total quality management), approaches that had emerged out of a distinctive Japanese way of thinking and doing: a way that emphasized community, harmony, slow patient increments (rather than "quick fixes"), and a long-term view.

Perhaps the most widely used framework for understanding culture – the "Seven S's" – was developed at this time (see figure 7.2). Hatched by four McKinsey & Co. consultants (Anthony Athos, Richard Pascale, Tom Peters, and Robert Waterman), the 7-S's formed the basis of Pascale and Athos's book, *The Art of Japanese Management*. This argued that whereas US managers focused on *strategic* plans, organizational *structures*, and *systems* of control, Japanese managers embraced the "soft S's" – a concern for *staff, skills* development, their corporations' *style*, and greater or *superordinate* goals (which would later be rephrased as "shared values").[3] This, according to Pascale and Athos, was why Japanese companies were more successful than those from other nations.

Beyond contrasting American and Japanese cultural practices, Dutch academic Geert Hofstede examined the cultures of 53 different nations and categorized

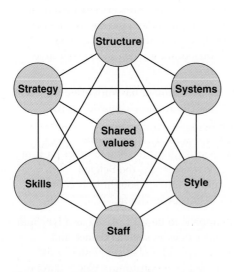

- **Strategy:** What it is and how is it implemented?
- **Structure:** How is the company organized? What processes does it employ to get things done?
- **Systems:** How the company operates on a day-to-day basis.
- **Skills:** Core competences of the organization vs. key competences.
- **Staff:** "Demographic" description of important personnel categories within the firm.
- **Style:** Symbolic behavior of management – what does it consider important?
- **Shared values:** Company culture and corporate identity.

Figure 7.2 McKinsey's 7-S framework

them according to five dimensions[4] of: (1) power-distance, (2) individualism versus collectivism, (3) masculinity, (4) uncertainty avoidance, (5) long-term versus short-term orientation (these are described more fully in the following chapter, Crossing Borders).

These different orientations can be seen to affect many things that relate to strategy: from the type of management theories that one nation develops or favors (Hofstede was particularly concerned to show how American management theories might not apply outside of the US) to the way staff behave and develop and implement strategy, to a particular nation's customer values. Herein lies an explanation why a company's advertising for cooking products will show male and female partners cooking together in the Netherlands while the same ads are adapted to feature two female friends in Germany;[5] and why some argue that Marlboro cigarettes were more successful in Asia than Camel because the Camel symbol represented a lonely figure whereas the Marlboro cowboy was implicitly part of a group.[6]

While many interesting discussions have stemmed from this sort of analysis of national character and how it affects corporations, there is always the danger that simple categorizations lead to stereotypes and, subsequently, inaccuracies. To better understand character one must look deeper at organizational particularities.

Organizational Culture

Building on the success of Pascale and Athos's application of the 7-S's to Japanese management, Tom Peters and Robert Waterman used the framework as a basis for learning about the characteristics of high-performing American firms. Peters and Waterman found that successful US firms also emphasized the softer S's, particularly **shared values**.[7] In their now famous book, *In Search of Excellence*, they claimed that these firms tended to exhibit a particular type of culture, namely one that exhibited eight traits: a bias for action; being close to the customer; valuing autonomy and entrepreneurship; emphasizing productivity through people; being hands-on and value driven; sticking to what they know best; having a simple structure and lean workforce; and being simultaneously centralized and decentralized.

Another good framework for analyzing the components of a corporate culture is "the cultural web" developed by Johnson, Scholes, and Whittington (see figure 7.3). By describing the distinctive rituals, stories, symbols, power, and organizational structures, and control systems that contribute to the organization's paradigm (or world-view), one can more clearly characterize an organization's culture.[8]

The "symbols" of an organization are broad ranging (e.g. from the clothes staff wear, the logo or brand, to the buildings the organization is housed in) but particularly telling with regard to culture. For example, much has been written on how the dominant architecture of a period characterizes the sensibilities of a particular society, and for organizations it is no different: *architectural style is the organization itself.*

Sir John Harvey-Jones, the famous British television management guru, exclaimed an experienced observer of business can tell a great deal about the character and ethos of these firms, their aspirations and values, their culture, just by looking at,

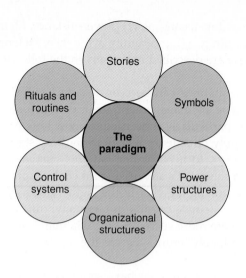

Figure 7.3 The cultural web (Source: Johnson, Scholes, and Whittington (2005))

and entering, their premises. For instance, if one went to almost any town in the UK during the early 1990s, bank branches were grand affairs located in prestigious high street positions, with ornate stone exteriors and beautiful interiors of rose wood paneled counters, marble floors, and expensive brass fitments, all symbolizing permanence, prosperity, and importance. If one looks at the stunning new steel, chrome, and glass buildings in London today, many occupied by professional service firms, a strong message is being stated.

Peters and Waterman concluded that "without exception, the dominance and coherence of culture proved to be an essential quality of excellent companies," a finding endorsed by Collins and Porras's more recent investigation in their book called *Built to Last*, which went on to claim that the key factor in sustained exceptional performance is a culture so strong that it is not dissimilar to a "cult."[9] However, a culture this tightly knit can be both a curse as well as a blessing. While a strong unified culture can help people act quickly and efficiently, it can blinker companies from re-thinking their assumptions as the environment changes. IBM had a strong culture, and this strength contributed to the company-wide belief in the 1980s that desktop computers of the sort brought to market by Apple at that time would not catch on.

Unfortunately, while attempts to characterize organizational cultures turned over much fertile ground and caused a whole generation of managers to take what Peters and Waterman described as the "softer side" of strategy seriously, there did emerge a tendency to believe that there was one best type of culture. This led to attempts to ape Japanese approaches in the West, approaches that only made sense within the deep context in which they emerged, and attempts to try to insert new culture into organizations as one might insert a new carburetor or air conditioner into a car. Needless to say, most of these attempts failed, and when the new culture did take hold it generally succeeded only in making companies more like those they were competing with – something that goes against one of strategy's main tenets and runs contrary to what corporate character should bring to a business.

One means to move beyond this tendency to "sameness" when thinking of character is to use the analogy of an individual: to think of an organization as if it were a human identity, or a personality, having its own distinctive soul or spirit or ethos. This is particularly helpful because while we might tend to aggregate and look for *similarities* in national and organizational cultures, terms like "identity" focus us on *differences*. In this view, just as we all have – and should nurture – a unique personality, a distinctive spirit, or a particular ethos, so too should an organization.

This is the thinking underlining a chapter called "Strategy as Ethos" from the book *Images of Strategy*.[10] It argues that organizations will have a clearer understanding of the strategic choices they should make if they have a good understanding of the organizations' *ethos* (defined as "the characteristic spirit, prevalent tone of sentiment, 'genius' or distinctive spirit of a people or institution"). The concept is somewhat critical of stakeholder analysis' (see chapter 1) instruction to firms to outline their responsibilities to a vast array of constituents, claiming that this stretches organizations too thin and hamstrings decision making. Instead it applies Aristotle's view that the man who tries to be friends with all will not be seen as a friend by any, implying that organizations, like people, must make difficult choices about who and what relationships they really care about and prioritize.

People can develop a clearer understanding of their company's ethos by thinking of it as if it were a living being and by asking questions like:

- If our organization was a person, what sort of person should it be?
- What sort of characters would our competitors be?
- How are we different from those characters?
- What sort of actions would this different character, or ethos, encourage us to take in order to be consistent to ourselves?

The Expressive Organization, by Schultz, Hatch, and Holten Larsen, examines similar themes, claiming that successful organizations are those that understand their distinct identity and their brands but also regularly and consistently express their identities internally and externally through their actions.[11]

This analogy of the organization as an identity brings us into some fairly "soft" areas not usually considered part of the realm of strategy. But given that these sorts of ideas are increasingly being taken very seriously by those whose job it is to design products and services, strategists should be thinking this way too. Steve Jobs, founder of Apple, is often quoted as saying that "Design is the fundamental soul of a man-made creation [and] we don't have a good language to talk about this kind of thing." By implication, we need to think more about how we might express the soul of a product, a service, or the brand or company that delivers these things. A recent *Business Week* review of the automobile industry concluded that after a decade-long drive to close quality and engineering gaps, the number one selling point is now a car's particular personality and the emotional response that this elicits. Consequently, it claims that the number one *strategic* element in car manufacture is design.[12] As Jean-Marie Dru exhorts in the book *Disruption*, the brands that represent corporate identities must be

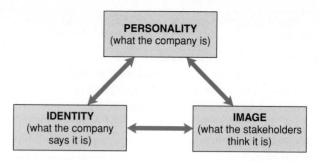

Figure 7.4 Elements of corporate reputation

understood not as "nouns but verbs. [Hence] Apple opposes, IBM solves, Nike exhorts, Sony dreams, Benetton protests . . ."[13]

Such notions bring strategy into close contact with marketing concepts like branding and image. However, it is important to recognize that while branding is an increasingly important strategic consideration, an effective corporate character must reflect a consistency between the external face and internal reality of an organization. One way of understanding how these elements can be joined *and* differentiated is shown in figure 7.4, taken from Davies and Miles's *What Price Reputation?*[14]

The Expressive Organization makes a similar distinction between image and identity, seeing the former as relating to external stakeholders, the latter to those within the corporation. But both works identify the key requirement as maintaining a good fit between a company's projected image and actual identity. These distinctions illustrate that, for a corporation's character or personality to effectively drive its image and strategic planning, it must be **authentic**. Lewis and Bridger make this point in their book *The Soul of the New Consumer*.[15] They explain that today's consumers are very savvy to corporations "selling their image." If a company is going to make claims about its character, they will only be respected and taken seriously if they are clearly linked to real places, times, and events. Hence, HP can claim the character described at the outset of this chapter, but another company could not do so to good effect.

This emphasis on the organization has encouraged some to even encourage applying the five human senses to better articulate an organization, product, or brand's character. In the book *Lovemarks*, Kevin Roberts explains why we should focus on understanding the distinctive taste, feel, sound, look, and even smell, of an organization to ensure we have a character that stands out. While this may sound far fetched, Roberts provides some compelling examples, such as the millions spent by car manufacturers trying to achieve the right feel of a leather trim, or the right sound a glove compartment or car door makes when it is opened and closed; Harley-Davidson's attempt to patent the sound that its motorcycles make (to prevent other firms replicating this key element of its competitive advantage); and Crayola's awareness of the importance of how its crayons smell (it's the 18th most recognized smell in America – coffee being first, peanut butter second – so Crayola will do anything to protect and preserve it). The importance of the connection between how products or services look and feel, how this links into corporate character, and, ultimately, strategic success is also increasingly plain to see. The UK Design Council recently produced a stock market index of firms that had won design awards. In the 10 years to 2004, shares in the 61 companies in their "design index" rose by 263%, compared with the FTSE 100's 57%.

Vision, Mission, and Values

The focus on seeing the firm as a living character has also encouraged the trend toward developing compelling and unique visions, mission statements, and values that guide and inspire strategy.

A vision articulates a view of what the company wants to achieve. Good visions generally adhere to **five principles**. They are: *brief* (not long-winded "hero sandwiches of good intentions," as Peter Drucker complained many vision statements were); *true to the particular company's focus and character; understandable* to all employees; *inspirational;* and *verifiable,* so that progress and ultimately success can be determined. Starbucks successfully drove its strategy with the vision: "2000 stores by the year 2000." Henry Ford's vision, published in 1907, is considered a classic: "To democratize the automobile. To build a motorcar for the great multitude . . . It will be so low in price that no man making a good salary will be unable to own one . . . The horse will have disappeared from the highways and the automobile will be taken for granted."

Mission statements should also adhere to the tenets above, apart from verifiability. This is because a mission is not so much a goal or a picture of where you want to get to in the future, but rather a philosophy or way of proceeding that is acted out day after day. Some classics include: Walt Disney's "To make people happy"; Marks & Spencer's "To continually improve the standards of working men and women"; or Wal-Mart's "Give ordinary folks the chance to buy the same things as rich people."

Corporate value statements have also become popular. In these, a firm lists a number of values that it will strive to uphold. Again, a firm's value statement should adhere to the five principles outlined above for a vision and they must be adhered to authentically – otherwise it will be fairly empty and meaningless. It is worth mentioning that Enron listed its values as communication, respect, and integrity.

In assessing all that has been written on corporate character and how it might be related to strategy, the key appears to be understanding the nature of an organization's character, its elements and where they come from, and how this might add to an organization's differentiated competitive advantage if properly harnessed. Strategists must realize that character runs deep and so be careful to avoid dealing with it mechanistically. Crucial in harnessing character for strategic advantage is attempting to nurture what is unique and inimitable about the organization and letting its character drive the corporation's strategy in a way that ensures that the company's unique individuality is authentically and consistently developed. Tina Brown, renowned magazine editor, expresses the importance of this "consistent individuality" in describing her key test for any magazine: "You should be able to throw a magazine on the floor at any page and know what magazine it is."

Given the growth of multinational organizations, and multibranded business, this is becoming increasingly challenging for strategists, as they must increasingly consider "families" of characters in addition to one unitary character that holds across their business. Then, too, they must integrate on some character dimensions and differentiate on others. However, perhaps the best aim in this situation, given what has been said above, is outlined by Trompenaars and Hampden-Turner in their book *Riding the Waves of Culture*, namely, to be sensitive to the character of each country, organization, or business unit, and integrate the best from each.[16]

What this chapter on Corporate Character has shown us, particularly when combined with the previous chapter on Living Strategy, is that companies are not as different from people as we might once have thought. They, like us, are social individuals.

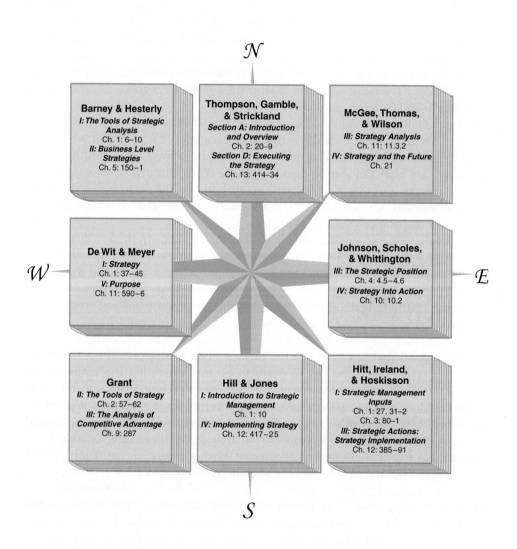

Pokemon versus The Little Engine That Could

Examining how the national context influences a company's strategic development has been commonplace since serious studies of strategy began. However, in 1992 Virginia Hill Ingersoll and Guy Adams published a paper that looked far beyond the sort of contextual factors generally seen as important environmental considerations. This paper, entitled "The Child is 'Father' to the Manager," argued that traditional national or regional tales shape the perceptions of children, and that these perceptions may continue to influence the way that adult managers perceive work, organization, and strategy.

For example, the focus in American children's stories on equal opportunity, clear links between individual attitude and effort and particular outcomes, and individual achievement and fulfillment against the odds through making tough choices and sacrifices, practice and hard work, underlie many widespread American preconceptions with regard to business. They also relate these preconceptions to what is often referred to as The American Dream. Stories from "The Little Engine That Could" (where a small steam train who is roundly dismissed and put down by his bigger peers reaches his particular "mountain top" – which is, in his case, actually steaming to the top of a particularly steep mountain – through secret training and single-minded determination) to the Rocky movies and other Hollywood fables sponsor and reinforce widely held American values.

Japanese children's stories generally have a very different focus. They tend to involve different characters bringing together particular skills to restore harmony by solving a problem that affects a whole community. Being an esteemed member of the team sees each character's status reinforced and enlarged. This is obvious in traditional Japanese fables, but it also underlies more modern Japanese tales. A recent article in *The Economist*, entitled "Pokemania v Globophobia," wrote of how Pokemon's "little monsters still teach distinctively Japanese values about the importance of team-building and performing your duties. The only way to succeed at the game is to cooperate with others – and the easiest way to fail is to neglect to care for your charges." German tales are different again, traditionally emphasizing the importance of sticking to the known path – dark things happen to those who wander off the beaten track, who go it alone into the forest. Mexican stories for children often emphasize the importance of having fun and Polynesian stories stress the importance of community and extended family.

What might all of this have to do with management and strategy? Well, take a popular management theory like Abraham Maslow's *hierarchy of needs*. Maslow's hierarchy, developed in the United States in the 1940s and 50s, will be familiar to any student of management or sociology and it is still taught as explaining the universal essence of human motivation. One can see how its scale of needs, starting with the satisfaction of basic physiological needs, such as food and water, and moving up to safety, belongingness, status, and finally self-actualization as the pinnacle (see figure 7-1.1) makes sense in an American context.

However, by focusing on the context set by children's stories, one can also see how such attitudes might be relative. Many people from Asian backgrounds, for example, accept the framework when it is taught to them, but will later confess to be perplexed by the idea that "self-actualization" could be more important than "status" within one's community. Polynesians might alternatively see

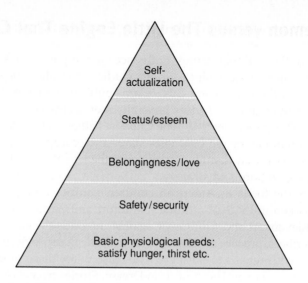

Figure 7-1.1 Maslow's hierarchy of needs

belongingness, particularly with regard to the extended family, as the pinnacle. The implications for how one might manage strategic human resources or goal setting in different social contexts, for example, in the light of this deep-set relativity, could be profound.

Perhaps the particular values inculcated through stories could also shed light on one of the most controversial assertions in strategic management in recent times. In a *Harvard Business Review* paper in 1996, American strategy guru Michael Porter argued that "Japanese companies rarely have strategies [as they] rarely develop a distinct strategic position." In 2001 Porter went further, claiming in the *Wall Street Journal* that the Japanese are inherently "bad at strategy." However, Porter's classic American view of strategy is one where the heroes are strong managers who take the lead in setting off down one path or another, a focus on cost or a focus on differentiation, for example. The Japanese view, on the other hand, is generally one that sees strategy as something that emerges slowly over time out of the collective interactions of many employees and which seeks a harmony between cost and quality rather than choosing a focus on one over the other.

1. *Do you think that the values promoted in different nations' or regions' popular tales could influence different views of strategy and what is important at work?*
2. *What other elements might influence national or regional character and, thus, views of strategy?*
3. *Can you relate the American children's stories described above to Hewlett-Packard's corporate character described at the beginning of this chapter?*
4. *Can you relate the different American and Japanese stories outlined above to Hofstede's cultural dimensions?*
5. *Which do you think is the better view of strategy: the mainstream American view, represented by Porter, or the Japanese view?*

◄◄◄ Pokemon versus The Little Engine That Could: Some Ideas . . .

1. *Do you think that the values promoted in different nations' or regions' popular tales could influence different views of strategy and what is important at work?*

While this is difficult to prove scientifically, the national stories do seem consistent with Hofstede's widely regarded analysis of national cultural differences, and they can be related to the conventional American view of strategy as being about vision, planning, and positioning and the mainstream Japanese view of strategy as a more communal and emergent practice. Thus, it would be useful for strategists to at least consider the influence that such traditional tales might have on national and thus corporate character. Indeed, it might be useful to think yourself about some of the popular children's tales in your region and how these might influence particular attitudes to work and strategy in later life.

2. *What other elements might influence national or regional character and, thus, views of strategy?*

Other elements that could influence national or regional character could be: traditional notions of asset ownership (e.g. individual or community based; communist or free-market); key historical events (e.g. wars; previous eras of strength or weakness); geographical and weather characteristics (e.g. mountainous or flat; arid or wet; hot or cool); beliefs about what's important in life (e.g. financial security or having a good time in the present; extended family or nuclear family); and views of time (e.g. punctuality). There might be others that you can think of.

3. *Can you relate the American children's stories described above to Hewlett-Packard's corporate character described at the beginning of this chapter?*

Yes, indeed, the Bill and Dave story is quite close to The Little Engine That Could or Rocky. A couple of nerds that one might expect not to succeed work hard, are resourceful, inventive, and determined, try and try again and succeed, bringing themselves great fame, fortune, and self-actualization. As explained at the beginning of this chapter, it is because the HP story, and thus character, fits so well with its regional and national value system that it is authentic and works extremely effectively.

4. *Can you relate the different American and Japanese stories outlined above to Hofstede's cultural dimensions?*

Three of Hofstede's cultural dimensions in particular can be related, with varying degrees of ease, to the American and Japanese stories. First, on individualism versus collectivism, they reflect Americans' propensity to value individual achievement and Japan's propensity to value communities working together. Second, on uncertainty avoidance, we might relate the desire to act individually to an American being more likely to take risks and the Japanese value of gaining consensus as related to being more risk averse. Third, although less obviously linked to the stories described, one could relate games like Pokemon's ongoing or never-ending character to a long-term focus and Rocky or Little Engine's focus on the achievement of a single goal to a more short-term orientation.

5. Which do you think is the better view of strategy: the mainstream American view, represented by Porter, or the Japanese view?

If one takes the themes in this chapter seriously, the answer must be both or neither. Their national characters shape the conventional Japanese and American views of strategy and one cannot say objectively, or with certainty, that one nation's character (and thus approach to strategy) is inherently better than another's. As the conclusion of this chapter explains, it is likely to be more advantageous for strategists to recognize the differences, understand from where these differences stem, see the merits of each, and be able to work with and apply them both where they are best suited to the situation.

► ► ►

Vikings and Anglos

A few years ago, we were discussing strategic decision making with the senior managers of a Swedish–British company (a steel-making organization). In many respects the merger was highly successful. They had joint HRM policies, had agreed on a common organizational structure, and had put in place a large number of cross-postings, with Swedish managers working in Britain and vice versa. However, it was when strategic decisions over what was core business and to what extent the firm should outsource key activities (for example) were presented that difficulties began to emerge.

The Swedes took significantly longer to get to the point of authorization than the British (generally, at least 6 months longer than their British counterparts). They spent longer negotiating and analyzing any problem (and usually identified a few additional problems in the process). "We like to achieve both high participation levels and consensus," one Swedish manager told us, "so we invest time in working the problem before we commit ourselves, then we can implement the decision quickly and without much further conflict or negotiation."

The British managers approached the same problems by seeking closure at every meeting. They wanted to narrow down the alternatives quickly so that the decision could be about a choice between a very small number of alternatives. The Swedes, on the other hand, specialized in opening up the number of alternatives at the same meetings and, in turn, raising fresh problems. This was one of the commonest causes of frustration and conflict between the British and Swedish managers. The tensions thus caused were a key factor in the eventual de-merger of the organization only a few years after the merger had taken place.

*　*　*

(left margin) CORPORATE CHARACTER

In addition to the obvious organizational culture clashes that can frustrate corporate mergers, the huge increase in cross-border M&A activity has highlighted how differences in national culture can also influence the way in which mergers unfold. This is not just a recognition of differences in language but an acknowledgement that, at a fundamental level, firms are embedded in their social contexts and this influences behaviors and assumptions over how business is done and for what purpose. Unfortunately, however, oftentimes (particularly in acquisition situations) managers tend to believe there is one right way of doing things, which tends to ignore the reality that the acquired or merged business is likely heavily customized to its operating environment. This is a prime reason for the fear felt by local employees and communities when foreign firms move in, and underlies the argument that cross-border acquisitions are corrosive of the local social and economic fabric.

A classic example of a post-merger situation that was heavily influenced by national differences is that between pharmaceutical firms Pharmacia of Sweden and Upjohn of the USA in 1995. Many rows ensued following this merger, with great falls in productivity, because of the Americans banning alcohol at lunchtimes and scheduling meetings during the Swedes' national holidays, which caused uproar. There was additional friction between the two decision-making styles as the Swedes preferred open and full discussion of issues at meetings to arrive at consensus whereas the Americans preferred short meetings to rubber-stamp decisions made informally in advance. As distrust between the two sides grew, a new corporate head office was established in London – supposedly neutral territory. But neither the Americans nor the Swedes would close their own "head offices" so the result was another layer of management that duplicated existing structures and increased inefficiencies – a somewhat ironic outcome when one of the primary reasons for the merger in the first place was to increase efficiencies.

1. *Use the Porter Diamond to outline why it might be that Sweden and the USA could have an international competitive advantage in the production of pharmaceuticals.*
2. *Use the Porter Diamond to analyze why a particularly successful industry that you are familiar with in your region might have an international competitive advantage.*
3. *Use Hofstede's dimensions to explain why the Swedes and the Americans sponsor such different corporate characters and perspectives.*
4. *What strategies would you have employed to make this merger run more smoothly?*

Sydney chainsaw massacre

In July 1986, two of Australia's best-known advertising agencies, Mojo and Monahan Dayman Adams (MDA), merged to form Mojo MDA. Mojo brought with it a reputation as the most dynamic "boutique" agency in Australia, while MDA was larger, more established, and more low-key. John Singleton, the well-known advertising man, described the merger as being akin to the Beatles combining with the post office.

Mojo's offices were in Paddington, entry being via a long, narrow, paved driveway lined with ferns, which then opened out into a large courtyard with willow trees and a fernery. The offices surrounded this courtyard. Those on the ground floor opened on to the courtyard, while those on the upper level opened on to a wisteria-covered balcony that overlooked it. MDA's offices were quite different, located in the concrete and glass high-rise area of North Sydney.

The agencies had also brought to the merger quite different staffing structures. Mojo's practice was to employ mainly highly paid senior staff who were given a high level of independence. They operated with a flat organizational structure of few hierarchical levels. This arrangement has been described as being "like freelancing under the umbrella of a company with the bonus of the companionship of like minds." MDA had a much more traditional pyramid structure of a few senior staff supported by large numbers spread over several hierarchical levels.

Mojo had a reputation for being undermanaged. For example, no one holding a position in the company had a clear job description specifying the duties and responsibilities for that position; there was no such thing as formal meetings, and the use of written memoranda was just not an acceptable practice. Some people, including many in Mojo, interpreted "undermanaged" to mean poorly managed. Consequently one of the attractions of the merger with MDA for such people was that MDA had a reputation as a well-organized "professional" company. For MDA, the parallel attraction was the highly regarded skills of Mojo's creative staff. Together they constituted the largest Australian-owned agency. Size was also a major consideration in the merger. Both agencies were proud of their independence from foreign ownership and wished to maintain this situation while also enlarging to a size where they felt they could successfully take on the advertising giants of New York and London.

Mojo MDA was building a new office at Cremorne which would house all its staff, but until that was completed it was decided that all creative staff (copywriters, art directors, and production staff) would move to Paddington while all management staff (the "suits") would be located at the North Sydney offices. One of the Mojo people required to move was its Finance Director, Mike Thorley, who moved to North Sydney where he was to work under Stan Bennett, MDA's Finance Director, who had been put in charge of finance for Mojo MDA. He describes the situation and what followed.

Thorley was one of the original Mojo employees and, as such, did not really think of himself as an employee, more as a partner. That he was not a partner was brought home forcefully at the time of the merger. Like the rest of the staff he had no warning that Mojo was going to merge with MDA and was shocked and angered by the announcement.

Thorley was referred to as the shop steward of Mojo: he looked after the staff, molded them into a team, and was at least partly responsible for giving the agency its character. However, after the merger he was banished to North Sydney to work for Stan Bennett. He did not go quietly.

To try to make the Paddington people feel at home in North Sydney at MDA, management installed a bar so the staff could follow their usual custom of a few drinks after work. But it was a modern black laminate structure running around the edge of the room. It looked like some up-market suburban pub. It was nothing like the solid white bench in the kitchen at Paddington and it seemed to Thorley that it summed up the differences between the two agencies: it was a symbol of how Mojo had let its people down. In an act of defiance he took a chainsaw to the work one morning and cut the bar in two.

---

1. *Draw two cultural webs, one outlining what you might think MDA's Rituals, Stories, Symbols, Power and Organizational Structures, and Control Systems were before the merger, the other doing the same thing for Mojo.*
2. *Having done this, how would you describe the **paradigms** of first MDA and then Mojo?*
3. *Knowing the deep differences in the characters of the two firms, how might you have sought to manage this merger?*

Virtue Finance: bore values

Recently, two academics were employed to conduct a review of a well-respected financial services company's core values. Virtue Finance had, like many of its competitors, recently sought to define its values and had employed leading consultants to help them. The seven agreed core values now adorned the company's walls and documents. The values were:

- creativity
- integrity
- respect
- commitment
- professionalism
- teamwork
- humor

Reviewing the value statements of the company's main competitors, the thing that immediately struck the academics was how similar they all were. They were quickly able to demonstrate that all of Virtue Finance's core values, apart from "teamwork" and "humor," were common across the lot, and that teamwork was still common to most. As the General Manager proclaimed on the academic's presentation of this finding: "If everybody has the same values then they are just hygiene factors. What we need is some added-value values."

To this end, the academics began by exploring its one somewhat unique corporate value – "humor" – and probing what Virtue Finance's people actually took that to mean, beyond the abstract adjective. Rather than focus on defining further nouns and verbs that expressed what humor meant in their company, they asked the staff to think of stories or anecdotes that expressed why and how humor mattered at Virtue Finance. The process teased a number of good stories, including this:

> "There is a particular broker who is a Spurs [Tottenham Hotspur Football Club] supporter who always calls us as opposed to our bigger rivals (even though he's advised otherwise) because he enjoys the mid-week banter with the people here who support other London teams. The banter usually takes longer than the business!"

This may not seem much. However, unlike the somewhat bald and sterile value statements common to many companies, it indicates several differentiating virtues. For example, the football banter story expresses the following:

• Virtue Finance is about developing personal relationships with its buyers and suppliers.
• Virtue Finance is about keeping staff for lengthy periods so it can develop these relationships.
• Unlike many of its competitors, Virtue Finance is not large and grey and all business.
• Not being the biggest is a weakness but Virtue Finance's smallness can be made a virtue or a strength if it works at it.

---

1. *Do you think the core values outlined by the consultants were authentic to Virtue Finance?*

2. *Do you think the core values outlined by the consultants are more "nouns" or "verbs"?*

3. *If you don't think they were authentic, or verbs, what would have led the consultants to suggest them? (You may want to refer back to chapter 2, Movers & Shakers for further guidance in answering this question.)*

4. *Why might the focus on the more unique values, like humor, and the active stories that can be related to these, have more power in terms of conceptualizing Virtue Finance's character and building strategies from this?*

From Jack Dee to 2-D and back

In the early 1990s Jerry Goldberg, Brand Manager at Scottish Courage Breweries, oversaw the appointment of an up-and-coming deadpan comedian Jack Dee as the spokesperson for John Smith's Bitter. "When John Webster at DDB [the advertising agency responsible for the campaign] suggested Dee, we weren't worried about whether he'd be big," reflected Goldberg. "The fact was that his personality suited the brand's 'no-nonsense' positioning." Five years later, the Jack Dee campaign, with 50 awards to its name, was widely regarded as having helped propel John Smith's from number 16 to number 4 in the UK beer market, toppling Tetley's from its market-leader perch in the Bitter segment for the first time. In December 1995, John Smith's sales were almost two percentage points behind Tetley's. Three years later, they were 4.5% ahead.

In 1998, Scottish Courage decided to replace Jack Dee as the personification of John Smith's.

The Jack Dee campaign had re-energized a beer with a long, solid history; a beer that had personified the honest, straight up, "no-frills, just good taste" ethos of a bitter first brewed in Tadcaster, Yorkshire 240 years ago. Now a new creative team from the agency GGT came up with *No-nonsense Man*, a cardboard cut-out synthesis of the essential "average bloke" pictured, in various guises, silently holding a pint of John Smith's. Jerry Goldberg's successor as Brand Manager explained that the new No-nonsense Man campaign would take "the 'no-nonsense' proposition one step further – our new frontman is the ultimate no-nonsense celebrity." Scottish Courage's Marketing Manager claimed, "No-nonsense Man aims to show the beer's down-to-earth positioning in an involving way. It conveys all the product values. It has the potential to become a cult star."

Even though Jack Dee was by no means everybody's favorite comedian, the momentum generated by the Jack Dee image had helped put John Smith's in a position where it looked well placed to leapfrog Guinness as the UK's third top-selling beer (after Carlsberg and Fosters). However, after the launch, a survey by *Campaign* magazine showed that 67 percent of people thought that the No-nonsense Man image was less effective than Jack Dee. A year on and the general consensus among industry and media commentators was that No-nonsense Man lacked the impact of the previous campaign and that, despite Scottish Courage not giving up on him, he was not catching on. No-nonsense Man had not become a cult star. John Smith's had not overtaken Guinness.

In a twist of fate, Jack Dee was chosen to host the British Advertising and Design Awards in 1999. One magazine's review of the night describes how "the audience loved it when he riffed about 'the days when John Smith's advertising used to win awards' and baited 'Anyone here from GGT?' with a 'You haven't won anything'."

Four lean years after ditching Jack Dee, Scottish Courage returned to the comedy circuit for a human face to replace No-nonsense Man. They selected the up-and-coming North-of-England comic Peter Kay, who, while different in many facets, in many ways represents a Jack Dee for the new decade. With No-nonsense Man folded away, Kay was shown taking a no-nonsense "blokey" approach to sports. The first ad, called *Ball Skills*, shows a group of young soccer players earnestly warming up by practicing their "keepy uppy" skills. After each player keeps the ball up for a time he effortlessly passes it on to the next man, until it reaches the solid figure of Kay – who promptly "wellies" the ball into a neighbor's garden while exclaiming "'ave it!" The ad closes with Kay overlooking the half-time orange segments and going straight for a can of John Smith's instead. "Research shows that John Smith's enduring association with a no-nonsense attitude plays a big part in its appeal to consumers and everything about Peter reflects this," said John Botia, the new Powerbrands Director at Scottish Courage.

The Peter Kay campaign returned the brand to the limelight. It has received a string of awards, including best British campaign of the year for 2002/3. The judges described the ads as "a brilliant campaign that has entered people's everyday lives while boosting sales and winning fans, plaudits, and column inches galore in the process." Analysts enthused that: "The Peter Kay campaign created massive awareness. It successfully communicated the brand's positioning in a way that

199

people could really engage with. As a result people feel closer to the brand, which ultimately has had a positive impact on sales . . . The TV commercials have been talked about in offices and pubs across the country, and sayings such as ''ave it!' have entered the everyday vernacular."

---

1. Use the 7-S framework with Jack Dee or Peter Kay at the center to represent John Smith's shared values, and then build up a picture of the corporate character of the brand by filling in the Style, Skills, Staff, Systems, Structures, and Strategy that these shared values should sponsor.
2. Why do you think that Jack Dee and Peter Kay seemed to be helpful in determining and developing the corporate character of this organization whereas the cardboard cut-out No-nonsense Man wasn't?
3. While Jack Dee and Peter Kay are popular comedians, they were probably not the most popular comedians or actors of their age. Would John Smith's have been even better served by choosing the most universally popular comedian's image to represent its identity?
4. Why does the association of an identity or character seem to work so well with certain products or brands? (Go online and check out the affection that Brazilians have for the turtle associated with the Brahma brand of beer, or that felt by Chileans for Becker Beer's "black sheep" for more ideas.)

Safer communities together

The New Zealand Police have a reputation as being one of the least corrupt law-enforcement bodies in the world. Up until the early 1990s, this simple ethos or mission guided them:

> "To work with the community to maintain the peace."

Generations of policemen and women took great pride in living up to this ideal.

However, as was often the way with public service organizations in the 1990s, the New Zealand Police Force was increasingly encouraged to become more "professional," to employ modern management thinking to bring it into line with approaches used in the private sector. The Force was urged to utilize external consultants to help it move closer toward "best practice," to develop more rigorous methods of managing performance, and be seen to be more "accountable."

One of the first services that such consultants generally offered was the creation of a new mission statement. Hence, after much development work, 1992 saw the launch of NZ Police's new mission:

> "To contribute to the provision of a safe and secure environment where people may go about their lawful business unhindered and which is conducive to the enhancement of the quality of life and economic performance."

Curiously, while the later statement is five times longer it says no more of substance than the first (indeed, by making no mention of how, or by what strategy, its stated aims should be achieved – contrast "To work with the community . . ." with "To contribute . . ." – it says less). Subsequently, the second statement is far less memorable and more confusing in terms of how it might be operationalized.

According to members of the Force it was not a great success. Many policemen and women on the ground now claim that it confused rather than guided them and admit that they paid little attention to the new mission, instead continuing to look up to the earlier statement and the ethos that it embodies. It is perhaps not surprising then that recent times have witnessed a re-appreciation of simpler times. The New Zealand Police's new motto is: "Safer Communities Together," which says more or less the same as "To work with the community to maintain the peace." However, it is even easier to paint on to the side of a police car!

---

1. *Why do you think the NZ Police's original mission might have been more effective than that developed by consultants in 1992? (Applying the five principles of a good vision might provide some interesting insights.)*
2. *Why might using consultants in this way actually diminish rather than add to an organization's character?*

Natural History

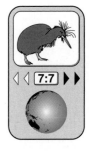

Natural History New Zealand (NHNZ) has been around for 30 years based at the "end of the earth" in one of the world's southernmost cities: Dunedin. Michael Stedman has been with the company for 21 of those years and CEO over the past decade.

Extinction was a real possibility just a few years ago. NHNZ was a department of Television New Zealand (TVNZ) and dying a slow death. It was making local programs about local wildlife – which it had by this point filmed many times over – aimed at a very small local audience (New Zealand's population is just over 4 million). When the previously state-owned TVNZ was privatized, it began to focus more on cost cutting. NHNZ was an obvious target. TVNZ put NHNZ up for sale, and much to its surprise it received ten offers for NHNZ from all parts of the globe.

In a decision that Stedman attributes to some strange sense of antipodean loyalty, an Australian company was TVNZ's preferred buyer. "But it was a company that we could have bought. They were too small. They couldn't have given us anything that we couldn't already give ourselves." Stedman told TVNZ executives that he would leave and take the rest of NHNZ's staff with him to set up their own company before he'd watch it be sold to the Australian buyer. TVNZ eventually relented and agreed to sell NHNZ to Stedman's preferred choice: Rupert Murdoch's Fox Corporation.

By combining its particular expertise with Fox's global empire of distributors, partners, and buyers, NHNZ has quickly become the world's second largest nature programming production company behind the BBC's Natural History Unit, something that Stedman is very proud of. "The reaction from the BBC when they heard that we were 'going global' was interesting. First they were amused. Then, when we didn't go under, they thought 'hmm.' Then when we started stealing business off them they got annoyed. Now they hate us. We steal a lot of business from them." Stedman is certain that NHNZ will overtake the BBC within the next couple of years.

More staff have been hired in Dunedin (NHNZ is Dunedin's largest employer after the local university and local government authorities). The audience for NHNZ's programs now spans 130 countries and is measured in millions rather than thousands, and, as it has spread its wings, it has picked up an increasing number of awards. Last year a series, co-produced with Animal Planet, called *Twisted Tales* (which traces the strange relationships between particular animals and humans) won an Emmy for Outstanding Achievement in a Craft in News and Documentary Programming for NHNZ writer-zoologists Ian McGee and Quinn Berentson. The next installment of the series has been nominated again this year. Berentson claims that the series was "quite easy to write because we both have twisted minds and we both think along the same lines."

Programs like *Twisted Tales* indicate a willingness to broaden NHNZ's scope beyond films of animals. This means moving, in Stedman's terms, into a number of "natural extensions." In the word of NHNZ's public relations and marketing people: "We don't just work with wildlife. Our experience extends into genres such as adventure, travel, and science, where we venture just as boldly to produce a variety of quality programming . . . We now bring our traditional pioneering spirit to our work in every continent and throughout the world's oceans in pursuit of compelling, often unique, stories." Particularly high hopes are held for a series entitled *Kill or Cure: The Bizarre and Curious History of Medicine*.

Beyond the access to new markets provided by Fox, to what does Stedman attribute NHNZ's global success? "Being from New Zealand is our biggest asset," Stedman explains. "Whenever we entertain potential clients we really play this up – New Zealand wine, New Zealand food . . . the whole thing." He reasons that people really like the association with New Zealand. It triggers positive associations for those who have had contact with New Zealand before, and a positive curiosity for those who have not.

NHNZ's corporate prospectus also highlights the importance of its Kiwi heritage. "NHNZ is founded on a passion for telling the stories of New Zealand's unique animals," it explains. Having been one of the first islands to have broken from the earth's primeval land mass, New Zealand's animals are certainly curious – a mix of prehistoric lizards and strange birds, many of which have evolved to the point of no longer being able to fly on account of their not having to share the land with mammalian predators not born before New Zealand was set adrift. While not as vibrant or spectacular, in plumage or deed, as their better-known Australian and Asian cousins, they are just as idiosyncratic.

Stedman believe there is a strong link between the nature of a company and the lay of its land: "this is [partly] why we get on so well with the Japanese – having grown up on a rugged isolated island pocketed with communities. They're always saying that we're like them, a bit quiet and introverted, relational, community oriented. They say we have very similar senses of humor." Japan is NHNZ's fastest growing market. "Australians on the other hand are much more extrovert; big and bold. It's a big wide-open land. I think this is why Murdoch gets a bum rap. He's no worse – and probably a lot better – than other media moguls, but he's out there being up-front and telling it straight. So others, particularly the British, label him a brash upstart Aussie . . . he he he [laughs], the British hate him."

NHNZ's corporate symbol and mascot, New Zealand's indigenous mountain parrot, the kea, also says much about the company's distinctive spirit. "[Our symbol has] been the kea for a long time now," Stedman explains. "We recently revisited it but we decided that we were pretty happy with it. I mean the obvious choice would have been a f***ing kiwi, but who wants to be a fat, dozy, dull, nocturnal, flightless bird." Examining the nature of the kea makes it easy to see why NHNZ prefers this association. It is a bird of paradox: "Hooligans, vandals, and killers; but superb parents and resourceful providers," says one source. "Endearing and mischievous," says another. The New Zealand Department of Conservation's website's entry on the kea (www.doc.co.nz) runs as follows:

> To survive in its harsh alpine environment, kea have become inquisitive and nomadic social birds – characteristics which help the kea to utilize and find new food sources. It is thought to have developed its own special character during the last ice age by using its unusual powers of curiosity in its search for food. Their inquisitive nature often causes kea to congregate around novel objects and their strong beaks have enormous manipulative power.

One suspects that Stedman may also take a perverse pleasure in stories of kea tormenting and often killing that other lumbering New Zealand stereotype – the sheep. "You know, a Swiss scientist has determined that on its level of intelligence the kea should be classified as a primate," he says proudly. This "intelligence" enables the development of sophisticated business relationships. "It is all about relationships," Stedman says, and coming from where NHNZ does provides a point of differentiation here as well.

He struggles to put his finger on what it is exactly: "New Zealanders seem to be unusually curious, and it's a genuine curiosity, but they seem to also be quite sensitive to cultural differences, so they don't push too hard. At the same time there's also an inquisitive naivety, but with brains." [I mention a statistic that Air New Zealand use a lot in their marketing – that New Zealanders on average travel more miles in their lifetime than people from any other nation. "Yes, that makes sense," he says.] However, what he is trying to say becomes clearer as he relates one story from his past and two from NHNZ's present.

"One of my early coups came when I happened to be in LA. I went to a just-released movie called *Star Wars* and thought it was great. I was in my twenties working on a children's television program for TVNZ and thought it would be great if we could do a feature on it, show a bit of footage, you know. So the next day I rang up the Marketing Manager of 20th Century Fox and we had a bit of a chat. I asked if he could let me have some stuff. He said "Sure" and asked where I was staying. The next morning, a huge package arrives, full of film, posters, all sorts of paraphernalia. My US friends asked how I'd managed to pull it off, so I told them that I called the guy up and asked. They would never have thought of doing that. I was too stupid to know that I shouldn't. But the guy didn't seem to mind. New Zealanders often don't feel bound by the 'can'ts' and 'shouldn'ts' that you find in other places.

"It's important to treat people how they like to be treated, but you have to make an effort to find out what this is. A few weeks ago I sent a fax to a Japanese manager and got nothing back. What do you do? Should I fax him again, should I phone him up directly? I mean, you don't want to be pushy. Anyway, I managed to get through to talk to his assistant and asked if I should send another fax. He said, 'Yes, keep sending faxes, he has a big pile of them on his desk; he likes getting them; sooner or later he'll come in and your fax will be on the top and he'll get back to you.' So, I kept sending the faxes and he did, eventually, get back to me.

"A lot of selling supposedly happens at these huge trade conventions. But after days of viewing and being sold to, a lot of people glaze over. You can sense this pretty quickly and if somebody's zombied there's not much point trying to sell to them. It's better to sit back and chat about something completely different; you can always send them an e-mail a couple of days later when they're more relaxed, away from the madness."

Returning to an earlier reference to close the circle, Stedman says, "Yeah, I think one of the reasons why Air New Zealand is such a good airline is that the staff seem very canny about what each customer wants, who wants to be left alone, who wants to chat, be flattered and asked questions, and so on. They're open, they don't have preconceptions, but they very quickly seem to figure out what's going to go best. I'm not sure whether it's conscious, but it's good to watch."

All of this seems to give NHNZ a real, albeit intangible, competitive advantage. Stedman relates what he believes to be perhaps the most satisfying thing he has ever been told by a client. "A manager of a Japanese company said 'you are the least arrogant company that we deal with.' You've no idea how much that meant to us." He contrasts the approach of some his competitors. The BBC? "The BBC seems to still walk about with the remains of a colonial outlook; they think they're doing everybody a service by coming in to film other countries with the British approach. Plus they have a huge millstone around their neck – David Attenborough. I mean he's good, but it's hardly ground-breaking." ("I'm more of a David Bellamy fan," he adds, not surprisingly. "I like his passion.") The Americans? "I was at a convention in Japan last week and this group of Americans decides to go out to dinner, on their own . . . for pizza! I mean, how stupid is that?"

1. *How would you characterize NHNZ's corporate character?*
2. *To what extent is NHNZ's character a function of its geographical location?*
3. *How important is this character to NHNZ's strategic success?*

5 to Five

I don't want 500 television channels. I just want the one channel that gives *me* what *I* want to see.

Nicholas Negroponte, MIT Media Lab

Channel 5, Britain's newest terrestrial (non-cable) television channel, has a problem. It, unlike its competitors, does not have a personality. Consequently, viewers do not know what to expect from it and, subsequently, seem less likely to tune in or build a relationship with it.

British researchers have recently demonstrated that viewers tend to have clear images in their minds about the personalities of the television channels they watch. BBC1 was seen as staid and establishment, but reliable – "the Queen Victoria of channels." BBC2 was seen as an "enthusiastic educator – something between an old professor and a trendy teacher, with a touch of social worker keen to save the world." ITV was seen as jolly, lively, and "more normal," but also a bit "dodgy," with something of a "used-car business" about it. Channel 4 was identified as a "Richard Branson" – entrepreneurial, dashing, and risk-taking, often pushing the boat out a bit too far, but then this suited its character.

The researchers also found that people do not apply the same standards to each channel. For example, it appeared that one reason for making a customer complaint was if a program delivered something at odds with the customer's anticipations of the channel's personality, thereby causing dissonance that led to the relationship between viewer and channel to be questioned. A racy program shown on Channel 4 would receive fewer complaints than the same program shown on BBC1 – partly because of the profile of the people tuning in to each (those watching Channel 4 were likely people who had already decided that their ethos was okay with them), but also because of viewer expectations. Using the same logic, when Channel 4 recently took over the rights to show cricket matches from the BBC, it knew that it would have to show them in a more dynamic, less traditional way – otherwise viewers would wonder "what on earth is happening to Channel 4?" The message seems to be that, as with the people in their every-day relationships, customers will tolerate difference between different companies far more than inconsistent behavior from one company.

Channel 5's problem in this regard is that their programming seems particularly inconsistent: an unruly mix of half-baked game shows, soft-porn, and 1960s wildlife programs. It is hard to see any positive pattern to it and thus it is hard for any significant segment of the population to connect with it. This is partly due to circumstances beyond its control. It is young and it could be said that it is still finding its way – no infant arrives with a personality completely intact. Plus, just after a highly successful launch, when the Spice Girls were used as the channel's spokespeople (indicating a bright, optimistic, youthful image), the five Spices became four, and those four seemed to go their own separate ways, making it difficult for Channel 5 to build on the initial success of the launch.

Eighteen months after the "personality research" described above came out, confusion still prevailed regarding what 5's character should be. Channel 5 executives recently announced that the channel was going to reposition itself dramatically – moving away from its salacious programming to become a "family broadcaster emphasizing popular entertainment." However, this did seem to have been compromised somewhat when one Channel 5 senior executive was reported to be demanding that his channel be allowed to show more explicit sex.

Channel 5 is not the only channel that is working on its personality. ITV has recently launched separate cable-only channels, with related but slightly different personalities, that will allow it to show a more diverse range of programming without compromising its flagship identity, and the BBC is reportedly not entirely happy about the staid Queen Victoria image. The BBC's public service remit is to "serve all people" and, in response to what its own research defines as an increasingly fragmented and multicultural market with different delivery methods and more consumer choice, it is currently asking itself how BBC1, in particular, should change its personality to better match the new environment.

Postscript: By the end of 2002, Channel 5 did seem to be beginning to establish an identity in the market. In the *Independent Review*, critic Thomas Sutcliffe wrote the following: "Evidence that even the most incorrigible miscreants can mend their ways was also available on Channel 5, which formally relaunched itself after months of stealthy self-improvement. The [garish] "Dolly Mixture" logo [around the number 5] has now gone to be replaced with a classy sans-serif text [of the word "five"]. Even more mind-bogglingly, it has been running a series of documentaries on ecclesiastical art and architecture [called *Divine Designs*], presented by a genial anorak called Paul Binski . . . It's as if you were to go on an 18–30 holiday and find that the pool-side entertainment was a lecture on 14th-century choir-stall carving. On Tuesday night, Binski referred to the medieval church's attitude to its congregation: 'We're actually sinful, vicious, oversexed, greedy, stupid creatures,' he said – a perfect summation, as it happens, of the world-view which appeared to govern Channel 5's early schedules. Now [this appears to have] given way to a [blend] of the high minded and cheap and cheerful. *Divine Designs* is not finely wrought television. The final credits list just 13 people in total . . . In television terms, this is one man and a dog he's borrowed for the day, but that hardly matters. Binski overflows with enthusiasm for his subject. Some medieval historians might have winced at the suggestion that church gargoyles were 'the 14th-century equivalent of *The Simpsons*,' but it got the point across – and you won't find such a conjunction anywhere else on television. The Channel 5 button on my remote control has remained in factory condition until now – I have a feeling it might be getting shinier." Sutcliffe's comments were typical of a number of other favorable reviews of the relaunch of Five.

---

1. Why do you think 5's initial attempts to develop an effective corporate character failed?
2. Do you think that the direction that Five is now following (outlined in the postscript) might be more successful? If so, why?
3. Do you think that the BBC should seek to replace its Queen Victoria character?
4. Since this case was written the BBC has expanded its portfolio of channels. This now includes additional channels such as BBC3, BBC News 24, BBC Children's, BBC History, and a number of others. How would you seek to manage this portfolio or family of characters?
5. What can we learn from the Five case about the link between corporate character and strategy?

> You may say I'm a dreamer, but I'm not the only one; I hope some day you'll join us, and the world will live as one.
>
> *John Lennon (1940–1980)*

> When I am at Milan, I do as they do in Milan; but when I go to Rome, I do as Rome does.
>
> *St. Augustine (354–430) Roman theologian and philosopher*

During the 1990s, James Dyson, a British inventor, created a revolutionary new vacuum cleaner that didn't use a dust bag and was significantly more efficient than competitor products. It was an immediate hit in the UK market and soon Dyson was selling his product overseas. Dyson followed this triumph by inventing a revolutionary washing machine containing two contra-rotating drums to give greater performance than other models. Such successful entrepreneurialism earned Dyson national recognition. So, imagine the shock when, in 2003, he announced that his factory in Malmesbury, England, was to close and all manufacturing moved to Malaysia for a 30% saving in production costs. There was widespread outcry in the UK press and from the trade unions. "This latest export of jobs by Dyson is confirmation that his motive is making even greater profit at the expense of UK manufacturing and his loyal workforce. Dyson is no longer a British product" (Derek Simpson, joint General Secretary of Amicus; Neil Collins, *The Daily Telegraph* (August 25, 2004)). Not only would 865 jobs be lost, but this also seemed to symbolize so much of British industrial history: the loss of yet another world-beating product overseas. Why would Dyson, a hero of British entrepreneurialism, risk the wrath of his countrymen for the sake of profit?

Dyson is an example of a small fast-growing company that rapidly succeeds in its home market, quickly begins to export its products, and then moves production overseas. This raises a number of questions central to international business. How recent is this phenomenon of internationalization? Why do firms trade across national boundaries? Why do countries seem to specialize in different types of commercial activity? Why do some international firms leave their home country for another? What are the obstacles to crossing borders? What strategies are used for competing internationally? Which borders should be crossed? What methods can be used to enter different countries? How can firms structure themselves for competing across borders?

Why Do Firms Trade Across National Boundaries and Countries Specialize?

Although a relatively new academic subject, international business itself is not new. Evidence survives of the Phoenicians mining for tin in Cornwall, England in 500 BC. The Cistercian monks engaged in pan-European wool trading in the 13th century. In the 15th century, the rise of the city republics, such as Venice, saw substantial integration into international trade. Soon afterwards, in the Age of Empires, the Portuguese, Spanish, Dutch, French, and British controlled and traded with many far-flung countries. The political power of these countries rested upon the economic power of trade, which came to be dominated by trading companies such as the East India Company (India), Hudson Bay Company (N. America), and Inchcape (Asia).

In essence, trade results in a higher level of economic well-being for its participants. This logic at the level of the parent nation was articulated famously in Adam Smith's **theory of absolute advantage**: "If a foreign country can supply us with a commodity cheaper than we ourselves can make it, better buy it off them with some part of the produce of our own industry, employed in a way in which we have some advantage."[1] Each nation, then, should specialize in producing goods in which it has a natural or acquired advantage. For example Scotland has an absolute cost advantage over Spain in producing whisky. Grant[2] gives a good example of how the firm Nike is benefiting from the absolute advantages of different countries as it is carrying out R&D in the US; fabric, rubber, and plastic shoe component production in Korea, Taiwan, and China; and assembly in India, China, the Philippines, Thailand, and other low-wage locations.

What if a country has no natural advantages? To address this question, in 1817, David Ricardo developed a **theory of comparative advantage**,[3] which examined the relative costs of production between goods in each country. On this basis, countries should produce and trade in goods that they are best equipped to produce, even though their cost of producing other goods may still be lower than the countries with which they are trading. Traditionally, these theories focused on natural resource endowments, population, and capital, but critical roles are now recognized for social and cultural factors such as human capital and management capabilities.

To improve on the rather static nature of the early theories, a more dynamic model was proposed by Hecksher (1919) and Ohlin (1933). Their **HOS model of factor endowments** argues that as a country specializes in a particular product, the main factor of production, such as land, labor, or capital, becomes increasingly scarce and expensive. As a consequence, countries that may have a large labor force, encouraging labor-intensive production, are likely to experience rising wages. To compensate for such pressures, countries need to develop other advantages. In order to explain the development of Japan and the catching-up process of industrialization, Kaname Akamatsu coined the term "The flying geese pattern of development." This model was presented to the world's academic audiences in 1961. It explains Japan's post-war transition away from cheap labor, through acquiring technology and developing capabilities, as reflected in changing industry emphases on textiles, chemicals, ship building, cars, and electronics. It also explains the rapid rise of NICs (newly industrialized countries) by recognizing that comparative advantage shifts across countries over time. Such Tiger economies, including Singapore, Taiwan, Malaysia, and Korea, now have firms that are beating Japanese industry in many areas and some, such as Samsung, can now claim to be world leaders at the forefront in several product areas.

Why Do Firms Leave Their Home Countries?

Within these broad national trends, firms attempt to adjust to changing contexts. For firms such as Samsung, with growing demand for its products in overseas markets, direct investment in production capacity abroad becomes increasingly attractive to reduce logistic costs. As the product becomes standardized, production may be moved to areas where manufacturing costs are low. This dynamic is captured in Raymond Vernon's article "International Investment and International Trade in the Product Life Cycle." Vernon suggests an **international product life cycle**[4] theory to explain why the location of industries changes. "As production and consumption increase, production costs decline and markets expand, so exports increase. With increasing competition, price cutting forces production to shift to cheaper countries." On this basis we have an explanation for the transfer of Dyson's manufacturing as well as the cataclysmic decline in traditional British industries such as textiles and shipbuilding.

Some firms may be more likely than others to internationalize. Firms that own hard-to-replicate proprietary advantage, such as technology, brand name, or distribution, may come to dominate the home market and later overseas markets.[5] This does not fully explain all differences between firms and industries. For instance, Tesco, which has been the undisputed leader in the UK supermarket industry for some years, is still primarily a domestic operation. This oligopolistic theory was refined in John Dunning's **eclectic theory**, which centered on **ownership**, **location**, and **internalization** (OLI). The firm has to: have some ownership of specific unique assets that can be transferred (O) and which will offset the additional costs of competing overseas; locate where cheap capital, labor, and other resources can be obtained and where logistics costs can be minimized in terms of transportation and tariffs (L); be able to make transfers internally to retain control of revenue generation (I). Those firms that derive most from internalizing activities will be the most competitive in foreign markets. The eclectic theory suggests that where a firm's OLI advantages are high, firms are more likely to prefer an integrated mode of entry across borders.[6]

Firms, then, are motivated to cross borders to exploit new market opportunities and to reduce labor costs. They may also be motivated by needing lower cost supplies and/or securing procurement. The rising costs of R&D and technology may need investment greater than can be sustained in the domestic market. Having operations in overseas countries may reduce the risk of fluctuating exchange rates and also allow arbitrage benefits by using resources in one country to benefit another. The "Californianization of society," or globalization of tastes, increases pressure for universal brands and products. This can be as much at the personal level, with products such as MP3s and iPods, as with business consumers wanting similar service and products around the world for all their subsidiaries. Such standardization suits high-tech products with low cultural content, and encourages economies of scale and scope in producers. Other pressures encourage the integration and coordination of operations in different countries. When the blockbusting film *The Matrix* was launched, it had the distinction of being the first film to open simultaneously around the world. Where there are short product life cycles, such as with movies and computer software, it is now essential to have coordinated global product launches to reduce the time for competitive response and illegal copying. Microsoft's Windows, for instance, now launches simultaneously worldwide. Coordination also allows learning through the transfer of best practice, people, and information. These advantages of gaining new markets, reducing costs, timing benefits, learning, and arbitrage opportunities are real but have to generate a competitive advantage for the firm. Numerous obstacles exist which may impair their realization.

What Are the Obstacles To Crossing Borders?

Obstacles can be classified into four types: (1) political and legal barriers, (2) commercial factors, (3) technical issues, and (4) cultural factors.

Political and legal barriers occur through the use of regulation, duties, and quotas that can limit free flow of people, cash, and products. For instance, to impede the importation of Japanese electronics, the French required all imported goods of this type to go through a single customs point, located in the mountains. Ownership policies, such as refusing total ownership (particularly if the industry is perceived as strategic) and only allowing joint ventures, for instance, may disrupt attempts to improve international coordination of business.

Commercial factors may include limited access to distribution networks, the need for customization, and differentiated approaches to sales and marketing.

Differences in technical standards can increase costs and transportation difficulties can reduce the benefits of economies of scale and standardization. There may also be a spatial need to be present locally, for instance in the provision of health care.

Cultural barriers may exist as differences in social attitudes, beliefs, and norms and in terms of language, etiquette, and way of interacting. These may hamper interactive communication and reduce the benefits of standardization. For instance, the British are notorious for using language in an opaque way. Where the British say "I hear what you say," foreigners will understand this to mean "He accepts my point of view." In actual fact, what is meant is "I disagree." When the British say "that's an original point of view," foreigners will tend to think that their ideas are interesting and liked, whereas what is meant is that "you are mad, or very silly." In some countries, great emphasis is placed on getting to know the people one is negotiating with, whereas other countries focus more on the transaction. For one large UK company that recently acquired a firm in Spain, the UK Director decided to visit the Spanish MD for a discussion about strategy. As time was tight, and in order to be efficient, the UK Director requested a working lunch over sandwiches. The Spanish MD regarded this as a personal slight as removing lunchtime also removed the time, necessary in his eyes, for the building of relationships – critical for doing business in Spain. Furthermore, where was the Spanish firm to get sandwiches from?

From our examples, one can perceive many different aspects of national culture. Studies aimed at crystallizing such differences have concentrated on: (1) ethological perspectives, such as Hall's study[7] on silent differences such as the importance of time, social and physical space, material goods, friendship, types of agreement, and the relative importance of context versus content; (2) country cultures such as Huntingdon's work[8] identifying civilization clusters by language, religion, beliefs, and institutional and social structures; (3) economic cultural differences such as Whiteley's work,[9] which examines business systems and forms of capitalism; and (4) country cultures based on managerial values. Probably the most famous, and certainly the largest survey into managerial values, is by Dutch academic Geert Hofstede, who surveyed 116,000 IBM employees across 53 different nations to assess national cultures based on work-related values.[10] With subsequent refinements, Hofstede categorized them according to five dimensions:

1. *Power-distance*, or the degree of inequity among people that a country's population sees as normal.
    Countries such as the USA, Germany, and the Netherlands scored low on power-distance, while Russia and China scored high.
2. *Individualism vs. collectivism*, or the degree to which people prefer to act as individuals rather than as members of groups.
    Countries or regions such as Hong Kong, Indonesia, and West Africa scored low on individualism; while the USA and the Netherlands scored high.
3. *Masculinity vs. femininity*, or the degree to which values often labeled masculine (e.g. assertiveness, competitiveness, performance orientation) prevail over those often labeled feminine (e.g. relationships, solidarity, service).
    Scandinavian countries, the Netherlands, and Russia scored low on masculinity; Japan, and Germany scored high.
4. *Uncertainty avoidance*, or the degree to which people preferred structured rather than unstructured situations.
    Countries such as Hong Kong, Indonesia, and the USA scored low, while Japan, Russia, and France scored high.
5. *Long-term vs. short-term orientation*.
    Countries such as Japan and China scored high on long-term orientation, whereas the USA and Britain scored low.

These different orientations can affect many things that relate to strategy, from the type of management theories that one nation develops or favors, to a nation's preference for certain types of action over others, to the way staff behave, develop and implement strategy.

While Hofstede's work has been criticized for focusing on a single organization, other researchers, such as Laurent,[11] have sampled more broadly and still identified systematic patterns of national differences among managers in their assumptions concerning power, structure, roles, and hierarchy. Later research by Fons Trompenaars and Hampden-Turner, following in Hofstede's footsteps, has identified cultural discriminators[12] by examining value-oriented differences.

Dimensions such as those identified by Hofstede are amenable to further empirical testing. They have been used extensively by international business researchers to understand variations in implementing strategies in different national contexts.[13]

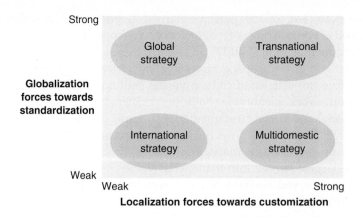

Figure 8.1   Global integration/local responsiveness grid (Adapted from Prahalad and Doz (1987))

The four categories of obstacles to global integration identified above push firms away from standardization towards local customization. While this means that scale advantages are harder to achieve, there are benefits of being focused more locally. These include being more responsive to customers, enabling a better understanding of their needs and being able to adapt more quickly to their demands. A useful framework for capturing this tension between the attractions of globalization and localization is captured in Prahalad and Doz's (1987) global integration/local responsiveness grid (see figure 8.1).[14]

What Strategies Can Be Used For Competing Internationally?

The degree of pressure from globalization forces requiring standardization and localization forces requiring local cultural richness will determine the strategies that firms will adopt. Figure 8.1 identifies the following four dominant styles. **International strategy**, where firms have (a) just begun to expand overseas but do not perceive a dominance of either dimension and (b) no need to customize a product, and its high and distinctive value gives few incentives to invest in scale economies. This may be a pre-competitive state, so new competitors may force choices. **Global strategy**, which emphasizes economies of scale through the standardization of products and services. This strategy lends itself towards high-volume production and very efficient logistics and distribution systems. A weakness is geographic concentration of such activity and isolation from target markets. **Multidomestic strategy**, which emphasizes differentiating products and services through adapting to local market needs. Customization, through tailoring packaging and service at the point of sale, incurs greater costs but there are advantages in greater flexibility and responsiveness to local demands, as well as allowing differential pricing across different markets. **Transnational strategy**, seeks to optimize the tradeoffs between global and multidomestic strategies by dispersing the firm's resources according to their most beneficial location. Typically, activities close to the customer are more decentralized and those further away are more centralized as less adaptation is required. The potential risks are whether the value of local adjustment is really realized, and the difficulties in managing the tensions internalized within the organization (see Cummings and Angwin (2004)).

Which Borders Should Be Crossed?

With forces pushing firms to expand overseas as well as opportunities attracting them to other countries, firms need to decide on where to expand or move to, and what method(s) to use. Through entering another country, firms ought to earn a return higher than the risk-adjusted weighted average cost of capital (WACC). This focuses attention on both the opportunities, in terms of market prospects and competitive conditions, as well as the risks of operating in that territory.

Analytical techniques outlined in chapter 1 can be used to assess the macro-environment of a new country. There exists considerable macro data on economic variables (e.g. GDP per capita, disposable income, investment rates), social data (e.g. urbanization levels, socio-economic distribution), demographic factors (e.g. population profile), and institutional variables (e.g. government spending, quality of infrastructure) on websites of the Economist Intelligence Unit (www.eiu.com), the World Bank (www.worldbank.org), and Business Environment Risk Intelligence (www.beri.com). These data allow regression analyses to identify drivers of spending/potential spending patterns. For instance, one important relationship recognized through this approach is the **middle-class effect**, which shows that an increase in GDP per capita can have a disproportionately larger positive effect on middle-class disposable income. A small increase in GDP, therefore, can result in great increases in spending on aspirational goods, such as digital cameras and flat screen TVs, by the middle classes.

Further insight into a country's competitive advantage can be gained through the application of Michael Porter's country Diamond.[15] The framework (discussed in chapter 7, Corporate Character) is based on the principle that the national environment exerts a powerful *dynamic* influence on the performance of the firm. The level of domestic rivalry in particular is critical for promoting improvements in other local factors – such as skilled labor, R&D capability, and infrastructure – and geographical concentration magnifies the interaction between these factors. The framework, while useful, has received criticism for being based on data for ten countries with greater economic strength/affluence than most countries in the world. The roles of chance and government seem to be presented in a positive way, but chance is unpredictable and both can act against the interests of business. While the Diamond is presented as a technique for national analysis, it must be applied in company specific terms because "firms, not nations, compete in international markets."[16] Porter contends that only outward foreign direct investment (FDI) is valuable in creating competitive advantage and that inbound investment or foreign subsidiaries are never a solution to a nation's problems. This conclusion has been challenged empirically.[17] The model also does not adequately address the role of the multinational enterprise (MNE) and perhaps this ought to be listed as the third outside variable. For MNEs, their competitiveness is more influenced by the configuration of Diamonds outside of their home countries and this may impinge on the competitiveness of home countries.[18] For different countries, then, different Diamonds need to be constructed and analyzed.

For smaller countries, such as Canada, Finland, and Norway, there could also be a case for using a "double Diamond."[19] Canadian firms, for instance, needed greater economies of scale than could be obtained entirely within the domestic market. They now produce for the North American market as a whole and so are in direct competition with firms operating in a Diamond of their own in the US. They can no longer rely entirely upon their home country's Diamond and natural resource base. For corporate strategy this means that the two countries of Canada and USA are integrated into a single market and for this reason a Canadian/US double Diamond is appropriate.

Porter suggests that countries, and regions within countries, can form clusters that are attractive for business development. Examples of such clusters might be Silicon Valley in the US, Sassuolo near Bologna in Northern Italy for ceramic tiles, and around Banbury, Oxfordshire, England for Formula 1 racing cars. Clusters promote competition, concentration, and reinforcement. Networks of businesses and supporting activities in a specific region, where flagship firms compete globally, may include private and public sector organizations, think tanks, support groups, and educational institutions. It is no surprise that high-tech clusters have formed successfully around universities in the UK such as Cambridge, Oxford, and Warwick.

What Methods Can Be Used For Crossing Borders?

Having decided on which country to enter, the firm has to decide on an entry strategy and its timing. The entry strategy will be determined by, among other things, the firm's resources and capabilities for establishing an overseas presence and the transaction costs[20] of negotiating, monitoring, and enforcing agreements, the costs of transportation, and information costs. The least exposure or involvement in the overseas country would involve licensing; a contractual arrangement whereby products/process technology are transferred to a licensee for commercial exploitation for royalties. Other methods used where direct investment is not justified include **franchising** and the use of **agents** and **distributors**. The latter two are frequently used by small and medium enterprises (SMEs), the former for the logistics of stocking, transporting, and billing, the latter more for taking orders and as a salesperson. Where low intensity of investment remains but greater ownership is required, a representative office is used. This is also a popular method, being perceived as a stepping stone for future and greater engagement. Where greater investment is intended, although ownership is limited, then the firm may engage in a **strategic alliance**, which can include a **joint venture** or being part of a **consortium**. Joint ventures are the main form of foreign direct investment in emerging markets and are often encouraged by the governments of the overseas country so their citizens can engage in industrial development without loss of control. For the entering firms, they gain local market knowledge and contacts with decision makers. Often joint ventures have a limited life-expectancy and can end up being wholly owned by one of the founding companies. A good typology of joint ventures can be found in the book by Dussauge and Garrette[21] and suggestions for effective management in Hamel, Doz, and Prahalad's paper "Collaborate with your Competitors – and Win."[22] If firms entering the country wish for this complete level of control and a substantial investment, then they may either opt for a wholly owned subsidiary or a cross-border acquisition. With these forms of ownership, it is vital to manage local obstacles as discussed above. Setting up a wholly owned manufacturing facility is the way that Dyson, our opening example, has gone. Through complete ownership, the quality of production can be controlled and the Dyson vacuum cleaner can benefit from the lower cost labor force provided local obstacles are navigated. For a discussion of cross-border pitfalls in post-acquisition integration, see Angwin's book *Implementing Successful Post-acquisition Management*.[23] Cross-cultural integration skills are at a premium for managing across borders.

Some would see these entry strategies as a sequence from low to high exposure based on experience.[24] Although this might resonate with Anglo-Saxon history, there is now substantial evidence to suggest that this unidirectionalism is too simple because contextual changes can lead to reversals in the sequence. Also, in sectors such as high-tech start-ups, the stage process is leap-frogged, with rapid internationalization almost immediately without passing through all the developmental stages of a low to high exposure model.

The timing of entry is important because firms can either aim to gain first-mover advantages or wait and become fast followers. The problems with first movers are significant investment and having to handle all uncertainties without guarantees of sufficient return. However first movers can pre-empt resources, establish their presence in terms of brands and standards, and have a head start in understanding local needs. Fast followers often need substantial resources and different strategies from first movers. They are unlikely to be the only entrants, so competition is greater. However, they are in a position to learn from the experiences of the first mover and so reduce their risks.

How Can Firms Structure Themselves For Competing Across Borders?

As companies spread around the world, new organizational challenges arise. The need for coordinating and controlling, as well as adapting to local demands, places organizations under tension. The relative importance of each will vary depending on the nature of the industry. Where the need for global standardization (and, so, centralized control) is dominant, a centralized hub form is an ideal structure. Where local responsiveness is more important than global standardization, a decentralized federation is likely. To reflect an equal emphasis on being global and local, a hybrid form was developed by ABB. The "matrix" structure was very popular at the end of the 1990s, with its dual command structure, in its simplest form, allowing employees to respond to both regional and product managers. However, its complexity led to internal confusion over responsibilities and absorbed a great deal of time in meetings and discussions necessary for coordination. Firms have begun to move away from the matrix form and even ABB has now finally abandoned this structure. Bartlett and Ghoshal[25] suggested an alternative for the global/local dilemma. They proposed a "transnational" design, which combines functional, product, and geographic designs into networks of linked subsidiaries. Within the network are nodes for coordination. The important feature of the

215

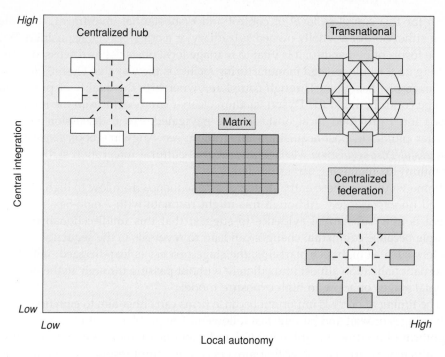

High

Central integration

Low

Low   High

Local autonomy

Figure 8.2   Border-crossing designs (Adapted from Bartlett and Ghoshal (1989))

transnational design is that it doesn't focus on structure but on management processes and culture. Managerial behavior is more important to them than structure and so a particular form is not prescribed.

At the heart of crossing borders, a paradox remains for managers: whether the international context is moving towards Leavitt's conformity or whether this is something of a myth, as argued by Douglas and Wind, and it will remain fragmented. Should businesses anticipate and encourage convergence and aim to realize global synergies, accepting some local value destruction, or exploit local diversity at the expense of global efficiencies? To some extent the answer to this question lies in the cultural richness of products and it is here that Dyson's decision, discussed at the beginning of the chapter, is seen to be based on products with little cultural richness. The opportunities to reduce costs for Dyson outweighed the value of localization. Dyson also recognized that global business is dynamic and that all firms have to continue to fight to preserve their competitive advantages. However, there is no one right best response for doing this in the face of the crossing borders paradox. It is for each organization to find its own way.

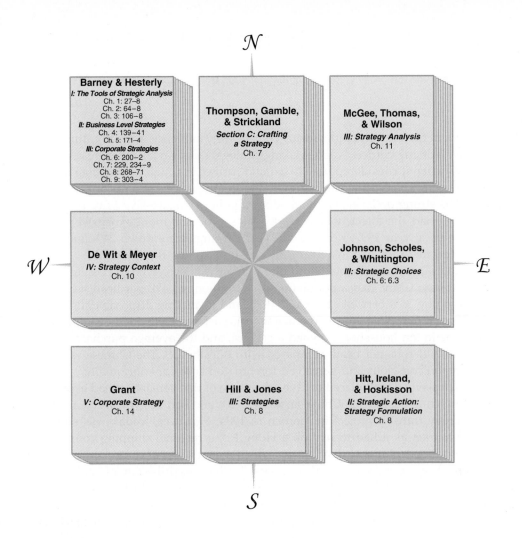

Barney & Hesterly
I: The Tools of Strategic Analysis
Ch. 1: 27–8
Ch. 2: 64–8
Ch. 3: 106–8
II: Business Level Strategies
Ch. 4: 139–41
Ch. 5: 171–4
III: Corporate Strategies
Ch. 6: 200–2
Ch. 7: 229, 234–9
Ch. 8: 268–71
Ch. 9: 303–4

Thompson, Gamble, & Strickland
Section C: Crafting a Strategy
Ch. 7

McGee, Thomas, & Wilson
III: Strategy Analysis
Ch. 11

De Wit & Meyer
IV: Strategy Context
Ch. 10

Johnson, Scholes, & Whittington
III: Strategic Choices
Ch. 6: 6.3

Grant
V: Corporate Strategy
Ch. 14

Hill & Jones
III: Strategies
Ch. 8

Hitt, Ireland, & Hoskisson
II: Strategic Action: Strategy Formulation
Ch. 8

Do you feel lucky?

'When the tiger comes down from the mountain to the plains, it is bullied by the dogs.'

Chinese proverb

When you are out of your element, your power/influence is greatly diminished and yet crossing borders is about taking strategic risks. Kodak faced this challenge in 1997 when it considered how to expand further in China. In its home markets it had been experiencing slow growth and the incursions of a major competitor, Fuji. The strong dollar helped Fuji adopt a policy of aggressive price reductions and also had the effect of making Kodak's products more expensive abroad. For the fiscal year 1997, Kodak's full year earnings were down 24% and it was estimated that they had lost 3% of the consumer photo-film market.

At the same time China's photo film market was perceived to present a huge opportunity: China had a population of 1.2 billion, a GDP per head which had increased by 36% between 1990 and 1995, and increasing disposable income (as the Chinese Government covered major costs such as health and housing). Fewer than one in ten households owned a camera, and the average purchase of films was only 0.1 rolls per head, compared with 6 in the US. The Chinese were also very brand conscious and perceived foreign goods as superior quality.

Kodak seemed well placed to take advantage of this demand. It had experience of conducting business in China since the 1920s and had been awarded a specific technology transfer project in Xiamen in 1984. However, Kodak was suffering in the market as it had to rely on a Hong Kong regional shipping company to ship products to Chinese distributors, which meant a loss of control over product quality. The excessive transit differences also increased the rate of spoilage and rendered less certain the delivery and availability of products. Such practical obstacles threatened to damage Kodak's reputation.

Kodak was also not alone in the market. Lucky Film Corporation, China's largest and most profitable state-owned enterprise (SOE), controlled 25% of the Chinese market and benefited from Government support. The Ministry for Internal Trade helped Lucky set up a national sales network to market its products and also approved substantial loans and grants.

Kodak approached Lucky by proposing large investments and taking a large share in the firm. However, the Chinese refused to permit foreign majority ownership and the removal of the Lucky brand name. Lucky was also a supplier to the Chinese military and this strategic importance meant a foreign owner was unlikely.

The other main competitor at the time was Fuji, which had adopted an aggressive market penetration and investment strategy. Fuji had a solid distribution channel through China-Hong Kong Photo Products Holdings Ltd and had made significant investments in manufacturing with the explicit intention of shifting all compact camera production to China and Indonesia to decrease the costs of manufacture. However, it was also well known that the long tumultuous history between China and Japan meant that the Chinese community (investors, consumers, Government officials) would rather trust *Meiguo* (America/beautiful) than *Riben Guizi* (Japanese devils).

Kodak CEO, George Fisher, an executive passionate about China and with direct experience of FDI projects in his former role at Motorola, knew that Kodak had advantages over Fuji and had to expand into China, but what were the risks? Would they be lucky?

---

1. *Why is Kodak considering expanding into China?*
2. *In what ways might Kodak be a tiger in relation to local Chinese competition and why might it be that, as the Chinese proverb suggests, "although you may be a superior force, in unfamiliar territory you may be weaker than local forces"?*
3. *What strategy should Kodak pursue?*
4. *In negotiating with the Chinese, what insights can be gained from models in this chapter?*

◀◀◀Do You Feel Lucky? Some Ideas . . .

1. Why is Kodak considering expanding into China?

There is a mixture of push and pull factors acting on the firm. Contextual factors, such as the strengthening dollar, were favoring Kodak's competitors' aggressive pricing strategies. The overall industry was also stagnating. The evidence of the pressure was Kodak's decline in profits. In contrast, China offered a vast, largely untapped market with strong consumer demand for foreign products. The recent strong growth in GDP per capita can be assumed to have greatly increased middle-class incomes and their aspirations for Western goods meant that the sale of cameras would be likely to increase substantially.

2. In what ways might Kodak be a tiger in relation to local Chinese competition and why might it be that, as the Chinese proverb suggests, "although you may be a superior force, in unfamiliar territory you may be weaker than local forces"?

Kodak has considerable strengths as a company with international operations. Its state-of-the-art technology was superior to anything owned by the Chinese, and the firm was well resourced financially. However, operating in the Chinese market was causing Kodak's capabilities to be undermined. The practical difficulties of getting its products to the consumer in a fit state were damaging its reputation. Even though Lucky, the main player in the Chinese market, was inferior to Kodak, it had close and preferential links with the authorities, which allowed it to be subsidized and sponsored. The fact that the Chinese also did not permit foreign ownership also removed Kodak's strength as a well-resourced company to influence the situation. Perhaps in attempting to purchase a substantial share of Lucky, Kodak had been acting as a tiger?

It is worth noting that, for China, having Kodak and Fuji as two tigers was beneficial: as they fended off each other to claim the coveted venison, the Chinese deer slowly transforms into a dragon, which neither of the two can defeat – the Chinese would continue to support Lucky.

Kodak clearly began to make much more progress when they approached the Chinese situation in a culturally more sensitive way. This approach was undoubtedly helped by having a CEO who had prior experience of FDI projects in China and who was passionate about the country.

3. *What strategy should Kodak pursue?*

Given that Kodak should expand into China, there are a number of options that might be pursued. Kodak can continue to attempt to link strongly with Lucky either as a major investment partner or through some form of alliance, or indeed continue to try to persuade the Chinese authorities that some sort of merger might be in Lucky's and China's best interests. If a major commitment could be put in place, this might give Kodak a major advantage over Fuji in terms of market share as well as close links with Chinese authorities. However, there is also the risk that a major tie up may cause Kodak to be severely hampered in how its Chinese operations would actually function, and once such a large commitment was made, it might be difficult to reverse.

Kodak might decide to try to do something different and arrange joint ventures or other types of alliance with other Chinese partners. As these firms were small in size, many such alliances might be necessary to gain scale and this could take a lot of time to put in place and take considerable efforts to manage/coordinate effectively. It is unlikely that this approach would really provide robust competition for Fuji, although the size of the Chinese market and its growth rate mean that there is considerable scope for competitors at this time.

Ideally Kodak needed a step change in the size of its Chinese operations and needed to control every aspect of product quality and distribution process. While a greenfield site was not politically acceptable, negotiations with the Chinese authorities might allow a compromise that would be better options to the ones considered above. In terms of an optimal strategy, if something along these lines could be worked towards, Kodak should also be continuing talks with Lucky to prevent the chance that Fuji might take this opportunity and completely dominate the market.

4. *In negotiating with the Chinese, what insights can be gained from models in this chapter?*

Hofstede's dimensions suggest major differences between American and Chinese cultures (see figure 8-1.1).

Substantial differences are clear for power-distance, individualism, and long-term orientation. These differences should be taken into account by the Americans (on the basis that this deal is in a Chinese context). Kodak will need to adapt its negotiation style to recognize that, for the Chinese, building trust and aiming for long-term relationships are important, underlining the key issue of long-termism. For the Americans, where there is greater emphasis on rapidity and a focus on getting a contract signed, learning to be patient is important. They must recognize that for the Chinese this is more about building a long-term relationship. The American top-down decision style and use of only a few specialists in a negotiation team will be faced, provided that the negotiation is important, with a large Chinese delegation among

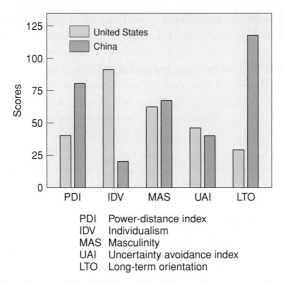

PDI	Power-distance index
IDV	Individualism
MAS	Masculinity
UAI	Uncertainty avoidance index
LTO	Long-term orientation

Figure 8-1.1   Geert Hofstede's 5D model comparing China and the US
(Source: www.geert-hofstede.com/hofstede_china.shtml)

whom decision making is consensual. To Westerners, the opaqueness of the Chinese decision-making approach will necessitate the use of Chinese experts and contacts to make headway.

▶ ▶ ▶

Biggles does Korea

Flying from London to Seoul on Korean Airlines turned out to be a very interesting cultural experience. Predictably for such a long flight (some 13½ hours), the aircraft was a Boeing 747, and in Korean Air livery. Passengers were greeted in Korean and English by smart and courteous cabin staff, in neatly pressed blue and white uniforms. Clearly the cabin crew were of Asian origin but while seated on the plane, awaiting takeoff, it was hard (for a Westerner) not to note the many unusual clues on-board as to the Asian-ness of the aircraft and its service.

However, after the aircraft took off, and after being lulled into this authentic Oriental ambience, we were suddenly subjected to a rude awakening as a clipped English public school accent punctured the air: "This is Basil your captain here. Spiffing weather today at our cruising altitude of 32,000 feet. Hope you enjoy the flight. Toodle pip!" It was hard to fathom. Surely, nobody today actually speaks like that – it was as if Biggles, the 1920s fictional flying ace, was captaining the aircraft!

The rest of the flight continued in this rather bizarre fashion, with cabin staff moving quietly, efficiently, and discreetly around the aircraft while abrupt "English toff" style interjections periodically came from the flight deck. In attempting to make sense of this incongruous mixture, I determined that Korean Airlines might be using a tape recording to make English-speakers feel more at ease. However, in attempting to make the commentary as English as possible, they had alighted upon a rather over-dramatic actor for impact. Why would the airline have gone to such trouble?

In the late 1990s, people became increasingly concerned about the poor safety record of Asian airlines. Of the five airlines that have had four or more serious crashes in the last decade, four of them are Asian. And researchers identified Korean Airlines as having the world's worst safety record. The airlines with the best records were mostly from Anglo-Saxon English speaking countries like Britain, Australia, Canada, Ireland, and, particularly, the US. In 1998, *The Times* ran a story on this research with the headline "Asian culture link in jet crashes." One can begin to understand why an Asian airline might want to promote Anglo influences.

However, things may not be as clear as the first cut of the data might suggest. One London-based expert specializing in risk assessment claimed: "It is notoriously difficult, even misleading, to try to draw meaningful conclusions from 'snapshots' in aviation." And many commentators are quick to point out that the Japanese, with a similar socio-cultural background to some of the worst performers, have one of the world's best safety records. Despite these warnings, some analysts have begun to look at the extent to which national cultures affect pilot performance by comparing flight data with cultural characteristics.

Research done by Dutch academic Geert Hofstede in the 1970s and 1980s demonstrated that Asian nationals scored higher on dimensions of collectivism, power-distance, and uncertainty avoidance than their Western counterparts. Those groups that score high on *collectivism* recognize their interdependent roles and obligations to group consensus, aspects indicative of a "strong" culture. Those on the high end of the *power-distance* scale expect and accept that power is distributed unequally, accept the necessity of hierarchies, and are less likely to challenge authority. Members of high *uncertainty avoidance* cultures prefer rules and set procedures to contain and resolve uncertainty, whereas low uncertainty avoidance cultures tolerate greater ambiguity and prefer more flexibility in responding to situations.

Aviation researchers have identified that total reliance on the autopilot facility is dangerous in potential crash situations, that captains can make fatal errors of judgment that can often be corrected by other crew members, and that the speed and decisiveness of decision making is usually vital. A more recent study carried out by psychologists from the University of Texas indicates that 100% of Korean pilots claim to prefer deferring to the autopilot and always used it (the highest percentage of the 12 countries surveyed), and showed greater shame when making a mistake in front of the crew than pilots from other countries.

1. *Why was I surprised by Biggles during the flight to Seoul? Why would Korean Airlines be hiring British pilots?*
2. *Why might culture be part of the explanation for the poor safety record of Korean Airlines?*
3. *What other factors may also play a part?*
4. *What solution could you suggest for this difficulty?*

Lo-glo Barbies

In "The Globalization of Markets," published in 1983 in the *Harvard Business Review*, Theodore Levitt famously predicted an increasingly homogenized world. Here, the "Model-T Ford" approach of the same standard essential product for all would be vindicated, as efficiency became *the* universal criteria for decision making. Levitt explained that multinational corporations have been "thoughtlessly accommodating" in "willingly accepting vestigial national differences, not questioning the possibility of their transformation, not recognizing how the world is ready and eager for the benefits of modernity, especially when the price is right." He went on to claim that this traditional "accommodating mode to visible national differences [wa]s medieval" or like paying homage to an "obsolete institution." By contrast, the modern corporation of the future will seek to:

> . . . constantly drive down prices by standardizing what it sells and how it operates. It treats the world as composed of few standardized markets rather than many customized markets. It actively seeks and vigorously works toward global convergence. Its mission is modernity [hence] the global corporation accepts and adjusts to . . . differences only reluctantly, only after relentlessly testing their immutability, after trying various ways to circumvent and reshape them.

At the same time as Levitt was advocating moves in this direction, Barbie began to move the opposite way. In the early 1980s, Barbie's makers Mattel, criticized for promoting an American ideal of beauty worldwide by selling the same blonde-haired, blue-eyed, high-busted doll everywhere, began localizing its dolls. The "Dolls of the World" initiative now numbers over 70 different forms: from Ghanaian to Moroccan, from two types of Eskimo to three Native American Indians, and from Korean, Thai, and Polynesian to Polish and Portuguese. Just how sensitive Barbie and her makers are is open to debate: after all, the Dolls of the World still seem to promote popular stereotypes, only now they are more localized stereotypes rather than just American ones; and the classic American doll continues to be far and away the most popular Barbie sold worldwide. Perhaps it is fairer to say that Barbie is swinging both ways: local and global.

However, our diverse world keeps throwing up examples of local differences refusing to bend to the will of global corporations and causing big companies to think hard about the complexity of operating in different national or regional contexts as they internationalize. A few such examples are listed below:

- A global clothing manufacturer's Italian subsidiary adopted a new human resource system module, which required automated recruiting and selection procedures. However, this proved counter-productive, because informal, face-to-face recruitment was the accepted norm in this region. Recruiting performance actually declined until the automated parts of the new module were bypassed and personal interviewing was revived.
- Similarly, an international bank introduced a standard system for mortgage application processing, based on customers submitting their applications electronically. While this system worked well in certain countries where the bank operated, in others it actually slowed down the application process because customers did not have access to the internet.

- Josephine Green, Director of Trends and Strategy at Philips and a regular guest speaker at WBS, likes to tell the story of how many consumer electronics companies started to use Italy as a launch pad/test market for new technology products after their data showed them that Italians adopted mobile phones incredibly quickly. This data, they presumed, indicated that Italians were unusually adaptive and receptive to new technology. But, several failed initiatives later, this was discovered not necessarily to be the case. If somebody had stopped to think about the context, Josephine says, they might have figured out that the Italians, generally speaking, do not so much love new technology more than the rest of the world does – they simply love fashion and they love to communicate (as spending even a small amount of time in Italy would tell you). Mobile phones had enabled them to indulge both of these passions at once.
- Wal-Mart entered into a joint venture to build and run supermarkets in Brazil, but failed to fully factor the shopping habits of the locals into projected traffic flows. In Brazil, almost nobody shops during the week and the new stores were built with car parks and shopping aisles too small to accommodate the weekend rush.
- For a long time, a well-known and highly successful European homeware and furniture brand did not know what to make of the sales data from some of its new American branches. This data showed unusually low sales of the company's drinking glasses and unusually high sales of its vases. (Perhaps you can figure out some reasons to account for this data. There is a clue in the experience of Land Rover, which had to significantly re-size and strengthen its cup-holders for the US market.) The same company struggled to sell its beds in the US until it realized that US bed linen did not fit its standard models.

1. *Why might the world be "Californianizing"?*
2. *What forces exist for localization?*
3. *How might the bank in the case address the need for global efficiencies on the one hand and the pressure for local customization on the other?*
4. *Why did Philips and Wal-Mart misinterpret their foreign consumers?*

8:4

Different Guyanas

Spain's European neighbors watched, jealously, as her imperial domain in Latin America sent home countless treasure galleons. Apart from unofficially condoning acts of piracy on these ships, and raids on Spanish colonial territory, these neighbors also strove to find riches of their own. Guyana, on the north-western coast of the South American continent appeared to provide untapped possibilities for the English, the Dutch, and the French.

Sir Robert Dudley made inquiries about the area when his ship pulled in to Trinidad in 1594. Soon after, the English were sending expeditions rushing up the rivers to penetrate the interior of Guyana, where they hoped they would find the fabled empire of El Dorado and its vast golden riches there for the taking. They withdrew their efforts soon after, however, following heavy casualties from disease and with nothing to show for their efforts. El Dorado had not yielded the quick gains they had wished for.

The Dutch, on the other hand, had a different agenda. At the end of the 1590s, they began to settle along the coast, dug in for the long term, and set about the less swashbuckling task of clearing large areas of land to be turned into plantations and putting the area's resources (along with local and imported slave labor) to work.

The French, meanwhile, did things differently, too. French Guiana was settled in 1604 and the area was to become a cog in the broader French Empire. It was made as French as possible and was given the task of contributing to "Greater France" by becoming its most notorious penal colony. This was closed in the 1950s but soon after French Guiana became the base for European Space Agency launches. It is still in French possession – the only non-independent country in South America.

While wars between the English, Dutch, and French saw the colonies change hands, and strategies for development change, over time (for example, the English began to follow policies quite similar to the Dutch in the 19th century), the result of these different types of conquests, acquisitions, and mergers is three different countries: Guyana, Surinam, and French Guiana. While their geographical proximity makes them similar in many ways, it is said that their many differences can be traced to the styles of those quite different "conquistadors" who came to claim (or prevent their competitors from claiming) what they saw as untapped resources in the 16th and 17th centuries and the ensuing historical paths this set them upon.

1. *Why might the three European countries have acted differently in Guyana?*
2. *Why did the different approaches lead to different types of outcome?*
3. *Why did the English adjust their approach towards that of the Dutch?*
4. *What lessons can we learn about the differences between Guyana, Surinam, and French Guiana today?*

Cultural icebergs

Vodafone PLC, under Chris Gent, chose Christmas 1999 for the launch of the biggest ever hostile takeover – an offer of DM 135bn (£83bn) for Mannesmann of North Rhine Westphalia, Germany.

The announcement of the takeover was met with something approaching hysteria in Germany, which was living through the agonies of BMW wrestling with the "English Patient" (namely, Rover Cars). At the political level, the German Chancellor, Schröder, announced: "Hostile takeovers destroy corporate culture." Similarly, Jurgen Ruttgers, leader of the CDU in the North Rhine Westphalia, said, "an unfriendly takeover *does not fit* with the rules of the social market economics which have been very successful for 50 years." Others remarked that "we should hold on to our culture and that implies our business culture as well." Indeed, drastic action was taken in the past when foreign companies aimed to buy German firms, such as when the Austrians were close to buying the Salzgitter steel company from Preussag in North Rhine Westphalia, the regional government stepped in with DM 1bn of public money (its budget for 2000 was DM 90bn). Comments and actions such as these were bluntly criticized by European Central Bank President, Wim Duisenberg, who said they did not enhance the image of being an increasingly market-driven economy across the Euro-area.

Klaus Esser, Mannesmann's Chairman, took a contrary view, believing that national culture and historical foundations were unhelpful: "We could really do without the national pathos; it doesn't suit our time." Esser was seen as a new breed of German CEOs who were used to acquisitions, understood the concept of shareholder value, and saw the advantages of Anglo-American financial markets. Controversially, Esser publicly stated that he would fight a clean fight and would concede victory if Vodafone secured more than 50% of votes – even though in theory he could still frustrate the bid. By eschewing court actions, white knights, poison pills, and other US-style defense tactics, Esser laid the foundations for one of the cleanest, fairest, and most investor-friendly takeover battles.

For Esser, the case for keeping Mannesmann independent was based largely on the strengths of his own company's prospects. However, he also attacked Vodafone's strategy and commented on the volatility of its share price.

Esser's road show through the US argued that Mannesmann was growing more rapidly than Vodafone (forecasting a 39% compound earnings growth for 2000–3 versus 24%), controlled leading mobile operators in three of Europe's four largest markets, and was well placed to be European partner of choice. The offer would also involve replacing Orange with Vodafone's UK business despite the former substantially outperforming the latter. In essence, Esser was arguing predominantly for organic development coupled with strategic alliances.

Gent decided to make the offer under German takeover rules rather than UK rules because this allowed Vodafone to raise its all-stock offer at a later stage, although Vodafone stated it had no intention of so doing. His case for the deal was that, even if Mannesmann remained independent, it would soon have to merge with a large US player to be able to compete in a fast-moving global industry. Indeed, there was concern over Vodafone's continued independence if the deal did not go through. Standing alone and waiting for some future alliance would take time in a world of mobile data and internet time, where time is of the essence. On this basis, acquisition is the only sustainable approach to growth as organic growth is too slow.

Esser lost some of the early initiative in the deal because some big Mannesmann shareholders were also concerned to protect their investments in Vodafone, which would suffer if the bid failed. In addition, the concerns of shareholder power were not as strong as in the UK and US, where many investors were based. Throughout the battle, there was controversy over the amount of Mannesmann shares held in Germany, with Mannesmann suggesting the figure to be around 40% whereas Vodafone believed it to be nearer 25%.

Although Mannesmann revealed excellent preliminary figures on January 7, 2000, showing a 70% rise in earnings (EBITDA) to €2.2bn, which it argued represented outstanding results for shareholders, they were perceived as being in line with analysts' expectations and appeared to offer little additional support for Mannesmann.

To avoid falling foul of the European competition authorities, Vodafone announced its intention to spin off Orange, the UK wireless carrier.

As this was unfolding, the sentiment in the stock markets was bullish and, at the same time, a blockbusting deal between AOL and Time Warner was announced. As the elapsed time of the bid increased, both Mannesmann's and Vodafone's shares increased in value. This proved problematic for Esser, as Mannesmann's defense document stated that Mannesmann was worth €250 a share, and he was on record as saying a fair price would range from €300–350, and now they stood at around €350 a share; an increase of 46% on the price at bid launch. He therefore switched focus towards the amount of shares in the combined company that Mannesmann shareholders would receive, arguing for 58% rather than the 47.2% being offered.

On February 4, 2001, Mannesmann capitulated, with the Vodafone offer valuing Mannesmann shares at €353 and the German group's shareholders taking 49.5% of the combined company. Esser became an Executive Director on Vodafone's Board until summer and then became a Non-executive Deputy Chairman. In Chris Gent's words, "It's been a long run, but it's been a pretty friendly hostile. Mannesmann – a great company – will be better with Vodafone." The new Vodafone emerges as Europe's largest publicly traded company and the world's largest telecoms group – a global giant to compete with NTT DoCoMo of Japan, WorldCom and AT&T in the US, and Deutsche Telecom in Germany. As the undisputed champion of the European telecoms sector, it stands at the centre of the continent's wireless-internet revolution.

1. *Why did Vodafone lauch its hostile bid for Mannesmann?*
2. *Why was there German outcry at the prospect of Vodafone acquiring Mannesmann?*
3. *Why did Mannesmann lose the contest?*
4. *Was this a good outcome for all stakeholders?*

Burgers and cola

Coca-Cola's iconic worldwide campaigns – like "I'd like to buy the world a Coke," "Always Coca-Cola," and "You can't beat the Real Thing" – represented an age of global standardization and homogenization. However, Coke's new millennium began with CEO Douglas Daft announcing the abandonment of its worldwide campaigns and global policies. According to Coke's British head of external affairs, Ian Muir, "We used to say that we thought globally and acted locally. Now we are thinking locally and acting locally." Events in Britain provide a good example of why Coke now feels the need to move this way. Perhaps the most successful soft-drink in the UK in recent times has been Tango, a brand spurred on by campaigns determined to connect to the quirkier aspects of British humor. (Anyone who has seen the ads will recognize that they would not go down well in most other cultures.) Coke's global campaigns appeared bland and pallid by comparison.

Moreover, American Cola giants like Pepsi and Coke are suffering from some local consumers taking a political stand against them. Witness the growth of *Mecca-Cola* launched at the end of 2002. (Sales pitches for the brand include: "No more drinking stupid, drink with commitment" and "Don't shake me, shake your conscience.") The brainchild of French businessman Tawfik Mathlouthi, Mecca-Cola is now imported into a growing number of North African states. The first African bottling plant, recently opened in Casablanca, locally produced and sold 300,000 units in its first week and there are plans for more such operations. Similar "ideological" opponents to Coke, such us *Muslim Up* and the British-based *Qibla-Cola*, are also doing well. More humorous in its approach, but also doing well on the back of anti-American sentiment, is Turkey's *Cola Turka*. A new series of ads starring Chevy Chase show the American becoming more and more Turkish (sprouting a mustache, cooking stuffed grape leaves, and bursting into rousing Turkish songs) the more he sips on a Turka. This new campaign coincided with what was seen as the heavy-handed seizure of Turkish soldiers by US troops in northern Iraq. Cola Turka's share of the Turkish cola market is already 10%.

In response to these sorts of local uprisings, Daft's first move when he took over at Coca-Cola was to send executives out of Atlanta and closer to local customers and give creative leeway to branches to produce their own promotions. On March 27, 2000, Daft, an Australian, outlined his vision for the company:

> "Even though our historical strength came from operating as a 'multi-local' business that relied heavily on the insight of our local bottling partners, we knew we had to centralize control to manage expansion. [Thus], we have headed in a direction that had served us very well for several decades, generally moving toward consolidation and centralized control. That direction was particularly important when we were 'going global.'
>
> "The world, on the other hand, began moving in the 1990s in a different direction . . . as globalization accelerated, many national and local leaders understandably sought to ensure sovereignty over their political, economic, and cultural identities. As a result, the very forces that were making the world more connected and homogeneous were simultaneously triggering a powerful desire for local autonomy and preservation of unique cultural identity.
>
> "Consequently, what we learned was that the next big evolutionary step of 'going global' now has to be 'going local.' In other words, we had to rediscover our own multi-local heritage. We must lead a Coca-Cola that not only has the expertise and structures required for success in a globalized economy, but which is also able to act nimbly and with great sensitivity in every local community where our brands are sold.
>
> "So, we are placing responsibility and accountability in the hands of our colleagues who are closest to individual sales. We will not abandon the benefits of being global, but if our local colleagues develop a strategy that is the right thing to do locally, then they have the authority and responsibility to make it happen. Our local people are ready to take on their shoulders the authority and accountability that naturally belongs to them.
>
> "In our recent past, we succeeded because we understood and appealed to global commonalities. In our future, we'll succeed because we will also understand and appeal to local differences. Think local, act local. The 21st century demands nothing less."

But while Coca-Cola goes local, that other American icon, McDonald's, has surprised analysts recently by bucking localizing trends with its new standardized global advertising campaign.

Over nearly 50 years McDonald's knitted together one of the world's most recognizable brands on the back of campaigns created by its regional agencies that each expressed the character of the country it was marketing in. But, at the end of 2003, it unveiled a global tagline ("I'm lovin' it") and supporting series of ads for the very first time. McDonald's Executive Vice-President and Global Chief Marketing Officer, Larry Light, claims that: "This first-of-its-kind borderless approach will let us capitalize on the powerful energy of our worldwide system."

However, some observers are questioning the merits of McDonald's adopting a global line. "People are reacting to US cultural imperialism, and what McDonald's is doing is responding by being more culturally imperialist than ever before," says one agency executive. Furthermore, Sydney-based food marketing consultant Gawen Rudder says McDonald's global campaign "is a complete disconnect" from its latest local image in Australasia. "Recently there has been a completely new look," he says. "It's a healthier, more logical, less energetic approach to the brand that has been encapsulated in Salads Plus. In the face of the debate over obesity it has been absolutely admirable." But, Rudder says, the global campaign will force two identities on the local market. "It is nice branding, slickly done, but I now have two conflicting personalities to think about. Then again, McDonald's don't make too many mistakes."

Australian marketing manager Nick Rodd is quick to downplay simplistic suggestions that the overarching borderless approach necessarily means that regional McDonald's initiatives will be stymied. "We will still do Australian campaigns," he says. Recent McDonald's advertising in the region has borne this out with the "I'm loving it" series being supported by parallel campaigns that are very local in both their form and content. Indeed, Larry Light stresses that the point of the global campaign is to give the brand a "consistent message" while at the same time allowing tailoring to regional markets to continue. In other words, the company must "Think global and local; act global and local."

---

1. *What were the benefits to Coke of going global?*
2. *How was this global approach mirrored in Coke's organizational structure?*
3. *Why has Coke now decided to go local?*
4. *What effect might this new local strategy have on Coke's organization?*
5. *Why has McDonald's persisted with a global approach?*
6. *What risks does McDonald's face with this strategy?*
7. *Where would you position Coke and McDonald's on the global integration/ local responsiveness grid?*

The world's local bank

From humble beginnings as a regional bank established in 1865 to finance international trade along the coast of China, HSBC (Hong Kong Shanghai Banking Corporation) has grown astronomically over the past decade. It has grown both organically and through astute acquisitions to become one of the world's biggest companies. From its early history as a collection of banks connected through British Empire or Commonwealth ties (early principal members included The British Bank of the Middle East, The Saudi British Bank, and the Cyprus Popular Bank), HSBC now employs over 218,000 staff based in 79 territories that serve 110 million customers in more than 200 countries. The recent growth spurt can be traced to 1991, with the formation of HSBC Holdings, a holding company for the entire group with its shares quoted in both London and Hong Kong.

Unusually for a company of its size, however, HSBC has always championed the importance of local diversity rather than the importance of scale. In the words of Group Chief Executive Stephen Green, "We do not aspire to be a unicultural company." This is down to the belief that, according to Group Chairman John Bond: "People do not appreciate the one size fits all approach commonly associated with global corporations."

But how do you continue to grow and coordinate and focus a company that operates across so many borders? One way was to adopt a unified brand. This brand, featuring the letters HSBC next to a red and white hexagon (a stylized version of the original 19th century HSBC flag based on the cross of St. Andrew) was launched in 1998. Within a couple of years, this symbol and the letters HSBC were well recognized, but according to HSBC's Head of Marketing, Peter Stringer, people were not really sure what they stood for. They weren't sure about the values or the character behind the HSBC name and symbol.

At around about this time, a group of UK-based HSBC executives on an executive development program settled down to discuss the ethos of their corporation and its current strategy. As part of an exercise they began to think of the HSBC in terms of its personality. In other words, to think on the question: "If our company was a person, what kind of person could it and should it be?"

While this was not an easy task, one thing that surfaced very quickly in the ensuing discussion was these execs were sure that one of their leading competitors had recently got its "personality" all wrong. Barclays Bank had just launched a media campaign extolling the virtues of its "bigness." Celebrities like Anthony Hopkins and Robbie Coltrane told the camera that "people want things 'big' – and they want a big bank." According to the HSBC execs, while people may have wanted some of the benefits that a big bank offered, they also liked the idea of dealing with a bank that "felt" small and which valued particular personal relationships.

Eventually, having split themselves into three smaller groups, each group came up with a possible personality: James Bond, the current CEO of the Bank, and Michael Palin.

After some discussion, Palin was thought best. Although the idea of Bond appealed to many, particularly the male members of the team, it was quickly decided that while his British, suave demeanor and his unruffled "shaken not stirred" character could fit nicely, his risk taking and attitude to women (an interesting character to have a "fling" with, but not a very safe long-term bet) probably did not fit the image the bank wanted to present. Many thought that having a well-liked CEO step forward and lead the company from the front, in the spirit of Victor Kiam or Richard Branson, would have been particularly powerful. However, others countered that his personality could be problematic given that it was not well known to those outside the company and that the "heart" would be pulled out of the corporation when he, eventually, left. So, in the end it was Palin – the decent, good-humored, charitable, stoic, and curious ex-Monty Python turned world-traveling documentary maker – who won out. (If you are unfamiliar with Michael Palin, you may want to consult www.palinstravels.co.uk/) He was British, but had made a second career of combining this very British nature with embracing foreign cultures and appearing completely sympathetic to their differences. His TV shows were the epitome of the "when in Rome . . ." ethos. He was also, said one manager, "a nerd, but with a broad good nature and a sense of humor underneath it – unlike James Bond you can associate this with a bank. Particularly with our bank."

The executives placed Palin firmly in the middle of the conventional competitive advantage distinction between costs and differentiation. "It's a very Palin-like position," said one manager. "He just understands different perspectives." This was something also indicated by his wide-ranging appeal ("you can watch his show with the kids and even teenagers kind of like him because of the Monty Python connection").

"I guess this fits with our strategy," another manager continued. "Like all banks we're increasingly having to cut processing costs. Globalization is increasingly giving up opportunities to do that. At the moment we're switching a lot of our data processing and clearing stuff to India and places like that."

Another interjected: "But we maybe have to be careful about this, what with concerns with business ethics and so on."

"Sure, sure, we can't abuse different people – maybe the Palin image can help us formulate our approach to that. No matter what, though, we have to cut costs to compete. But, at the same time, one of the strongest things our market research is telling us is that most of our customers like having a branch. They like the idea of a branch manager or someone they can talk to in a branch about what concerns them. So, one of the ways that we are going to try and differentiate ourselves increasingly is by having a strong local branch presence while others are closing theirs down. So I guess what I'm saying is that we have to look both ways – toward new suppliers for cost saving and to existing and new customers to differentiate, even though keeping the branches open and staffed costs us a lot."

There was general agreement about this logic. Another manager expanded on it: "And we do, through our traditional presence on the world's high streets, have a broad appeal – in fact we have to cover a lot of fixed costs so we really have to be broad to shift the 'units' needed to perform."

Nobody present knew whether Mr. Palin would have been available to approach with a proposal that could have led to these ideas being used in a public arena. But perhaps this didn't matter. A group of managers had a clearer idea of what their organization was and what it was not and could, from there, begin to think about how they would move into the future.

And, indeed, future developments at HSBC, while not involving Mr. Palin, did increasingly seem to bear the stamp of his spirit.

In 2002 a new advertising campaign was developed, with the strap-line "HSBC: The World's Local Bank". This campaign, with which you are probably already familiar, focuses on how things are done differently, or how the same things can mean different things, in different local contexts. The television ads in particular follow a travelog style and ethos that is very Palin-esque. Thus, they illustrate the importance of HSBC's "local knowledge and tailored service" approach. According to Head of Marketing, Peter Stringer, the campaign "makes a clear and powerful statement of what we stand for . . . we think the world is a diverse place, full of interesting people, and it is these people that we want to help go about their business."

On a more practical level, too, the Palin ethos of respecting and learning from local cultural norms seems to be ringing true. For example, recent initiatives include:

- having specialist branches in the UK for Indian businesses
- establishing a north London branch, situated among a large orthodox Jewish population, that opens on Sundays
- being the only UK high street bank to offer a *sharia*-compliant mortgage for Muslim customers
- operating a number of women-only branches in Saudi Arabia

Moreover, the past few years have witnessed HSBC increasing its investment in local philanthropic initiatives. For instance, it spent over US$34m on a wide range of educational and environmental projects in 2003.

And finally, in introducing the publication of a new history of HSBC in 2004, Group Archivist Edwin Green emphasized that "We are international in a way very few companies of any kind can claim. What is distinctive about the group is not how early it gets into markets, but that it stays with them through thick and thin: crises, wars, emergencies, social upheaval, HSBC has seen them all."

---

1. *HSBC has grown primarily through acquisitions. What are the virtues of this approach?*
2. *Why was James Bond not the best choice of personality for HSBC?*
3. *Why does Michael Palin resonate so strongly with HSBC executives?*
4. *HSBC claims distinctiveness in persistence and commitment to markets. How is this possible and why might it confer advantage?*
5. *How can HSBC compete effectively by championing local diversity and yet proclaiming itself as a global bank?*

The Trojan Rover

Four years after its management buyout from BMW, MG Rover was struggling. Sales continued to fall sharply from levels of 200,000 vehicles per year under BMW to 144,000 in 2003. To fund the development of a single mid-sized car to replace the aging Rover 45, assets had to be sold off, including the valuable parts business. As for the small car range in its portfolio, the group would clearly struggle to finance its development. Even the new mid-sized car due for launch in 2004 had to be postponed to 2006, prompting speculation over Rover's ability to survive with dwindling revenues.

MG Rover then announced its plan for a wide-ranging strategic collaboration with the state-owned Shanghai Automotive Industry Corporation (SAIC). Negotiations were in the final stages of approval by the Chinese Government, at the time of writing.

When cleared, SAIC would pump funds into the venture to finance an ambitious development and production program. The first phase of the alliance would last until 2010 and would create a range based around the medium-sized car that Rover had been developing to replace its Rover 45/MG ZS models. SAIC was also expected to provide a solution to the problem of Rover funding the development of a small car range to replace the Rover 25/MG ZR.

The cars would be built at MG Rover's Longbridge plant near Birmingham and in Shanghai. This would help to reverse Rover's decline and increase employment in the longer term. It would also give Rover exposure to the Chinese market. SAIC would gain access to MG Rover's dealer networks across Europe and in other overseas markets. It would also benefit from technology transfer from MG Rover's 322 engineering workforce.

Traditionally, China's auto industry was comprised mainly of joint ventures producing western manufacturers' vehicles under license for the fast-growing domestic market. However the Chinese Government has a clear goal to create a fully integrated auto industry capable of exporting to the world. In this sense, Rover might be viewed as a Trojan Horse for the Chinese industry.

At the same time Honda had just opened a stunning glass-walled and marble-floored £1m dealership in Shanghai. This "temple," with pagoda-like entrance and spotless 27-bay service department that stays open for emergency repairs 24/7, is revolutionary and clearly attracting significant attention from upwardly mobile Chinese anxious to trade in their bikes for Western style freedom. In this rapidly growing market, which is building up to becoming the second largest car economy (behind the USA), blasting horns are now drowning out the ringing bells of bicycles. Indeed, it seems the Chinese cannot ditch their bicycles fast enough as the capitalist culture of car ownership becomes embedded.

Honda is not known for taking risks when it comes to establishing new car production outposts around the world. However the arrival of the Chinese built Honda *Jazz* hatchbacks at showrooms around the world is very significant. While other manufacturers have poured £6.8bn into establishing manufacturing bases in the world's most important new economy, Honda is the first to ship substantial numbers of "made in China" models to Europe. Mindful that consumers could be sensitive to perceived quality differences of Chinese goods, the President of Honda Automobile China, Hironori Kanayama, is adamant that the Jazz will not compromise on quality. The existing factory, which has been manufacturing Odyssey people carriers, Accord saloons, and Jazz saloons since 1999, is the winner of a company quality poll across 19 overseas plants. He also maintains that his young workforce, averaging just 28 years old and earning around £2,700 per year, delivers cars that consistently earn high satisfaction index ratings from the domestic JD Power consumer car quality benchmarker.

1. *Why would Rover try to enter into a strategic alliance with SAIC?*
2. *What are the attractions for SAIC to enter into the alliance with Rover?*
3. *Why has Honda chosen to manufacture and distribute for itself in China rather than using some form of strategic alliance?*
4. *What insights can international business theories give us in comparing the expansions of Rover and Honda into China?*
5. *What are the implications for the two international strategies in the UK car market?*

California sunlight, sweet Calcutta rain,
Honolulu starbright, the song remains the same.

Led Zeppelin

You can never step into the same river twice.

Heraclitus

Wisdom lies neither in fixity nor in change,
but in the dialectic between the two.

Octavio Paz, Mexican poet

Any strategic development will, of necessity, involve managing some degree of change to structures, technologies, products, services, culture, or processes. But over the past two decades the flow of change that organizations have sought to keep pace with has increased dramatically – to the point, indeed, where commentators like Christopher Bartlett and Sumantra Ghoshal have claimed that the levels of change have in many instances outpaced the human capability to cope with change.[1] While organizations must move to keep pace with a changing environment, the strategist must also ensure constancy and consistency with regard to stakeholder relationships and corporate character, among other things. The change management challenge paradoxically requires ensuring both movement and stability in optimal measure.

Since the 1980s there has been a dramatic expansion in the number of ideas and frameworks to deal with guiding change. These can be divided into two camps: conventional or straightforward "one-best way" methods, or frameworks that promote more nuanced or differentiated approaches.

Conventional or "Straightforward" Approaches to Managing Change

Despite a great expansion in numerical output, a review reveals a similarity among conventional approaches to managing change. This can be seen by the way that John Kotter's method, currently the most widely used framework for managing change, replicates most of what has been said in applied management fora on this subject.[2] Kotter claimed that a successful change process goes through a series of eight phases or steps. These steps are shown at the top of figure 9.1. Other commentators may have outlined their ideas about managing change in other ways, but they are easily assimilated into Kotter's steps.[3]

The main reason for the homogeneity of conventional change management theories in the 1980s and 1990s may be history. In the early 1950s, Lewin discovered

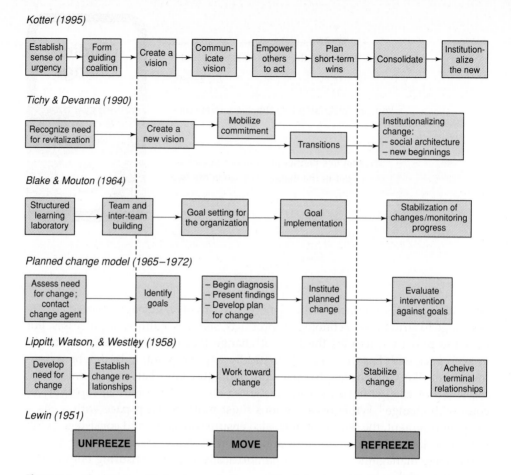

Figure 9.1 The incremental development of conventional change management frameworks since 1950 (Source: Cummings (2002))

what textbooks to this day call the three basic steps that summarize what's involved in the process of changing people and organizations: unfreezing → moving → refreezing.[4] Figure 9.1[5] shows how others (all the way up to Kotter in the mid-1990s) would subsequently follow Lewin's lead, building on his classical approach, adding details or splitting levels but maintaining Lewin's three simple steps. This homogeneity is underpinned by a number of assumptions about change:

- Change is a generalizable linear input → process → output process: hence we can determine "one-best way" approaches to it.
- Change comes from the top or outside in and then works its way down. In Kotter's (1995) words, top people must firstly provide a vision for change.
- We can break down the complexity of change into its "component parts" that can then be ordered into a series of steps.
- Change and constancy are seen as an either/or choice: conventional approaches would have difficulty comprehending the quotation by Octavio Paz at the head of this chapter.

While almost all of the authorities mentioned above and in the related notes are American, Kotter's eight steps seemed to also ring true with the best of European theory. Pettigrew and Whipp's *Managing Change for Competitive Success* presents ideas very similar to Kotter's eight steps. In a study of competitive change in a number of UK industries, Pettigrew and Whipp identified nine key aspects: (1) building a receptive context for change, legitimization; (2) creating a capacity for change; (3) constructing the content and direction of change; (4) operationalizing the change agenda; (5) creating a critical mass for change within senior management; (6) communicating the need for change and detailed requirements; (7) achieving and reinforcing success; (8) balancing the need for continuity and change; and (9) sustaining coherence.[6] Of these nine steps, the only thing that the American works generally do not incorporate is the notion of "balancing continuity and change."

All of these straightforward general models can be used effectively to develop and communicate change programs. However, given that we can now see them as somewhat similar, and hence limited, perhaps we should look at additional frameworks that may inspire us to think about managing strategic change differently.

Unconventional, or Nuanced, Frameworks For Guiding Change

The frameworks for guiding the management of change outlined in the section above are both useful and heavily used. They are used because they are simple, easy to remember, and easy to communicate. However, often managing change is not so straightforward. No two change initiatives are exactly the same and the following differences are worth investigating:

- Change occurs at *different* organizational and conceptual levels.
- There are often *different* needs and objectives that organizations are seeking to achieve and subsequently *different* styles of crafting change.
- Change can be instigated by *different* types of individuals or groups.
- Change initiatives meet with *different* forms of resistance that the skillful strategist will want to take account of.
- Finally, human nature and capabilities require that change be combined with continuity, to *different* extents, depending on the circumstances.

These complexities, which require good managers to take a more dexterous or nuanced approach, rather than just implement an eight- or nine-step plan, are explored in more detail in the sections that follow.

Different Levels of Change

Change can occur at different conceptual or practical levels. Mintzberg and Westley's framework (see figure 9.2) provides a useful means of separating out, and seeing the interrelationships between, the more organizational versus the more strategic aspects of change and relating these to different levels of thought versus action.[7] For example, changing an organization's vision for the future will necessitate

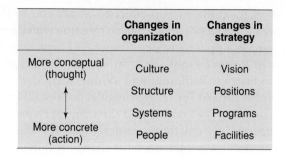

	Changes in organization	Changes in strategy
More conceptual (thought)	Culture	Vision
↑	Structure	Positions
↓	Systems	Programs
More concrete (action)	People	Facilities

Figure 9.2 Strategic changes related to organizational changes (Source: Mintzberg and Westley (1992))

Degree of change	Level of change	Characteristics
Status quo	Can be both operational and strategic	No change in current practices. A decision not to do something can be strategic as well as operational
Expanded reproduction	Mainly operational	Change involves producing "more of the same" goods or services etc.
Evolutionary transition	Mainly strategic	Sometimes radical changes occur but they do so within the existing parameters of the organization (e.g., existing structures or technologies are retained)
Revolutionary transition	Predominantly strategic	Change involves shifting or redefining existing parameters. Structures, processes and/or technologies likely to change.

Figure 9.3 Levels of operational and strategic change (Source: Wilson (1992))

changing the organization's culture if this new vision is to be achieved, all of which will require a lot of conceptual work. This should then trickle down to more practical, but congruent, actions relating to the organization's facilities and people or human resources to ensure consistency of corporate identity.

It can also be useful to develop a clearer understanding of whether what is envisaged is a more strategic- or more operational-level change, and what differences of approach this might necessitate before embarking on the change. For this purpose David Wilson's framework, pictured in figure 9.3, is very helpful.[8]

Different Change Needs and Styles

Different organizations in different settings have different needs for change. For example, organizations in industries or societies that are quickly undergoing fundamental changes may require a complete *revolutionary* transformation, a

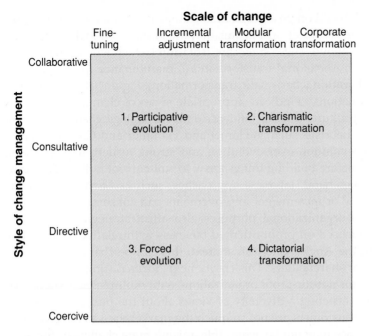

Scale of change

	Fine-tuning	Incremental adjustment	Modular transformation	Corporate transformation
Collaborative				
Consultative	1. Participative evolution		2. Charismatic transformation	
Directive	3. Forced evolution		4. Dictatorial transformation	
Coercive				

(Style of change management — vertical axis)

Figure 9.4   Different scales and styles of change (Source: Dunphy and Stace (1990))

change program that is broad in scope, necessitating sharp changes to most if not all of its procedures. Where the firm is facing collapse, its turnaround would necessitate revolutionary change – a complete rethinking of the nature of the business and how it competes, and radical and immediate surgery for survival.[9] In a calmer setting or a more conservative industry, a more *evolutionary* approach and some fine-tuning to just a few aspects of the organization's activities will be more appropriate. Figure 9.4 provides a useful means of characterizing different change needs and then thinking through the sort of management approaches and programs required to satisfy those needs.[10]

There are four main styles of change:

1. **Participative evolution** is appropriate when the organization is either "in fit" with its environment, or it is "out of fit" but time is available, and key interest groups favor change.
2. **Charismatic transformation**, led by a popular change agent, is appropriate when the organization is out of fit, the need to change is urgent, and key interest groups or stakeholders support substantial change.
3. **Forced evolution**, driven by a strong leader, is appropriate when the organization is either in fit but needs minor adjustments or is out of fit and, although time is available, key stakeholders oppose change.
4. Widespread **dictatorial transformation**, imposed from above, is appropriate where the organization is out of fit, time is short, and key stakeholders oppose change.

A particular context where there are varying needs for change is *post-acquisition* integration. The target company has been acquired but will have different degrees of organizational and strategic fit with the acquiring company and varying amounts of time available for change. Duncan Angwin (2000)[11] has developed a contingency framework based on post-acquisition change in UK mergers and acquisitions and suggests four types of post-acquisition integration style which resonate with the framework above. These styles are **isolation** (which would be forced evolution), **subjugation** (dictatorial transformation), **maintenance** (participative evolution), and **collaboration** (charismatic transformation). Figure 9.4 can be usefully applied to such situations to indicate appropriate styles of change.

Different cultures can also influence different strategic change styles. For example, American theorists, such as Hamel and Hammer and Champy, have tended to advocate revolution over evolution and strong leaders wiping the slate of the past clean before building things anew to suit current rather than former needs.[12] On the other hand, Japanese approaches, such as *kaizen*, have favored slower evolutionary or incremental improvements and consensus-driven change.[13]

Different organizational purposes also affect strategic change styles. So far we have focused on profit-oriented business with relatively clear objectives and aims – in the Anglo-American context, this can be characterized as the pursuit of profit for shareholders. This clarity helps focus during organizational change. However, for not-for-profit organizations with multiple, non-aligned stakeholder pressures, reflecting a diversity of views about the purpose of the organization (where the customers are not so much the marketplace as the provider of funds), this coherence may not be achievable, raising huge challenges for organizational change. If there is any doubt about the massive complexity and difficulties involved in changing not-for-profit organizations, one only has to look at the agonies of the UK National Health System, the problems of improving state education, and the consequences of privatizing the national railway system.

Different Instigators of Strategic Change

We tend to associate strategic change initiatives with those at the top of an organization. While leaders and the roles they play do have a large influence on how change is enacted in an organization, the dexterous manager of strategic change will recognize that change can also be driven by individuals with unique insights at lower levels of the organization, or by groups or communities rather than individuals.

That leaders shape change seems an obvious statement. However, different leaders lead in different ways, and different organizational situations require different styles of leadership. The Leavy and Wilson scale (shown in figure 9.5)[14] is an excellent means of thinking through what type of leadership will best suit the challenge faced.

Perhaps just as often, however, innovative individuals who can see beyond current conventions and practices and create new visions of the future are often the drivers of change. Writers and artists such as Joyce and Picasso challenged established beliefs and in turn transformed our understanding and appreciation of literature and art. Political figures such as Luther and Gandhi overturned the establishment in similar ways. While it is tempting to think of organizational leaders as drivers of change in much the same manner, such leaders, in the mold of Richard Branson for example, are in fact remarkably rare.[15] This is probably inevitable. Corporations themselves have become incredibly analytical, seeking

Change	**Build:** here leader/founders must build their respective organizations at the formative stage of their development, often imbuing the organization with their own distinctive personalities
↑	**Transform:** transformers radically change the strategic direction of their organizations (e.g., take it into a new area of core business)
	Revitalize: revitalizers operate within the already established basic characteristics of their organization, but try to raise it to a new plane of development (e.g. more of the same, but more effective)
	Turnaround: leaders in this situation must chop and change the basic, already established characteristics of the organization (e.g. emphasize one or more areas while de-emphasizing others)
↓	**Defend:** defenders work with mature organizations protecting their established market positions (e.g., they ensure sustained competitiveness)
Continuity	**Inherit:** inheritors focus on consolidating and building on the progress made by their predecessors

Figure 9.5   The locus of influence of leadership related to change versus continuity (Source: Leavy and Wilson (1994))

to mitigate risk by doubting their hunches, passion, and gut-feelings and employing sophisticated logarithms to plot their course instead.[16] Moreover, the higher up the establishment people are, the less likely they may be to question the very processes that enabled them to get where they currently are. It is important to remember that the likes of Joyce and Gandhi did not employ managerial risk analysis techniques and were nowhere near the top of their fields or societies when they began their transformational quests.

The same is true in business organizations. Often the people with the most innovative ideas, the ones that could really shake-up or change an organization for the better, are not those who have been in senior management positions for a decade or more. Remember the 3M example in case 6-8? It is doubtful that any of 3M's executives could have hatched Post-It Notes. However, what 3M execs did do was create an environment in which people from all over the organization had the confidence and systems in place to enable them to contribute innovative ideas that could drive change in the organization.

Creating an environment where bodies other than executives can drive change is also important when it comes to unleashing the change potential of communities of practice – those informal networks of influential people that we discussed in chapter 6, Living Strategy. Communities of practice can be powerful drivers of change because they can solve complex problems quickly; they facilitate the transfer of new practices; they continuously develop professional skills and the knowledge base of the organization; they can help attract and retain new people. The best communities of practice tend to form naturally, but skillful managers can also encourage their emergence. However they come to be, it is crucial that they are supported by an adequate infrastructure. Because they tend to lack the legitimacy and budgets of more formal groups, communities of practice can be vulnerable without this kind of support.

Strategy	Commonly used	Advantages	Disadvantages
Education + communication	Where there is a lack of information or inaccurate information and analysis	Once persuaded, people will often help with the implementation of the change	Can be very time comsuming if lots of people are involved
Participation + involvement	Where the initiators do not have all the information they need to design the change and others have power to resist	People who participate will be committed to implementation. Any relevent contributions can be integrated	Can be very time consuming if partici- pators design an inappropriate change
Facilitation + support	Where people are resisting because of adjustment problems	No other approach works as well with adjustment problems	Can be time consuming, expensive and still fail
Negotiation + agreement	Where somebody with considerable power to resist will lose out	Sometimes a relatively easy way to avoid major resistance	Can be too expensive if it alerts others to negotiate for compliance
Manipulation + co-optation	Where other tactics will not work or are too expensive	Can be a quick, inexpensive solution	Can lead to future problems if people feel manipulated
Explicit + implicit coercion	Where speed is essential, and the change initiators possess considerable power	Speedy, and can overcome any kind of resistance	Can be risky if it leaves people mad at the initiators

Figure 9.6   Dealing with resistance to change (Source: Kotter and Schlesinger (1979))

Managing Different Forms of Resistance to Strategic Change

One of Machiavelli's most often quoted lines gets to the nub of why many well-planned change initiatives fail: "The innovator makes enemies of all those who prospered under the old order and only lukewarm support is forthcoming from those who would prosper under the new." Many change initiatives do not gain traction due to failing to anticipate and manage such individual and organizational resistance that Machiavelli's quotation suggests is inevitable.

Most of these failures are due to insufficient communication and thus uncertainty about what change is coming, why it is coming, and what the implications of the change will be for people. Kotter and Schlesinger's table articulates different communication strategies that can be used to work through resistance, where they should be used, and their relative advantages and disadvantages (see figure 9.6).[17]

Blending Strategic Change and Strategic Continuity

The book *Recreating Strategy* argues that one way to think beyond conventional straightforward models of change is to explore how change might have been seen differently in societies other than our own.[18] The ensuing interrelated elements were identified as crucial.

1. *A vision that joins the past and future:* A vision for change not only has to show a different future but also has to acknowledge past glories and how these had shaped the present organization so as to not belittle the achievements, or jar with the values, of those key people who have been with the organization for some time.
2. *Interweaving future, present, and past:* Change programs should work to ensure that structures in the *present*, vision for the *future*, and mythology or history from the *past* resonate and are congruent with one another. This notion often gets lost in modern change management initiatives, which can suffer as a result. For example, it is no good maintaining matrix structures and employing a vision of "increased efficiency and accountability." While both have been fashionable in recent times, one undermines the other (matrix structures by nature require more time of organizational members). This forces members to make their own choices as to which "master" they will serve and which they will compromise, with confusion being the result.
3. *Integrating material and mythic dimensions:* An appreciation of an organization's myths or stories is often overlooked nowadays (although the current vogue for "strategic story-telling" – see chapter 6, Living Strategy – may reconnect us with it). Hence, we observe many managers today being either too aggressive in managing such aspects, seeking to impose or transplant external "hero" myths and stories from the top down, or being too passive, avoiding learning about and developing these local stories in favor of issues of structure or technology, which are more easily grasped.
4. *Change requires continuity:* In The Physics, Aristotle develops the idea that "there must always be something that underlies, out of which things come to be," examining how we are only able to recognize something as having changed if something about it or what it does has *remained the same*. In keeping, managing change paradoxically requires providing continuity. Many managers overlook this, approaching the process as a matter of replacing old with new, always asking "how will we change?" but seldom asking "how will we stay the same?" The most obvious recent manifestation of this view in management theory is seen in the "start with a clean sheet of paper" and "wipe the slate clean" rhetoric of business process reengineering. This last element reconnects us with that one element of Pettigrew and Whipp's nine steps for managing change that was substantially different from conventional change frameworks: "balancing continuity and change."

While there is no shortage of frameworks that can be used to enhance the chances of successfully implementing change, it is important to realize that many of the conventional mainstream frameworks draw on quite similar assumptions and are consequently fairly simplistic. Blending these approaches with an understanding of the unique setting or context in which the change initiative must work and some of the other, less-straightforward ideas related here will enable you to be a more effective manager of strategic change.

Given all that has been outlined above there are two important questions that should always be in the mind of the manager of strategic change. One relates to the end of the process, the other to the beginning. With regard to the end, the biggest problem is that once a program for change is complete and the change agents move on or lose focus, the powerful pull of the old culture can drag the company back into old habits. The test is to ask yourself, having "completed" the change path: "Would it now be as difficult to go back to the former valley as it was to reach the new plateau?" If the answer is "no" then you must keep moving because the slope back down beckons. The message: change should not be something that ends – so long as the environment keeps changing, the organization must change, or else drift out of fit.

Paradoxically, the most important question with which to begin your change analysis is: "What aspects will we preserve and maintain?" This is true now more than ever before for two reasons. First, there are very few completely bad organizations any more. Increased global competition has run them out of business or forced them to improve. Almost every company does one or a few things well and these should be built on. Second, research now suggests that good employees are having difficulty keeping up with, and are consequently frustrated by, the change programs that some companies are constantly launching at them. And, we know that these days companies cannot afford to frustrate good people. Despite the need for change, people crave continuity. It is this dialectic – the interplay between forces for consistency and forces for change – that the strategy pathfinder must constantly navigate.

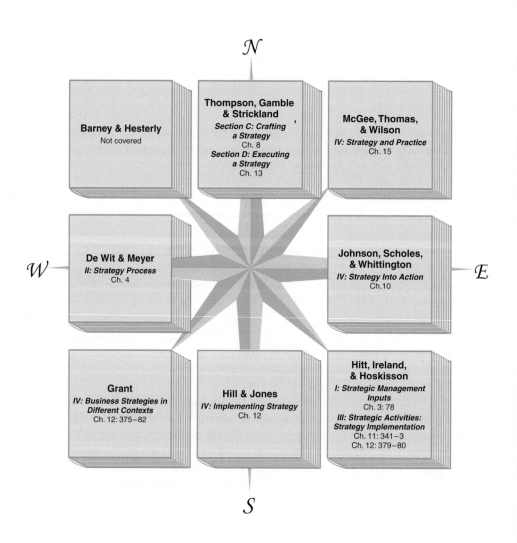

Hanging by a thread

Pringle of Scotland is a knitwear company with a long and proud history. Established in 1815 in the Scottish Borders and based around the town of Hawick, its trademark argyle sweaters and golf-wear became increasingly popular in the middle of the 20th century, when it found fans among the early "Sweater Girls" – who included sophisticated leading ladies like Jean Simmons, Deborah Kerr, and Margot Fonteyn – and the dapper Edward, Duke of Windsor. However, the later part of the 20th century saw a decline in the company's fortunes. A perceived "stale-ness" of the brand and falling sales saw a company that once employed 4,000 people in the region shrink to a quarter of that size. In June 1998, a further 720 jobs were shed with the closure of two factories in Scotland. With just 200 employees left at the Hawick factory, and Nick Faldo seemingly entrenched as Pringle's poster-boy for the past 20 years (a good golfer but hardly a fashion icon any more), many feared that Pringle was not cut out for the modern world of business. The company was put up for sale.

Kenneth Fang of SC Fang & Sons, a Hong Kong Knitwear manufacturer, bought Pringle in March 2000 and immediately poached a young manager from Marks & Spencer's to head up the company. Kim Winser was responsible for trebling the turnover of aspects of M&S's clothing business, but she recognized that Pringle presented a much tougher challenge.

On a positive note, however, the recent post-modern love affair with things retro has seen the successful resurrection of a number of "former glories" like Pringle. For example, Daks – the label that introduced the first self-supporting waistband for women's trousers – has adapted its style to changing times. Recently, the label invited fashion students from the Royal College of Art to give it a 21st century makeover: with the proviso that its trademark shades of camel, vicuna, and black were kept to the fore. LVMH, whose portfolio includes brands such as Dior, Givenchy, and Louis Vuitton, has gone from strength to strength under the impressive Bernard Arnault. Burberry is another label that has enjoyed a renaissance after new managers and new designs were introduced in 1997, and successful diversifications were made into other product ranges. Since then, celebrity devotees have helped regenerate Burberry's image.

Indeed, the recent craze for all things vintage has given such companies an inimitable source of advantage: an ability to recreate their iconic lines. Boucheron, the haute jewelry company, launched its Vintage Limited Edition collection in 2002, re-releasing designs from the 1970s. Its creative director, Solange Azagury-Patridge, plans to add vintage pieces from the 1980s in the next few years. "Boucheron is 150 years old and has a really rich archive, with pieces that are so great and so appropriate that it is a shame not to revisit them again," she says. However, this new trend to revisit the old is not simply about scoring some quick sales; it is also a clever external marketing and internal strategy initiative. Azagury-Patridge points out that "reissuing pieces from the past is a way of conveying the essence and character of the brand." In other words, it is an "event" that can create a buzz and whip up enthusiasm for customers jaded by the homogeneity of global shopping, while raising awareness of what the company stands for and the standards it is trying to achieve and maintain.

However, there seem to be just as many failures as success stories with attempts to rejuvenate luxury brands. Since fading into obscurity in the 1980s, Jaeger has made repeated attempts to update its image by redesigning product lines and ranges. However, these attempts did not win enough new customers and traditional followers felt alienated. Shares in the cash-strapped Luxury Brands Group, which owns the Hardy Amies brand, were recently suspended because of a rumored takeover bid and shares in Printemps-Redoute, the French retailer that is the majority owner of Gucci, fell over 50% in the first half of 2002. Prada, the fashion house, has had to cancel its float three times for fear of a poor response from the market. The effect of September 11 and wealthy tourists staying away from Europe has been blamed for adding to the struggles of smaller businesses of a similar ilk. Dawson International, the cashmere company, issued profit warnings in 2002 at about the same time as June Chester Barrie, the Savile Row tailor, had to call in the receivers. Even traditional stalwart Fortnum & Mason, the "Queen's grocer," which was privatized in 2001, is fighting for its life. It has frozen staff pay and been forced to open its doors on Sundays – something previously unthinkable – in an attempt to revive its fortunes. Managing Director Stuart Gates told staff, "The company has to face hard decisions critical to the future of the store."

Maceira de Rosen, an analyst at JP Morgan, says that the luxury goods labels that remain intact will be those that have a strong brand that is "balanced geographically, whose sales are spread over regions, like Burberry. It also helps to have good management with experience of tough times and capable of flexibility in terms of cost-cutting."

So, what has Kim Winser overseen in her first 2 years in charge at Pringle? She began by finding out, and then explaining, just how dire the situation was. She characterized her and her staff's task as: "Rescuing the heritage of a great British brand."

Following this she instigated an aggressive trimming of existing product ranges (out went lesser quality lambswool jumpers and underwear, for example). "We only make beautiful cashmere knitwear," she explained. She then sought greater efficiency in the Hawick factory. The potentially infinite number of different Pringle jumpers on the market – a function of allowing some retailers to order alterations to colors, buttons, and sleeve lengths – has been discontinued, with Winser claiming that "we must have one very clear range, one message, which must not be broken. If people don't like our sleeves or our buttons I suggest that they don't buy Pringle."

While a strategic decision has been made to continue and invest in the factory in Hawick (at a time when so much manufacturing is being relocated out of the United Kingdom to the Far East), the existing Factory Manager was relieved of his duties. Winser promoted a younger more energetic character from the floor to take his place and then worked closely with him to improve processes and facilities.

While the previous Pringle design team was retained, new blood was also injected. The first collections under Winser's reign showed a heavy emphasis on updating the signature argyle knits and promoting the traditional Pringle Lion logo in interesting new ways. The new head designer drafted in to breathe further life into Pringle's venerable history is Stuart Stockdale, a 33-year-old with diverse credentials. Stockdale graduated from Central Saint Martins in London before completing an MA in womenswear design at the Royal College of Art. Since then he has covered both ends of the fashion market, working as assistant to the Italian designer Romeo Gigli before cutting his teeth in commercial design with J Crew – purveyor of basic casual-wear to the US masses. This experience gave him a great understanding of the American market – a market that is crucial to Winser's plans for resurrecting Pringle. Since returning to the UK, Stockdale has set up his own label in London as well as launching Jasper Conran's first luxury menswear collection. Now he works for Pringle. "When I first saw the archive, I was totally inspired," Stockdale claimed. "There is so much potential. There was nothing else like Pringle on the market. My challenge is to break out from the knits, yet everything I design must come from the heritage of the knitwear." Stockdale is well placed to understand what he is taking on. He was born just a stone's throw away from Pringle's Hawick home.

Winser set her staff tough targets. Within 12 weeks of her joining the company, she reversed a previous decision not to show a new Pringle range at the world's biggest menswear fair in Florence, and soon after this wanted to launch completely new menswear and womenswear ranges in Pringle's first live catwalk shows since the 1950s. While it was a close-run thing, both targets were met successfully, providing a tremendous boost to staff morale.

Nick Faldo has been removed as the personification of Pringle's identity (although he has been retained to promote golf-wear in certain markets). David Beckham has been identified as an appropriate update of Faldo, and American anglophiles such as Madonna and Julia Roberts reinforce his British presence. The aim of these changes is to refocus the company identity around an "old-world take on modern elegance."

Pringle's London headquarters has been moved from Savile Row, which Winser saw as too fusty and not fashion-oriented enough anymore, to a setting described as "retro-chic" – a converted 1960s warehouse just around the corner. A new emphasis on retailing has been signaled with Pringle "signature stores" being developed in Milan, New York, Tokyo, and London. The latter will replace Emporio Armani's flagship store in Bond Street. Bill Christie, who played a significant part in the successful regeneration of Burberry, has been employed as the new head of retail. Mr. Christie is promising VIP customers complimentary single malt Scotch whisky in the "libraries" within these stores, where the men's range will be displayed.

The signs, so far, are positive and Winser is proud to communicate the company's recent achievements. Sales are up by a third. Many new high-fashion retailers are now buying Pringle. The number employed in Hawick is up by a quarter. The American market is still tough, but Winser claims that Pringle is not suffering like some and that "we're well placed for when things pick up." It is speculated that Winser has even begun to cast her eye over some of Pringle's traditional competitors (like those mentioned above) which have fallen on hard times, but she claims to be holding back at the moment: "I think it's best to focus on [the brand that] we have already." However, new international licensing deals are now enabling Pringle to take the label into related diversifications such as leather goods, children's clothes, and home-wear, and increase production quickly and effectively.

The *Sunday Times* has described Pringle's progress as "a great British success story." Winser herself is more circumspect: "Is the company saved? Not completely. But we've made a very good first step."

> 1. What are the key elements of managing strategic change in the luxury brands sector?
> 2. What has made Kim Winser such an effective manager of change at Pringle?

◀◀◀ Hanging by a Thread: Some Ideas . . .

1. What are the key elements of managing strategic change in the luxury brands sector?

While the effective management of change will require an understanding of the particular organization in question, this case seems to suggest at least one general characteristic in this sector. It seems important to be very cautious about revolutionary change because a luxury brand often relies on a mystique created by its associations and relationships with the past – and this must be preserved at all costs. Often the guardians of these relationships are long-serving staff or suppliers or customers, so they must be treated with care. However, often these firms have fallen out of fit with the modern business environment, and subsequently on hard times, by not questioning old processes, inherited inefficiencies, or outdated production methods. Managing change in this sector appears to require a very dexterous change agent who can effectively blend evolutionary and revolutionary approaches, going through each item of the value chain, asking what should be preserved and what should be changed, and asking if every item does actually contribute to a great enough extent to justify its costs.

2. What has made Kim Winser such an effective manager of change at Pringle?

One can quite easily break down Winser's success using a straightforward change framework like Kotter's eight steps. Using this we can see that Winser:

1. emphasizes the urgency of the situation
2. works hard to form coalitions (with the existing design team and the new Factory Manager, for example)
3. expresses a clear vision, both in word and in deed
4. communicates the change with everything she says and does
5. sets tough targets and then lets people get on with achieving them
6. uses these targets, once achieved (e.g. the fashion shows), as exemplars of short-term wins
7. communicates to consolidate these successes
8. recognizes that the current success is just a start and that there is more change to come

However, this sort of analysis only tells part of the story. As the ideas for the previous question suggest, managing change in this sector requires a dexterous approach that blends different types of evolutionary and revolutionary methods. In this light, it is interesting to look at how Winser exhibits a number of different change management styles in this case. For example, she exhibits all four of Dunphy and Stace's four change styles at different phases, and on different issues, when appropriate. And, she is a combination of a Transformer, Revitalizer, Turnarounder, Defender, and Inheritor, according to the Leavy and Wilson scale. Consequently, she also uses different strategies to manage resistance.

She seems to focus strongly on the importance of consistency across the operational and strategic levels, and the culture and the strategy of the organization, to preserve the corporate or brand identity. Moreover, she seems to understand the heritage of the brand and the importance of blending the best of the new with the old stories and the traditions to keep existing customers happy while reaching out to new ones. Finally, she acknowledges that the change program is not over. No matter how successful these early steps have been, they are still first steps on a long onward journey.

▶▶▶

The awakening giant

ICI was one of Britain's largest manufacturing firms. In 1981 it was ranked the fifth largest of the world's chemical companies. *The Awakening Giant* project examined ICI's attempts to change its strategy, structure, and culture over the period 1960–84. ICI's four largest divisions and its corporate headquarters were studied. However, this case only summarizes some of the key elements of study.

ICI had developed its scale and scope early in the development of the global chemicals industry. The company had been a great technological innovator and its position was helped through its market dominance in "The British Empire" that had been ensured by the pre-WWII cartels that dominated the industry. After the War, with the cartels and other political agreements dissolving and a wide range of new players entering the industry with newer and larger plant, ICI found itself in a more competitive context. Spurred by the increasing success of US chemical companies in Europe, the platform for growth in Europe provided by the birth of the EEC, pressures from within ICI for innovation coming from some of the newer divisions (such as organics, plastics, and synthetic fibers), and some inauspicious financial results in 1958 and 1961, ICI began the new decade in an atmosphere of challenge and change. Thus, around the early 1960s, ICI management began to cohere around four strategic changes that it hoped would improve the company's competitive position:

1. dramatic improvement in the size and efficiency of ICI's manufacturing plants
2. energetic attempts to improve labor productivity
3. repositioning market focus away from Britain and old Empire markets towards Europe and North America
4. moving ICI's culture and organization toward a greater concern with marketing and financial competences and away from its technocratic culture and power system and purely functional bureaucracy

This plan for change coincided with the anointing of Sir Paul Chambers as Chairman – the first "outsider" to occupy the position within ICI.

By 1972, ICI was still Britain's biggest industrial company, and, according to prevailing rates of exchange, the biggest chemicals company in the world. However, not all of the above strategic changes were realized with the purpose and energy that many within and outside ICI would have liked. It still had scale and it had scope; it was still active in all major industrial and most non-industrial countries; and it was, product-wise, one of the most diversified chemical companies in the world.

However, ICI was, in culture and management, almost entirely British. About two-thirds of the total workforce were employed in Britain; British factories were by far the most important part of ICI's manufacturing interests; and 63% of total sales were derived from UK assets. ICI remained divided into nine largely autonomous and profit-accountable divisions, answering to the main Board. The Board and Executive Directors were resident at ICI's head office in Millbank, London, SW1. They maintained effective strategic control over the divisions through having the final say over the investment decisions that determined ICI's future shape and being the final arbiter of personnel policy.

As ICI entered the 1970s, Anthony Sampson had placed the jibe "slumbering giant" around ICI's neck. During the 1970s it would increasingly find itself prone to its dependence on an inflation-ridden and declining British economy, and an industry where the premium of chemical growth over general rates of growth was reduced and in some sectors eliminated. By the end of the 1970s, there was massive over-capacity in the European fibers, petrochemicals, and plastics industries and ICI was having to learn to live with the increasingly confident use of trade union power and government intervention in business. Some within the company had seen these problems coming. One of Chambers' likely successors, Lord Beeching, departed rapidly from ICI in 1967 for sensing problem areas and recommending action that his Board colleagues could neither appreciate nor act on. Many of Beeching's recommendations were not to be implemented until 12 years later.

Things took a further dramatic turn around 1980. The arrival of the Thatcher Government and its pursuit of strict monetarist economics led to high interest rates, a recession in industrial production, and mounting unemployment. The further fall in ICI's UK customer base and the sharply rising value of sterling in relation to the US dollar and Deutsche Mark meant cheaper chemical imports from Europe and the US and a trend for British chemical prices to move out of line with those on the Continent. The net effect was a dramatic worsening of ICI's performance in the early 1980s and an end to the belief that success would come from investment in huge, efficient complexes producing heavy chemicals. The situation was once again ripe for major change.

John Harvey-Jones had joined ICI in his early 30s from a career in the Royal Navy. Harvey-Jones, like Chambers before him, was not "an ICI man." However, in addition to this, Harvey-Jones was incredibly charismatic and extremely shrewd. He was appointed to the main Board in 1973 and spent much of the 1970s orchestrating an "educational process" – trying to "open ICI up to change." Crucial to this process was a need to change the mode, style, composition, and problem-solving processes of the Board. This required persistence and patience as well as

250

the articulation of a vision of a better future for ICI. However, Harvey-Jones had no simple-minded or clear-cut vision for ICI. Insofar as there was a vision amongst Harvey-Jones and the "for change caucus" on the Board, it was imprecisely clarified through additive implementation. Harvey-Jones became Chairman of the Board in 1982 as the context for change, outlined above, was ripening.

The new Chairman and other key executives sought to replace some of the old beliefs about the potency of capital expenditure, cash management, and a risk-averse, consensual, and operational style of management, with a new ideology. This emphasized a sharpening of market focus, a greater entrepreneurial emphasis on decentralized units, and a lessening of bureaucracy and central control. This cultural shift was linked to major changes in structure, systems, and human resource management.

Real changes in ICI's strategic direction followed the shift in organizational culture. Assets in the two biggest loss-making divisions, Petrochemicals and Plastics, were closed, and then the two were merged. Three other divisions all lost assets. Service functions, such as engineering, R&D, purchasing, and personnel, were rationalized. ICI's UK employees fell by 31% between 1979 and 1983. In 1986, all of the UK heavy chemicals divisions – Agricultural, Mond, Petrochemicals, and Plastics – were merged into one group, allowing further fixed costs to be taken out. In addition, ICI finally began to realize the intentions of the 1970s and significantly increase its business in high added-value products, consolidate its position in Europe, and build up its presence in the US. Toward the end of the 1980s, ICI was actively seeking new acquisitions and was cultivating high growth in new markets in the Pacific Basin.

---

1. *What were the change needs facing ICI by the time Harvey-Jones took up the reins? How would you subsequently describe Harvey-Jones' change management approach? (You may find figures 9.3 and 9.4 and the surrounding text helpful in analyzing these issues.)*
2. *Can you use Mintzberg and Westley's framework (outlined in figure 9.2) to suggest why it was important for Harvey-Jones to shift the culture of ICI?*
3. *How would you characterize Harvey-Jones' change leadership locus according to Leavy and Wilson's scale?*
4. *Can you use Kotter's eight-step model of change to outline Harvey-Jones' strategy for changing ICI?*
5. *Why do you think Harvey-Jones was a more successful change agent than his predecessors had been at ICI?*

9:3

Leopards, tigers, and bears

The New Zealand Social Policy Agency (SPA) exists to provide policy advice and was established by combining a number of pre-existing Government departments. The New Zealand Government at the time the SPA was established hoped that it would provide a counterbalance to other advisory agencies, particularly the Treasury, whose advice was perceived by many to be overly driven by dry economic analysis. The organization had been up and running for almost a year before it was decided that a change initiative was required to focus the SPA toward more tangible business objectives.

Developing these objectives presented certain difficulties. After being subject to a number of restructurings, as the Government increasingly brought in business consultants to review the operations of organizations like the SPA, many staff were skeptical with regard to the worth of such change initiatives. In addition, many of the departments that were brought together to form the SPA had been plucked whole from previous Government bodies. Hence, the subcultures within the organization were stronger than the culture of the SPA as a whole, making it likely that people would have a far greater sense of their own local needs and wants as opposed to those of the body corporate.

It was decided that the best first step toward developing a focus on new objectives would be to randomly select people from across the SPA, distribute them into four groups, and then ask each group to think of a non-business metaphor that described what the SPA was like. The groups presented the following four metaphors (two mechanistic, one organic, and one something in between): *stationary engine, electric generator, leopard cub,* and *racing yacht.*

The first two groups' metaphors were similar, as was their reasoning. They saw the SPA as turning inputs (e.g. coal/statistics) into outputs (e.g. energy/policy advice) through a series of interrelated processes. The racing yacht group said that the organization was best seen as a collection of individuals each with unique specialist skills who had to work together if the whole was to be greater than the sum of the parts. Additionally, the SPA was an organization that needed a clear strategy, but one that could be quickly adjusted if and when environmental conditions changed. Those who associated the SPA with a leopard said that the organization was like a cub because it was young and needed to find its feet in the "jungle." However, like the leopard it "could not change its spots." It had to realize that most of its staff had a long history of working in government organizations and it therefore had to be understood that they could not change overnight – certainly not into the sorts of people that many of the previously enlisted consultants had insisted were imperative in the "new business environment." The strengths of this history should be recognized rather than swept, wholesale, under the carpet.

The groups were then asked to discuss the achievements that would be necessary for their metaphorical identities to be successful.

The generator/engine groups pointed out the importance of *good quality inputs,* be they coal or statistics, if outputs of a regularly high standard were to be produced. Plus, *regular maintenance* of the parts that made up the organization was crucial.

If the racing yacht was to be successful, two things were thought imperative. While the specialist units needed to maintain their particular skills, ways needed to be found whereby they could develop an *appreciation* of how those skills related to the skills of others. Secondly, systems that enabled the organization to *quickly learn* about environmental changes were required.

Learning was also critical to the leopard cub as it grew. But just as important was a developing *sense of identity* – that it become aware of what it meant to be a leopard, and how this made it different from other animals. This developed sense of identity would also help others understand it, what it did, and why.

After this exercise, five objectives were developed, which, perhaps not surprisingly, reflected the analogies that had been developed (these are provided in brackets at the end of each objective). The new objectives are listed below with the name of the individual chosen to take responsibility for maintaining the organization's focus on their achievement beside them:

Alan   (a) To have secured quality inputs that enable us to provide an excellent policy service. (Engine/Generator)

Craig   (b) To be an organization that recognizes and continuously maintains and updates [through training etc.] the value of our core assets and puts them to optimal use in providing quality social policy advice. (Leopard Cub and Engine/Generator)

Clifford   (c) To be an organization that benefits from the synergy between its diverse elements. (Racing Yacht)

Rose   (d) To become an organization with a "learning culture" with systems in place to enable the regular questioning of assumptions and methods in light of environmental change. (Leopard and Racing Yacht)

Aroha   (e) To have a distinct identity that is recognized and respected by clients and stakeholders. (Leopard Cub)

It was generally agreed that these objectives and the other developments that came out of this change management initiative were a great success, particularly given an environment that had been resistant to previous initiators for change.

---

1.   *How would you characterize the strategy for change outlined in this case using Kotter and Schlesinger's framework (reproduced in figure 9.6)?*
2.   *Outline the reasons why you think this sort of change strategy worked in this case.*
3.   *In what other situations do you think a strategy like this might be usefully applied? And, in what sort of situations do you think another strategy might be more appropriate?*

The plastic pig

During the 1970s, Reliant was the second largest independent British producer of cars in the UK, with 360 cars a week coming off its production line. Reliant was noteworthy for the three-wheeled Reliant Robin as well as the up-market sports car estate, the Scimitar, once favored by Princess Anne. The three-wheeled Robin consisted of a fiberglass body and an 850cc aluminum engine capable of 60 miles per gallon, all of which was made in-house.

After a long period of decline, Reliant went bust three times during the 1990s. (A brief history of the firm and its cars can be found on www.3wheelers.com/

reliant.html.) While in administration, Jonathan Haynes, an ex-Jaguar engineer, decided to attempt a rescue of the ailing firm. Haynes's father had been famous for designing the E-type Jaguar, a famous racing car, and son, like father, also had a passion for sports cars. He was attracted by Reliant's illustrious past even though sports cars hadn't been made since the early 1990s. Just before Reliant entered administration, the firm was only producing the Robin, which had been dubbed "the plastic pig." To get the factory working again, Haynes would have to focus on production of the Robin and postpone any thoughts of a more glamorous future. How could he possibly turn the tide?

On arriving at the site, he found total disarray as the administrators had left the site in a real mess. The machines had lain idle and had seized up and rusted. One employee commented that it was a good collection a museum would be proud of. Haynes' first task in getting production restarted was to hire back the original engineers, as they knew how to make the Reliant Robin. It was a testimony to their loyalty to the car that they even considered this very uncertain future.

Suppliers proved very awkward. They had lost money when Reliant went into administration. Even for such small items as bulbs costing 10p each they wouldn't supply until Reliant's cheque was cashed. There were other demands on working capital as well. Employees needed to be paid and, to get production moving as soon as possible, Haynes had to pay for large amounts of overtime.

Robin Reliant customers are passionate about their cars. Around 44,000 were registered and many had bought seven or eight cars over a sustained period of time. The Reliant Robin had a strong image at the time, as it featured in a favorite BBC comedy *Only fools and horses* and was also the object of many jokes by the comedian Jasper Carrott. Although laughed at for its quirkiness and down-market image, many also regarded the Robin Reliant fondly – indeed, the jokes were seen as free advertising. Part of the attraction may have been the unusualness of a three-wheeled car, and the camaraderie of an ownership club. The car was certainly popular among market traders and farmers. The loyalty of the customers meant a continuous demand for spare parts and updates, although many competitors were filling this demand.

Haynes forecasted that the firm had to build 50 cars per week to pay his rehired 60-strong workforce and to balance the books. Fortunately when he took charge, he had discovered 14 Robins in nearly complete form. With little effort these cars were finished and sold.

One of Haynes's early priorities was to meet with the dealers to hear their views on what the customers wanted. Throughout the first year, Haynes was close to the dealers, but also demanded quick and prompt payment from them.

At the factory he placed a salesman into a position that he regarded as the most important in the firm – to sell off spare parts to generate £2,000 per day. This target was soon doubled. In his words: "Sell anything! Sell, sell, sell!"

Haynes was conscious that traditional attitudes in the company had to change. Many employees had lived through the previous three collapses and were very cynical that anything would really change. In the day-to-day operations of the business, Haynes detected the attitude of "The answer's no, but perhaps we can do it, but the answer's no!" In response he would quote John Neil of Unipart: "The answer's yes – now what's the question?"

Haynes was worried by his 20 employees involved in making the bodies of the car, entirely by hand. This seemed overly labor intensive and outdated, as chopper guns existed which could do the task more quickly and would require fewer employees. In forceful discussions with his production manager they agreed to test out the new technology.

Haynes underachieved his target of 50 cars per week, producing 36 cars at the deadline. Reasons included reliance on new employees who had to be taught the job. However, support from Haynes's backers continued. A special edition Robin Reliant was launched in racing green and was well received by customers. At this time Haynes also hired a designer to draft images of a new sports car.

At the end of the first year, Haynes relaxed at his farm and reflected on the trials and tribulations of his first year. At one stage they had almost come close to bankruptcy, with just £400 in the bank. He had pushed all his employees hard with long hours, tough discussion, and with only the promise of an uncertain future. Indeed, his own farm had suffered as he put all his attention into Reliant. However, it seemed now that Reliant was back onto a firm footing and Haynes savored the prospect of the unveiling of his new four-wheeled sports car at the Birmingham motor show the following month.

---

1. *Suggest why Reliant was declining prior to Haynes's arrival.*
2. *What barriers or resistance to change did Haynes encounter?*
3. *Why did Haynes have to take more of a revolutionary or transformational approach rather than an evolutionary one?*
4. *Despite the more revolutionary process outlined in this case, what aspects of Reliant's past would you look to try and continue with into the future? Give reasons why.*
5. *Outline Haynes's change strategy and suggest why you believe it was successful in this instance.*

Four weddings and a funeral

In an article in the *New Republic* at the beginning of 2000, Joseph Stiglitz, former Chief Economist with the World Bank, offered a stinging critique of his former organization and the IMF (International Monetary Fund), "fixer" of the economies of poor countries. Wrote Stiglitz: "Critics accuse the institution of taking a cookie-cutter approach to economics and they are right. When the IMF decides to assist a country, it dispatches a mission of economists. These economists frequently lack extensive experience in a country; they are more likely to have first-hand knowledge of five star hotels than of the villages that dot its countryside. They work hard, poring over numbers deep into the night. But their task is impossible. In a period of days or, at most, weeks, they are charged with developing a program sensitive to the needs of the country. Needless to say, a little number-crunching rarely provides adequate insights into the development strategy of an entire nation." Given their limitations, Stiglitz claims that country teams have been known to "compose draft reports before visiting. I heard stories of team members copying large parts of the text for one country's report and transferring them wholesale into another. They might have got away with it, except the 'search and replace' function on the word processor didn't work properly, leaving the original country's name in a few places."

The views of Tony Smith, Principal of Baraka Agricultural College, appear to support Stiglitz's. "The models used by the IMF and World Bank," he explains, "tend to judge development in terms of industrialization. So, if countries like ours want funding, they have to show how it will be channeled into big industrial projects." Not only are such projects potentially damaging to the sensitive ecosystems within the countries that the IMF seeks to help; Tony explains that they are often simply not feasible in countries where the infrastructure – electricity, clean water, roads – is not yet able to support existing needs. At present, for example, the college has to make preparations for at least three lengthy power-cuts a week.

Baraka College was founded in 1974 by a group of Franciscan Brothers. Its ends are more or less the same as the IMF: "to respond to the needs and aspirations of the poor." However, its stated philosophy indicates very different means: "Baraka promotes sustainable agriculture and rural development through education, training, and extension programs that focus on recognizing the environment, natural and human resources as the foundation of economic and social activity. In the current demographic, economic, environmental, and social realities of East Africa, the most appropriate response is that of *Sustainable Agriculture and Rural Development*."

From humble beginnings, Baraka now attracts students from all over East Africa. It seeks to train these students to get more out of their land, and enable them to spread this knowledge when they return to their homes. In contrast to some of the grander IMF-sponsored projects, Baraka's latest initiative is the promotion of and training in beekeeping. This is an activity that is easily set up, does not take away resources from soil crops (indeed the bees' activity improves yields of traditional crops such as coffee, bananas, and sunflowers), and provides small farmers with invaluable extra income. In a land where subsistence farming is still very much the way of life and the dominant mode of production, the college believes that this sort of from-the-ground-up development is far more practical and beneficial to local people at this point in time than industrialization imposed from on-high.

* * *

At the end of another disappointing English football season, Liverpool Football Club took what seemed to be a fairly insignificant step in May of 1998. In a small article in *The Times*, Nick Szczepanik reported it thus: "Manchester United recently claimed to have moved football shirt design forward with their new zip-front shirt design, but Liverpool have moved in the opposite direction with a distinctly traditional look to their new home shirt, launched today. The design, more or less identical to that of the Bill Shankley era [Liverpool's 'golden age' of the 1960s and 70s] is bound to evoke memories of Ron Yeats, Ian St. John, and John Toshack [famous past players]." Indeed, while Manchester United has been far and away the best team in the UK over the past decade, Liverpool is perhaps the one English team that could boast a past more glorious than United's. At the turn of the millennium, *The Times'* ranking of all English Football League clubs, based on their performance since the League's inception in 1872, showed Manchester closing in fast from second place but Liverpool still as number one. Szczepanik, however, seemed somewhat skeptical of the shirt change: "One unfortunate side-effect could be that the underachievement of the present squad may be thrown into even sharper relief by the similarity of their new kit to that worn by multi medal-winners of the past."

However, with the benefit of hindsight, one might see this change of kit as symbolic of a more substantial rejuvenation at Liverpool. Shortly afterwards, Gérard Houllier, a Frenchman who spent a good part of his youth in Liverpool studying for his Masters and teaching in Liverpool schools, was given sole charge of the team. After 18 months at the helm, Liverpool's aim of consistently finishing in the top three of England's Premier League ("a financial necessity," explains Liverpool Director Noel White) appears a realistic one for the first time in a long time. Both die-hard fans and shareholders alike seem united behind Houllier, quite an achievement given the general sense of suspicion regarding a "foreigner" being appointed, and the "divisive" and "unprofessional" influences that were at work in the clubhouse when he took over.

On reflection, most commentators see the secret of Houllier's success as his "going back to old values to heal new divisions," "blending foreign and local talent," or his ability "to thread foreign players' technique with the ebullience of the emerging players from Liverpool's youth academy." Many feared that Houllier's appointment would see the club's grass-roots undermined as the side followed the approach of other English clubs under foreign leadership, with more emphasis on signing overseas talent and less on "growing their own" (London's Chelsea, for example, now often played without any Englishmen in their team). However, Houllier is clear that "our best signing is probably our youth academy. It represents an investment of £12m. [But] the tradition of players going through the youth development system has got to be kept." Liverpool's traditional strength of investing in home-grown youth means that while clubs like Arsenal and Chelsea bypass English youth to buy wholesale from abroad, Liverpool fielded seven players from the local region in the 1999/2000 season. While Liverpool must buy in certain players to remain competitive on a global scale with Manchester United, Real Madrid, and Juventus, Houllier believes that the investment in the Academy is a crucial element in maintaining continuity with the past.

And now the team is playing with almost the same passion, perseverance, and commitment that Houllier claims to have "loved" when he first watched Liverpool from the Anfield terraces in 1969. "What we have is embryonic," he says. "The team is starting to have some personality . . . and we're leaving the century in a good way."

*   *   *

At the beginning of the year 2000, Robin Cook, the British Foreign Secretary, approved a new campaign to "rebrand" Britain. Twelve new posters were designed to replace decorations in British Embassies and Councils that had not been updated since the 1960s. While calculated to show that traditional images of Morris Dancers and crooked teeth, flatulent beef-eaters, and glossy Kodachromes of

Castles have been eclipsed, the posters sought to illustrate a sense of continuity with the past. Each is split down the middle, connecting *Old England* with *New Britain*. A frock by Sir Hardy Amies, the Queen's most respected couturier, is cut in half and joined with the right half of an outfit by John Galliano, the flamboyant Englishman who designs for Christian Dior. Julie Christie, the face of the "swinging sixties," fades into Kate Winslet. Sir Geoff Hurst, in his 1966 World-Cup-winning England kit, kicks at a ball that is melded with the one being chased by England's most recent international football sensation, Michael Owen. The late Benny Hill is paired with Mr Bean, and a horse painted by George Stubbs in the 18th century is "cross-bred" with Damien Hirst's infamous 1990s *pickled sheep*. Embassy staff and the general public have welcomed the campaign, as has Mark Leonard, who writes on national identity for the independent "think-tank" Demos. "It is a good use of money," says Leonard. "We could do with some of these posters at British airports and the Eurostar [train] terminal, too, just to remind us – as well as visitors – what Britain is about."

*   *   *

Hewlett-Packard was founded by Bill Hewlett and Dave Packard in a garage in a small mid-western town in the United States at the height of the Depression in the 1930s. Along with IBM, it grew to become the most successful computer company in the world, and, all the while, the company's existing employees and its new recruits were inspired by the circulation of what were called "Bill and Dave stories." However, in the 1980s and 1990s the company fell upon relatively hard times and appeared to be losing its focus in a market where differentiation was becoming increasingly important. On November 15, 1999, under the leadership of new CEO Carly Fiorina, HP announced a new global campaign. "We must reinvent ourselves," proclaimed Fiorina. At the heart of this reinvention was a theme of "going back to the garage." Advertisements featured a small wooden garage at twilight with a light burning inside, over the top of which were printed messages such as: "The original company of inventors started here. It is returning here. The original start-up will act like one again."

*   *   *

A former state-owned enterprise in New Zealand had just been privatized and bought by an American corporation. The new controllers brought about many changes. They needed to if the organization was to be successful in its new guise. Most managers were gung-ho about the structural changes that had been put in place and felt that the culture of the organization would not take long to catch up. "From a structure point of view, there's very little left to do," claimed one senior manager. A senior director claimed that, "We have a people and a 'mind set' problem. We were 25,000; we are now 15,000. Of those 15,000, 13,500 worked for the old organization. We don't have a structure problem."

However, things did not come around as quickly as they had hoped. "From a culture point of view," said the first manager quoted above, "there are quite a lot [of problems] because the people who are still here from the old organization are not in tune with the new direction and the values that the new management has

258

Figure 9-5.1

put in place. Theirs is a culture that does not work in a trading organization – sorry, full stop, end, not any of it. It has to be completely new."

A year later, many believed that, on reflection, a lot of the teething problems that the organization suffered in the first 2 years after the change were caused by the original assumption that "everything must go" – that the old culture held nothing within it of use to the service organization of the future. Staff members expressed their frustration and disappointment at the way things had developed by faxing cartoons to one another, like the ones pictured in figure 9-5.1. (Spot the Dog, an agreeable little terrier who would go anywhere and do anything to help people out, was the company's "spokesperson".)

The Head of Corporate Strategy, a veteran with the company and one of the many we interviewed, summed up the feelings of many looking back – with the benefit of hindsight – at the change process:

> "The old organization had a very strong ethic; a strong sense of 'family.' There was a strong sense of public responsibility and I think many who stayed in the organization over a long period of time stayed because of these values and a sense of service . . . I think at the moment the family sense is shattered or strained. I think the sense of service, the spirit of service, is not there because too many issues are being reduced to issues of profitability, accountability, and incentivization, and this emphasis is devaluing those things."

1. *Why can evolutionary approaches to strategic change be more successful than revolutionary approaches?*
2. *If you were involved in managing change in these organizations how would you look to incorporate myths or stories from the organizations' pasts as they move into the future?*
3. *Why do managers of business organizations often favor revolutionary rather than evolutionary approaches to change, and more tangible things like structures or technology than less tangible things like stories?*
4. *In hindsight, do you think that Houllier should have taken a more revolutionary or transformation approach to improving Liverpool FC's fortunes?*

Three in one

The new vicar of St. Margaret's rose to address the assembled congregations of St. Margaret's, St. Barnabus, and Trinity church.

St. Margaret's vicar: "I'm pleased to see so many of you here this afternoon to discuss the future of our three churches and how we may move forward as a unified body. Our churches already work together in a number of ways, such as a shared parish newsletter, occasional shared services, and the rotation of priests on a bi-monthly basis. This is very much in the spirit of the Church of England's wishes that ecumenicalism, the working together of different branches of Christianity, is the road we must follow. When I was appointed to my position at St. Margaret's, it was made clear to me by the bishop that we must embrace our differences as a source of strength. With this vision in mind, we must also confront the practical challenges of everyday existence in our parish. Our congregations are aging and dwindling and we have very significant costs in the upkeep and running of three church buildings. We are also expected to increase our contributions to the diocese from our collections and bequests. The vicars of St. Barnabus and Trinity have had many meetings on this subject and this evening are proposing we consider worshiping more closely together under fewer roofs. This will also have the welcome effect of reducing our costs.

"As you know, St. Barnabus's is a grade 1 protected listed building and so cannot be changed in any way. The focus of attention is therefore on what we should do with St. Margaret's and Trinity church. Trinity is located on the main street of our town and a large number of people pass daily. Local interest is evident in the very successful coffee mornings held on Saturday. However, Trinity is in very poor condition and will need a complete restoration in the next few years or a rebuild – I believe some architects have been contacted informally and they recommend the latter course of action. Needless to say either course is very expensive even taking into account the subsidy we may receive via the bishop. St. Margaret's is a very large Victorian building with a seating capacity of 700. It is less well located, being set in attractive memorial grounds, in a quiet leafy side road some way from the town center. Apart from regular Sunday morning services, its large seating capacity makes it attractive to local schools for their special events. St. Margaret's size is also a drawback as the older members of the congregation complain that it is cold and there is no doubt that it costs a lot to heat.

"I would now like to ask all of you for your thoughts on how we might go forward in realizing our aims of greater ecumenicalism, and reducing our costs."

Trinity church's vicar: "Thank you for your opening words, vicar. I would like to suggest that the forces of St. Margaret's and Trinity combine to create a stronger, unified congregation. I believe either church would be large enough for this to happen. The arguments for making Trinity our preferred option are its excellent location and it could be rebuilt to be a striking new presence on the high street. St. Margaret's, on the other hand, could be redesigned to suit the needs of an enlarged pluralist congregation."

Congregational member of St. Margaret's: "When you say 'redesign St. Margaret's,' what do you mean exactly?"

Trinity church's vicar: "Well, our style of worship at Trinity is more intimate than that of St. Margaret's. We prefer a more conversational style in smaller spaces, rather than the, dare I say it, 'pomp and splendor' of the high church style of St. Margaret's. I would like to suggest that architects are employed to see how St. Margaret's could be partitioned into a series of meeting rooms and glass screens used to separate the main worship space from the body of the church."

Congregational member of Trinity church: "Because St. Margaret's has such large spaces, microphones and amplification have to be used. We oppose the use of such 'technology' – it interferes with the word of God!"

Organist of St. Margaret's: "If you partition St. Margaret's, you will be losing the finest acoustic in the county. I don't know the actual revenue figures, but a number of chamber orchestras and other instrumental groups use the building on a regular basis to make recordings for CD and radio broadcasts. They also hire the organ and piano, both of which are outstanding instruments. These fees help maintain them and the building."

Accountant to St. Margaret's: "I'm surprised to hear that St. Margaret's is financially unhealthy. Although our congregation is dwindling, our receipts from bequests are actually increasing and, as the building is in superb condition, I don't anticipate any capital expenditures for years to come."

Congregational member of St. Margaret's: "Of course the congregation of St. Margaret's would welcome the congregation of Trinity church if they chose to join us."

Congregational member of Trinity church: "Thank you for your welcome, but we would need to be sure that we could have our normal service, led in our own way at 9.30 AM."

Congregational member of St. Margaret's: "Well I'm not sure that's possible as our service starts at 10 AM, so your service would have to start at 9 AM or 11.30 AM."

Congregational member of Trinity church: "Why should we have to adjust our service times? We are the ones who would be sacrificing our building to move to your building. We also have many very elderly members in our congregation and getting to church for 9 AM on a wet winter's day would not be possible. Why can't St. Margaret's move its services?"

Vicar of St. Barnabus's: "Before we get into the detail of changing St. Margaret's, maybe we should think about St. Margaret's congregation moving to Trinity church. Rebuilding Trinity with a modern design in a prime location is bound to attract attention and visitors. Now that businesses can open on Sundays, the church has to face competition for its services. St. Margaret's is really too far from the center of town. A new Trinity church would be an excellent visible statement of the progressiveness of the church. To fund this new building, I suggest that St. Margaret's be sold off for development, as it is a large area of land in a very desirable residential area, where there is a shortage of parking space."

At this point, an elderly lady struggled to her feet, her outstretched arm shaking with rage.

> **Elderly lady:** "Do you mean to tell me that St. Margaret's would be turned into a parking lot – how dare you even suggest such a thing?! My husband is buried in those memorial gardens, as are the loved ones of many people in this meeting. How can you even think of building over them?!"
>
> **Congregational member of St. Margaret's:** "I agree – how can you consider demolishing St. Margaret's? I have worshiped there all of my life – for 60 years. I was married there and my children christened there. You cannot destroy St. Margaret's. Anyway, who are you to say what should happen to St. Margaret's? What has your congregation got to do with it? You don't worship there – you don't care!"

Later that evening, the new vicar of St. Margaret's reflected on the situation and despaired. She had had no idea of the difficulties that "working together" would entail. There was even a question mark over her future already. Why would there be a need for two vicars in the same church? She was the most recent arrival and the other two vicars seemed to be against her. The telephone rang:

> **Congregational member of St. Margaret's:** "Sorry I couldn't be at the meeting this afternoon, vicar. I gather it didn't go very well – I bet the other two churches ganged up on us? Anyway, I have great news. In anticipation of those problems, I have applied to have our church listed as a building of important architectural interest – so it may be protected after all from change. . . ."

The caller continued, but all the vicar could think about was tomorrow morning's meeting with the bishop and his parting words from the last meeting:

"We really have to move things on, you know. Your parish is in the vanguard of change – everyone will be looking to see how you have handled this highly desirable move towards our ecumenical goals. I really hope you can tell me what steps you are taking towards this aim and the progress you have made when we next meet. Don't let me down."

> 1. *What are the drivers for change at the three churches?*
> 2. *What are the barriers to change?*
> 3. *What ways forward can you suggest for the new vicar?*

According even to middle-of-the-road popular opinion, capitalism is at best a regrettable necessity, a useful monster that needs to be bound, drugged, and muzzled if it is not to go on the rampage . . . Capitalism, if guided by nothing but (its) own unchecked intentions, would be wicked, destructive and exploitative – bent on raping the planet and intent on keeping the poor outside the capitalist West in poverty.

The Economist, January 20, 2005

My great-grandfather's vision was to provide affordable transport for the world. I want to expand that vision for the 21st century and provide transportation that is affordable in every sense of the word – socially and environmentally, as well as economically.

Bill Ford, Ford Motor Company, 2005

"Beyond Petroleum" . . . It's beyond belief.

Editorial, Sunday Telegraph, July 6, 2002

At the beginning of the new millennium, British Petroleum relaunched itself as "Beyond Petroleum," proclaiming its concern for the environment and championing its own efforts with regard to developing alternative energy sources. While this re-branding may have been beneficial internally as the firm sought to integrate new acquisitions such as Arco and Amoco together into one shared identity, the move was widely criticized externally. In an editorial entitled "Oil Slickness," London's *Sunday Telegraph* pointed out that: "less than 1% of BP's revenues come from renewable sources of energy and well over 90% of its income still comes from fossil fuels and derivative businesses such as chemicals and petrol retailing." Other media commentators and the general public also didn't buy it, and the Beyond Petroleum marketing was quickly scaled back while the company rethought its position.

BP, like many companies, is concerned not just with short-term profits but also with its ability to sustain itself and its business environments for the long term. This "sustain ability" comes in two parts. First, companies are concerned with developing a sustainable competitive advantage against other similar companies, and, as we have seen in previous chapters, this requires developing a position or character that is different from competitors and difficult to replicate. In this context BP might have thought that taking the environmental high ground through Beyond Petroleum would set them apart from the likes of Exxon and establish relationships that would be difficult for competitors to copy. Second, BP was well aware of the need to be concerned about environmental change. Because changes in the availability of resources like oil would impact on its future prospects, the well-being of the world and its corporate well-being were intertwined. The company needed to be a socially responsible corporate citizen. However, to succeed, BP has found that it has to deal with an increasingly skeptical and informed audience.

Just looking at some recent exposés of companies behaving badly would be enough to make even the most trusting individual a little bit cynical. Consider, for example:

- the high-level chicanery at firms like Enron and WorldCom aided and abetted by auditors with equally questionable values
- the exploitation of gullible investors by "entrepreneurs" and analysts with vested interests during the dot-com bubble
- the environmental devastation wreaked, for example, by the *Exxon Valdez* on the ocean and by logging companies on underdeveloped forested countries
- the egregious level of financial compensation conferred on senior executives while they are in the job and when they are sacked
- the cavalier attitude to consumer health demonstrated by various tobacco, pharmaceutical, and building companies as they orchestrated silence and deception about the effects of their products
- the blind eye turned to the exploitation of offshore workers, including children, by some of the most famous branded goods companies in the world
- the connivance with corrupt officials and governments by some extraction companies keen to protect valuable leases and mining rights
- the popular movies and books, such as *The Corporation* or Michael Moore's works, which have presented these sorts of infamy to an increasingly receptive audience

These, and many other, examples raise questions about the corporate world. Are these merely examples of "rogue" companies or is this the tip of a large rubbish dump wherein the best that can be said of the remainder is that they have not yet been caught? Society's answers to these questions and the actions and attitudes adopted by business in general, and individual organizations in particular, will have a significant influence on the degrees of strategic freedom enjoyed by firms in the 21st century. Thus, in this chapter we explore sustainable development, a recent paradigm that might redefine the role of the firm and capitalism. Sustainable development, according to some of its most zealous advocates, goes beyond dealing with how firms should look to protect and sustain their competitive advantage across the long term and how they should act as good citizens concerned with sustaining or preserving our shared environments for the future. It goes to the heart of what a firm actually is.

Sustainable Development

Students and practitioners of strategy are familiar with the concept of sustainability in the context of a **sustainable competitive advantage**. Advantage is sustainable if the underpinning sources are not substitutable or imitable. The durability of any advantage is a function of the isolating mechanisms impeding copying (see chapter 5 Perfect Positioning). However, the concept of sustainability has taken on broader connotations since the World Commission on Economic Development (WCED) drew attention to the need for **sustainable development** as "... development that meets the needs of the present generation without compromising the ability of future generations to meet their own needs."[1] This broad concept results from the convergence of the principles of **environmental integrity**, **economic prosperity**, and **social equity**. This convergence denotes a significant change.

Historically, economic development (notably through firms) was viewed in many ways as being a tradeoff with environmental concerns and social equity. Pollution, logging, and land abuse, for instance, have been viewed as negative externalities or "collateral damage" of the value-creating process and the under-payment of women and minority groups, for example, viewed as necessary in the interests of the "main" stakeholders: managers and shareholders (see chapter 2 Movers & Shakers). Public, media-driven shaming, or direct control through legislation and hence prosecution were often seen as the necessary forces to make firms keep the public and environmental good in mind.

Another change that had been evolving before the WCED report, but was further stimulated by it, was an increasing focus at a lower level of analysis. Sustainable development had traditionally been discussed as an intraglobal issue at the level of the nation state. So it is nations which sign or do not sign the Kyoto agreement on carbon emissions, for example, even though it is organizations within nations that do the emitting, and it is nations which make trade and tariff agreements although firms do the trading. It is also nations which have been measured on a sustainability index. However, in modern industrialized nation states the firm is becoming (willingly or not) a focus for sustainable development rather than an involved but not necessarily committed bystander. This seems logical to some commentators because "corporations . . . control most of the resources of our global society. If we are to have effective leadership of the sustainability movement, then much of the movement must come from the corporate sector."[2]

There has been a paradigm shift in that businesses are being asked to become manifestations of the planet's requirement for environmental integrity *and* economic prosperity *and* social equity, rather than uneasy equilibria of tradeoffs between the three. This mirrors the evolutionary biologist's perspective that ecology and economy are interdependent and inseparable dynamics.[3] In response to this shift, increasing numbers of businesses are demonstrating a commitment to sustainable development (or at least its language and reports) through reporting on the so-called **triple bottom line** of economic, environmental, and social performance. Such sustainability reporting is becoming commonplace, with laggards under more scrutiny to explain their lack of transparency. To some companies, this is no more than dealing with one of the pests of PEST, or ESTEMPLE, but to others it is a strategic necessity not only in terms of diffusing potentially hostile political and social forces, but also in terms of potential reputational disadvantage in the minds of environmentally sensitized customers. Indeed, the quotation by Bill Ford at the beginning of this chapter is a good example of how these three bottom lines have become a part of today's strategic language.

Corporate Sustainability[4]

Mirroring the global concept of sustainable development is the firm-based concept of **corporate sustainability (CS)**. Again the concept resists tight definition but can best be understood as an amalgam of *corporate environmental integrity*, *corporate social equity*, and *corporate economic prosperity* (see figure 10.1).

Corporate environmental integrity emphasizes a firm's responsibility to manage its processes and products so as to minimize their impact on the physical environment. At the most reactive end of the continuum, this calls for businesses to simply act responsibly in the way they dispose of the waste and by-products of their processes. A more progressive approach, however, would involve seeking

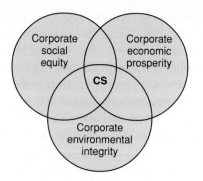

Figure 10.1 The three legs of corporate sustainability (CS)

ongoing improvements and/or innovation, to reduce and eventually eliminate such pollution (pollution prevention[5]). Further on from this, so-called "cradle to grave" responsibility encourages firms to design products for minimal energy usage both in manufacture and in use, to use less material and components, and to use material least harmful to the environment both as an input and with regard to eventual disposal. Some predict that legislation will increasingly demand that firms accept the disposal ("grave") end of the product process as their responsibility. As an example, the "take-back" law in Germany already makes auto manufacturers responsible for disposing of their products at the end of their useful life.

Much of the language of the above paragraph reflects a "do no harm" and "minimize depletion" orientation and would be familiar to most managers today. Many claim, however, that true sustainability demands a more constructive response whereby companies actively seek to *improve* the world's environmental integrity. The concept of an "ecological footprint"[6] captures the daunting scale of this problem. It takes 10.3 hectares (the footprint) to supply the basic needs of the average US citizen compared with 0.8 hectares in India – yet even India's total footprint is larger than the country itself. If the remainder of the world comes to enjoy the same level of consumption as the US, then the known resources of the world would need to triple to accommodate that growth unless a major reorientation takes place in those companies fulfilling that consumption. Logging companies who plant more trees than they chop down are a simple example of this sort of reorientation. Monsanto's shift to genetically modified (GM) crops that are more productive and inherently resistant to disease and pests without use of protective chemicals is a further example of how technology might increase the available footprint by increasing yields and reducing pollutants at the same time. (Note that GM food is not problem-free and Monsanto has many virulent critics, as micro-case 10-2 below illustrates.)

The **corporate social equity** leg of the corporate sustainability stool is manifest as *corporate social responsibility*[7] (CSR) or *corporate citizenship*. The discussion around this dynamic, associated with the older concept of business ethics, dates back at least to the governing bodies of the ancient Greeks.[8] From one extreme, it is argued that a firm's social and ethical responsibilities are fully discharged in maximizing long-run returns to shareholders and are captured in the aphorism "the business of business is business."[9] *The Economist*, for example, is unapologetic in asserting that "managers . . . ought not to concern themselves with the public good: they are not competent to do it, they lack the democratic credentials for it, and their day jobs should leave them not time even to think about it. If they merely concentrate on discharging their responsibilities to the owners of their firms, acting ethically as they do so, they will usually serve the public good in any case."[10] The diametrically opposing perspective is that "social responsibility is the managerial obligation to take action to protect and improve both the welfare of society as a whole and the interests of organizations" and, within this perspective, maximizing shareholder value is *neither a necessary nor a sufficient component*.[11] Hence, while *The Economist* stresses "acting ethically" while pursuing shareholder value, others suggest that it may be the pursuit of shareholder value per se that is the problem.

These arguments are often expressed in terms of the relative gains and losses of various **stakeholders** and the extent to which the needs of some *direct stakeholders of the firm* (e.g. shareholders, senior managers) are privileged over the needs of others, who may be directly or indirectly involved (e.g. employees, customers, local community, and society in general). The heat in the argument is generated most when the actions of businesses harm some stakeholders while pursuing the interests of others. *Roger and Me*, a 1989 film by the ever-controversial producer Michael Moore, captured this dynamic by showing the negative economic and social consequences for Moore's home town, Flint in Michigan, when General Motors (then under the stewardship of Roger Smith) closed down its Flint manufacturing facility with a loss of 30,000 local jobs. Current arguments along this line concern such matters as putting local people out of work by "offshoring" their functions to lower cost countries, the sale of socially harmful products (e.g. high-sugar and high-fat foods), the use of child labor, and dealing with corrupt regimes.

Beyond the level of the individual firm, there are a number of typologies of CSR. Some suggest a longitudinal pathway from one general orientation to another while others indicate a continuum of similar dynamics co-existing in different ways in any cross-section of businesses. Table 10.1 illustrates an historical perspective with different phases of social responsibility having emerged because of different pressures at different times.[12]

An alternative suggestion is that while social change – for example, in the form of increasing pluralism and global awareness, and a far wider share ownership – has indeed forced a change in orientation in business in general, it is more realistic to view different organizations as having different perspectives contingent on their specific histories and contexts. Like people, companies can range from socially responsible to irresponsible, from being careful to preserve a legacy for tomorrow's

Table 10.1 Development of sustainability orientation in developed countries

Phase	Time	Orientation
I: Profit maximizing	Post-Industrial Revolution	Maximize profits within the law
II: Trustee management	1920s–1980s	Equitable balance among competing claims of internal and external stakeholders
III: Quality of life management	1980s–now	Broad economic, social, and environmental responsibility

Table 10.2 Business types and societal roles

Type	Societal role
I: Profit maximizer	An *economic entity* with the sole objective of making legal profits. Labor is an input factor to be bought and sold like land and capital
II: Good employer	A *human development entity* with obligations to develop and use employees to their fullest capability by providing a stimulating work environment and meeting both the hygiene and motivational needs of its workers
III: Good citizen	A *civic entity* with obligations to support its local community with money and effort and to be fair and open in its dealings and not engage in deceptive or unsafe market or product practices
IV: Social worker	A *societal entity* with obligations, within and beyond its local context, to actively protect and enhance both the physical environment and social equity

citizens to being cavalier with that heritage in optimizing today's benefits.[13] Table 10.2 describes an evolution in firm orientation in this respect, with each higher level "type" incorporating and developing on an earlier level.[14]

The table should also be taken to suggest that each firm has elements of each of the four types and so both context and firm character are important in determining which characteristic predominates. In underdeveloped countries, where most businesses may be type I (through competitive and other contextual forces), there will be some that are higher up the social responsibility scale and the increased proportions of firms in the type II–IV categories in developed countries may say more about the local political and social context than about the fundamental "personality" of those businesses. And so companies that might otherwise be classified as type IV (e.g. Nike, Shell) have been accused of turning a blind eye to labor exploitation (Nike's Asian suppliers)[15] or corrupt dealings (Shell's links with the Nigerian Government)[16] when outside their home markets (contexts). Cynics suggest that inside every (socially constrained) type IV firm there is in fact a type I genie bursting to get out.

Corporate economic prosperity (i.e. creating value and prosperity through producing and selling goods and services) is the fundamental rationale underpinning the existence of firms and the capitalist system. The value created (or value added) is shared between the business and other direct stakeholders/members of society dependent on the extent to which the price obtained by the firm is greater than the overall economic costs of creating and distributing its offerings. In some intensely competitive industries, businesses are forced to sell at prices below economic costs for long periods and hence value is transferred to consumers (airlines and mass-producers of cars have been placed in this position over various business cycles). When prices exceed costs, then the firm captures the value it creates and is able to enhance the prosperity of managers, shareholders, and other direct stakeholders.

While this might seem the "no-brainer" leg of the corporate sustainability stool, a more controversial aspect is captured in the idea of using it to develop a business case for corporate sustainability. In other words, as a "hook" for the "greed is good" business community, some social/environmental champions have dangled the bait of making money from being "good" by arguing that environmental opportunities can become a major source of revenue growth: ". . . few executives realize that environmental opportunities might actually become a major source of *revenue growth* . . . most companies fail to recognize opportunities of staggering proportions."[17] Indeed, it has been noted that the combination of high shareholder returns and a strong focus on social welfare has long been a characteristic of outstanding companies.[18] In line with this, the Dow Jones Sustainability Index (which tracks the share prices of international companies considered leaders in sustainable development) has often outperformed the Dow Jones Global Index. This seems to offer prima facie evidence that corporate sustainability is indeed a function and a driver of corporate economic prosperity, corporate environmental integrity, and corporate social equity (figure 10.1). Three broad theoretical thrusts, all with some empirical support, propose reasons behind this relationship.[19]

1. **The organizational slack perspective**: those firms which earn good returns can devote more resources to social equity and environmental integrity.[20]
2. **The positive synergy perspective**: combining the idea of resource availability and good management, the advocates of this view suggest that, along with all the other things they do well, good managers in firms with available resources also do well in terms of social equity and environmental integrity.[21]
3. **The social impact hypothesis**: the actual costs of social equity and environmental integrity are small compared with the higher risk entailed by failing to meet these requirements. Increasingly those firms that are indifferent to broader stakeholder demands will pay a price in terms of reputational disadvantage and/or a higher risk premium on debt/equity.[22]

These models can be contrasted with the tradeoff approaches mentioned earlier in which social equity and environmental integrity are claimed to entail additional costs that will financially disadvantage the "do-gooder" against more opportunistic and less principled competitors. This is most often expressed by regretful companies attributing their loss of integrity to the lack of a level playing field whereon all competitors must play to the same ethical and environmental rules. It is more subtly expressed in terms of a review or renewal of "the contract between business and society."

The argument that sustainability authors make against the business case orientation is that it is inherently a **contingent concept**, as captured in: "The business case is not a generic argument that corporate sustainability strategies are the right choice for all companies in all situations, *but rather something that must be carefully honed to the specific circumstances of individual companies operating in unique positions within distinct industries*"[23] (emphasis added). This orientation puts economic prosperity at the top of the company's agenda and other aspects of sustainability, such as environmental integrity and CSR, will follow *when and if* it is (economically) sensible for them to do so.[24] The concept of corporate sustainability makes economic prosperity, environmental integrity, and social equity equal and ever-present partners (figure 10.1). There is no "if . . . then" contingency (e.g. "*if* it is good for shareholders *then* we will do it"); there are no "ors" (e.g. "we can be socially responsible *or* we can maximize shareholder value"); there is only "and" (e.g. "we will make profits *and* improve society *and* improve the environment").

BP has continued to persevere with "Beyond Petroleum" and appears willing to learn from its previous mistakes with it. At the end of 2002, Beyond Petroleum bubbled back to the surface as part of the company's new "It's a start" campaign. This featured "ordinary people" sharing their concerns for our environmental future before BP explains what it was doing about these concerns. For example, one billboard announces: "Our goal is to make solar a $1 billion business by 2007 . . . it's a start." *The Times* of London remarked that it seemed "astonishing that the company should plug 'beyond petroleum' after the roasting it received from the British press in July 2000 when it announced the re-branding." Its article explained that while steps such as the installation of windmills at some service stations to generate electricity for the fuel pumps "may seem more of a gimmick than a business opportunity for a company that sells petrol . . . BP is not like that; it has invested $200 million in a solar power business that has yet to turn a profit. It was the first oil company to state publicly that climate change was a problem linked to carbon emissions. It declared its support for the Kyoto Protocol and set itself a more aggressive target – to reduce carbon emissions by 10 per cent below 1990 levels."

While other commentators have not been so positive (e.g. Daniel Gross on MSN's *Moneybox* program slated the new campaign as audacious and dishonest), public opinion sees something more authentic, and thus viable, about BP's words this time. Most of the reader feedback posted to Gross's MSN column gives BP the benefit of the doubt, with one reader responding: "Gross's point [that] BP is still a carbon-belching behemoth trying to garner some mostly undeserved cachet with a mostly superficial eco-marketing campaign and some small forays into

Business will promote sustainable development	Business will not promote sustainable development
The long-term viability of a business and its ability to deliver ongoing shareholder value is contingent on a viable social and physical planet. Hence the enlightened self-interest of business managers will promote global well-being in much the same way as new products have enhanced quality of life as an unintended side-effect since the Industrial Revolution. In terms of table 10.2 all that is required for social and environmental welfare is for firms to be diligent Type Is and then, for their own and everbody else's good, to evolve to Type IVs. The vastly increasing wealth, health, and general well-being of the world thus far is evidence that the system works	Due to free-rider problems (wherein one selfish firm can benefit at the expense of many enlightened ones), the pressures of "sub-goal optimization" (wherein the urgent, short-term imperatives of business – such as achieving this month's budget – inevitably drive out the long-term sustainability goals), and the inevitability of "moral hazard" (dishonesty) from some companies, the world cannot rely on businesses to embrace sustainable development as a natural consequence of profit optimization. Continued deforestation, global warming, dwindling fish stocks, pension mis-selling, and many other examples of firm self-interest dominating the well-being of society is evidence that legislation and surveillance are essential for the planet to thrive and that the current dalliance with CSR is failing

Figure 10.2 Poles of opinion regarding the relationship between corporations and the current emphasis on sustainable development and corporate sustainability

alternative fuels, is absolutely true. But still . . . it's a start. I'd rather have big oil companies do what BP is doing than actively fight against alternative energy – by lobbying against tax breaks and government incentives – or do nothing at all, which is what some companies are doing."

As with the BP example in this chapter (and the micro-cases attached to it) this chapter attempts to present dilemmas rather than generic solutions. The most intriguing aspect of this major new arena is that there is little or no disagreement as to the desirability or validity of the overarching sustainability principles or goals. The major divide lies between those who firmly and genuinely believe that the corporate world, through enlightened self-interest, will embrace and drive sustainable development (left-hand pole in figure 10.2), and those who believe that in the business world the profit imperative of the individual firm will inevitably undermine any collective will towards sustainability.

One thing is for certain, however. The days of businesses claiming not to care, or not wanting to engage with these debates, are gone. At the very least, all the wider community will expect that organizations consider, develop, and defend a view of where they stand with regard to corporate sustainability: at one pole, or the other, or somewhere in between.

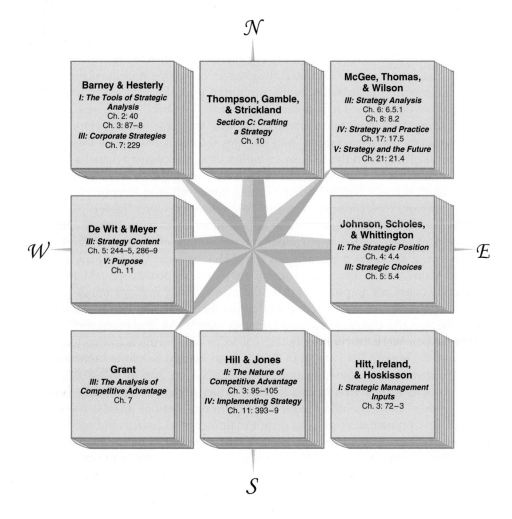

McAttacked

I'm lovin' it

McDonald's 2005 tag line

As one of the most famous brands in the modern world and *the* foremost emblem of "fast food" in the 21st century, McDonald's is only ever one over-cooked French fry from controversy. In August 2005, California's Attorney General asked for a court order requiring McDonald's and eight other restaurant chains to warn customers that their fries may contain the potential carcinogen, acrylamide. A by-product of the chemicals and heat in cooking, acrylamide is found in low levels in several foods but at higher levels in fried offerings such as fries and potato chips. Such stories, whatever their truth, dent the reputation of well-known brands more than their lesser known rivals. Since 1984, when James Huberty killed 21 people in San Ysidro, California by raking one of its restaurants with gunfire, McDonald's has come to understand that there *is* such a thing as bad publicity.

From its earliest marketing campaigns using the lovable clown Ronald McDonald, McDonald's implicit characterization of itself has been one of good, clean, fun-like wholesomeness. This was symbolized in the innocence of the children in its advertising, operationally embodied in Ray Kroc's obsession with cleanliness and friendly service in its restaurants and is the essence of the basic "bread, meat, and potatoes" of its products. The company has spent enormous sums developing and maintaining this image and has been famously litigious in protecting it from encroachment and debasement. An Australian rugby supporter, Malcolm McBratney, found this out in 2005 when he tried to register his nickname "McBrat," which he was using as a (clothing) logo in his sponsorship of his local team. McDonald's opposed this on the grounds that it owned the "McKids" (toys) trademark and that there would be a confusion between the two. In an earlier case, the company sued a Scottish café owner called McDonald for infringement in using the name "McMunchies" even though it was a family business dating back well over a century.

The company took umbrage again in 2003 when the word "McJob" – defined as "low paying and dead-end work" – appeared in the *Merriam-Webster Collegiate Dictionary*. As well as the implications for the morale of workers in its 30,000+ restaurants, a spokesmen pointed out that "McJobs" was the company's trademarked name for its training program for handicapped people. McDonald's eventually chose not to pursue this line of attack, being perhaps mindful of the negative publicity generated from the UK "McLibel" trial. This began in June 1994 when the firm did choose to sue two British protestors for libel contained in pamphlets the pair were distributing outside of McDonald's outlets in London. After 314 days, the longest libel action in British legal history concluded with £60,000 damages awarded to the company (later reduced on appeal to £40,000). The judgment was widely viewed as a Pyrrhic victory given two and a half years of negative press coverage and the fact that the judge did not dismiss the allegations of environmental, work, and health malpractice as untrue, but merely that the protesters could not prove their claims. In a further blow to the company's image, the European Court of Human Rights found that the laws under which McDonald's was successful breached the protestors' rights to a fair trial and freedom of expression. The UK Government changed the laws accordingly.

More importantly for McDonald's, the issues at the heart of the McLibel case, and, in particular, the criticisms of its major products, have refused to go away. In 1999, the veteran French activist José Bove achieved international exposure when he was jailed for 3 weeks after leading a group of farmer-activists in the destruction of a branch of McDonald's. He thus became a martyr for both the anti-globalists (Ralph Nader invited him to the Seattle WTO conference) and the opponents of the industrialization of food production. His attack on "malbouffe" (bad food), although perhaps aimed at protecting French farming interests, resonated on a number of fronts with a mounting tide of condemnation of McDonald's style food across the US and Europe.

So-called "lifestyle-related" illnesses from smoking, drinking/drugs, and, in particular, obesity, are the most significant precursors of serious health problems in the industrialized world. While people are living longer in general, they are at the same time manifesting health problems that are costly to society as lost productivity, diminished quality of life, and, what cynics suggest is the major issue, ballooning healthcare expenditure. The fast food industry, epitomized by McDonald's, has been targeted by governments and, in the US, by lawyers as being at least partially responsible for the modern epidemic of obesity and obesity-related illnesses. In a move reminiscent of the tobacco industry, obese US plaintiffs began a series of court actions claiming their obesity to be the responsibility of McDonald's and seeking (astronomical) damages in compensation and damages. In 2004, the US House of Representatives passed the "cheeseburger bill" (The Personal Responsibility in Food Consumption Act) banning such actions.

While seemingly protected from obesity lawsuits, McDonald's is still faced with the fact that increasingly it is seen as a purveyor of unwholesome products to customers whose eating habits the company has influenced since their childhood. The fate of the potential McDonald's "addict" was dramatized in the documentary *Super Size Me* in which the film's producer, Morgan Spurlock, ate nothing but McDonald's food for 30 days. This resulted in liver toxicity, a 55 point increase in blood cholesterol count, a 25 lb weight gain, depression, and loss of libido. Through such high-profile challenges, the restaurant chain is being forced to address the question of its degree of responsibility for the food its customers eat, both in terms of its ingredients and quantity. Proponents of healthy eating have proposed that, like tobacco and alcohol suppliers, fast food outlets should be offering "health" warnings to customers in their restaurants. These warnings should specify such things as the amount of saturated fats and salt in the order compared with the recommended daily average and indicating that fast food should not be eaten more than once or twice a week.

A stock response from McDonald's spokespeople has been that what people eat "is all about personal responsibility and individual decisions." But as more headlines appear like "McDonald's Salads Fattier than Burgers," "Shock News: McDonald's Makes You Unhealthy," and "The Invisible Extra with a Happy Meal McCarrot" (revealing that carrot sticks are kept "healthy looking" by being dipped in hydrogen peroxide) the company comes under increasing pressure to respond with more than "caveat emptor."

---

1. *To what extent do you think companies like McDonald's are responsible for the eating habits of their customers?*
2. *What should McDonald's do?*

◀◀◀**McResponse: Some Ideas . . .**

There is no doubt that for McDonald's and other fast food restaurants the issues touched on in the case are significant *political* and *social* forces that must be systematically dealt with as part of their ongoing *non-market strategies*. It is unlikely, for example, that the House of Representatives passed its "cheese-burger bill" without at least some lobbying from industry representatives. It is also logical that new menus should be developed with healthier options, that calorie counts for all the items on the menu should be provided (in some McDonald's restaurants, these are on the tray mats), and that cooking styles should be (publicly) modified, as McDonald's has done by switching to vegetable oil instead of beef fat in its frying. Notwithstanding these strategic responses, there remains the question of the extent to which McDonald's can or should be held accountable for the eating habits of its customers. Although this might be argued to be a generic "ethical/legal" issue for all companies, it is particularly emotive for those companies, like McDonald's, that target children as a critical market segment.

On one side of the **corporate social responsibility (CSR)** continuum, it can be argued that because the company targets children in their formative years it takes on more than a customer–supplier relationship with these **stakeholders**. In sponsoring such programs as *Sesame Street* and idealizing eating in their restaurants, the companies are doing more than inviting informed consumers to trade with them (the standard trading relationship). By shaping the tastes, expectations, and aspirations of children, they have no choice but to also take on some of the parental responsibilities to prevent those children unwittingly harming themselves by developing poor eating habits with negative health consequences in their adulthood. In the same way that liquor companies, for example, are increasingly required to promote responsible drinking and to not glamorize alcohol to the young, so too should fast food companies be made to face up to their broader social responsibilities.

On the other side there is an argument that children do not walk into these restaurants by themselves and, as with skateboards, video games, baseball bats, or chocolate sweets, it is parents who train and shape their children into being good citizens and having appropriate self-regulation when it comes to eating or behavior of any kind. The company must, of course, not provide products that are harmful in themselves but, as any food is harmful in excess, it comes back to parents to instill this lesson and not the company. If a child spends 20 hours per day watching television then this is unlikely to be good for his or her long-term social development and yet the television company is not held to account for such excessive viewing – parents are.

Others emphasize the role of government in regulating both consumers and industries. It is often forgotten, for example, that "hard" drugs like heroin and cocaine were once legal. With legal "drugs" such as alcohol and tobacco, the government regulates who can buy and sell and how (or even if) these products can be advertised. While minors are not allowed to purchase alcohol, the onus remains on the seller to ensure that the customer is the legal age – others buying alcohol for children are also held legally liable. This sense of legal liability for the actions of others is spreading so that with the problems associated with drink-driving, for example, many countries have enacted legislation putting the legal onus on serving staff (and their hotel/restaurants) to not sell alcoholic beverages to customers already showing signs of inebriation. While the juxtaposition of food and drugs/alcohol may seem a "stretch," it has in fact been suggested by some of the more extreme critics that McDonald's, through overuse of fats, salt, and added flavoring, creates a form of addiction in the young consumers, who may develop a preference for fast food over a more healthy (but less "tasty") diet. Could we see a time when a fast food restaurant will be held liable for selling fat-enhancing foods to already obese patrons?

Whatever McDonald's does, it needs to remain aware that these complex issues are not going to disappear overnight. The fact that companies (or people) firmly believe themselves to be paragons of moral and ethical conduct can sometimes blind them to the obvious fact that such judgments are always made in the eyes of the observers – no matter how unfair those judgments may seem. McDonald's probably sees itself selling nutritious meals to willing customers while being unjustly attacked by gold-digging opportunists citing one-sided "junk science." There are equally sincere opponents who are horrified at what they see as McDonald's unfettered, capricious purveyance of addictive junk food to vulnerable consumers who lack the capability for informed choice and stand in need of protection. And between those two extremes lie a plethora of positions that shift with each new headline.

▶ ▶ ▶

Growing the future?

Monsanto is an American-owned international agro-chemical and food conglomerate, with nearly US$5.5bn in sales and capitalized at over US$16bn (2003/4).

> "Monsanto . . . is consciously developing new competencies . . . It is betting that the bioengineering of crops rather than the application of chemical pesticides or fertilizers represents a sustainable path to increased agricultural yields." (Hart, 1997: 73)

Monsanto's View Of Its Own Ethics

- "Sustainable development is going to be one of the organizing principles around which Monsanto and a lot of other institutions will probably define themselves for years to come."
- "We can't expect the rest of the world to abandon their economic aspirations just so we can continue to enjoy clean air and water. That is neither ethically correct nor likely to be permitted by the billions of people in the developing world who expect the quality of their lives to improve."
- ". . . current agricultural practice is not sustainable . . . You have to get twice the yield from every acre of land just to maintain current levels of poverty and malnutrition . . . new technology is the only alternative to any one of two disasters: not feeding people . . . or ecological catastrophe."
- "If economic development means using more stuff, then those who argue that growth and environmental sustainability are incompatible are right."

- "We can genetically code a plant . . . to repel or destroy harmful insects. That means we don't have to spray the plant with insecticides. Up to 90% of what's sprayed on crops today is wasted. Most of it ends up on the soil . . . Can we develop plants that will thrive in salty soil . . . create less thirsty plants suited to a drier environment?"
- "Because of Monsanto's history as a chemical company, we have a lot of employees – good people – with a recurring experience like this: their kids or their neighbors' kids or somebody at a cocktail party asks them what kind of work they do and then react in a disapproving way because of what they *think* we are at Monsanto. And that hurts."
- "At Monsanto we're trying to invent some new businesses around the concept of environmental sustainability."

The Views Of Others On Monsanto's Ethics

- "In the 1980s, Monsanto Corporation got a bad name for polluting every square foot of the planet with noxious PCBs, dioxin, and harmful pesticides. Now Monsanto is a leader in the biotech revolution that threatens to engineer the genes of every food crop on the planet with potentially desasterous (*sic*) consequences for the environment." (www.mcspotlight.org)
- "In 1962, Rachel Carson's book *Silent Spring* first drew people's attention to the slow death of nature being caused by the pesticide DDT. In response, Monsanto published *The Desolate Year*, a parody about a DDT-free USA being overrun by a plague of locusts. The book was sent *free* to over 5,000 media outlets. In 1968, DDT was banned in North America and Europe." (www.mindfully.org)
- "Monsanto is in the process of acquiring and patenting their newest technology . . . "Terminator Technology." If used by Monsanto on a large-scale basis, it will inevitably lead to famine and starvation on a worldwide basis . . . seeds have been genetically engineered so that when the crops are harvested, all new seeds from these crops are sterile . . . This forces farmers to pay Monsanto every year for new seeds . . . half the world's farmers are poor and can't afford to buy seed every growing season, yet poor farmers grow 15 to 20% of the world's food . . ." (www.ethicalinvesting.com)
- "Recent research is beginning to confirm that dairy foods produced using *Monsanto's genetically engineered Bovine Growth Hormone (BGH) may speed the growth of human breast and prostate cancers.*" (www.ethicalinvesting.com)
- "Monsanto is part of the chemical industry . . . It is important to expose the unethical practices of specific companies as their behavior is often indicative of the entire system." (www.mcspotlight.org)
- "New York's financial community is now convinced that successful protests from consumers and environmental groups in Europe have hurt Monsanto's growth prospects and its stock market rating so badly that the only option to realize some value for investors would be some kind of sell-off . . . Big investors and analysts have become increasingly worried as concerns in Europe about genetically modified foods have spread around the world . . ." (*The Guardian*, October 22, 1999).

> 1. *What do you think about Monsanto's position and where do you stand?*
> 2. *What would you do if you were CEO of Monsanto today?*

The Credo

Johnson & Johnson's Credo below is likely the most widely respected statement outlining a corporation's duties with regard to stakeholders.

Our Credo

We believe our first responsibility is to the doctors, nurses and patients, to mothers and fathers and all others who use our products and services.
In meeting their needs everything we do must be of high quality.
We must constantly strive to reduce our costs in order to maintain reasonable prices.
Customers' orders must be serviced promptly and accurately.
Our suppliers and distributors must have an opportunity to make a fair profit.

We are responsible to our employees, the men
and women who work with us throughout the world.
Everyone must be considered as an individual.
We must respect their dignity and recognize their merit.
They must have a sense of security in their jobs.
Compensation must be fair and adequate and
working conditions clean, orderly and safe.
We must be mindful of ways to help our employees fulfill
their family responsibilities.
Employees must feel free to make suggestions and complaints.
There must be equal opportunity for employment, development
and advancement for those qualified.
We must provide competent management, and their actions
must be just and ethical.

We are responsible to the communities in which we live and work
and to the world community as well.
We must be good citizens – support good works and charities
and bear our fair share of taxes.
We must encourage civic improvements and better health and education.
We must maintain in good order the property we are privileged to use,
protecting the environment and natural resources.

Our final responsibility is to our stockholders.
Business must make a sound profit.
We must experiment with new ideas.
Research must be carried on, innovative programs developed
and mistakes paid for.
New equipment must be purchased, new facilities provided
and new products launched.
Reserves must be created to provide for adverse times.
When we operate according to these principles,
the stockholders should realize a fair return.

Johnson & Johnson

While its seemingly unwieldy length may cause some to mock that its staff could never remember it, most Johnson & Johnson employees pride themselves on knowing the Credo. Indeed, I once made this mistake of questioning whether or not it could be remembered in front of an MBA class – without realizing that there were two Johnson & Johnson employees present. They quickly took me to task, and then proved their point by reciting it, sight unseen, almost word for word.

The Credo is indeed something that Johnson & Johnson see as a very important guide to their decision making. Its prominence has contributed greatly to the company's deserved reputation as one of the world's most ethical companies. However, some cynics have questioned whether the existence of a statement such as this indicates an ethical corporation. They cite a number of examples to illustrate this point.

At the end of 1982, Johnson & Johnson fell victim to industrial terrorists who claimed to have injected cyanide into an unspecified number of Tylenol capsules. Seven people in the Chicago area died. A leading strategy textbook outlines what happened next:

> "Johnson & Johnson immediately withdrew all Tylenol capsules from the US market, at an estimated cost to the company of $100 million. At the same time the company embarked on a comprehensive communication effort targeted at the pharmaceutical and medical communities. By such means, Johnson & Johnson successfully presented itself to the public as a company that was willing to do what was right, regardless of the cost. As a consequence, the Tylenol crisis enhanced rather than diminished Johnson & Johnson's image. Indeed, because of its actions, the company was able to regain its status as a market leader within months."

The Credo, it was argued, had shown Johnson & Johnson the way.

However, in February 1986 another person died in New York after taking a tainted Tylenol capsule and many commentators revisited the case. In 1983, shortly after the first crisis, Johnson & Johnson had developed "caplets," smooth-coated capsule shaped tablets that could not be penetrated with a foreign substance. Some now argued that if Johnson & Johnson's first responsibility really was to "doctors, nurses, patients, and mothers and fathers" (see the first line of the Credo), then the capsules should have been replaced with caplets. James Burke, then Chairman of Johnson & Johnson, countered that if "we get out of the capsule business, others will get into it" and that to do so would be, in any case, a "victory for terrorism." Others though, pointing to Johnson & Johnson's huge investments in capsule-making facilities, cited a survey that 59% of capsule users would not be willing to switch to caplets, and projections that such a move would result in a $150 million pre-tax charge against first-quarter earnings and cost the company between 60 and 80 cents a share. These things, they argued, made doing "what was right" seem like the wrong thing to do. It was claimed that, in reality, Johnson & Johnson's "final responsibility," to stockholders (first line of the Credo's final paragraph), had triumphed over its first.

But is it really a drug company's role to act as "big brother"? Surely, was it not the case that all Johnson & Johnson could do was offer people advice and alternatives, then it was up to the individual? If Johnson & Johnson had done all that these critics seem to have expected, it would soon be bankrupted, which would compromise all of its other stakeholder responsibilities. The FDA concluded that it should not direct or pressure Johnson & Johnson into such an action, and that the decision was "a matter of Johnson & Johnson's own business judgment."

In any event, it is hard to see how the Credo, on its own, could provide Johnson & Johnson with the best judgment as to what the company ought to do in a situation like this. However, Johnson & Johnson's being charged with heavy fines by the authorities after admitting in 1995 that one of its businesses had shredded important documents to hinder a federal investigation into the marketing of one of its products seems somewhat more problematic.

Also problematic is a growing recognition among companies like Johnson & Johnson that statements like "we are responsible to our employees" (first line of paragraph two in the Credo) are difficult to apply as organizations increasingly act across national boundaries. Does a statement like this mean that companies are "responsible" in the same ways to employees in all the countries in which they operate? Should these employees' healthcare benefits, insurance, and even salaries be the same? These increasingly asked questions, in combination with increasingly bold lawyers and litigious interest groups, are now making companies balk before committing their duties to paper.

---

1. *Whereabouts would you place Johnson & Johnson in terms of tables 10.1 and 10.2 from the chapter?*
2. *How might this placement contribute to Johnson & Johnson's sustainable competitive advantage?*
3. *What are the strengths and weaknesses of the Credo from a strategic management perspective?*
4. *Would you advise other corporations to develop their own Credos to help guide their strategy making in an ethical way?*

SUSTAIN ABILITY

Codes and conduct

Enrico Marcos gazed ruefully at the Code of Conduct poster on the wall of his office in his factory in the Southern Philippines. The output of the Ethical Team of the biggest customer for his sporting footwear, it comprised five points making up the acronym "WORTH" (figure 10-4.1).

Enrico had worked in a factory in his youth and hence could only applaud the sentiments behind the poster. Excess working hours, often in the form of compulsory and unpaid overtime, had been the norm for himself and his parents. Resigning was out of the question, as even the meager wages on offer were better than nothing, and to complain only increased the verbal and physical abuse from harried supervisors. While forced into excessive, underpaid efforts during peak periods, workers would be told to stay at home or were not paid when orders dried up. The occasional foolhardy firebrand who attempted to enforce his or her legal rights, or to form a union of other brave rebels, soon found him/herself out of a job and often in detention at the local police station.

> The Marcos Company recognizes the **WORTH** of all its workers and their rights to dignity and security in employment. The owners and management acknowledge their responsibilities to all staff and commit to working within the **WORTH** guidelines, which they accept to be minimum standards of conduct.
>
> **W**orking hours will be reasonable
>
> **O**vertime will be voluntary
>
> **R**ates will be fair
>
> **T**rade unions will be accepted
>
> **H**arassment will not be tolerated
>
> *Signed*: Enrico Marcos, CEO

Figure 10-4.1 Marcos Company WORTH poster

When Enrico had started up his own small workshop 14 years ago, he had vowed that if ever he became an employer he would not be one that allowed the same conditions that made his factory life so miserable. His workshop was soon employing others as his diligence and attention to detail garnered him increasing numbers of repeat customers. After 6 years he had rented a cheap, disused building on the outskirts of town and started up his own factory. Sales grew and the Marcos Company enhanced its reputation as a reliable supplier of quality products and a place of work where employees were treated with fairness and respect.

Although the Ethical Team visited every 2 years or so, members of his customer's Buying Team were in his office at least every quarter and often more frequently. The team comprised aggressive, ambitious young executives, all intent on fast-tracking their careers through performance that was noticed by superiors. They mocked the Ethical Team as "ETFAP" (i.e. "ET – From Another Planet") and declared that they were interested in "value" not WORTH. Their guidelines were the "5Fs." They needed **F**ast delivery times to meet the needs of their giant retailer customers as well as **F**lexibility of response should things change – as they always did. If suppliers did not meet their deadlines and targets the costs would be passed on to them as **F**ines for poor performance. Finally, and most crucially, they needed increasingly **F**rugal pricing to keep margins high enough to sustain the payments to celebrities whose endorsements were essential to sell the product.

"You said there were five Fs," Enrico pointed out. "That's only four." The smartly dressed twenty-something buyer smiled her dazzlingly white smile: "That F is what happens if the other four don't work; we will be **F**inished with the supplier, but I'm sure that will never apply to you Enrico."

Enrico could not pinpoint exactly when it was that conditions in his factory began to change but change they certainly had. The incessant pressure for price decreases had forced him to save in the only place he could and that was in labor costs. As he was required to supply more items for lower prices, he passed this on to his workers in higher piece-rate targets. Initially he had asked his workers to work overtime only for special rush orders and they had been happy to help, particularly as the extra hours were paid. These days the extended working day was the norm and the fines from customers, often for things outside of Marcos's control, had eaten into the funds available to pay for extra time. As the workers worked faster they made more mistakes; in response the supervisors had instituted a practice of offsetting quality costs against the worker's pay where the individual who made the error could be identified. To further reduce ongoing costs the company now hired workers on temporary contracts and rotated the labor frequently to avoid paying the entitlements due to permanent employees. It had also found that female workers tended to be more compliant with extra workloads and lower pay and so females now made up the vast majority of the workforce. Complaints from some of his longer staying workers made Enrico aware that some supervisors were bullying workers to hit their targets and to maintain their silence about working conditions – he felt ashamed.

He felt ashamed also about how he had systems in place to keep the factory working in the way that it was while reporting a different ethos. Audited once every 2 years by the Ethical Team, the Marcos Company had become adept at keeping false time records to hide the excessive hours as well as two payroll records, one that reflected actual pay and the other to satisfy the WORTH requirements. Each audit was announced well ahead of time and, in preparation for the inspection and the interviews, the factory was thoroughly cleaned and painted and selected workers were trained in how to deal with the interviewer's questions. Some of these interviewees were given extra money but for most the threat that the factory might be closed down if the audit results were negative was sufficient inducement. The Marcos factory was an unpleasant place to work but the pay was enough to prevent starvation – the only other available option.

1. *Discuss the "causes" of the maltreatment of workers as presented in this case.*
2. *What can Enrico do?*
3. *How can these problems be overcome?*

Handi Ghandi Curries

There are many chains of Indian takeaway restaurants throughout the world, and a chain created on Australia's Gold Coast is not too different from most of them – apart from its quirky name and catchy advertising.

Handi Ghandi Curries has grown quickly through franchising and there are now stores using the Handi Ghandi Curries name and logo being opened in Australia's major cities. The company, which primarily delivers a large range of Indian-style curries in American-style Chinese takeaway boxes, uses the slogan "Great curries . . . No worries," has a logo featuring a cartoon image of Mahatma Gandhi tucking in to a Handi Ghandi box, and a jingle featuring a man singing "I am Handi Ghandi, eat my curries" in an accent like that used by the actor Ben Kingsley in the popular film version of Gandhi's life.

However, as the company has grown, its exploits have attracted more attention and it turns out that the Mahatma's family is not at all pleased with this use of his image. His great-grandson Tushar, managing trustee of the Mahatma

Gandhi Foundation, was outraged that the Gandhi name had been used to sell meat curries (even though it had been misspelled). Mr. Gandhi described the act as offensive, saying it went against all the renowned vegetarian's beliefs. Especially offensive was the sale of beef curries by Handi Ghandi, as cattle are considered sacred to Hindus.

On June 16, 2005, *The Calcutta Telegraph* reported the story as follows:

> The Mahatma has been many things to many people. But when an Australian company portrayed him as a cook to sell beef curry, his great-grandson decided things had gone too far.
>
> Tushar Gandhi today requested Prime Minister Manmohan Singh to take up the matter with the Australian Government and stop the New South Wales-based Handi Ghandi Pvt Ltd from abusing the Mahatma's memory.
>
> Tushar Gandhi would have had no problems as long as the Mahatma sold the company's samosas, vegetable curries, parathas, naans, chutneys, salads, and biryanis. It was the Beef Madras, beef vindaloo, lamb rogan josh, Bombay Fish, and butter chicken that got his goat.
>
> "I have nothing against non-vegetarian food," the relative said, "but using Bapu's [Gandhi's] image to sell meat curry is too much. I probably would not have raised the issue if the company had promoted vegetarianism and health food."
>
> The great-grandson has written to the Prime Minister's Office, the Ministry of External Affairs, and the Union Law and Judiciary Department to take the issue up at a diplomatic level with Canberra.
>
> "Bapu's image is protected by the Indian Constitution," he said. "It is the equivalent of a national flag or any other Indian emblem (in sanctity)."

Although Mahatma Gandhi's name and image are protected under India's Constitution and national emblem laws, they are not protected outside of India, so legal action could not be taken in Australia. Indeed, the Handi Gandhi brand and logo were approved by and registered with the Australian trademark authorities.

However, in response to the Gandhis' protests the company issued the following statement on its website and announced the change of its logo from a drawing of Gandhi to a caricature of a more generic Indian man.

> "A recent press release distributed with comments from Tushar Gandhi, the great-grandson of Mahatma Gandhi, stating his concerns over the use of a caricature contained in our company trademark has been viewed widely around the world. Our company has never at any stage intended any offence or disrespect to the great Mahatma Gandhi or his family and Indian nationals. In a sign of good faith our company has decided to alter its corporate logo."

Handi Ghandi hoped the alteration of its logo would placate the Gandhi family – but it didn't.

The *Lismore Northern Star,* a local paper in the area where Handi Gandhi was established, reported Tushar Gandhi's response on June 25:

> THE great-grandson of Mahatma Gandhi has called on Northern Rivers residents to boycott Handi Ghandi takeaway restaurant chain if it refuses to alter its name.
>
> If the restaurant complied, Tushar Gandhi said he would eat the Lennox Head-based company's curries himself.

In an email interview, the Mumbai resident said he was sending an appeal to the residents. "To those of you who work for Handi Ghandi and for those of you who are their clients, prevail on them . . . to change the name, remove the mis-spelt but still related name of my illustrious great-grandfather . . . from their brand name and stop the use of the very offensive jingle," he said.

"May peace and joy be your eternal neighbours."

International protests have been sparked by the company selling curries in the name of vegetarian pacifist Mahatma Gandhi.

A caricature logo of the leader attracted complaints from Australian Indians and the Mumbai-based Mahatma Gandhi foundation.

Even Indian Prime Minister Dr Manmohan Singh has joined the protest, adding his name to a letter demanding the company drop the use of the image and change its name.

The protesters won a partial success last weekend when Handi Ghandi decided to change its logo; swapping an image of Mahatma Gandhi for a picture of a bearded man in Indian garb. But the company co-owner and managing director Troy Lister said the name would not change.

"It is a legally registered tradename," Mr Lister said.

Mr Lister has said the name of the takeaway franchise was deliberately mis-spelled to prevent it relating directly to Mahatma Gandhi.

Mr Gandhi [also] wants the people of Ballina to know the Handi Ghandi jingle parodying the Indian accent is demeaning to Indians.

"It is a racist image of the Indian accent," he said.

"[The Handi Ghandi promotion] is as offensive to us as if the name and images of Jesus [were used] to sell products or, for the British, if the Queen's image as a sales woman [was used]."

[However, Mr Ghandi] said he would be the first to thank Handi Ghandi if they complied. If Handi Ghandi changed its name "I would not hesitate to patronise their business," he said.

Some Western media did not take these protests quite so seriously, however. Under the heading "What's Next, Martin Luther Burger King Jr.?" *CMO Magazine*'s Constantine von Hoffman made light of the situation: "The family of Mahatma Gandhi is upset just because some Aussie company is using the great guy's name and image to sell curry. Some people are just sooo sensitive."

And, the *Calcutta Telegraph* did point out that Tushar himself had faced public criticism in 2001 when he was accused of trying to sell the Mahatma's image to a US-based licensing company for use in a film advertisement for a credit card. CMG Worldwide had offered $51,000 per year for the use of the image.

---

1. *Why do you think Handi Ghandi Curries is so resistant to changing the name of the company?*
2. *What do you think Handi Ghandi Curries should do now? Can you think of a way that the company can satisfy the Gandhi family, be seen as a good corporate citizen, and help develop its sustainable competitive advantage?*

The Il Ngwesi: eco-warriors

Tourism is currently the world's largest growth industry. But with a growing number of tourists comes increasing pressure on natural resources, and an increasing number of international investors in the industry looking to make quick returns rather than foster sustainable development. Recognition of the need to preserve and protect natural environments for the long term has led many countries to focus on ecotourism. The United Nations is also seeking to promote ecotourism, not only in terms of managing the impact of tourism on the natural environment, but also because of the positive effects it can have on human environments. In other words, the UN believes that encouraging local communities to conserve their wild surroundings, and educate visitors about the value and fragility of their land, can lead to a greater respect for and promotion of their own well-being and cultural legacy. Recognizing the global importance of this sort of initiative, the United Nations designated the year 2002 as the International Year of Ecotourism.

Ecotourism aims to conserve the environment while benefiting local communities in sustainable ways. It generally takes place in poorer, less-developed areas that attract a higher proportion of independent travelers, and often involves smaller companies with more local commitment. However, even with smaller local companies in charge, ecotourism can reduce local access to natural resources, disrupt community groups, and have a damaging effect on the livelihoods of poor people in the area unless the process is properly managed.

Just a few hundred kilometres from Baraka College (see case 9-5), one of the UN's exemplar ecotourism projects is going from strength to strength. Il Ngwesi is a communally owned ranch that combines sustainable farming, local development, and ecotourism. The local Maasai people of the Samburu region run the Il Ngwesi Community Conservation Area (INCCA) in central Kenya. They have built a 16,500-acre group ranch owned collectively by the 499 pastoral households, comprising 6,000 people that inhabit its diverse environment. It operates as a community-owned trust with a Natural Resource Management Committee responsible for land management.

On one portion of this ranch, people have moved their cattle off the land in favor of wildlife. On this site in 1996, an exclusive ecotourism facility, Il Ngwesi Lodge, was established – Kenya's first community-owned and managed tourist destination. The lodge, built using funds donated through the Kenya Wildlife Service, was constructed using materials from the local area. It employs 28 people from the local community, half of whom work in the lodge looking after visitors while the other half work as Il Ngwesi's ranger force, providing security for the animals and people in the region. From the lodge, visitors can spot elephant, buffalo, bushbuck, kudu, and the occasional big cat. The local Samburu community who live there and run the lodge now earn much more revenue from tourism than they ever did from cattle. Although the original construction of the lodge was funded by donors and built with the assistance and support of the Lewa Wildlife Conservancy (www.lewa.org/IlNgwesiGR.htm), Il Ngwesi is now financially independent.

Earnings from the lodge are dispersed as wages to employees and as dividends to members. For these workers and their families, these wages provide security and consistency. The lodge operates as a separate company but revenue from the lodge and other ecotourism activities is also put back into the community in a variety of other ways: to pay for education, infrastructure and medicines, measures to bring an end to cattle rustling and banditry that meant losing valuable assets and income, and access to better emergency healthcare through a new radio and vehicle to provide emergency access to the nearest hospital.

Ten years ago, it was unsafe to travel through this area of Kenya because of the risk of attack from armed bandits. Today, thanks largely to the security infrastructure funded through the increased revenue from ecotourism, Il Ngwesi is a safe and peaceful place for tourists to visit, while the local community no longer has to fear that their village might be raided at any time.

The stable conditions created through the Il Ngwesi Trust and the clear responsibility to protect and maintain the wilderness area have resulted in the lodge going from strength to strength. A Water Use Association has been established to deal with misuse, overconsumption, and pollution in the area, and this, combined with the use of solar power for water heating and electricity in the lodge rather than wood or fossil fuel, has added to Il Ngwesi's reputation as an ecologically sound tourist destination. Meanwhile, protection from logging, overgrazing, and poaching of wildlife such as elephants and zebra thanks to enhanced security has helped Il Ngwesi to become a recognized safe haven for wildlife. A collaring and monitoring program for lions and elephants has been established and the Kenya Wildlife Service is now beginning to translocate various game to enhance the present diversity near the lodge, including an endangered hand-reared black rhino.

And, beyond already being an internationally acclaimed tourist destination, Il Ngwesi is also sharing its experiences with others through educational tours that are helping other communities to see just how it is done. Indeed, it recently featured as one of five such ecotourism projects in a television series made by TVE (The Television Trust for the Environment) and hosted by Anita Roddick. The TVE website provides more details (www.TVE.org/network.html).

This website also provides a summary of the key aspects that can be learned about implementing successful ecotourism strategy from the Il Ngwesi experience. These are paraphrased below. Ecotourism projects should:

- ensure that all partners are involved in the development of an ecotourism strategy from the outset, especially local villagers (particularly important for villages near protected wildlife areas because local villagers have traditionally been the custodians of natural resources and have specific skills and knowledge to take on responsibilities within the development of ecotourism)
- encourage local people to be involved in staffing the project
- hold democratic communal meetings to discuss revenue distribution, management policies, registration of new members, and election of a management committee that carries out day-to-day management
- ensure that benefit-sharing between ecotourism partners is equitable, with established legal agreements that should address issues of respect towards the local culture and indigenous knowledge of the community
- ensure that at least a portion of revenue should be used for development of social services, bursaries, self-help groups, etc.
- be supported by national policies that encourage community-owned, sustainable ecotourism activities, as well as provide incentives toward the development of ecotourism initiatives

- be market driven and commercially viable, in addition to being environmentally sound and supportive of local communities
- aim to become self-sufficient as quickly as is practically possible
- seek to encourage a sense of pride among local people about their local culture and environmental legacy

> 1. *Why do you think Il Ngwesi's strategy has been so successful?*
> 2. *Why do you think "ecotourism" is a growing industry?*
> 3. *The Il Ngwesi's sustainable competitive advantage is obviously connected to sustainable development. But do you think this is necessarily the case for all corporations these days?*

Sustaining Postman Pat?

In December of the year 2000, the British Post Office announced that its corporate figurehead, Postman Pat, an animated character whose television show has been entertaining children in Britain and other parts of the world for decades, would be dropped from its promotional and charity work. (If you are not familiar with Postman Pat you may want to check him out at www.postmanpat.co.uk) Among other measures, Post Office employees will no longer be encouraged to visit local schools, fêtes, and children's wards dressed as Pat. Instead their volunteer work will be directed toward a new campaign to encourage literacy. In the Post Office's defense, a press officer said that it was nothing personal: "We're not anti-Pat. We're just reassessing our priorities."

These are certainly challenging times for the Post Office. Courier companies, many of them well-known global corporations, are eroding market share in what once was largely a monopoly for the Post Office. Society's values are also changing. However, David Thomas of *The Independent* has put up a spirited defence for the long-serving Greendale-based postie:

> I realise of course, that, judged by the ruthless, market-driven standards universally prevalent today, Pat is a hopeless case. From the moment when, just as the day is dawning, he climbs into his bright red van, his life is a catalogue of professional misconduct. The Post Office was quick to confirm that his habit of letting Jess, his black-and-white cat, ride in the front of his van was a blatant contravention of health and safety procedures.
>
> Similarly, the incidents [from his television and book adventures] that repeatedly cause post to be lost, misdirected or damaged (one thinks, for example, of the occasion when Pat entrusts the school mail to young Bill Thompson, who promptly drops it in a puddle) would be matters requiring disciplinary action. "This is a very serious matter for a postman," said my source.
>
> But his most persistent failing is his seemingly incurable habit of allowing his close relationships with local folk to distract him from the swift delivery of the mail. "We do like a postman to be community minded," I was told by the Post Office spokesperson. "But he's there first and foremost to do his job."

286

This is something that Pat would do well to remember. No one could deny his fundamental enthusiasm. He's determined to do his deliveries, come wind, rain or snow. He has been known to use methods as various as inline skates, sledge and motorised super-speed scooter to help him on his rounds. But there's no escaping the degree to which other matters are liable to intrude.

In Postman Pat's Washing Day, for example, he begins his rounds with the observation that Granny Dryden has neglected to hang out her washing, despite the sunny, breezy weather. He stops to discuss the matter with the rheumatically afflicted pensioner, who reveals that her washing-machine has broken. Taking her dirty togs, Pat promises to deliver them to Mrs Pottage. He then drives to see Dorothy Thompson, with whom he has tea and a slice of cake, before discussing laundry issues with the Rev Timms, Ted Glen, Miss Hubbard and George Lancaster . . .

On the following morning, Pat delivers Granny Dryden's laundry to Mrs Pottage and stops for yet another cup of tea, only for his uniform jacket and hat to be thrown into the washing-machine along with the old biddy's unmentionables. This is by no means the only occasion on which Pat causes damage to his uniform (one remembers, with a shudder, the white paint he left all over his trousers on the occasion of Granny Dryden's redecoration), despite being contractually responsible for its upkeep. But the fact that Pat has to complete his round in a tweed jacket and deer-stalker hat belonging to Mr Pottage is far less significant, in the great scheme of things, than the blatant time-wasting that has gone on beforehand.

Here is a man with no concept whatever of productivity or time-and-motion. And he is not alone. Consider Ted Glen, the local handyman. Pat visits him during his search for Katy Pottage's lost doll. Ted has agreed to mend toys, television sets, cookers, cake-stands, bikes, roller-skates, farm machines and house machines, "more than you could count." Yet he has no idea when he will fulfil these contractual obligations. Even when he does, his service is abysmal. Among his goods is a watch of Miss Hubbard's, of which he remarks, "She brought it to be fettled, last Christmas."

The service economy has made little headway on Greendale. But is the region's apparent refusal to move with the times really so counter-productive? Here we have a rural community that can sustain both a sub-post office (run by Pat's superior, Mrs Goggins) and Sam Waldron's mobile store. At a time when households are shrinking and the increasing autonomy of individuals as social and economic units is producing side effects of isolation and alienation, Greendale folk evince a strong sense of community.

When Granny Dryden's ceiling needs painting, Miss Hubbard provides dust sheets, Dorothy Thompson donates spare time while both Pat and Ted Glen volunteer their time to do the job for free – a task rewarded by cake and tea . . .

This is a world which has no need for social workers, a world that looks after its own. When Ted Glen's design for Pat's scooter causes chaos, people do not sue or seek compensation. Instead they take the matter to PC Selby. He, in turn, talks to Mrs Goggins. She has a quiet word to Pat, who abandons his machine without complaint, secure in the knowledge that Dr Gilbertson is having words with his superiors in Pencaster to ensure that they get him a proper trolley for his parcels.

People feel better living in a world like that, and there are clear economic benefits. The Government spends £120bn on social security, much of which could be saved if people were empowered to take local voluntary community action . . .

Pat and Ted's working methods are less wasteful than they may appear to corporate accountants, who seem incapable of seeing the financial wood for the budgetary trees. In a country plagued by the longest working hours in Europe, staff everywhere find themselves burdened with ever greater responsibilities, while being offered diminishing professional security. No wonder that more than two-thirds of TUC safety representatives identify stress as the greatest health and safety concern in the workplace.

Stress is now the single biggest cause of absenteeism, and costs corporate Britain anything between £9bn and £19bn per annum in compensation payments, quite apart from the mammoth cost of lost days of work. The Government spends about £8bn in incapacity benefits every year, quite apart from the drain on NHS resources.

If more of us were more like Pat – or if we were allowed to be – the social and economic benefits would be enormous.

Beyond the decision to drop Pat and the publication of Thomas's defense of Pat's worth, there has been good and bad news with regard to the Post Office's maintenance of its traditions. In a bid to sound more global and meaningful and relevant to today's business world, the Post Office changed its name to Consignia. But it changed it back again in 2002, after 2 years of public confusion as to what Consignia stood for and public dismay that terms that they had become familiar with, like "the Post Office" and the associated "Royal Mail," could have been discarded so brusquely and without discussion. Not long after this, however, on June 20, 2003, it was announced that the Post Office branch that had inspired Postman Pat was to be closed. The author of Postman Pat, John Cunliffe, reportedly wrote the books after listening to conversations in the Beast Banks branch in the Lake District town of Kendal. *The Independent* reported that the closure of Beast Banks would be one of 350, mostly rural, Post Offices that would be closed in 2003.

1. *Do you think the Post Office's management should have handled the relationship with Pat differently?*
2. *How might the association with Pat be a part of the Post Office's sustainable competitive advantage? Develop a business case (or strategic rationale) that would support bringing back Pat as the symbol of the Post Office's character.*

You can't be remarkable by following someone else who's remarkable . . . The thing that all great companies have in common is that they have nothing in common.

Seth Godin (2003) Transform Your Business by Becoming Remarkable

The "surplus society" has a surplus of *similar* companies, employing *similar* people, with *similar* educational backgrounds, coming up with *similar* ideas, producing *similar* things, with *similar* prices and *similar* quality.

Kjell Nordtrom and Jonas Ridderstrale (2002) Funky Business

In 2002, David Martin, president of corporate branding consultants Inter-brand, attributed clothing label Banana Republic's declining performance to a lack of *"maverick-ness."* According to him, "They've got to give it more uniqueness, Banana's got to stand for something that I can't get anywhere else." Martin said BR's parent company, The Gap, was also beginning to suffer from the same malaise. Why have former mavericks like The Gap and BR, who led a casual clothing revolution in the 1980s and 90s, become so difficult to distinguish? What took the maverick out of these companies' strategies? And what should they do to get back on track?

For Jesper Kunde, many companies are "now more or less identical" thanks to the rise of best practice benchmarking and copying.[1] Correspondingly, research by Philip Nattermann proved that companies in industries where best practice benchmarking was seen to be good strategy generally suffered from declining margins and Clayton Christensen's work suggests that many companies that increased their investment in getting strategy right have tended to copy "best practice" and become homogeneous with their competitors, subsequently facing mounting price pressure.[2] Indeed, in the late 1990s, sensing that strategies were becoming less concerned with differentiation, Michael Porter published a paper in the *Harvard Business Review* which argued that strategy – which Porter defined as about "performing different activities from rivals' or performing similar activities in different ways" – was being confused with operational effectiveness (or "performing similar activities better than rivals").[3]

The rise of "risk management" and "accountability" certainly has not helped this situation either. As managers were increasingly held to account for performance in the short as well as long term, they sought to mitigate their risks, and they increasingly turned to management consultants who employed similar generic techniques as a kind of "quality guarantee." Instead of daring to be unorthodox, most companies followed whoever their advisors identified as "the leader." Nattermann quotes Warren Buffett to explain the phenomenon: "As a group, lemmings may have a rotten image, but no individual lemming has ever received bad press."

David Koepp, co-writer of *Jurassic Park*, believes a similar logic explains the growth in movie sequels: "Approving a sequel is a non-fireable offence. If a sequel doesn't work, they can still say, 'It wasn't my fault! It was a no-brainer.'"

However, companies who have fallen into the **copycat strategy trap** now find that they must stand out more than ever. With consumers facing myriad choices from around the globe in every product category, companies must either be the lowest cost producer or stand out in some other way – they must be mavericks: unorthodox and independent-minded. Now the biggest risk is to not take any risks. This is the age of the **maverick strategy**.

Indeed, there are many stories of organizations that did not fall into copycat traps. Companies can look to them for inspiration in this regard. For example:

- Anita Roddick's Body Shop largely redefined how cosmetics are developed and sold by challenging the industry's previous assumptions.
- Cirque du Soleil, a Canadian circus troupe in a dying industry, effectively collapsed two industries into one: theatre and circus. This saw Cirque open up entire new venues and a new audience (who were prepared to pay higher prices).
- Swatch challenged the assumption that a watch was a luxury or high-tech item that people only needed one of. It sold watches as collectable fashion accessories.
- Some 20 years after sparking a revolution in computing, Apple's iPod is revolutionizing the way the music industry thinks and operates.

While an emphasis on thinking differently or creatively to add value in strategy is increasingly recognized as crucial to securing an organization's future, there are many who argue that such things cannot be taught. There is a famous story about Anita Roddick beginning a guest lecture to an entrepreneurship class by saying that if any of them were actually cut out to be entrepreneurs they would not be sat there being taught how to do it – they'd be out there doing it. However, researchers like Kim and Mauborgne are less dismissive. Their database of 30 of the world's highest performing companies shows that those that created new markets generally followed a systematic path.[4] While you cannot be a maverick by following a formula, organizations can develop systems and cultures that help to instill a maverick orientation and help animate people to engage in maverick acts. Beyond the inspirational stories listed above we believe there are some general lessons that can be proposed as to how to foster strategic maverick culture. This chapter provides eight maverick steps that companies should consider.

1. Build Awareness of Maverick Strategies and Their Value to the Organization

It is important to convey a sense of how an organization's health depends on maverick strategies. There are many examples that can help bring this home. For example, Kim and Mauborgne's research shows that while 86% of business or product launches are line extensions, or incremental improvements, they only account for 62% of corporate revenue and 39% of profits. Value innovations (the remaining 14% of launches) account for 38% of revenue and 61% of profits.

A prominent framework that makes the case for new strands in an organization is the **S-curve**, introduced in Richard Foster's 1986 book *Innovation, the Attacker's Advantage*.[5] It shows how a product will hit a plateau where further improvement will either be impossible or prohibitively expensive. Corporate performance over the long term thus requires different products, markets, or approaches being brought into the picture – even though they will take time to pay off and may even fail.

At the same time, it is important to convey that maverick strategies are not just about innovation for its own sake. They can come from simply connecting old thinking from different spheres or re-looking at an existing product from an unusual perspective. This is a theme of Kim and Mauborgne's promotion of **value innovation** – an approach that ensures that maverick strategies focus on providing added value to customers rather than just invention. Hence, the selling of books without bookstores, or nappies that are disposable, or flights that operate more like buses are as much "value innovations" as the iPod. Thus, maverick strategies can be developed by anybody – you do not need to be a "creative type." Indeed, Kim and Mauborgne suggest that value innovation can be advanced by any manager asking structured questions like:

1. What factors could be eliminated that an industry has taken for granted? (For companies like Egg and First Direct it was that banks need branches.)
2. What product/service elements could be reduced below the industry standard? (For Ryanair and Southwest it was food and beverage services.)
3. What elements could be lifted above the standard? (For Dyson and Alessi it was that things like vacuum cleaners and teapots could have designer styling.)
4. What should be introduced that the industry has never offered the customer? (For Swatch it was the idea that you could launch watches like fashion collections.)
5. Could a new offering win buyers without any marketing hype? (The Smart car or new Mini created demand simply through people seeing them on the streets.)

2. Promote Your Organization's Particular Maverick-ness

Because companies have become used to looking to what other companies are doing for the answers, engendering maverick-ness thus firstly requires that this mind-set be de-programmed. Each organization should be aware of and actively develop its **legitimate strangeness**, to use a term promoted in Stephen Cummings' book *Recreating Strategy*. This partly reflects social trends (for the first time ever, Nike is finding that young people in its surveys claim to aspire to being "themselves" rather than Michael Jordon or Michael Johnson, which indicates that customers are increasingly seeking difference and individuality) and is partly because it makes good business sense (recent studies show how continually chasing and measuring oneself against the competition leads to declining performance).[6]

So, a firm's orientation must shift from following the leader to continually getting better in your particular "category of one." As Jerry Garcia of The Grateful Dead put it: "You do not merely want to be the best of the best. You want to be considered the only ones who do what you do." Fostering this maverick attitude requires some changes in emphasis: moving away from following customers ("companies should be idea-led and consumer informed," claims Doug Atkin, Director of Strategic Planning at advertising and branding consultancy Merkley, Newman, Harty, because the world is moving too fast for consumers to understand what is possible and following focus groups can only result in averages and incremental developments); questioning strategic supplier relationships (Wayne Burkan's *Wide-Angle Vision* claims that suppliers who make you question your practices are more likely saviors than those designed to fit efficiently into your existing modus operandi); and moving away from an emphasis on promoting "best practice" copying of competitors.[7] Alternative mindsets with regard to this last point include:

- focusing on "**next practice**" (an idea advocated in *Recreating Strategy* and inspired by Sony's attitude of looking at its competitors' accomplishments merely as conventions to be overturned rather than achievements to aim for)
- focusing on promoting "**good practice**" (an idea advanced by IBM, which now discourages staff from talking of "best practice" because it implies that there is only one best way that cannot be surpassed, thus encouraging complacency)
- focusing on identifying particular "**promising practices**" (an idea developed by the AIM research network in the UK, which is interested in identifying how companies sponsor and bring through emergent new approaches)
- focusing on understanding and discussing "**worst practices**" (an approach sponsored by David Snowden of the think-tank Cynefin because, he claims, "striving to avoid failure is more compelling than imitating success")

In a nutshell, a company's people need to understand and be animated to act on a particular maverick orientation. According to Seth Godin, if you can't explain such an orientation "in eight words or less, then you don't have one."[8] But some claim that an organization's maverick-ness should be even easier to see. Jean-Marie Dru's book *Disruption* claims that the following companies are greatly aided because their names imply a single unique and inspiring verb. It is widely understood that Apple *opposes*, IBM *solves*, Nike *exhorts*, Virgin *enlightens*, Sony *dreams*, and Benetton *protests*.[9]

3. Encourage Diversity

According to Arthur Koestler, "Invention or discovery takes place by combining ideas. The Latin verb cogito for 'to think' means 'to shake together' . . . the creative act, by connecting previously unrelated dimensions of experience, is an act of liberation – the defeat of habit by originality."[10] Koestler's philosophy underpins the recent promotion of **diversity management**: the idea that if you want to encourage inventive thinking in an organization you need a dissimilar workforce who will look in different ways, then challenge and shake up one another's habits. An inspiring anecdote in this regard is that of Andrew Higgins, who was charged with building landing craft for the American army in World War II. He turned out 20,000 craft (that Eisenhower credited with winning the war) by hiring all sorts of people other than engineering graduates. Higgins argued that they spent too much time teaching you what you can't or shouldn't do at engineering school.

A number of Bob Sutton's *"Weird Ideas That Work"* from the book of the same name are also useful spurs here. Sutton claims that you should: hire people that make you uncomfortable; use job interviews to get new ideas, not just to screen candidates; never try to learn anything from people who seem to have solved the problems you face; decide to do something that should fail, then convince the people working with you that they will succeed and see what happens; or simply hire people you don't seem to need.[11]

4. Provide Time and Space For Mavericks To Operate

Sutton's last point implies that maverick-ness (like knowledge – see chapter 6 Living Strategy) requires "slack" – mavericks need to be provided with time and tools with which to think. This may be as simple as giving people time out to try new things or to actively encourage the prototyping of new ideas. "Effective (i.e. quick) prototyping may be the most valuable core competence an innovative company can hope to have," claims Michael Schrage – because *"Innovation occurs as people see, deconstruct, and rebuild prototypes."*[12] Thus, mavericks need to be encouraged to try, fail, learn, and try again.

Good thinking tools that can encourage maverick thinking include scenario planning, which we discussed in chapter 6, and "blue ocean" thinking. **Blue ocean strategy** is a term developed by Kim and Mauborgne in an attempt to get beyond strategy's "wrong-headed militaristic foundations."[13] These foundations suggest that firms, like armies, are competing for finite pieces of territory. Mavericks look beyond such territorial boundaries and blue ocean thinking encourages managers to think across and beyond established industries, traditional buyer groups or suppliers, or the traditional functional or emotional orientation of an industry. Apple's PC revolution in the 1980s stemmed from this sort of thinking. By assembling a group of employees that IBM would never have hired, Apple took a new type of computing (fun, stylish, cheap, easy to operate) to a group of buyers that the industry hadn't really paid much attention to.

5. Elevate People From Spheres Where Difference Rather Than Compliance Is Key

Most senior positions in organizations are occupied by people from law, engineering, and accountancy backgrounds. Such fields are concerned with compliance, with being mindful of past precedent, general standards, and established practice. This makes them unlikely mavericks or supporters of maverick-ness. Jesper Kunde's book *Unique*, consequently describes most executives as having "no idea how to add value in a metaphysical world. But that is what the market will cry out for in the future. There is no lack of 'physical' products to choose between."[14] People from backgrounds such as design or advertising are better able to understand the importance of uniqueness, the particular emotional ties that a brand or product can convey, and of standing out from the crowd. Companies would do well to bring them into the boardroom. Their leadership, by its very nature, will also be difficult for other companies to replicate.

6. Match Entrepreneurial Thinking With Financial Flair

Maverick strategies require people to be entrepreneurial rather than just accepting what has passed for a good product or strategy before. It is hard to define an entrepreneur, but one way of doing so is to think of them as a person with an ability for innovation, a vision or "memory" of the future (that is, an ability to see the future as a different place requiring different things), and a desire to take risks. These innovative, risk-taking, and visionary characteristics, if effectively combined, have an ability to inspire and instill confidence in others to follow these entrepreneurs on their maverick path. Such entrepreneurs may be CEOs like Richard Branson or Rupert Murdoch, or inventors like Steve Jobs or James Dyson, or even people operating at lower levels of companies (who are often termed "intraprenuers" – people who are entrepreneurial within an organization). Susan Segal-Horn suggests that lower level employees can become entrepreneurial if they cease to be "implementers of top-down decisions" and become instigators of corporate actions. Often, because these people go against the grain, they are seen to be odd or misguided. A few organizations recognize this – Tait Elder at 3M famously said that "we expect our champions to be irrational." However, companies need them if they are to seize or create new opportunities and growth. Moreover, they need to fund them – new ideas seldom get off the ground without sponsorship. But deciding to back such people and their ideas generally means using judgment and taking calculated financial risks rather than following rational financial criteria to the letter.

7. Don't Follow Frameworks Blindly: Conceive of Your Organization As Unique

While the pioneers of strategic management believed that an organization's structure would be determined by its choice of strategy, since the 1980s it has been accepted that strategic choices are also shaped by a company's structure. Thus, a centralized firm will not be as responsive to local environmental changes as a highly decentralized firm. Thus, in order to promote maverick strategies we must simultaneously promote seeing in terms of individualized structural configurations. In a 1999 *Harvard Business Review* articled titled "Organigraphs: Drawing How Companies Really Work," Henry Mintzberg advocates moving away from representing companies with standard generic organization chart hierarchies, toward an individualized approach of drawing the unique things that each organization does and how it does them.[15] Figure 11.1 provides an example.

One should take a similarly maverick approach to using strategic frameworks. In chapter 2 we described how leading theorists and their frameworks can act as movers and shakers but that this can sometimes blinker independent thought. For example, try asking an MBA student how many forces there are in an industry. They will generally tell you "five." Ask them why and they will cite Porter's Five-Forces. In reality, of course, the world is a more diverse and open-ended place, and a maverick approach is more likely to come from ignorance of

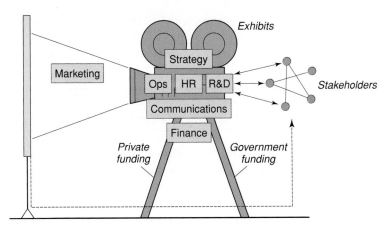

Figure 11.1 An organigraph of a national museum

such blinkers or by looking beyond them. Asking, for example, what Apple's iPod is in relation to the music industry (is it a buyer, a new entrant, a competitor, a substitute, a potential supplier, or all of the above, or does it represent something new – another force?) will lead to stimulating discussion on new approaches to strategy. Some industries should be analyzed in terms of more than five forces: government or technological change could be incorporated, for example; but any future-focused analysis would do well to keep an open mind and look to stretch and customize established theories and frameworks, which were, after all, based on past practice.

A good example of this is the value chimera. In a recent article titled "The Future Shape of Strategy," Cummings and Angwin outline a number of future imperatives in strategy. However, they claim that successful strategies cannot afford to leave past imperatives behind. Things like structure, efficiency, and cost and risk reduction are still important, but new necessities, like nimbleness, agility, and individuality, must be achieved in tandem with these. They go on to propose the **value chimera** (a customized value chain) as one way of thinking through and depicting how a firm might seek to achieve the best of both worlds. Rather than a generic line with a single point of contact with customers, the value chimera can be drawn with any number of differentiated heads targeted at different markets fused onto a single body of shared resources and core competences (figure 11.2). An auto manufacturer like the VW Group, with its emphasis on keeping brands

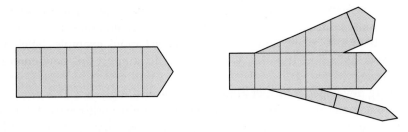

Figure 11.2 From generic value chains to customized value chimera

like Audi, Seat, Skoda, and VW distinct, *and* developing commonality of parts and enhancing purchasing power across the whole group is a good example of a value chimera, but every company's chimera should be unique.[16]

> ## 8. Recognize That There Is More Than One Approach To the Strategy Process

The conventional definition of strategy (with which this book began) was that laid down by Alfred Chandler in 1962: "Strategy is the determination of the basic long-term goals and objectives of an enterprise and the adoption of a course of action and the allocation of resources necessary for carrying out these goals." Chandler matched this view with a generic triangular-hierarchical view of organizational structure. Putting his definitions of strategy and structure together, one could identify and distinguish strategic, tactical, and operational levels of the firm and see strategy as the preserve of those at the top. Other definitions of strategic management followed Chandler's key premises. Hence, strategy was seen to be about: top managers rationally determining the *position* that the company will assume relative to its competitors and developing the *plans* by which these would be achieved.[17]

However, in recent years a number of leading thinkers have argued against there being one best view of the strategy process, or how firms develop strategy. Maverick strategy theorists like Henry Mintzberg argue that if we want to see unique or independent-minded strategies, then we need to recognize that there is more than one way of developing a strategy and that different companies should follow an approach that suits their differences.

Mintzberg's challenge to the conventional one-size-fits-all approach to strategy began in 1973 with his book *The Nature of Managerial Work*. This looked not at what we might think managers should be (rational, analytical, measured, calculating) and should do (plan, direct, and position) but what they actually *did*. He found that managers were far more chaotic, political, expedient, and opportunistic than the textbooks suggested.[18]

Mintzberg's ideas in this regard came to a head in a series of published debates with Igor Ansoff and a book called *The Rise and Fall of Strategic Planning*.[19] Here he put forward the view that the classical approach to strategy was dead and that a new view was rising to take its place. He argued that strategies in reality arose not from senior managers analyzing and planning, but from patterns of behavior that *emerged* from the day-to-day interactions of those at lower levels and from chance events and culture shifts. (He drew an analogy between the way an artisan crafts a piece of clay on a potter's wheel to illustrate that strategists must craft strategy by responding to what emerges as one is working rather than just "plan" and then "do.") Now famous examples, such as the emergence of 3M's Post-It Notes, were invoked to support this new **emergence view** of strategy.

Mintzberg developed a further approach in the ensuing years. This argued that there were actually many different schools of thought with regard to strategy. These were outlined in the book *The Strategy Safari*.[20] Summaries of them are listed in table 11.1.[21]

Table 11.1 Mintzberg's "different schools of thought about the strategy process"

The design school	sees strategizing as the result of senior managers using conscious rational analysis to design a fit between the internal strengths and weaknesses of the organization and the environmental opportunities and threats
The planning school	reflects most of the design school view except that strategizing is decomposable into distinct steps delineated by checklists and supporting frameworks like the value chain or the Five-Forces of industry
The positioning school	views strategy as a process of selection from generic options or frameworks (e.g. the generic strategy matrix) based on the formalized analysis of the specific industry and market situation
The environmental or impositional school	concentrates on the environment's influence in steering firms toward or mitigating strategic options. Unlike the first three schools, senior managers are seen here to have far less agency and control over strategic decisions. They are "imposed" upon by the "movers and shakers" or "industry dynamics"
The cognitive school	is concerned with understanding the mental processes of the strategist that lead to particular strategic decisions. Kenichi Ohmae's *The Mind of the Strategist* is written in this vein
The learning school	views the strategy development process as emerging incrementally over time through trial, error, and learning. Strategists and other influences on strategy can be found throughout the organization; great attention is paid to environmental shifts and questioning present assumptions
The cultural or ideological school	concentrates on the influence of culture in promoting particular strategic choices
The consensus school	is similar in nature to the cultural school. However, unlike the cultural school where consensus is established around a common belief system, the consensus school views strategy as emerging from the mutual adjustment of a company's key stakeholders as they learn from each other to establish a common strategic perspective
The power school	sees strategizing as influenced by *micro-power* (which suggests that the strategy process is entirely political, involving bargaining, persuasion, and confrontation between various interested parties) and *macro-power* (which relates to the power dynamics that exist between the whole firm and its strategic partners and other networks)
The entrepreneurial school	represents a move away from precise designs or plans, towards more vague notions such as "visions" and "perspectives" – typically articulated through metaphorical statements or a "sense of mission" embodied by the CEO or senior management

Table 11.1 Continued

The process school	sees the strategic role of senior managers as the definition and control of the processes by which strategy is developed. The determination of actual strategies is left to others at lower levels
The configuration school	views organizations as coherent but time-varying "states" or clusters of resources, characteristics, and behaviors. The strategic development process then becomes one of defining a desired end state (configuration) relative to the current state, and mapping out a series of steps to move from one to the other. The configuration school can be seen to draw upon many of the other schools

It has been argued that these schools of strategy are mutually incompatible. However, using the famous analogy of six blind men grasping separate parts of an elephant and claiming they each had a hold of something quite different, *The Strategy Safari* claims that each school is just focusing on and emphasizing different parts of the same multifaceted being. It adds that "the greatest failings of strategic management have occurred when managers took one point of view too seriously" and that as strategists we should be able to utilize them all to look at strategy. This is in no small part because different organizations will adhere more closely to particular approaches depending on their history, resources, and corporate culture. Hence, we should acknowledge the strengths of both the classical and emergent perspectives. Organizations may tend towards one or the other depending on the nature of what they do (e.g. larger cost-focused low-tech manufacturers should plan a lot; smaller high-end innovators should organize to allow new ideas and approaches to emerge quickly from interactions with the environment), but today all firms should aim to exhibit "strategic agility" – the ability to move quickly to, and away from, set plans as the environment shifts. A similar approach is advanced by Bob De Wit and Ron Meyer. They claim that strategy comes from each individual firm's resolution of paradoxes such as: the need to be logical *and* creative; to be focused *and* allow scope for opportunities to emerge; to attempt to move with the environment *and* be true to one's unique configuration of resources; and so on.[22]

A further attempt to get beyond the one-size-fits-all definition of strategy is advanced in the book *Images of Strategy*. It argues that we should focus less on a definition of where strategy comes from and more on what good strategies do: they *orient* (or provide a sense of what an organization is and where it is heading) and *animate* (motivate people to move toward and beyond this) (see figure 11.3). This can come from top-down planning or emergent ideas or an emphasis on knowledge or a strong brand or a clear design philosophy or any combination of forces such as these, depending on the nature of the particular organization in question.[23]

These wider-ranging views of strategy reinforce Godin's quote at the head of this chapter: great firms will do strategy in different ways, ways that suit

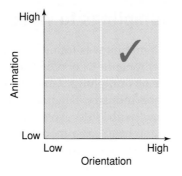

Figure 11.3 Strategies can come from anywhere to provide orientation and animation

their particular resources and capabilities. They will take a maverick approach to developing strategy, an approach that can be guided by the steps described above. Rather than sticking to the norm they will be out on the edge, because, as Kurt Vonnegut put it: "out on the edge you can see all kinds of things you can't see from the center."[24]

Epilogue

In recent times, Mintzberg has published another new book bemoaning the traditional MBA degree's role in churning out the "similar" people described in the quotation with which this chapter began and who subsequently diminish the likelihood of maverick-ness.[25] However, it is important to recognize that he is not (or he should not be in any case) critical of MBAs per se, but rather he warns that the notion of a generic education can dull people's ability to think independently and to take risks if one does not guard against this.

Thus, the maverick strategist, indeed the expert strategist in general, should not forgo the conventions and theories of strategy; he or she must learn from them, and become expert. They provide a conceptual toolkit from which he or she should draw to skillfully create endless different combinations that provide greater insight into strategic problems and solutions. True experts, however, are not bound by frameworks but are masters in their creative application to their own individual situations and circumstance. Picasso, for example, became a great artist by first learning well the conventions he would later knowingly twist around and adapt to suit his own particular maverick approach. The skilled strategist, the strategy pathfinder if you will, must similarly be both a traditionalist and a maverick.

Given that maverick strategists are called upon to think freely in new and unconventional ways, we felt it would be inappropriate to include the pathfinder compass in this chapter.

Dumplings to villas

Synear Quick-Frozen Food Company was founded in 1994 by a group of young and ambitious Chinese entrepreneurs in one of China's southern provinces. It began life as a manufacturer of dumplings. China's "dragon head," or leading player, in the quick-frozen food industry, Sanquan, was located just 1 mile from Synear's base. As a newcomer with little experience in the industry, Synear's founders perceived this "dragon head" as a model and aimed to copy Sanquan's factory layout, administrative systems, training processes, supplier relationships, and recipes, as near as possible. They set out to become, in their words, a "mini-Sanquan."

While this approach enabled Synear to get its operations off the ground, it created a number of problems. Perceiving Sanquan as "best practice" and duplicating its products made it hard for customers to differentiate the two company's offerings. Inevitably, this led to a price war that Synear, given its much smaller operating base, was in no position to win. Synear management found that the only way it could shift sales in this environment was to offer its dumplings on credit, but the difficulties associated with deferred payments by customers led to a serious cash-flow problem.

Synear responded in two ways. First, to improve cash flow, it integrated forwards into restaurants that utilized Synear products but enabled bigger margins and improved cash receipts. Second, it began to think about how it could differentiate its dumplings from those of Sanquan. This it did in two ways that might be seen as contradictory by followers of classic Western strategic management theory.

On the one hand, Synear abandoned what it described as "high-income" customers and focused instead on those with middle or low incomes who would sacrifice some degree of quality for a lower price. This enabled it to focus on every step of the processes it had copied from Sanquan and examine how costs could be cut. For example, Synear decided not to sell its dumplings to wholesalers and stores in traditional small packets, but in bulk cartons from which shoppers could pick the amount they wanted and pay by weight at lower prices. Synear was soon able to market its wares as the lowest priced dumplings on the market, knowing that Sanquan, whose success was wedded to its broad appeal to all income groups and traditional dumpling manufacture techniques, would find it difficult to follow.

On the other hand, however, Synear sought to differentiate its dumplings in ways that appealed to younger people like themselves. Synear's managers had watched with interest the emerging awareness of environmental issues among younger consumers. To match these interests they decided to go after the newly developed Chinese "green product certificate," which assured customers that a product was made of natural or organic ingredients and that the manufacturing process did not pollute the environment. Additionally, it introduced natural dyes to some products to create green dumplings in addition to the traditional white color. This made Synear dumplings stand out in the marketplace and attracted attention to the green policy. A yellow coloring was also added in honor of the Yellow River, a "being" of great cultural and spiritual significance in the region.

While its lack of experience in frozen foods had been seen as something of a hindrance when Synear started life, it was now beginning to use the fact that its people weren't ingrained with traditional approaches and could therefore think about making and selling dumplings in new and different ways. Other innovative approaches that Synear developed included:

- Convincing Sanquan to develop an alliance that would give the companies added muscle to jointly procure produce at lower prices.
- Using some of its underutilized frozen food facilities to develop a range of ice cream.
- An alliance with a local sales agent willing to put money into the company. This agent became the company's second largest shareholder. The cash injection enabled dumpling and ice cream production to double.
- Another alliance with a regional agent who had a strong hold over the market in three provinces in China's southwest region, provinces where companies like Sanquan had yet to establish a presence. This provided a ready market for the increased production described above. While ensuring this agent's cooperation required an agreement to sell to him at little more than cost, his networks enabled Synear to dominate the frozen dumpling market in these provinces within a matter of months.
- Broadening its portfolio by buying the recipes for proven products (a particular regional black sesame dumpling, for example) from smaller companies that lacked the finance to develop the market for such items.
- A commitment to developing very good and very professionalized relationships with banks and government agencies – relationships that over time would help with obtaining the capital and permits required for further developments. This was something that traditional and less entrepreneurial Chinese companies had generally not focused on.

The development of these new strategies meant that business was getting much better for Synear, but as time went by the partners became increasingly aware of the relatively low margins that the dumpling and restaurant businesses provided. It was time to diversify further. However, once again the direction the company took might be seen by some to make little sense when analyzed using classical Western decision-making models.

Synear's managers made the decision to enter the real estate business. However, this time they realized that they needed to differentiate themselves from the competition from the outset. There were literally tens of thousands of property development businesses in China and most of them much the same as one other, but Synear sought to mark itself out as different by building on the ethos that had developed around the dumplings. Synear sought to focus on low-cost housing. This meant building some distance out from the city. But this then enabled a connection to another of Synear's tenets to come into play. Synear would build on newly developed forestland and would emphasize the green, environmentally sound, and tranquil aspects of their properties to young middle-income house buyers. Thus, Synear developed four principles around with it would focus its property development energies. They are as follows:

1. In Chinese cities most people live in apartments, and most are sick of concrete and steel buildings. People want houses – homes with gardens, grass, and flowers. All our buildings are villas.

2. All our buildings are far away from city noise. At least 20 kilometres away from the city so that people can plunge themselves into a paradise after a hard day's work.
3. The backgrounds of our houses are very green and tranquil. Our homes are built in a forest in surroundings that are like rural areas.
4. All our houses are near the "Mother" (or Yellow) River. People have a special emotion for the river and living near her gives them a feeling of harmony and relaxation.

The company that began as a frozen dumpling maker still makes dumplings. But it now makes much more, and each product in its diverse range (dumplings, restaurants, villas) reinforces the brand image of the other. The company has gone from strength to strength and its managers are now considering what their next move will be.

1. *Draw an organigraph or a value chimera of Synear. Why do you think this might be a more effective depiction of Synear than an organization chart or a value chain?*
2. *What were the strengths and weaknesses of Synear's initial strategy to copy and replicate Sanquan as the "best practice" model?*
3. *Work through Kim and Mauborgne's five "value innovation" questions to determine the value innovations that Synear's managers have achieved.*
4. *Can you also identify any examples of "blue ocean" strategies followed by Synear?*
5. *Define Synear's particular maverick-ness, or "legitimate strangeness," in eight words or less. How would a statement like this help orient and animate the company for the future?*
6. *What do you think Synear's next moves should be?*

Gray boxes

With 3 days to go before Christmas, a file landed on my desk with "most urgent" stamped on the cover. Inside was a memo from the Managing Director saying, "In the light of this bank's substantial exposure to this client firm, and the request from this client for further financing, we must review, urgently, the bank's position. A Board meeting has been arranged for Christmas Day to make a decision on this matter. Review all the documentation to date, including the current request, and present your summary recommendations at 10 AM, December 25th, in the Boardroom. Present will be myself, the Chairman and the Heads of Corporate Finance, the Credit Committee, and Risk Finance." Investment banking was living up to its reputation as 24/7.

The client firm had a reputation as an innovator in electronics and was well regarded in the industry. A number of innovations had been patented successfully and the firm continued to grow rapidly. However, the firm was highly indebted and most of this debt was held by our bank. Understandably, the bank was getting very nervous as the amount of outstanding debt continued to grow and there appeared to be no real sign from the firm that any of its products would really be a stellar performer. And now here they were, asking for a substantial increase in funds of £50m for a completely new product.

Shortly after the file landed on my desk, a gray box the size of a small briefcase arrived. It had a few dials and switches and weighed a ton. Attached was a technical note that was hard to follow, but it was clear that the device was supposed to be portable! How would it be carried? It wouldn't fit into anything but the largest of bags and it didn't have its own case. One would certainly be conspicuous carrying it down the street, but for all the wrong reasons.

Christmas Day arrived and my presentation began. The atmosphere was tense, as the Head of the Credit Committee had been supporting this client from the beginning and the Head of Risk felt that the bank was already too exposed. The new product, for which further financing was required, seemed to underwhelm the meeting, especially when it was revealed that it was supposed to be portable and yet was bulky, heavy, and ugly. In my presentation I had to point out that the battery life was extremely limited and the device only seemed to work effectively in relatively few locations. Indeed, it was more likely not to work at all. "What about using it in a car, as there would be a power source and its weight would be less significant?" suggested one Director. I replied that we failed to get it to work in a car, possibly because it was moving, or there was some sort of interference with the engine and other electronics.

Conscious of my career being on the line in front of such a senior audience, I gave a highly detailed and conservative analysis of the client's financials, and drew widely on industry experts for forecasts and market soundings. Using the bank's credit assessment techniques as well as a number of other evaluative methods, the figures, at best, were an either way bet. I had been asked to prepare a presentation for a credit committee, and therefore conservative, point of view. I therefore recommended the bank walk away from any further financing of the client as the numbers really did not support further exposure based on the bank's own criteria for loans. I also recommended the bank reduce its exposure to the firm by syndicating some of the debt. For the committee, the fate of the client hung in the balance. To refuse financing would imperil the client's future. There is no doubt that the client would have had a very hard time getting finance from another bank when its own bank had refused it.

The Head of Risk asked: "When should the bank stop lending to a firm that is really not showing results, and just keeps coming up with new products for which there appears to be no demand?" The Head of the Credit Committee responded by remarking that the client had never defaulted on an interest payment and then, to my surprise, said that the numbers were only part of the equation. What he wanted to know was: "What does the client MD think about when he gets up in the morning? What worries him when he is shaving in front of the mirror?" The Managing Director of the bank agreed, saying, "the key to good lending is *really* understanding the entrepreneur – a great idea in the hands of a poor entrepreneur is a disaster, a mediocre idea in the hands of a great entrepreneur is success."

There followed a spirited discussion between the Directors around which they largely agreed that the client MD was passionate about his firm and his products and that he would do anything to get his products to work. After a bruising meeting for all concerned, the Board agreed, late on Christmas Day, that they would support the client and finance the launch of its new product – even though the Head of Risk could not see why anyone would want an oversized, pig-ugly, temperamental gray box!

1. *Would you have supported the decision to lend a further £50m?*
2. *What are the main considerations for banks involved in this form of finance?*
3. *It is clear from the case that it was touch and go for the entrepreneur gaining the necessary finance for his product. Why was he successful in getting finance? Could he have improved his approach to the bank?*
4. *This is a real case. The identity of the client firm is revealed under Case Authors section following the References. Now that you are aware of the client firm's identity, does this affect your answers to the earlier questions? What lessons can be learned about the way in which early-stage finance and entrepreneurial endeavors work alongside each other?*

21st century cars

Democracy is the system where everybody gets what nobody wants.

Anon

The appearance of cars is changing. According to Hugh Pearman, cultural commentator with the *Sunday Times,* "manufacturers have been driven to take risks . . . to create market niches. Before, everyone wanted their products to look the same. Now, they want them to look distinctive . . . Good is bland, bad is good, and suddenly instinct is cooler than logic." This is culturally significant, claims Pearman, because "cars dominate our visual surroundings."

Examples of this distinctiveness are now coming to the fore. Ford may have led the way with its Scorpio ("bugged eyed and strangely proportioned, but you noticed it," says Pearman) and is now "going back to the future" with its Forty-Nine. Chrysler's new PT Cruiser is described by its makers as "a love it or hate it car too cool to categorize" (it looks like a 1950s American hotrod). The PT follows on from what Chrysler describes as its "yestertech" sports cars like the Prowler and Viper, combining retro styling and modern technology (their old-fashioned large-diameter steering wheels housing airbags). Only 41% of the company's focus-group members liked the PT (26% hated it, usually more than enough to kill off a prototype).

Why are such examples striking a chord? A decade-long drive where closing the quality and engineering gap among car manufacturers around the world was the main strategic focus has left the companies so similar technologically that they are being forced to compete increasingly on *different looks.* "The globalization of the car industry meant that all cars (and all car ads) came to look much the same everywhere," Pearman explains. "The aim of manufacturers was for the greatest number of people to be unoffended by the look of the product. This avoidance of risk was achieved through focus groups, and meant that national and marque differences were ironed out. Weird French cars ceased to be weird; Japanese cars stopped being ugly; the Americans toned down their once incredible styling in the name of international sales." Handling and performance differences also went the way of stylish eccentricity. The car market, says Pearman, "became like architecture's dogmatic modern phase." Homogenization meant it became impossible to express an individual identity through a new car. "But now the world's motor magnates are discovering the joys of pluralism. Retro cars, cute baby cars, plug-ugly cars, even modern cars – they're making them all."

Ray Hutton reports from the US that whereas "Not long ago the world car was the thing, car makers having declared that customer tastes had converged and that the latest designs would be as acceptable in Tamworth as they were in Tuscon or Tokyo. [But] it didn't turn out that way. Buyers wanted individuality." Toyota recently claimed that "Our global strategy used to center on 'world cars,' which we would modify slightly to accommodate demand in different markets. Today our focus is shifting to models that we develop and manufacture for selected regional markets." Subsequently, says Hutton, all sorts of niche cars are starting to appear and American cars are once more starting to look "distinctly American." Consequently, "Design is the No. 1 selling point these days," asserts James Kelly, professor of transportation design at the Pforzheim University of Applied Sciences in Germany.

The change of emphasis has caught some manufacturers on the hop. A few years ago Citroen, once leaders in quirky French styling, found that its new cars resembled last year's Fords and that consumers were unsure of Citroen's "identity." Renault's Head of Design, Patrick le Quement, describes the change that has happened in the car industry since: "When I joined Renault, my notion of bringing 'Frenchness' to the brand was heresy, we were living through the 'world car' phenomenon . . . but now people recognize that we are so much richer for having Britishness, Dutchness, and Germanness and so on."

These developments have caused many to question the stock traditionally placed on focus groups. Inventor James Dyson believes that you cannot have customers designing products because individual distinctiveness must be a key part of any successful product. "We have focus groups," he explains, "but I take a perverse delight in ignoring them." Dyson points out that one of the most boring British cars ever made – the Hillman Avenger – emerged from focus groups, whereas the Mini, one of the most memorable, was one man's local vision.

One company that didn't march to the tune of homogenization is Jaguar, and it did so in no small part because of its different approach to focus groups. It did not ask groups if they liked a proposed prototype. Instead it asked if they could identify a prototype, without any badging, as being a Jaguar. Unless upward of 90% of people could see a prototype as continuing the Jaguar legacy, first and foremost, that prototype would be dead in the water. In recent times, Jaguar has sought to make further capital out of its "difference" in this respect, with advertising campaigns focused around the uniqueness and Britishness of the marque. The strap line of one recent campaign ran: "In a city where everyone is anonymous the individual will always stand out."

However, Pearman is unsure whether these shifts have enough substance to make them significant for the long term. Consolidation in the car industry and advances in computerized design have made manufacturers adept at making marques appear different, when they are just the same model with a different skin. The new Beetle is just a Golf (or Seat?) in disguise and the Ka is just a Ford Fiesta with curves. "Pluralism is all very well," Pearman concludes, but the current appreciation of individuality and difference may be "just another passing phase."

However, there is evidence to suggest that this may be more than a phase. Two out of three of Jeremy Clarkson's trendsetting cars for 2002, which formed part of the *Sunday Times* "Good Car, Bad Car" guide, were individual retro hybrids: the new Mini and the PT Cruiser. And even the world's biggest manufacturer, GM, is said to be seeking to inject more "personality" into its cars so as to exploit the market niches that are opening up retro vehicles, convertibles, super-tough off-roaders, and what are now called "crossover vehicles." Finally, a *BusinessWeek* special report in 2004 concluded that using individualized design to create cars with a "unique personality" has never counted more. It concludes with a quotation from the Director of Innovation at PSA Peugeot Citroen, Robert Peugeot: "The executive committee [now] spends a lot of time on design: It's absolutely strategic."

1. *Why do you think that design has become "absolutely strategic" in the auto industry?*
2. *What other elements, apart from design, are important in automobile manufacture nowadays?*
3. *The case describes Jaguar's attempts to keep the brand individualized and distinctive. However, Jaguar is now owned by the Ford Group (that also comprises Aston Martin, Land Rover, Volvo, and Mazda). Why would large automobile companies be looking to buy up smaller brands? Can you use the value chimera to depict an organization like the Ford Group?*
4. *Why might listening to focus groups not be a good thing?*
5. *Why would companies like Citroen and Renault be seeking to "inject more Frenchness" into what they do?*

Breaking the chain; joining the customer

Levi-Strauss is a great brand name and it makes great jeans. But then so do a lot of other companies nowadays. To continue to be at the forefront of casual-wear and related products, Levi's is rethinking the way it conceives its value chain. Using the conventional linear, step-by-step, input-process-output view of adding value embodied in the conventional generic value chain, clothes manufacturers take inputs like fabrics and fixtures, use the company's information systems and knowledge to subject these inputs to value-adding processes (such as design and assembly), and then distribute outputs to customers who pay for the finished product and then go on their way. Levi's has attempted to deconstruct these assumptions and look at ways in which it can *involve* its customers in the value-adding process so that they become part of the company, and part of the "Levi's community," rather than an anonymous body beyond the company walls.

Flagship stores, such as those in San Francisco and London, now contain a "Levi's customization area." Here customers can photograph themselves and input these images into computer terminals that allow them to see what various outfits from the Levi's range would look like on them. Then they can become part of the value-adding design team by testing out how customized alterations (different cuts, or washes, or buttons, or pockets, or rips, or stitching, or patches and so on) would look on them. Finished designs can then be taken to an in-house construction team that works with the customer to develop what is wanted. Information on individual customers can be kept for return visits and aggregated to provide insights into popular trends.

Moreover, the London store has been refurbished into a combined store and club/arts venue. It incorporates a "chill-out" area, internet stations, plasma screens, ISDN links, a suspended two-tier DJ booth designed by DJ Paul Oakenfold, and a record outlet called Vinyl Addiction. It can be transformed into a 500 capacity venue with facilities to host club nights, live music, fashion shows, film screenings, comedy nights, and exhibitions. It can create and sustain "value" in many more ways than the traditional, "go in–browse–buy–leave" store.

A related approach has been used to great success recently by Build-A-Bear Workshop Inc., a retailer based in shopping malls across America (a distribution chain that many saw as a "dinosaur" with the rise of the internet). Build-A-Bear has experienced an average annual profit growth of 108% in the 3 years to 2005. The concept: kids come in and build their own soft toy, match it up with accessories and clothes as they wish, and get a birth certificate issued with the name of their choosing. The bears, dogs, and other creatures are priced at around US$32, but the extra trimmings hike up the price, and kids, little girls in particular, love being involved in creating a friend of their own.

The company is the brainchild of CEO Maxine K. Clark. Clark did not invent teddy bears, and indeed, the Build-A-Bear concept draws greatly on the earlier phenomenon of Cabbage Patch Kids, but Clark figured getting customers involved in the production process would revitalize a mature product. As she says: "Ray Kroc [the entrepreneur behind McDonald's] didn't invent hamburgers, he just invented a way of doing it differently."

Land Rover UK has attempted to achieve similar aims with its Land Rover Club (a concept not dissimilar to the old "car-clubs" of our grandfather's times). To stay involved with Land Rover drivers and keep adding value after a Land Rover is purchased, the Club seeks to link interested Land Rover customers to one another. Drivers are provided with free off-road driving lessons (it turns out that many new owners of four-wheel drive vehicles have little idea of how to get the most out of them), as well as being invited to off-road rallies, other special events, and "adventures." They are also kept informed of news with respect to Land Rover initiatives, off-roading, and other related spheres of interest, and involved in forums where they can provide ongoing feedback and raise any ideas or concerns. The idea behind the Club is to build on Land Rover's brand values and foster the idea that when people buy a Land Rover they are buying into something far more valuable than a collection of parts and technology assembled into a truck. The concept is now being adopted in other parts of Land Rover's global network.

1. *Where do you think Levi's "standard models" (like 501 jeans) sit on the S-curve? Why are Levi's taking the risk of developing the new customized approach described above?*

2. *Try drawing Levi's, incorporating its customization arm, using a generic value chain. How would you customize this chain to more usefully reflect Levi's new strategies? Do you think Levi's customization approaches will make its standard models obsolete?*

3. *Having incorporated customers into their processes, where do you think Levi's, Build-A-Bear, and Land Rover's strategies for the future are coming from? Is there a school of strategy, or combination of schools, that you think reflects this? Or does this represent another, new school of the strategy process?*

4. *Can you identify any examples of value innovation or blue ocean strategies that are described in this case?*

5. *Following Dru's approach described in this chapter, what verbs would you attach to the Levi's, Build-A-Bear, and Land Rover brands to capture their particular maverick-ness?*

The curate's egg?

In 2001, the financial services company Egg's call center in Derby (in England's Midlands) was nominated as one of the UK's "most creative and feel-good offices for the digital age." This was a surprising result, given that call centers were supposed to be the 21st century's sweat-shops – the equivalent of earlier times' dreary and mind-numbing factories – and that Derby lacks what one might call a "feel-good" reputation. But Egg's call center was designed to be different.

With the opportunity to design and build from the ground up on a greenfield site, Egg's vision was to create a vibrant and fun call center that would accommodate over 1,000 people. Its express purpose: to help attract and retain the highest quality personnel. Instead of relying on existing models, Egg's design consultants set about talking to potential staff members aged between 18 and 23 (a typical age for new call-center employees) to find out what sort of work environment would appeal to them.

The result is a huge white aircraft hangar-like building that looks like half an egg, sliced length-wise. It has almost no internal walls, office furniture is configured to enable people to cluster together in teams and to enable employees to reconfigure it as they see fit, and no set seating plan. (Although, it is worth mentioning that Egg employees do admit that despite no set structure, people's patterns did emerge and become ingrained fairly quickly after the Derby center opened.) In each of the four corners of the building are recreational spaces based around different themes (for example, a sports area with room for ball-games, pinball, and so on and a relaxing Mediterranean café) that staff can use depending on their mood.

Egg is not the first company in recent years to attempt to redesign the office or factory, but many consider the company at the forefront of a revolution that is continuing to spread and impact on all of our places of work.

Many trace the beginnings of the workplace revolution to the invention of Apple Computers. Apple made much of not being IBM – the industry standard. It didn't make computers for IBM-type people and the staff didn't work like IBM employees. No corporation uniforms, no strict timetables, no rigid job descriptions, no formal chains of command and time-weary procedures, no sitting alone in an allocated box. This was the story at least, but it was certainly played on in Apple's early advertising for models like the Macintosh and it has become the integral part of the Apple mythology.

Since this time, executives have been empowered to be different in the workplace, to "dress down" on Fridays, or to replace their suits and ties with chinos and soft collars on a more permanent basis. New terms like "open-plan" and "hot-desking" have entered the language, and more and more workspaces contain "chill-out rooms" and fitness centers. But is this revolution in making where we work more comfortable, or more like home, necessarily a good thing? A recently published essay on the trend, called "Game Over! Back to Work," by Jonathan Bell, is not so sure.

Bell claims that the modern office is beginning to resemble a playpen. Not only may all of this just be a ruse to increase productivity – to fool jaded employees into thinking that their company loves them so much that it wants them to have fun, so that these employees, in turn, feel that they owe the company – it may also be a ruse that doesn't actually work. Hence, we may not be too far away from "rediscovering the worth of workspaces that are workspaces rather than romper rooms."

Not that the revolution has been all bad: in many ways it has redressed the imbalance caused by the 20th century's first workplace mavericks. Ninety years ago, workplace architects, inspired by F.W. Taylor's new doctrine "Scientific Management," sought to rationalize the workplace and design out all vestiges of individuality. They built so as to maximize sterility and order. Modernism henceforth became the business world's architectural style of choice and offices came to resemble filing cabinets. But, as with most doctrines, this revolution went too far and by the 1980s the backlash that Apple personified was long overdue.

By the end of the 20th century, things had loosened up so much that for many the lines between work and play were becoming increasingly imperceptible. In 2001, a report entitled *Tomorrow's Workplace: Fulfilment or Stress?* envisaged the office of the future as a "recreational center," where the toys and tasks differed little from those found at home. Product designers are already seeing the boundaries blurring. Industrial designer Sam Hecht says that he is not sure if there is much of a difference anymore: "It's very hard [now] to distinguish between objects for the home and for the office."

At the same time, we are witnessing a blurring between work-time and play-time, with employees finding it increasingly difficult to determine whether they are at work or not. Thanks to "advances" in information technology, for many the workday now begins when they begin their commute, not when they sit down at their desk. For others, it never really ceases as they are constantly available on the end of a cell phone and most homes now contain a computer and an e-mail connection in a "home office."

Although not specifying exact working hours has become the norm for an increasing class of workers, it is generally understood that most "white-collar jobs" (an increasingly anachronistic term given the relaxation of dress codes) consume more and more of people's time. As Madeline Bunting's book *Willing Slaves: How the Overwork Culture is Ruining Our Lives* explains, in many parts of the labor market "the boundaries between work and play have been eroded: work is play, work is your hobby. Work becomes the organizing principle of your life."

This is fine for some, particularly those creative souls for whom their work is a consuming passion: it is where they find their identity and purpose. But it may be that many of us are not wired that way.

Says Bell: "It may be time to recognize that [the majority] do not find identity and purpose in vintage PacMan machines and bean bags. Innovations like hot-desking fail to recognize that most of us want a permanent workstation that allows us to get our job done. We are starting to realize that long hours spent in the office playing table football are not useful or clever. Many of us love our work [but] don't need side-shows or soft furnishings to keep the relationship alive."

Indeed, Bell believes that a new generation of offices will emerge that acknowledges that good ideas can come from people having the freedom to congregate, but at the same time recognize that a good office is about allowing individuals to focus on doing their jobs quickly and cleanly.

"It's a century since Frank Lloyd Wright's Larkin Building was completed in Buffalo, New York," concludes Bell. "This was perhaps the first modern office building. And here was order and communality, efficiency and common purpose. He may have been on to something." But, in the same year as Bell's essay was published, Egg won another prestigious national award, this time topping the list of call centers in the UK with the most motivated and productive staff.

1. *What effects might the way a workplace is designed have on the development of strategy?*
2. *How might the growing awareness of "diversity management" and the importance of "shaking together" different ideas and perspectives impact on the future shape of workplace design?*
3. *Which of the developments in workplace design described in the case do you think are value innovations and which are just innovations for the sake of innovation?*
4. *The case describes Apple's maverick approach setting off something of a revolution in workplace design. Do you think IBM and Apple's other competitors should have followed in Apple's footsteps in this regard?*
5. *Do you think there is one best approach to workplace design or should this design reflect the particularities of each organization?*

Crafting strategy

A criticism often leveled at management and strategic management theory is that because of a lack of diversity in those individuals or schools who are developing them, and a lack of critical questioning of the founding assumptions on which the field is based, what is advocated and promoted as "new!" is often unwittingly very similar to what was advocated in earlier times. It is often argued that our basis for developing such theory tries to be too universal and generally developed in American professional contexts.

For example, consider F.W. Taylor's ideas and those of the 1990s' most pervasive new management approach, Michael Hammer's *Business Process Reengineering*. Despite Taylor writing at the beginning of the 20th century and Hammer at the end, it is often hard to see the difference between the underlying forms of their theses. See if you can guess which of them wrote the statements below. (The statements are presented in pairs, with each pair containing one statement by Hammer and one by Taylor. The answers are listed in the Case Authors section following the References.)

1. Tradition counts for nothing. [This approach is] a new beginning. Managers must throw out their old notions about how businesses should be organized and run . . . the time has come to retire those principles and adopt a new set.
2. The defective systems of management which are in common use [must be substituted for] scientific methods.

3. [This approach] is so much more efficient than the old [ways].
4. [This approach] means doing *more* with *less*.

5. [This approach] must come from the top of the organization [because] people near the front lines lack . . . broad perspective . . . Their expertise is largely confined to the individual functions and departments that they inhabit. They may see very clearly . . . the narrow problems from which their departments suffer, but it is difficult for them to see a process as a whole.
6. All of the planning that under the old system was done by [people near the front lines], as a result of his personal experience, must of necessity under [this approach] be done by management in accordance with the laws of science. Because even if [he] was well suited to the development and use [of this approach], it would be physically impossible for him to work at his machine and at a desk at the same time.

7. The fundamental principles of [this approach] are applicable to all kinds of human activities . . . whenever these principles are correctly applied, results must follow which are truly outstanding.
8. [This approach] applies to any organization in which work is performed . . . [It is] the single best hope for restoring the competitive vigor of American businesses.

9. Fundamentally, [this approach] is about reversing the industrial revolution . . . We need something entirely different . . . [This approach] is to the next revolution of business what the specialization of labor was to the last.
10. In its essence, [this approach] involves a complete mental revolution.

Both Hammer and Taylor argue for throwing away all that has gone before, because their new ideas are more *efficient*. Both talk in terms of a *hierarchical system*

MAVERICK STRATEGIES

311

of relationships, with those at the top having a better view and thus being best placed to make key decisions. Both offer their theory as the new *universal "one best way"* (a term first used in a public forum in a magazine article relating Taylor's method in 1911). And both subsequently urge a *revolution* that will see their ideas save us all. While Hammer states that, "Reengineering rejects the assumptions inherent in Adam Smith's industrial paradigm" and seeks to overcome Smith's *taking apart and simplification of work tasks* into "meaninglessly thin slices," he appears to "replace" this with the *taking apart and simplification of processes*.

On August 27, 2001, *Time* magazine ran a special feature based on a three-month international study on quality carried out by dozens of its correspondents. Its cover headline read: "The Quest for Quality: Why Europe's Craftsmen are Still the Best." The main thrust: after decades of standardization, mass production, and globalization, the world is now beginning to "re-value things produced the old, careful way. And Europe, [which] has always been a place where the past and the future happily co-exist, where teens toting the latest cell phones stroll among 2,000 year old Roman ruins . . . is the center of this new appreciation for excellence." Europe, *Time* claims, "is the capital of quality."

Across 70 pages it ran dozens of case studies on organizations: Irish and Swedish crystal cutters; Scottish whisky distillers; Belgian jewelers; English car and stove manufacturers; Dutch florists; American-Venetian boat-builders; French patisseries, confectioners, tapestry weavers, and beaders; Spanish porcelain producers; Australian-Portuguese wine-makers; French-Italian cobblers; Swiss watchmakers; Danish furniture designers; Czech glassblowers, cosmetics, and liqueurs; Hungarian perfumeries; Austrian knitters; Polish woodcarvers; German bakers, brewers, and organ-builders; Swedish textile producers; Serbian filigree workers; and Finnish tool makers.

These case companies had a number of things in common: their "bringing forward" of centuries-old local traditions; their recognition that "in-with-the-new doesn't always have to mean out-with-the-old – good work and modern technology are not mutually exclusive" (indeed, traditions of old are now being blended with the latest management thinking as younger generations return to their families' businesses having completed MBAs and other business degrees); "an intangible value we call individuality"; and the fact that their very local enterprises are "thriving in the face of globalization."

"Machines give us precision, volume, economy," *Time* claimed, "they have democratized the making of things by putting quality goods within the reach of more than just the rich. But the articles whose construction demands the human hand, eye, ear – and, yes – heart, rarely come off a production line."

Time's conclusion with regard to "crafting the future" at the end of one of its longest ever features: "Artisans can teach the 21st century some old tricks."

---

1. *Why do you think that a lot of ideas in management and strategy that are claimed to be "new" might actually be quite similar to earlier thinking?*
2. *In the light of your answer to question 1, why might traditional craft organizations be better at thinking differently than larger more "professionally" managed companies?*

3. *What elements are these craft organizations now "shaking together," to use Kostler's term, that have not been combined before? And why might this shaking be difficult for larger, more conventional organizations to copy?*

4. *If you were a manager of a large professional company, what lessons would you learn from the examples of the "craft" organizations described in this case and in the* Time *story?*

Picture this!

Pretend you are playing the popular board game *Pictionary*, where you, as a team member, are given the task of drawing an article/animal/idea given to you on a card (which is hidden from other team members). They have to guess what you are drawing as quickly as possible.

When you have something to draw with, and are ready, draw **organization** in the space provided below or on a separate sheet of paper. (Do not look over the page until you have finished.)

Picture this (continued) . . .

We have used this game innumerable times with a wide variety of audiences: from undergraduates to senior executives. By far and away the most common drawing looks like figure 11-7.1. A triangular hierarchy of boxes and lines: a "classic organization chart." Around 80% of Western-educated people draw something like this.

However, this is not exclusively the case. Around 20% do draw something different: for example, a family, a group of people involved in a process, a spiral, a human body, or a house. For those people who do not have a Western business education the number of people drawing these "maverick" forms increases greatly.

If your picture looks like the one shown in the figure, then ask yourself the following question: Where is strategy located? (Most will point to the top box and point downwards). Now ask yourself: If organization had been drawn as a house or a factory building, where would strategy be? What might the advantages be of thinking of strategy in terms of these different pictures?

Why does this matter in terms of strategy development? Well, if most people who make key decisions with regard to business are walking around with triangles in their heads, then they may be steering us away from more creative or radical views of strategy. A recent article in *The Guardian* newspaper on a new book called *Experimental Houses* begins as follows:

> "Why don't people live in radical, experimental houses? Answer: Ask a 5-year-old child to draw a house. Whether from a rich or poor background, whether born in a council flat in Glasgow or a mock Tudor mansion in Weybridge, the result will almost always be the same. A funny little box-like house with a patched roof, smoking chimney, centrally placed door, a window on either side downstairs and two windows more or less symmetrically arranged above them."

The same idea can be applied with our perceptions of organization (although our understanding of "organization" is seemingly more "learned" and less "primal" than "house" – a young child can generally not draw organization without an

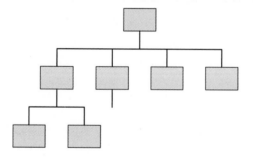

Figure 11-7.1

older person who has "learned" what an organization is first explaining the concept to them). Unless we question the preconceptions of organization structure that exist in our collective consciousness, any attempt to enact alternative or individualized approaches to strategy may be curtailed.

1. *From a "maverick strategy" perspective, what is wrong with the vast majority of people seeing organizational structure in much the same way?*

2. *When we gave a matched sample of arts and business students the* Pictionary *task outlined above, the arts students were far more likely to draw people interacting or "flow type" diagrams. Why might the arts students have been less likely to draw the standard triangular hierarchies?*

3. *One difficulty often encountered in organizational settings is how to expose common core assumptions. However, drawing and humor are two particularly acute methods for doing this. The cartoon shown in figure 11-7.2 is generally found to be humorous. The question is, why? What assumptions is it attacking?*

4. *While the triangular hierarchy may be a good way of depicting the classical planning, positioning, and design schools of strategy, what alternative shapes or forms would you draw to more accurately reflect some of the other schools or approaches described in table 11.1 in this chapter?*

5. *What are the advantages of using alternative forms and schools to think about strategy development?*

Figure 11-7.2

Strategize that!

Integration case

The aim of this book has been to aid people in their ability to turn theoretical understanding into practical strategies by encouraging them to think through what they would do in the real-life situations presented in our micro-cases. Having read to the end of *The Strategy Pathfinder* you should now be in a position to develop strategies for anything, from microwaves to paper clips. To test this out, choose one of the following images and imagine you are charged with developing strategies for a company that produces this product or service, and answer the questions below (which relate to the 11 paths presented in this book).

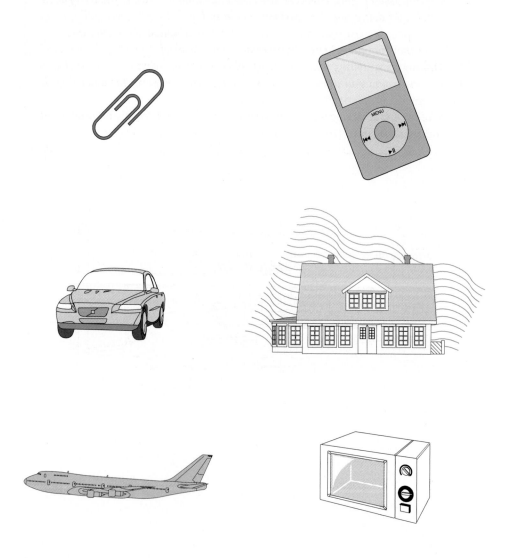

MAVERICK STRATEGIES

1. What macro-shocks might you anticipate impacting on the industry in which your product or service is located, and how would you configure your organization to cope with these?

2. What movers & shakers would be key in the industry in which your product or service is located, and how would you configure your organization to work with these?

3. Describe the terrain of the industry in which your product or service is located, and how you would seek to benefit from, or counter, this environment.

4. How would you seek to establish your product or service within the corporate structure of your organization?

5. Outline the competitive position that you would adopt for your product or service.

6. What organic or living approaches might you seek to take advantage from in developing strategy for your product or service?

7. Define the character of the product or service and outline how this might be significantly different from that of your competition.

8. How would you take your product beyond the local market?

9. How would you seek to strategically manage change as your product begins to compete in the marketplace?

10. What steps would you take to ensure that the competitive advantage and living character of your product or service is sustainable for the long term?

11. How would you seek to keep your product ahead of the norm in its industry? And, could you use your product or service's success as a springboard into other arenas?

NB. Other images are provided in a test bank on *The Strategy Pathfinder* website (www.blackwellpublishing.com/angwin). However, you can use any image you like to develop your strategizing ability in this respect.

Notes

1. Macro-Shocks

1. Stewart, I. (1989) *Does God Play Dice?* 2nd edn. Penguin Books. Stewart traces the origins of chaos to the original formless mass from which the creator molded the ordered universe.
2. Ginter, P. M. and Duncan, W. J. (1990) Macro-environmental Analysis for Strategic Management, *Long Range Planning*, 23 (6): 91–100.
3. Tomlinson, J. (1999) *Globalization and Culture*. Polity: Cambridge.
4. Beck, U. (2002) The Cosmopolitan Society and its Enemies, *Theory, Culture and Society*, 19 (1): 17–44.
5. Volberda, H. W. (1998) *Building the Flexible Firm*. Oxford: Oxford University Press.
6. Courtney, H., Kirkland, J., and Viguerie, P. (1997) Strategy under uncertainty, *Harvard Business Review*, 75 (6): 66–80.
7. Wack, P. (1985) Scenarios: Uncharted waters, *Harvard Business Review*, 63 (6): 139–51.
8. Ansoff, I. and McDonnell, E. (1990) *Implanting Strategic Management*. Upper Saddle River, NJ: Prentice Hall, Inc.
9. Wilson, I. (2000) From Scenario Thinking to Strategic Action, *Technological Forecasting and Social Change*, 65: 23–9.
10. Volberda, H. W. (1998) *Building the Flexible Firm*. Oxford: Oxford University Press.
11. Johnson, G., Scholes, K., and Whittington, R. (2005) *Exploring Corporate Strategy*, 7th edn. FT/Prentice Hall: 27–8.
12. Quinn, J. B. (1978) Strategic Change: Logical Incrementalism, *Sloan Management Review*, 20 (1): 7–21.
13. Romanelli, E. and Tushman, M. L. (1994) Organizational Transformation as Punctuated Equilibrium: an empirical test, *Academy of Management Journal*, 37 (5): 1141–61.
14. Hamel, G. (2000) *Leading the Revolution*. Boston MA: Harvard Business School Press.

2. Movers & Shakers

1. For a more detailed discussion of the separation of ownership and the delegation of authority to the agent, refer to the classic paper by Jensen, M. and Meckling, W. (1976) Theory of the firm: managerial behaviour, agency costs, and ownership structure, *Journal of Financial Economics*, 3: 305–60. The same paper gives details of agency problems but other references building on this include: Amihud, Y. and Lev, B. (1981) Risk reduction as a managerial motive for conglomerate mergers, *Bell Journal of Economics*, 12: 605–16; Jensen, M. (1986) Agency costs of free cash flow, corporate finance, and takeovers, *American Economic Review*, 76: 323–9; Shleifer, A. and Vishny, R. (1988) Value maximisation and the acquisition process, *Journal of Economic Perspectives*, 2: 7–20. For mechanisms to control agency costs, refer again to the Jensen and Meckling

318

(1976) paper but also look at Fama, E. (1980) Agency problems and the theory of the firm, *Journal of Political Economy*, 88: 288–307; Tosi, H. L. Jr. and Gomez-Mejia, L. R. (1994) CEO compensation monitoring and firm performance, *Academy of Management Journal*, 37: 1002–16; Byrd, J., Parrino, R., and Pritsch, G. (1998) Stockholder–manager conflicts and firm value, *Financial Analysts Journal*, 54: 14–30. An overview of agency in strategic management can be found in Angwin, D. N. (2006) Agency theory perspective, in Jenkins, M. and Ambrosini, V. (2006) *Strategic Management: A multi-perspective approach*, 2nd edn. Palgrave MacMillan.

2. The granting of options also raises accounting questions around how they are to be expensed and what their effect on the profit and loss account may be.

3. For a good discussion of the principal–agent model, read Eisenhardt, K. (1989) Agency theory: an assessment and review, *Academy of Management Review*, 14 (1): 57–74.

4. Cash might not be paid out if it is held for future as yet unidentified investments, or perhaps if the company is in a cyclical business downturn.

5. German banks were restricted in their ability to reduce their share holdings because of tax regulations on disposal. These are now being relaxed.

6. For a critique of the consulting industry, read Micklethwait, J. and Wooldridge, A. (1997) *The Witchdoctors. What the management gurus are saying, why it matters and how to make sense of it*, Mandarin paperbacks; Cummings, S. (2002) *Recreating Strategy*, Sage.

7. "Toff" is used in English to denote a class divide in general but may have academic overtones.

8. Cummings, S. and Angwin, D. N. (2004) The Future Shape of Strategy: Lemmings or Chimeras? *Academy of Management Executive*, 18 (2): 21–36; Micklethwait, J. and Wooldridge, A. (1997) *The Witchdoctors. What the management gurus are saying, why it matters and how to make sense of it*, Mandarin paperbacks.

9. Porter, M. and Kramer, M. (2002) The competitive advantage of corporate philanthropy, *Harvard Business Review*, 80 (12): 56.

10. For a more detailed discussion of the interaction between agency, agency problem, and stewardship, see Angwin, D. N., Stern, P., and Bradley, S. (2004) The Target CEO in a Hostile Takeover: Agency or Stewardship – can the condemned agent be redeemed? *Long Range Planning*, 37 (3): 239–57.

3. Industry Terrain

1. We follow Michael Porter (1980) *Competitive Strategy*, New York: The Free Press, in defining an industry as "the group of firms producing products that are close substitutes for each other" (p. 5). There can be several markets (i.e. groups of customers with similar needs) in an industry and so, for example, the automotive industry has markets for sports cars, sports utility vehicles, saloon cars, trucks and so on.

2. Perfectly competitive industries, like "rational" people, are not found in their theoretically pure form in the real world. However many markets exist where the final outcome of perfect competition (i.e. a lack of discretion in pricing) is evident (e.g. oil, wheat, coffee). A common mistake is the one of confusing commodity products (where the market is perfectly competitive) with the commodity producing industry, wherein large players with large (unused) capacity face large exit costs. The theoretical perfectly competitive industry earns normal returns (i.e. returns equal to the cost of capital). Sustained losses in capital intensive industries (e.g. the airline industry on many occasions) are an indicator of non-perfect competition. Empirical research indicates that if an industry is characterized by any two of over-capacity, many sellers, and homogeneous products, then prices tend to be forced down towards marginal cost and returns below the cost of capital. Besanko, D. et al.

(2004) *Economics of Strategy*, Harvard Business School Press, make this point in the context of discussions on perfect competition and the discussion in the chapter borrows heavily from their insights.

3. Much of the discussion of the life cycle is standard. Grant, R. M. (2005) *Contemporary Strategy Analysis*, 5th edn, Blackwell, offers a detailed treatment in his comprehensive strategy analysis text.

4. Information and communication technology has made imitation faster and more efficient across all domains of human endeavor. Hence comedians find their jokes have a very short life as original material as they whiz around the internet in nanoseconds and young sports hopefuls can record and imitate the new tricks of the champions in the comfort of their lounge room. It is no surprise to the thinking strategist that efficiency/cost-focused methodologies such as business process reengineering (BPR) and activity-based management (ABM) have significant impacts on managers in mature industries. Similarly it is no surprise that doom-mongering journal articles railing against the perils of such imitation-as-strategy also appear in regular cycles. Unfortunately, impassioned exhortations to "dare to be different!" or "invent the future!" or "innovate or die!" have as much credibility in many mature industries as the directive to "leap to the top of a large building in a single bound" has for most mature adults – no matter how many exclamation marks are used. Make no mistake, one adult may be able to leap to the top but, in the main, those that keep trying to do so lose out to those who use the elevator, just like everyone else. If someone does eventually leap to the top, his/her leaping methodology is quickly (and cheaply) copied and everybody goes a-leaping.

5. On decline, see Kathryn Harrigan (1980) *Strategies for Declining Businesses*, Lexington, and Kathryn Harrigan and Michael Porter (1983) End-game strategies for declining industries, *Harvard Business Review*, 61 (4): 111–20.

6. Oligopolies are industry structures where the dynamics of game theory most often emerge and, in particular, that part of game theory that deals with zero-sum games or, as they are more popularly known, the Prisoners' Dilemma. For example, although no one company in the industry might want to reduce prices (as buyers demand) or increase industry capacity, the fear that the others will drop price (and gain the business) or increase capacity (and hence reduce costs) drives all players to reduce prices and/or increase capacity to avoid being left out. After the decision, all competitors make less money because of the price reduction or, in the case of the capacity decision, because the industry is now plagued with chronic overcapacity and the associated increase in costs. A very readable book on this sort of problem is Poundstone, W. (1993) *Prisoner's Dilemma*, Oxford University Press.

7. Traditionally MES has meant *minimum efficient scale*, with the strategic emphasis being on scale-based cost reductions (i.e. increasing supply-side returns to scale). We use "size" for two reasons. First, there are other size-based cost dynamics, such as scope and experience effects, where the former is a version of scale but the latter is driven by cumulative volume (i.e. past "size") rather than current production capacity (scale/scope). Second, on the demand side, size is important in those (rare) industries that demonstrate **network effects** (i.e. where the value of the product to the customer is a positive function of the number of other users – increasing demand-side returns). Hence, in the traditional areas of telephones and in the current industry of web-based auction companies (e.g. eBay), the value of the product is a positive function of the number of others currently in the "network" and/or the potential customer's expectations of the number of future users. As with many other areas of strategy the potential for network gains has tended to be spectacularly hyped by some. Liebowitz, S. (2002) *Network Economics: The True Forces that Drive the Digital Marketplace*, New York: Amacon, counters the more extreme claims.

8. Note that size, per se, does not automatically engender monopoly power; it is the degree of contestability of the market/industry that underpins pricing discretion. If impediments to entry and exit (low exit costs context) are low then some monopolists are forced to maintain prices at a level that would prevail under competition as the ever-present risk of entry prevents the large firm from engaging in predatory monopoly pricing. This is an argument that some have used in support of Microsoft during that firm's frequent battles with industry regulators in Europe and the US. Microsoft argues (amongst other things) that the nature of the software industry is such that costs of entry and exit are low (the start ups of now-monsters, such as Google, support this view) and innovation such a constant threat to Microsoft's positional power that the firm is forced to continue to innovate and to keep its prices low – neither of which is consistent with monopoly power. Netscape might be forgiven for being somewhat incredulous.

9. Chapter 2 of Ghemawat, P. (2001) *Strategy and the Business Landscape*. Pearson Education.

10. Brandenburger, A. and Nalebuff, B. (1996) *Co-opetition*. New York: Currency Doubleday: 17.

11. Ibid.: 12.

---

4. The Big Picture

1. The seminal work on the emergence of the multidivisional structure was carried out by Alfred Chandler, a business historian, whose ground-breaking book *Strategy and Structure, Chapters in the History of American Enterprise* (Cambridge, MA: MIT Press), published in 1962, charted the rise of the M-form in the US and gave rise to the enduring dictum that "structure follows strategy."

2. This may seem a somewhat cynical observation but the basis of "agency theory" lies in the conflict of (self) interests between the owners of firms (shareholders) and their agents, the managers of firms. In this context, Michael Jensen has noted that owner–agent interests clash when it comes to the payout of "free cash flow" (i.e. "cash flow in excess of that required to fund all projects that have positive net present values when discounted at the relevant cost of capital"). While owners might logically expect such cash to be paid out to them, Jensen suggests that "managers of firms with unused borrowing power and large free cash flows are more likely to undertake low-benefit or even value-destroying mergers" (1986: 328). He strongly advocates high levels of debt as a device to ensure self-discipline on inherently wasteful managers. In a later provocative *Harvard Business Review* article (1989), Jensen argues that the leveraged buyout (LBO), with its high level of debt, is a business form that, due to its debt-enforced focus on efficiency and shareholder value, threatens the "Eclipse of the Public Corporation" (the title of his article).

3. This is an example of a potential "holdup" problem and is normally linked to "relationship-specific assets" (i.e. investments that one party makes that are specific to the needs of another party). It is often impossible to formally specify the nature of the relationship in such a way as to protect the vulnerable party from being exploited once the investment has been made ("incomplete contracting") and hence integration is often the preferred route. There are many specific texts on the complex arena of transaction cost economics but Besanko, D., Dranove, D., Shanley, M., and Schaeffer, S. (2004) *Economics of Strategy*, Boston: Harvard Business School Press, a general text, offers valuable insights in the context of strategy.

4. Rumelt, R. P. (1974) *Strategy, Structure and Economic Performance*, Harvard Business School Press, describes a major study on the relationship between performance and relatedness. He revisited the study in 1986, coming up with essentially the same findings of higher value from related diversification. While some authors were supportive of

Rumelt's main contentions, a significant body of research was in disagreement. Overall, using market-based measures of relatedness has produced equivocal evidence on the link between firm performance and the composition of the corporate business portfolio with few strong findings on either side and no consensus. For a summary of the situation and a discussion of possible causes for a lack of a relationship, the interested reader could usefully start with Robins, J. and Wiersema, M. F. (1995) A resource-based view of the multibusiness: empirical analysis of portfolio interrelationships and corporate financial performance, *Strategic Management Journal*, 16 (4): 277–99.

5. Peter McKiernan (1992) *Strategies of Growth*, Routledge, offers a detailed account of the boxes and, in particular, the problems that such classification bring when most businesses fall into the "dog" box, for which the theoretical strategic imperative is "divest."

6. In 1981, there were nine different matrices that managers could choose from, as rival consultancies developed their own frameworks to help beleaguered corporate managers shape their portfolio of business and allocate resources within it (Wind, Y. and Mahajan, V. J. (1981) Designing a product and business portfolio, *Harvard Business Review*, 59 (1): 155).

7. Each factor is given a weight for its importance (adding to a total of 1) and this is multiplied by a ranking (1–5) of how well placed the organization is against others in the industry. For example, if market share (part of competitive position) is deemed to have a weight of 0.3 and the business is well placed as the market leader (5) then the weighted score for market share is 1.5 (0.3 × 5).

8. Risk diversification was always difficult to justify as a benefit to shareholders because, as the capital asset pricing model tells us, it is only unsystematic risk that can be diversified away and shareholders can do this themselves. They can also do so with far lower transaction costs than a corporate entity that generally must buy all of a firm at a takeover premium to normal market price whereas a shareholder can buy a small part of a firm (via shares) at the non-premium market price. Diversifying non-systematic risk at the corporate level is a risk reduction strategy for managers not shareholders.

9. The seminal paper by Prahalad, C. K. and Bettis, R. A. (1986) The dominant logic: a new linkage between diversity and performance, *Strategic Management Journal*, 7 (6): 485–501, brought this cognitive perspective into the mainstream of strategy thinking and reminded us of the importance for synergy of how senior managers view the businesses (dominant logic) and the interbusiness mechanisms they put in place on the basis of this logic. The authors were responding to the narrowness of traditional product, process, or market measures of diversity/relatedness and stressed instead the importance of the "strategic variety" among the businesses.

10. Within the overall framework of the resource-based view (RBV – see chapter 5, Perfect Positioning) of the firm, Gary Hamel and C. K. Prahalad have emphasized that core competences are the "central subject of corporate strategy" (1994: 220) but that the organization of the typical multidivisional business into stand-alone business units militates against the development of such competences. Their article, "The Core Competence of the Corporation," in the *Harvard Business Review* (Prahalad and Hamel, 1990: 86) decries the "tyranny of the SBU" as it promotes its own autonomous functioning and fails to facilitate the complex interactions and sharing that are necessary for corporate-wide development and exploitation of core competences.

11. Porter, M. (1987) From Competitive Advantage to Corporate Strategy, *Harvard Business Review* 65 (3): 43–59.

12. Goold, M., Campbell, A., and Alexander, M. have published extensively but most of their major ideas are covered in their book *Corporate-Level Strategy* (1994), John Wiley and Sons.

13. "Cooper Industries' Corporate Strategy," Harvard Business School Case No. 9-391-095.
14. Research into multidivisional businesses routinely reveals the ingenuity of business managers in developing their own specific systems in the face of corporate hegemony.

5. Perfect Positioning

1. The debate between the impact of industry and the firm on company returns is an ongoing one. Richard Rumelt suggests that an intermediate position between the two is the most useful, with actual balance contingent on the particular industry: Rumelt, R. (1991) How much does industry matter? *Strategic Management Journal*, 12 (3): 167–86.
2. Despite what most MBA students believe, this insight pre-dates Michael Porter by some time. As far back as 1817 the economist David Ricardo pointed out that industry prices are set by the marginal (highest cost) producer and so other producers with lower costs (competitive advantage) make higher levels of profits: "The exchangeable value of all commodities, whether they be manufactured or the produce of mines, or the produce of the land, is always regulated, not by the less quantity of labor that will suffice for their production under circumstances very favorable . . . but by the greater quantity of labor necessarily bestowed on their production by those who have no such facilities, by those who continue to produce under the most unfavorable circumstance."
3. In his earlier version of this matrix, Porter (1980: 39) used the term "Uniqueness perceived by the customer" instead of "differentiation" advantage and it may have reduced confusion if he had stuck with the idea of uniqueness as an advantage and differentiation as a strategy aimed at building that uniqueness.
4. Mintzberg, H. (1998: 69) Generic Strategies: Towards a Comprehensive Framework, in Lamb, R. B. and Shivastava, P. (eds) *Advances in Strategic Management*. JAI Press.
5. Edith Penrose's (1959) book, *The Theory of the Growth of the Firm*, Oxford University Press, is not an easy read but sets out most of the concepts often hailed as new insights by authors in the 1980s/90s.
6. For instance, "Competitive advantage, whatever its source, ultimately can be attributed to the ownership of a valuable resource that enables the company to perform activities better or more cheaply than competitors . . . a valuable resource can be physical; intangible or a set of organisational capabilities . . ." (Collis, D. J. and Montgomery, C. A. (1995) Competing on resources: Strategy in the 1990s, *Harvard Business Review*, 75 (6): 118–28).
7. The definitional problems that beset RBV writings are legendary and we have no wish to offer yet another attempted solution. In this chapter we use "competency" and "capability" as interchangeable terms to mean those things that a firm is good at and these, along with tangible assets, people, location etc., are part of the resources a company can make use of in its efforts to survive and thrive. To stay in business a firm needs to be good at many things (i.e. have many capabilities, and so a "distinctive" or "core" capability/competency denotes that the firm has a competitive advantage in that area). The interested reader is recommended to consult Hamel, G. and Heene, A. (1994) *Competence-Based Competition*, John Wiley and Sons, and Sanchez et al. (1996) *Dynamics of Competence-Based Competition*, Elsevier Science, for a variety of papers on the RBV, including a stroll through the definitional labyrinth. The most influential article on core competence is that by Hamel, G. and Prahalad, C. K. (1990) The Core Competence of the Corporation, *Harvard Business Review*, May–June: 79–81, the most reprinted *Harvard Business Review* article ever.

8. Luck in strategy is neglected as a dynamic by theorists but recognized by managers who would "rather be lucky than smart" any day. Jay Barney is one academic author who does not discount luck and his 1986 paper, Organizational culture: can it be a source of sustained competitive advantage? *Academy of Management Review*, 11: 656–65, brings it into the strategy equation.

9. These points are made by many authors and summarized by Collis and Montgomery (1995). The alternative acronym, VRIO, stands for Value, Rarity, Imitability, Organization (Barney, J. B. and Hesterly, W. S. (2006) *Strategic Management and Competitive Advantage*, Pearson/Prentice Hall).

10. Alexander, R. C. (1988) *Fumbling the Future*. New York: William Morrow.

6. Living Strategy

1. Heidegger, M. (1962) *Being and Time*. Blackwell.
2. Kunde, J. (2002) *Unique: Now or Never – The Brand Drives the Company in the New Value Economy*. Prentice Hall.
3. Senge, P. (1990) *The Fifth Discipline*. Century Business.
4. de Geus, A. (2000) *The Living Company*. Harvard Business School Press.
5. Collins, J. C. and Porras, J. I. (1994) *Built to Last: Successful Habits of Visionary Companies*. HarperCollins.
6. Nonaka, I. (1991) The Knowledge Creating Company, *Harvard Business Review*, 69 (6): 96–104.
7. Shaw, G., Brown, R., and Bromiley, P. (1998) Strategic Stories: How 3M is Rewriting Business Planning, *Harvard Business Review*, 76 (3): 41–54. See also, Barry, D. and Elms, M. (1997) Strategy Retold: Toward a Narrative View of Strategic Discourse, *Academy of Management Review*, 22: 429–52.
8. Gardner, H. and Laskin, E. (1996) *Leading Minds: An Anatomy of Leadership*. HarperCollins.
9. Brown, J. S. and Duguid, P. (1991) Organizational learning and communities-of-practice: towards a unified view of working, learning and innovation, *Organization Science*, 2 (1): 40–57; (1998) Organizing knowledge, *California Management Review*, 40 (3): 90–111; (2001) Knowledge and organization: a social practice perspective, *Organization Science*, 12 (2): 198–213; Wenger, E. (1998) *Communities of Practice: Learning, Meaning and Identity*, Cambridge University Press; Wenger, E. and Snyder, W. (2000) Communities of practice: the organizational frontier, *Harvard Business Review*, 78 (1): 138–45.
10. Baker, W. (2000) *Achieving Success Through Social Capital*. Jossey-Bass.
11. Peters, T. and Waterman, R. (1982) *In Search of Excellence*. Harper & Row.
12. Krackhardt, D. and Hanson, J. (1993) Informal Networks: The Company Behind the Chart, *Harvard Business Review*, 71 (4): 104–11; Normann, R. and Ramirez, R. (1993) From Value Chain to Value Constellation: Designing Interactive Strategy, *Harvard Business Review*, 71 (4): 65–77.
13. Evans, P. E. and Wurster, T. S. (1997) Strategy and the New Economics of Information, *Harvard Business Review*, 75 (5): 71–82.
14. Foucault, M. (1977) *Discipline and Punish: The Birth of the Prison*, Allen Lane; (1980) *Power/Knowledge*, Harvester Press.
15. Foote Whyte, W. (1943) *Street Corner Society*. University of Chicago Press.
16. Barney, J. B. (1986b) Organizational culture: Can it be a source of sustained competitive advantage? *Academy of Management Review*, 11 (3): 656–65; (1991) Firm resources and sustained competitive advantage, *Journal of Management*, 17 (1): 99–120.
17. Michaels, E., Handfield-Jones, H., and Axelrod, B. (2001) *The War for Talent*. Harvard Business School Press.

18. The origins of the strategy as practice view can be located in the early work of Stewart, R. (1967) *Managers and Their Jobs*, Macmillan, and Mintzberg, H. (1973) *The Nature of Managerial Work*, Harper & Row. More recently it has received conceptual clarification as a domain in Whittington, R. (1996) Strategy as Practice, *Long Range Planning*, 29 (5) Special Issue: 713–36, and a future research agenda has been set out in Johnson, G., Melin, L., and Whittington, R. (2003) Micro Strategy and Strategizing: Towards an Activity-Based View, Guest Editors' Introduction, *Journal of Management Studies*, Blackwell Publishers, 40 (1): 3–22. The strategy as practice movement has an active website: http://www.strategy-as-practice.org and now has a conference track at the Strategic Management Society in the US: http://www.smsweb.org.
19. Cummings, S. (2003) Strategy as Ethos, in Cummings, S. and Wilson, D. (eds) *Images of Strategy*. Blackwell: 41–73.

7. Corporate Character

1. Porter, M. (1990) *The Competitive Advantage of Nations*. Macmillan.
2. Hofstede, G. (1993) Cultural Constraints in Management Theories, *Academy of Management Executive*, 7 (1): 8–21; Smircich, L. (1983) Concepts of Culture and Organizational Analysis, *Administrative Science Quarterly*, 28 (3): 339–58.
3. Pascale, R. and Athos, A. (1981) *The Art of Japanese Management*. Warner.
4. Hofstede, G. (1993) op. cit.
5. Hankinson, G. and Cowking, P. (1996) *The Reality of Global Brands*. McGraw-Hill: 44.
6. de Mooij, M. (1997) *Global Marketing and Advertising: Understanding Cultural Paradoxes*. Sage: 189.
7. Peters, T. and Waterman, R. (1982) *In Search of Excellence*. Harper & Row.
8. Johnson, G., Scholes, K., and Whittington, R. (2005) *Exploring Corporate Strategy*, 7th edn. FT/Prentice Hall.
9. Collins, J. C. and Porras, J. I. (1994) *Built to Last: Successful Habits of Visionary Companies*. HarperBusiness.
10. Cummings, S. (2003) Strategy as Ethos, in Cummings, S. and Wilson, D. (eds) *Images of Strategy*. Blackwell: 41–73.
11. Schultz, M., Hatch, M. J., and Holten Larsen, M. (2000) *The Expressive Organization: Linking Identity, Reputation and the Corporate Brand*. Oxford University Press.
12. Special Report: Designer Cars, *Business Week*, February 16, 2004: 40–8.
13. Dru, J.-M. (1996) *Disruption: Overturing Conventions and Shaking up the Marketplace*. John Wiley.
14. Davies, G. and Miles, L. (1997) *What Price Reputation?* Haymarket Business Publications.
15. Lewis, D. and Bridger, D. (2001) *The Soul of the New Consumer: Authenticity – What we buy and why in the new economy*. Nicholas Brealey.
16. Trompenaars, F. and Hampden-Turner, C. (1997) *Riding the Waves of Culture: Understanding Cultural Diversity in Business*, Nicholas Brealey; Cummings, S. and Angwin, D. N. (2004) The Future Shape of Strategy: Lemmings or Chimeras? *Academy of Management Executive*, 18 (2): 21–36.

8. Crossing Borders

1. Smith, A. (1776) *The Wealth of Nations*, Smith, A. (ed.) (1999) Penguin Books/South-Western Publishing.
2. Grant, R. (2004) *Contemporary Strategy Analysis*, 5th edn. Blackwell.
3. Ricardo, D. (1967) *The Principles of Political Economy and Taxation*. Homewood, IL: Irwin.

NOTES

4. Vernon, R. (1966) International Investment and International Trade in the Product Life Cycle, *Quarterly Journal of Economics*, 29 (2): 190 –207.

5. Hymer, S. (1970) The multinational corporation and the law of uneven development, in Bhagwati, J. (ed.) *Economics and World Order*. New York: World Law Fund.

6. Brouthers, J. E., Brouthers, K. D., and Werner, S. (1999) Is Dunning's Eclectic Framework description or narrative, *Journal of International Business*, 30 (4): 831–44.

7. Hall, E. (1960) The silent language in overseas business, *Harvard Business Review*, May 1st: 87–96.

8. Huntingdon, S. P. (1997) *The Clash of Civilisations and the Remaking of World Order*. London: Simon and Schuster.

9. Whiteley, R. D. (1999) *Divergent Capitalisms*. Oxford University Press.

10. Hofstede, G. (1980) *Culture's Consequences: International Differences in Work-Related Values*. Beverly Hills, CA: Sage.

11. Laurent, A. (1986) The cross-cultural puzzle of global human resource management. *Human Resources Management*, 25 (1): 91–102.

12. Trompenaars, F. (1993) *Riding the Waves of Cultural Differences: Understanding Cultural Differences in Business*, London: Nicholas Brealey; Hampden-Turner, C. and Trompenaars, F. (2000) *Building Cross-cultural Competence*, Chichester: John Wiley.

13. Kogut, B. and Singh, H. (1988) The effect of national culture on the choice of entry mode, *Journal of International Business Studies*, 19 (3): 411–33; Angwin, D. N. (2001) Mergers and Acquisitions across European borders: National perspectives on pre-acquisition due diligence and the use of professional advisers, *Journal of World Business*, 36 (1): 32–57.

14. Prahalad, C. K. and Doz, Y. L. (1987) *The Multinational Mission: Balancing Local Demands and Global Vision*. New York: Free Press.

15. Porter, M. (1990a) *The Competitive Advantage of Nations*, New York: Free Press; Porter (1990b) The Competitive Advantage of Nations, *Harvard Business Review*, 69 (2): March–April.

16. Porter (1990a), ibid.: 33.

17. c.f. Rugman, A. M. (1990) *Multinationals and Canada–United States Free Trade*, University of South Carolina Press; Crookell, H. (1990) *Canadian–American Trade and Investment under the Free Trade Act Agreement*, Quorum Books.

18. Dunning, J. H. (1993) Internationalizing Porter's Diamond, *Management International Review*, 33 (2) Special Issue: 7–16.

19. Rugman, A. M. and D'Cruz, J. R. (1993) The Double Diamond Model of International Competitiveness: the Canadian experience, *Management International Review*, 33 (2) Special Issue: 17–40.

20. Teece, D. J. (1986) Transaction cost economics and multi-national enterprise, *Journal of Economic Behaviour and Organization*, 7 (1): 21–45.

21. Dussauge, P. and Garrette, B. (1999) *Cooperative Strategy: Competing Successfully Through Strategic Alliances*. Wiley.

22. Hamel, G., Doz, Y. L., and Prahalad, C. K. (1989) Collaborate with your Competitors – and Win, *Harvard Business Review*, 67 (1): 133–9.

23. Angwin, D. N. (2000) *Implementing Successful Post-acquisition Management*. Financial Times/Prentice Hall.

24. c.f. Johansen, J. and Vahine, J.-E. (1978) A model for the decision making process affecting pattern and pace of the internationalization of the firm, in Ghertman, M. and Leontidaes, J. (eds) (1978) *European Research in International Business*, Amsterdam; Davidson, W. (1980) The location of foreign direct investment activity: country characteristics and experience effects, *Journal of International Business Studies*, 11 (2): 9; Barkema, H. G., Bell, J. H., and Pennings, J. M. (1996) Foreign entry, cultural barriers, and learning, *Strategic Management Journal*, 17 (2): 151–67.

25. Bartlett, C. A. and Ghoshal, S. (1989) *Managing Across Borders: the Transnational Solution*. Boston, MA: Harvard Business School Press.

9. Guiding Change

1. Bartlett, C. A. and Ghoshal, S. (1989) *Managing Across Borders: The Transnational Solution*. Boston, MA: Harvard Business School Press.
2. Kotter, J. P. (1995) Leading Change: Why Transformation Efforts Fail, *Harvard Business Review*, 73 (2): 59–67.
3. Identifying a compelling need for change or creating *a sense of urgency* is seen as crucial by Beer, M. (1987) Revitalizing organizations: Change process and emergent model, *Academy of Management Executive*, 1 (1): 51–6; Johansson, H. J. et al. (1993) *Business Process Reengineering: Breakpoint Strategies for Market Dominance*, Wiley; Tichy, N. (1993) *Handbook for Revolutionaries*, New York: Doubleday; Nadler, D. and Tushman, M. (1989) Organizational frame bending: Principles for managing reorientation, *Academy of Management Executive*, 3 (3): 194–204; Stace, D. and Dunphy, D. (1994) *Beyond the Boundaries: Leading and Recreating the Successful Organization*, McGraw-Hill; and a book published by consultants Price Waterhouse Coopers (1995) entitled *Better Change: Best Practices for Transforming your Organization*, Irwin. All of these sources and others, like Beck, R. N. (1987) Visions, values, and strategies: Changing attitudes and culture, *Academy of Management Executive*, 1 (1): 33–40, Chen, M. (1994) Sun Tzu's thinking and contemporary business, *Business Horizons*, 37 (2): 42–8, and Larkin, T. J. and Larkin, S. (1996) Reaching and changing frontline employees, *Harvard Business Review*, 74 (3): 95–104, emphasize the need to develop, effectively *communicate*, and *empower others* to work toward a *vision* of a future organizational state. We are reminded of the particular importance of being aware of the politics at work in an organization, gaining commitment, and *forming a guiding coalition* by Price Waterhouse Coopers (1995), Johansson et al. (1993), Tichy, N. and Sherman, S. (1993) *Control Your Destiny or Someone Else Will*, New York: Doubleday, and Nadler and Tushman (1989), while *emphasizing short-term wins* and *consolidating improvements*, integrating and *institutionalizing* new approaches, and forming a *platform for further change* are highlighted by reengineering exponents and most of the above.
4. Smither, R. D. (1994) *The Psychology of Work and Human Performance*, HarperCollins.
5. Cummings, S. (2002) *Recreating Strategy*, Sage. Original sources: Lewin, K. (1951) *Field Theory in Social Sciences*, Tavistock Publications; Blake, R. R. and Mouton, J. S. (1964) *How to Assess the Strengths and Weaknesses of a Business Enterprise*, Scientific Methods; Lippitt, R., Watson, J., and Westley, B. (1958) *The Dynamics of Planned Change: A Comparative Study of Principles and Techniques*, Harcourt, Brace; Tichy, N. and Devanna, M. A. (1990) *The Transformational Leader*, Wiley.
6. Pettigrew, A. and Whipp, R. (1991) *Managing Change for Competitive Success*. Blackwell.
7. Mintzberg, H. and Westley, Y. (1992) Cycles of Organizational Change, *Strategic Management Journal*, 13 Special Issue: 39–59.
8. Wilson, D. (1992) *A Strategy of Change: Concepts and Controversies in the Management of Change*. ITP.
9. Key works on turnarounds include Lovett, D. and Slatter, S. (1999) *Corporate Turnaround*, Penguin Books; Barker, V. L. and Duhaime, I. M. (1997) Strategic change in the turnaround process: theory and empirical evidence, *Strategic Management Journal*, 18 (1): 13–38; Grinyer, P., Mayes, D. G., and McKiernan, P. (1990) The Sharpbenders: achieving a sustained improvement in performance, *Long Range Planning*, 23 (1): 116–25.

NOTES

10. Dunphy, D. and Stace, D. A. (1990) *Under New Management: Australian Organizations in Transition*. McGraw-Hill.

11. Angwin, D. N. (2000) *Implementing successful post-acquisition management*. Financial Times/Prentice Hall.

12. Hamel, G. (1996) Strategy as revolution, *Harvard Business Review*, 74 (4): 69–82; Hammer, M. and Champy, J. (1993) *Reengineering the Corporation: A Manifesto for Business Revolution*, Nicholas Brealey.

13. Imai, M. (1986) *Kaizen: The Key to Japan's Competitive Success*. McGraw-Hill.

14. Leavy, B. and Wilson, D. (1994) *Strategy and Leadership*. ITP.

15. As Jim March reminds us: "most current leaders seem to be competent and analytical rather than imaginative and visionary . . . they seek to refine the establishment rather than challenge or transform it." March, J. (1999) *The Pursuit of Organizational Intelligence*. Blackwell.

16. Bonabeau, E. (2004) The perils of the information age, *Harvard Business Review*, 82 (6): 45–54.

17. Kotter, J. P. and Schlesinger, L. A. (1979) Choosing Strategies for Change, *Harvard Business Review*, 57 (2): 106–14.

18. Cummings, S. (2002) op. cit.

10. Sustain Ability

1. World Commission on Economic Development (1987) *Our Common Future*. Oxford: Oxford University Press: 43.

2. Dunphy, D., Griffiths, A., and Benn, S. (2003) *Organizational Change for Corporate Sustainability: A Guide for Leaders and Change Agents of the Future*. New York: Routledge: 83.

3. Elizabet Sahtouris combines evolutionary biology and spirituality to express this interconnectedness. Her writings are available from the website www.ratical.org/LifeWeb.

4. This version of the development of social equity, environmental integrity, and economic prosperity to their corporate equivalents is taken from Bansal, P. (2005) Evolving Sustainability: A Longitudinal Study of Corporate Sustainable Development, *Strategic Management Journal*, 26 (3): 197–218.

5. Stuart Hart is an influential writer in this area and several of the terms and ideas in this section are based on Hart, S. (1997) 'Beyond greening: Strategies for a sustainable world, *Harvard Business Review*, 75 (1): 71–91.

6. Wackernagel, M. et al. (1997) Ecological footprints of nations. How much nature do they use? How much nature do they have? Report prepared for the *Rio+5 Forum*.

7. For an insightful review of the CSR literature and its development see McGee, J. (1998) Commentary on corporate strategies and environmental regulations: an organizing framework, in Rugman, A. M. and Verbeke, A. (1998) *Journal of Strategic Management*, Special Edition: Editor's choice, 19 (4): 377–87.

8. Eberstadt, N. (1973) What History Tells Us About Corporate Responsibilities, *Business and Society Review*, 7: 76–81.

9. Friedman, as might be expected, espoused the view that CSR means maximizing shareholders' returns: Friedman, M. (1970) The social responsibility of business is to increase its profits, *Ivey Business Journal*, March/April: 1–5.

10. The good company: a survey of corporate social responsibility, *The Economist*, January 22, 2005: 16.

11. The broader definition quoted from Davis and Blomstrom (1975: 6) suggests that optimizing social good is a more diffuse outcome as a part of which maximizing shareholder value is neither a necessary nor a sufficient component. Davis, K. and Blomstrom, R. L. (1975) *Business and Society: Environment and Responsibility*. New York: McGraw-Hill.

12. Adapted from Hay, R. D., Gray, E. R., and Gates, J. E. (1976) *Business and Society*. Cincinnati, OH: Heath.

13. In book, movie, and television series, "The Corporation" presents the modern corporation as a "psychopath" that is self-serving, lacking empathy with others, and has no sense of remorse or guilt about its negative impacts.

14. Freely adapted from Zenisek, whose model specifically acknowledges a continuum of social responsibility from low (Type I) to high (Type IV): Zenisek, T. J. (1979) Corporate social responsibility: A conceptualization based on organizational literature, *Academy of Management Review*, 4 (3): 359–68.

15. Tim O'Connor of the NikeWatch campaign wrote in his report in 2001: "The Global Alliance's new report on Nike factories in Indonesia found evidence of serious labor abuses, including inadequate wages, forced and illegal overtime, denial of sick leave, menstrual leave, and annual leave, and unacceptable levels of sexual harassment and verbal abuse" (http://www.amnesty.org.uk/business/newslet/spring01/nike.shtml). In April 2005, Nike published a 108-page report acknowledging the truth of many of these allegations. The report followed 3 years of silence from the company following its payout of nearly £800,000 in settlement of a court case claiming it had made false statements about how employees were treated.

16. In 2004, Shell stated that it had inadvertently fed conflict, poverty, and corruption through its oil activities in Nigeria: http://news.bbc.co.uk/1/hi/business/3796375.stm.

17. Hart, op. cit.: 68 (emphasis in original).

18. Kay, J. (1993) *The Foundations of Corporate Success*. Blackwell.

19. Taken from Salzman, O., Ionescu-Somers, A., and Steger, U. (2005) The business case for corporate sustainability: literature review and research options, *European Management Journal*, 1: 27–36.

20. Waddock, S. A. and Graves, S. B. (1997) The corporate social performance–financial performance link, *Strategic Management Journal*, 18 (4): 303–19.

21. Ibid.

22. Cornell, B. and Shapiro, A. C. (1987) Corporate stakeholders and corporate finance, *Financial Management* 16 (1): 5–14.

23. Reed, D. J. (2001) *Stalking the Elusive Business Case for Corporate Sustainability*. Washington: World Resources Institute.

24. The commonly used "balanced scorecard" (Kaplan and Norton, 1992) reflects this orientation to ensure that all stakeholders and constituencies receive their due consideration *while pursuing the main goal of shareholder value* – i.e. all stakeholders are balanced but some are more balanced than others.

11. Maverick Strategies

1. Kunde, J. (2002) *Unique: Now or Never – The Brand Drives the Company in the New Value Economy*. Financial Times/Prentice Hall.

2. Nattermann, P. (2000) Best Practice Does Not Equal Best Strategy, *McKinsey Quarterly*, 2; Christensen, C. (2003) *The Innovator's Dilemma*. HarperBusiness.

3. Porter, M. (1996) What is Strategy? *Harvard Business Review*, 74 (6): 61–79.

4. Kim, W. and Mauborgne, R. (2003) Think for yourself – stop copying a rival, *New Thinking from INSEAD*.

5. Foster, R. (1986) *Innovation, the Attacker's Advantage*. Macmillan.

6. Cummings, S. (2002) *Recreating Strategy*. Sage.

7. Burkan, W. (1996) *Wide-Angle Vision: Beat Your Competition by Focusing on Fringe Competitors, Lost Customers, and Rogue Employees*. Wiley.

8. Godin, S. (2003) *Purple Cow: Transform Your Business by Becoming Remarkable*. Portfolio.
9. Dru, J.-M. (1996) *Disruption: Overturning Conventions and Shaking Up the Marketplace*. Wiley.
10. Koestler, A. (1976) *The Act of Creation*. Hutchinson.
11. Sutton, B. (2001) *Weird Ideas That Work: 11½ Practices for Promoting, Managing, and Sustaining Innovation*. Free Press.
12. Schrage, M. (1999) *Serious Play: How the World's Best Companies Simulate to Innovate*, Harvard Business School Press.
13. Kim, W. and Mauborgne, R. (2005) *Blue Ocean Strategy: How to Create Uncontested Market Space and Make Competition Irrelevant*. Harvard Business School Press.
14. Kunde, J. (2002) op. cit.
15. Mintzberg, H. (1999) Organigraphs: Drawing How Companies Really Work, *Harvard Business Review*, 77 (5): 87–94.
16. Cummings, S. and Angwin, D. N. (2004) The Future Shape of Strategy: Lemmings or Chimeras? *Academy of Management Executive*, 18 (2): 21–36.
17. Chandler, A. (1962) *Strategy and Structure: Chapters in the History of the American Enterprise*. MIT Press.
18. Mintzberg, H. (1973) *The Nature of Managerial Work*. Harper & Row.
19. Mintzberg, H. (1994) *The Rise and Fall of Strategic Planning*. Free Press.
20. Mintzberg, H. et al. (1998) *The Strategy Safari: A Guided Tour Through the Wilds of Strategic Management*. Free Press.
21. Richard Whittington provides a further outline of different views of the strategy process in *What is Strategy? And does it matter?* (ITP, 2000). His four generic approaches to the strategy process are: *classical* – stressing rationality and analysis; *evolutionary* – stressing the unpredictable nature of the environment that renders much of what is traditionally regarded as strategic analysis irrelevant; *processual* – a pragmatic view of strategy that recognizes the need to continually adapt and learn due to imperfections in the real world and our knowledge; and *systemic* – stressing the importance and relevance of culture and social systems, and their impact on strategic development in particular contexts.
22. De Wit, B. and Meyer, R. (1999) *Strategy Synthesis*. ITP.
23. Cummings, S. and Wilson, D. (eds) (2003) *Images of Strategy*. Blackwell.
24. As cited in Godin, S. (2003) op. cit.
25. Mintzberg, H. (2004) *Managers Not MBAs: A Hard Look at the Soft Practice of Managing and Management Development*. Berrett-Koehler.

References

Alexander, R. C. (1988) *Fumbling the future*. William Morrow: New York.

Amihud Y. and Lev B. (1981) Risk reduction as a managerial motive for conglomerate mergers, *Bell Journal of Economics*, 12 (2): 605–16.

Andrews, K. R. (1971) *The Concept of Corporate Strategy*. Illinois: Dow Jones-Irwin Inc.

Angwin, D. N. (2000) *Implementing successful post-acquisition management*. Financial Times/Prentice Hall.

Angwin, D. N. (2001) Mergers and Acquisitions across European borders: National perspectives on pre-acquisition due diligence and the use of professional advisers, *Journal of World Business*, 36 (1): 32–57.

Angwin, D. N. (2006) Agency theory perspective, in Jenkins, M. and Ambrosini, V. (eds) *Strategic Management: A multi-perspective approach*, 2nd edn. Palgrave MacMillan.

Angwin, D. N., Stern, P., and Bradley, S. (2004) The Target CEO in a hostile takeover: Agency or Stewardship – can the condemned agent be redeemed? *Long Range Planning*, 37 (3): 239–57.

Angwin, D. N. and Vaara, E. (2005) Connectivity in Merging Organizations – beyond traditional cultural perspectives, *Organization Studies*, 26 (10). Special Issue.

Ansoff, I. and McDonnell, E. (1990) *Implanting Strategic Management*. Upper Saddle River, NJ: Prentice Hall Inc.

Baker, W. (2000) *Achieving Success Through Social Capital*. Jossey-Bass.

Bansal, P. (2005) Evolving Sustainability: A Longitudinal Study of Corporate Sustainable Development, *Strategic Management Journal*, 26 (3): 197–218.

Barkema, H. G., Bell, J. H., and Pennings, J. M. (1996) Foreign entry, cultural barriers, and learning, *Strategic Management Journal*, 17 (2): 151–67.

Barker, V. L. and Duhaime, I. M. (1997) Strategic change in the turnaround process: theory and empirical evidence, *Strategic Management Journal*, 18 (1): 13–38.

Barney, J. B. (1986a) Strategy Factor Markets: Expectations, Luck and Business Strategy, *Management Science*, 32 (10): 1231–41.

Barney, J. B. (1986b) Organizational culture: Can it be a source of sustained competitive advantage? *Academy of Management Review*, 11 (3): 656–65.

Barney, J. B. (1991) Firm resources and sustained competitive advantage, *Journal of Management*, 17 (1): 99–120.

Barney, J. B. and Hesterly, W. S. (2006) *Strategic Management and Competitive Advantage*. Pearson/Prentice Hall.

Barry, D. and Elms, M. (1997) Strategy Retold: Toward a Narrative View of Strategic Discourse, *Academy of Management Review*, 22 (2): 429–52.

Bartlett, C. A. and Ghoshal, S. (1989) *Managing Across Borders: The Transnational Solution*. Boston, MA: Harvard Business School Press.

Beck, R. N. (1987) Visions, values, and strategies: Changing attitudes and culture, *Academy of Management Executive*, 1 (1): 33–40.

Beck, U. (2002) The Cosmopolitan Society and its Enemies, *Theory, Culture and Society*, 19 (1): 17–44.

Beer, M. (1987) Revitalizing Organizations: Change process and emergent model, *Academy of Management Executive*, 1 (1): 51–6.

Besanko, D., Dranove, D., Shanley, M., and Schaeffer, S. (2004) *Economics of Strategy*. Boston: Harvard Business School Press.

Blake, R. R. and Mouton, J. S. (1964) *How to Assess the Strengths and Weaknesses of a Business Enterprise*. Scientific Methods.

Bonabeau, E. (2004) The perils of the information age, *Harvard Business Review*, 82 (6): 45–54.

Bowman, C. (1988) *Strategy in Practice*. Harlow: Prentice Hall.

Brandenburger, A. and Nalebuff, B. (1996) *Co-opetition*. New York: Currency Doubleday.

Brouthers, J. E., Brouthers, K. D., and Werner, S. (1999) Is Dunning's Eclectic Framework description or narrative, *Journal of International Business*, 30 (4): 831–44.

Brown, J. S. and Duguid, P. (1991) Organizational learning and communities-of-practice: towards a unified view of working, learning and innovation, *Organization Science*, 2 (1): 40–57.

Brown, J. S. and Duguid, P. (1998) Organizing knowledge, *California Management Review*, 40 (3): 90–111.

Brown, J. S. and Duguid, P. (2001) Knowledge and organization: a social practice perspective, *Organization Science*, 12 (2): 198–213.

Burkan, W. (1996) *Wide-Angle Vision: Beat Your Competition by Focusing on Fringe Competitors, Lost Customers, and Rogue Employees*. Wiley.

Businessweek (2004) *Special Report: Designer Cars*. Feb, 16: 40–8.

Byrd, J., Parrino, R., and Pritsch, G. (1998) Stockholder–manager conflicts and firm value, *Financial Analysts Journal*, 54 (3): 14–30.

Chandler, A. D. (1962) *Strategy & Structure: Chapters in the History of the American Enterprise*. Cambridge, MA: MIT Press.

Chen, M. (1994) Sun Tzu's thinking and contemporary business, *Business Horizons*, 37 (2): 42–8.

Christensen, C. (2003) *The Innovator's Dilemma*. HarperBusiness.

Coase, R. (1937) The Nature of the Firm, *Economica*, 4: 386–405.

Collins, J. C. and Porras, J. I. (1994) *Built to Last: Successful Habits of Visionary Companies.* HarperCollins.

Collis, D. J. and Montgomery, C. A. (1995) Competing on resources: Strategy in the 1990s, *Harvard Business Review*, 73 (4): 118–28.

Cornell, B. and Shapiro, A. C. (1987) Corporate stakeholders and corporate finance, *Financial Management*, 16 (1): 5–14.

Courtney, H., Kirkland, J., and Viguerie, P. (1997) Strategy under Uncertainty, *Harvard Business Review*, 75 (6): 66–80.

Crookell, H. (1990) *Canadian–American Trade and Investment under the Free Trade Act Agreement.* Quorum Books.

Cummings, S. (2002) *Recreating Strategy.* Sage.

Cummings, S. (2003) Strategy as Ethos, in Cummings, S. and Wilson, D. (eds) *Images of Strategy.* Blackwell: 41–73.

Cummings, S. and Angwin, D. N. (2004) The Future Shape of Strategy: Lemmings or Chimeras? *Academy of Management Executive*, 18 (2): 21–36.

Cummings, S. and Wilson, D. (eds) (2003) *Images of Strategy.* Blackwell.

Davidson, W. (1980) The location of foreign direct investment activity: country characteristics and experience effects, *Journal of International Business Studies*, 11 (2): 9.

Davies, G. and Miles, L. (1997) *What Price Reputation?* Haymarket Business Publications.

Davis, K. and Blomstrom, R. L. (1975) *Business and Society: Environment and Responsibility.* New York: McGraw-Hill.

Davis, K. and Frederick, W. C. (1984) *Business and Society: Management, Public Policy, Ethics*, 5th edn. New York: McGraw-Hill.

de Geus, A. (2000) *The Living Company.* Boston, MA: Harvard Business School Press.

de Mooij, M. (1997) *Global Marketing and Advertising: Understanding Cultural Paradoxes.* Sage.

De Wit, B. and Meyer, R. (1999) *Strategy Synthesis.* ITP.

De Wit, B. and Meyer, R. (2004) *Strategy: Process, Content, Context; An International Perspective*, 3rd edn. Thomson.

Dru, J.-M. (1996) *Disruption: Overturning Conventions and Shaking Up the Marketplace.* Wiley.

Dunning, J. H. (1993) Internationalizing Porter's Diamond, *Management International Review*, 33 (2) Special Issue: 7–16.

Dunphy, D., Griffiths, A., and Benn, S. (2003) *Organizational Change for Corporate Sustainability: A Guide for Leaders and Change Agents of the Future.* New York: Routledge.

Dunphy, D. and Stace, D. A. (1990) *Under New Management: Australian Organizations in Transition.* McGraw-Hill.

Dussauge, P. and Garrette, B. (1999) *Cooperative Strategy: Competing Successfully Through Strategic Alliances.* Wiley.

Eberstadt, N. (1973) What History Tells Us About Corporate Responsibilities, *Business and Society Review*, 7: 76–81.

Eisenhardt, K. (1989) Agency theory: an assessment and review, *Academy of Management Review*, 14 (1): 57–74.

Evans, P. E. and Wurster, T. S. (1997) Strategy and the New Economics of Information, *Harvard Business Review*, 75 (5): 71–82.

Fama, E. (1980) Agency problems and the theory of the firm, *Journal of Political Economy*, 88 (2): 288–307.

Foote Whyte, W. (1943) *Street Corner Society.* University of Chicago Press.

Foster, R. (1986) *Innovation, the Attacker's Advantage.* Macmillan.

Foucault, M. (1977) *Discipline and Punish: The Birth of the Prison.* Allen Lane.

Foucault, M. (1980) *Power/Knowledge.* Harvester Press.

Friedman, M. (1970) The social responsibility of business is to increase its profits, *Ivey Business Journal*, March/April: 1–5.

Gardner, H. and Laskin, E. (1996) *Leading Minds: An Anatomy of Leadership.* HarperCollins.

Ghemawat, P. (2001) *Strategy and the Business Landscape.* NJ: Pearson Education.

Ghertman, M. and Leontidaes, J. (eds) (1978) *European Research in International Business.* Amsterdam.

Ginter, P. M. and Duncan, W. J. (1990) Macro environmental Analysis for Strategic Management, *Long Range Planning*, 23 (6): 91–100.

Godin, S. (2003) *Purple Cow: Transform Your Business by Becoming Remarkable.* Portfolio.

Goold, M., Campbell, A., and Alexander, M. (1994) *Corporate-Level Strategy: Creating Value in the Multibusiness Company.* New York: John Wiley and Sons, Inc.

Grant, R. M. (2005) *Contemporary Strategy Analysis*, 5th edn. Oxford: Blackwell.

Grinyer, P., Mayes, D. G., and McKiernan, P. (1990) The Sharpbenders: achieving a sustained improvement in performance, *Long Range Planning*, 23 (1): 116–25.

Hall, E. (1960) The silent language in overseas business, *Harvard Business Review*, May 1: 87–96.

Hamel, G. (1996) Strategy as revolution, *Harvard Business Review*, 74 (4): 69–82.

Hamel, G. (2000) *Leading the Revolution.* Boston, MA: Harvard Business School Press.

Hamel, G., Doz, Y. L., and Prahalad, C. K. (1989) Collaborate with your Competitors – and Win, *Harvard Business Review*, 67 (1): 133–9.

Hamel, G. and Heene, A. (1994) *Competence-Based Competition.* New York: John Wiley & Sons.

Hamel, G. and Prahalad, C. K. (1990) The Competence of the Corporation, *Harvard Business Review*, May–June: 79–81.

Hamel, G. and Prahalad, C. K. (1994) *Competing for the Future.* Boston, MA: Harvard Business School Press.

Hammer, M. (1990) Reengineering Work: Don't Automate, Obliterate, *Harvard Business Review*, July–August.

Hammer, M. and Champy, J. (1993) *Reengineering the Corporation: A Manifesto for Business Revolution.* Nicholas Brealey.

Hampden-Turner, C. and Trompenaars, F. (2000) *Building Cross-cultural Competence.* Chichester: John Wiley.

Hankinson, G. and Cowking, P. (1996) *The Reality of Global Brands.* McGraw-Hill: 44.

Harrigan, K. R. (1980) *Strategies for Declining Businesses.* Lexington, MA: D. C.

Harrigan, K. R. and Porter, M. E. (1983) End-Game Strategies for Declining Industries, *Harvard Business Review*, 61 (4): 111–20.

Hart, S. (1997) Beyond greening: Strategies for a sustainable world, *Harvard Business Review*, 75 (1): 71–91.

Hay, R. D., Gray, E. R., and Gates, J. E. (1976) *Business and Society.* Cincinnati, OH: Heath.

Heidegger, M. (1962) *Being and Time.* Blackwell.

Hill, C. W. L. and Jones, G. R. (2004) *Strategic Management Theory: An Integrated Approach*, 6th edn. Boston and New York: Houghton Mifflin Company.

Hitt, M. A., Ireland, R. D., and Hoskisson, R. E. (2001) *Strategic Management: Competitiveness and Globalization*, 4th edn. South-Western.

Hofstede, G. (1980) *Culture's Consequences: International Differences in Work-Related Values*. Beverly Hills, CA: Sage.

Hofstede, G. (1993) Cultural Constraints in Management Theories, *Academy of Management Executive*, 7 (1): 8–21.

Huntingdon, S. P. (1997) *The Clash of Civilisations and the Remaking of World Order*. London: Simon and Schuster.

Hymer, S. (1970) The multinational corporation and the law of uneven development, in Bhagwati, J. (ed.) *Economics and World Order*. New York: World Law Fund Industries.

Imai, M. (1986) *Kaizen: The Key to Japan's Competitive Success*. McGraw-Hill.

Jenkins, M. and Ambrosini, V. (2006) *Strategic Management: A multi-perspective approach*, 2nd edn. Palgrave MacMillan.

Jensen, M. (1986) Agency costs of free cash flow, corporate finance and takeovers, *American Economic Review*, 76 (2): 323–9.

Jensen, M. C. (1989) Eclipse of the Public Corporation, *Harvard Business Review*, 67 (5): 61–75.

Jensen, M. and Meckling, W. (1976) Theory of the firm: managerial behaviour, agency costs, and ownership structure. *Journal of Financial Economics*, 3: 305–60.

Johansen, J. and Vahine, J.-E. (1978) A model for the decision making process affecting pattern and pace of the internationalization of the firm, in Ghertman, M. and Leontidaes, J. (eds) *European Research in International Business*. Amsterdam.

Johansson, H. J. et al. (1993) *Business Process Reengineering: Breakpoint Strategies for Market Dominance*. John Wiley and Sons.

Johnson, G., Melin, L., and Whittington, R. (2003) Micro Strategy and Strategizing: Towards an Activity-Based View, Guest Editors' Introduction, *Journal of Management Studies*, Blackwell Publishers, 40 (1): 3–22.

Johnson, G., Scholes, K., and Whittington, R. (2005) *Exploring Corporate Strategy*, 7th edn. FT/Prentice Hall.

Kaplan, R. S. and Norton, D. P. (1992) The Balanced Scorecard: Measures that drive performance, *Harvard Business Review*, 70 (1): 71–80.

Kay, J. (1993) *The Foundations of Corporate Success*. Blackwell.

Kim, W. C. and Mauborgne, R. (2003) Think for yourself – stop copying a rival, *New Thinking from INSEAD*.

Kim, W. C. and Mauborgne, R. (2005) *Blue Ocean Strategy: How to create uncontested market space and make the competition irrelevant*. Harvard Business School Press.

Koestler, A. (1976) *The Act of Creation*. Hutchinson.

Kogut, B. and Singh, H. (1988) The effect of national culture on the choice of entry mode, *Journal of International Business Studies*, 19 (3): 411–33.

Kotter, J. P. (1995) Leading change: why transformation efforts fail, *Harvard Business Review*, 73 (2): 59–67.

Kotter, J. P. and Schlesinger, L. A. (1979) Choosing Strategies for Change, *Harvard Business Review*, 57 (2): 106–14.

Krackhardt, D. and Hanson, J. (1993) Informal Networks: The Company Behind the Chart, *Harvard Business Review*, 71 (4): 104–11.

Kunde, J. (2002) *Unique: Now or Never – The Brand Drives the Company in the New Value Economy*. Financial Times/Prentice Hall.

Lamb, R. B. and Shivastava, P. (eds) (1998) *Advances in Strategic Management*. JAI Press.

Larkin, T. J. and Larkin, S. (1996) Reaching and changing frontline employees, *Harvard Business Review*, 74 (3): 95–104.

Laurent, A. (1986) The cross-cultural puzzle of global human resource management, *Human Resources Management*, 25 (1): 91–102.

Leavy, B. and Wilson, D. (1994) *Strategy and Leadership*. ITP.

Lewin, K. (1951) *Field Theory in Social Science*. Tavistock Publications.

Lewis, D. and Bridger, D. (2001) *The Soul of the New Consumer: Authenticity – What we buy and why in the new economy*. Nicholas Brealey.

Liebowitz, S. (2002) *Network Economics: The True Forces that Drive the Digital Marketplace*. New York: Amacon.

Lippitt, R., Watson, J., and Westley, B. (1958) *The Dynamics of Planned Change: A Comparative Study of Principles and Techniques*. Harcourt, Brace.

Lovett, D. and Slatter, S. (1999) *Corporate Turnaround*. Penguin Books.

March, J. (1999) *The Pursuit of Organizational Intelligence*. Blackwell.

McGee, J. (1998) Commentary on 'corporate strategies and environmental regulations: an organizing framework', in Rugman, A. M. and Verbeke, A. (eds) *Journal of Strategic Management*, Special Edition: Editor's choice, 19 (4): 377–87.

McGee, J., Thomas, H., Wilson, D. (2005) *Strategy. Analysis and Practice*. McGraw-Hill.

McKiernan, P. (1992) *Strategies of Growth*. London: Routledge.

Mendelow, A. (1991) Proceedings of the Second International Conference on Information Systems, Cambridge, MA.

Michaels, E., Handfield-Jones, H., and Axelrod, B. (2001) *The War for Talent*. Harvard Business School Press.

Micklethwait, J. and Wooldridge, A. (1997) *The Witchdoctors. What the management gurus are saying, why it matters and how to make sense of it*. Mandarin paperbacks.

Mintzberg, H. (1973) *The Nature of Managerial Work*. Harper & Row.

Mintzberg, H. (1994) *The Rise and Fall of Strategic Planning*. Free Press.

Mintzberg, H. (1998) Generic Strategies: Toward a Comprehensive Framework, in Lamb, R. B. and Shivastava, P. (eds) *Advances in Strategic Management*. JAI Press.

Mintzberg, H. (1999) Organigraphs: Drawing how Companies Really Work, *Harvard Business Review*, 77 (5): 87–94.

Mintzberg, H. (2004) *Managers Not MBAs: A Hard Look at the Soft Practice of Managing and Management Development*. Berrett-Koehler.

Mintzberg, H., Ahlstrand, B., and Lampel, J. (1998) *Strategy Safari. A guided tour through the wilds of strategic management*. Prentice Hall Europe.

Mintzberg, H., Lampel, J., Quinn, B., and Ghoshal, S. (2003) *The Strategy Process. Concepts, Contexts, Cases*. Global 4th edn. Prentice Hall.

Mintzberg, H. and Westley, Y. (1992) Cycles of Organizational Change, *Strategic Management Journal*, 13, Special Issue: 39–59.

Nadler, D. and Tushman, M. (1989) Organizational frame bending: Principles for managing reorientation, *Academy of Management Executive*, 3 (3): 194–204.

Nattermann, P. (2000) Best Practice Does Not Equal Best Strategy, *McKinsey Quarterly*, 2.

Nonaka, I. (1991) The Knowledge Creating Company, *Harvard Business Review*, 69 (6): 96–104.

Nordtrom, K. and Ridderstrale, J. (2002) *Funky Business*. Pearson Education.

Normann, R. and Ramirez, R. (1993) From Value Chain to Value Constellation: Designing Interactive Strategy, *Harvard Business Review*, 71 (4): 65–77.

Pascale, R. and Athos, A. (1981) *The Art of Japanese Management*. Warner.

Penrose, E. (1959) *The Theory of the Growth of the Firm*. Oxford: Oxford University Press.

Peters, T. and Waterman, R. (1982) *In Search of Excellence*. Harper & Row.

Pettigrew, A. and Whipp, R. (1991) *Managing Change for Competitive Success*. Blackwell.

Porter, M. E. (1980) *Competitive Strategy: Techniques for Analyzing Industries and Competitors*. New York: The Free Press.

Porter, M. E. (1985) *Competitive Advantage: Creating and Sustaining Superior Performance*. New York: The Free Press.

Porter, M. (1987) From Competitive Advantage to Corporate Strategy, *Harvard Business Review*, 65 (3): 43–59.

Porter, M. (1990a) *The Competitive Advantage of Nations*. New York: Free Press.

Porter, M. (1990b) The Competitive Advantage of Nations, *Harvard Business Review*, 69 (2): March–April.

Porter, M. (1996) What is Strategy? *Harvard Business Review*, 74 (6): 61–79.

Porter, M. (1998) *The Competitive Advantage of Nations*. New York: Free Press.

Porter, M. (1999) Philanthropy's new agenda: creating value, *Harvard Business Review*, 77 (6): 121–31.

Porter, M. and Kramer, M. (2002) The competitive advantage of corporate philanthropy, *Harvard Business Review*, 80 (12): 56.

Poundstone, W. (1993) *Prisoner's Dilemma*. Oxford: Oxford University Press.

Prahalad, C. K. and Bettis, R. A. (1986) The dominant logic: a new linkage between diversity and performance, *Strategic Management Journal*, 7 (6): 485–501.

Prahalad, C. K. and Doz, Y. L. (1987) *The Multinational Mission: Balancing Local Demands and Global Vision*. New York: Free Press.

Prahalad, C. K. and Hamel, G. (1990) The Core Competence of the Corporation, *Harvard Business Review*, May–June: 79–81.

Price Waterhouse Coopers (1995) *Better Change: Best Practices for Transforming Your Organization*. Irwin.

Quinn, J. B. (1978) Strategic Change: Logical Incrementalism, *Sloan Management Review*, 20 (1): 7–21.

Reed, D. J. (2001) *Stalking the Elusive Business Case for Corporate Sustainability*. Washington: World Resources Institute.

Ricardo, D. (1817) *Principles of Political Economy and Taxation*. London.

Ricardo, D. (1967) *The Principles of Political Economy and Taxation*. Homewood, IL: Irwin.

Roberts, K. (2004) *Lovemarks: The Future Beyond Brands*. Powerhouse Cultural Entertainment Books.

Robins, J. and Wiersema, M. F. (1995) A resource-based view of the multibusiness: empirical analysis of portfolio interrelationships and corporate financial performance, *Strategic Management Journal*, 16 (4): 277–99.

Romanelli, E. and Tushman, M. L. (1994) Organizational Transformation as Punctuated Equilibrium: an empirical test, *Academy of Management Journal*, 37 (5): 1141–61.

Rugman, A. M. (1990) *Multinationals and Canada–United States Free Trade*. University of South Carolina Press.

Rugman, A. M. and D'Cruz, J. R. (1993) The Double Diamond Model of International Competitiveness: the Canadian experience, *Management International Review*, 33 (2) Special Issue: 17–40.

Rugman, A. M. and Verbeke, A. (1998) *Journal of Strategic Management*, Special Edition: Editor's choice, 19 (4): 377–87.

Rumelt, R. P. (1974) *Strategy, Structure and Economic Performance*. Boston, MA: Harvard Business School Press.

Rumelt, R. P. (1986) *Strategy, Structure and Economic Performance*, 2nd edn. Boston, MA: Harvard Business School Press.

Rumelt, R. P. (1991) How Much Does Industry Matter? *Strategic Management Journal*, 12 (3): 167–86.

Saloner, G., Shepard, A., and Podolny, J. (2001) *Strategic Management*. John Wiley and Sons.

Salzman, O., Ionescu-Somers, A., and Steger, U. (2005) The business case for corporate sustainability: literature review and research options, *European Management Journal*, 1: 27–36.

Sanchez, R., Heene, A., and Thomas, H. (1996) *Dynamics of Competence-Based Competition*. Oxford: Elsevier Science.

Schrage, M. (1999) *Serious Play: How the World's Best Companies Simulate to Innovate*. Harvard Business School Press.

Schultz, M., Hatch, M. J., and Holten Larsen, M. (2000) *The Expressive Organization: Linking Identity, Reputation and the Corporate Brand*. Oxford University Press.

Senge, P. (1990) *The Fifth Discipline*. Century Business.

Shaw, G., Brown, R., and Bromiley, P. (1998) Strategic Stories: How 3M is Rewriting Business Planning, *Harvard Business Review*, 76 (3): 41–54.

Shleifer, A. and Vishny, R. (1988) Value maximisation and the acquisition process. *Journal of Economic Perspectives*, 2 (1): 7–20.

Smircich, L. (1983) Concepts of Culture and Organizational Analysis, *Administrative Science Quarterly*, 28 (3): 339–58.

Smith, A. (1776) *The Wealth of Nations*, Smith, A. (ed.) (1999) Penguin Books/South-Western Publishing.

Smither, R. D. (1994) *The Psychology of Work and Human Performance*. HarperCollins.

Sorenson, J. (2005) Why Firms Differ, MBA Thesis, Warwick Business School.

Stace, D. and Dunphy, D. (1994) *Beyond the Boundaries: Leading and Recreating the Successful Organization*. McGraw-Hill.

Stewart, I. (1989) *Does God Play Dice?* 2nd edn. Penguin Books.

Stewart, R. (1967) *Managers and Their Jobs*. Macmillan.

Sutton, B. (2001) *Weird Ideas That Work: $11^1/_2$ Practices for Promoting, Managing, and Sustaining Innovation*. Free Press.

Teece, D. J. (1986) Transaction cost economics and multi-national enterprise, *Journal of Economic Behaviour and Organization*, 7 (1): 21–45.

Thompson, A. A., Gamble, J. E., Strickland, A. J. III (2004) *Strategic Management*, 13th edn. McGraw-Hill.

Tichy, N. (1993) *Handbook for Revolutionaries*. New York: Doubleday.

Tichy, N. and Devanna, M. A. (1990) *The Transformational Leader*. Wiley.

Tichy, N. and Sherman, S. (1993) *Control Your Destiny or Someone Else Will*. New York: Doubleday.

Tomlinson, J. (1999) *Globalization and Culture*. Cambridge: Polity.

Tosi, H. L. Jr. and Gomez-Mejia, L. R. (1994) CEO compensation monitoring and firm performance, *Academy of Management Journal*, 37 (4): 1002–16.

Trompenaars, F. (1993) *Riding the Waves of Cultural Differences: Understanding Cultural Differences in Business*. London: Nicholas Brealey.

Trompenaars, F. and Hampden-Turner, C. (1997) *Riding the Waves of Culture: Understanding Cultural Diversity in Business*. Nicholas Brealey.

Van der Heijden, K. (1996) *Scenarios: The Art of Strategic Conversation*. Chichester: Wiley.

Vernon, R. (1966) International Investment and International Trade in the Product Life Cycle, *Quarterly Journal of Economics*, 29 (2): 190–207.

Volberda, H. W. (1998) *Building the Flexible Firm*. Oxford: Oxford University Press.

Wack, P. (1985) Scenarios: Uncharted waters, *Harvard Business Review*, 63 (6): 139–51.

Wackernagel, M. et al. (1997) Ecological footprints of nations. How much nature do they use? How much nature do they have? Report prepared for the *Rio+5 Forum*.

Waddock, S. A. and Graves, S. B. (1997) The corporate social performance–financial performance link, *Strategic Management Journal*, 18 (4): 303–19.

Wenger, E. (1998) *Communities of Practice: Learning, Meaning and Identity*. Cambridge: Cambridge University Press.

Wenger, E. and Snyder, W. (2000) Communities of practice: the organizational frontier, *Harvard Business Review*, 78 (1): 138–45.

Whitley, R. D. (1999) *Divergent Capitalisms*. Oxford University Press.

Whittington, R. (1996) Strategy as Practice, *Long Range Planning*, 29 (5), Special Issue: 731–6.

Whittington, R. (2000) *What is Strategy? And does it matter?* ITP.

Wilson, D. (1992) *A Strategy of Change: Concepts and Controversies in the Management of Change*. ITP.

Wilson, I. (2000) From Scenario Thinking to Strategic Action, *Technological Forecasting and Social Change*, 65: 23–29.

Wilson, M. (2003) Corporate sustainability: What is it and where does it come from? *Ivey Business Journal*, March/April: 1–5.

Wind, Y. and Mahajan, V. J. (1981) Designing a product and business portfolio, *Harvard Business Review*, 59 (1): 155.

World Commission on Economic Development (1987) *Our Common Future*. Oxford: Oxford University Press.

Zenisek, T. J. (1979) Corporate social responsibility: A conceptualization based on organizational literature, *Academy of Management Review*, 4 (3): 359–68.

REFERENCES

Primary Chapter and Case Authors

All of the book's authors worked on each chapter, but primary authors for each were:

Macro-Shocks –	Duncan Angwin
Movers & Shakers –	Duncan Angwin
Industry Terrain –	Chris Smith
The Big Picture –	Chris Smith
Perfect Positioning –	Chris Smith
Living Strategy –	Stephen Cummings
Corporate Character –	Stephen Cummings
Crossing Borders –	Duncan Angwin
Guiding Change –	Stephen Cummings
Sustain Ability –	Chris Smith, Stephen Cummings
Maverick Strategies –	Stephen Cummings, Duncan Angwin

Case Authors

All of our cases should be viewed as starting points for discussion. They are intended for classroom use rather than as examples of good or bad strategic management practice.

1.1 "Ironclads versus canoes" – Duncan Angwin. This case draws on The New Grove Piano (1988); Ehrlich, C. (1990) *The Piano: A History*, Clarendon Paperbacks, Oxford University Press. Revised edition.

1.2 "Shock and awe" – Duncan Angwin. Crecy and Agincourt are not the only examples of heavy French defeat and English victory based on the principles described in the case. The same situation also occurred at Poitiers on September 19, 1356. The case is based on Tuck, A. (1999) *Crown and Nobility: England 1272–1461*, Blackwell classic histories of England, 2nd edn, Oxford: Blackwell Publishers; Allmand, S. (1997) *Henry V*, Yale University Press; Luecke, R. A. (1994) *Scuttle your ships before you advance*, New York: Oxford University Press; Taylor, F. and Roskell, J. S. (eds) (1975) *Gesta Henrici Quinti*, Oxford: Oxford University Press: 76–9, 91.

1.3 "Flower power" – Bob Galliers and Sue Newell.*

1.4 "Local actions, global response" – Stephen Cummings.

1.5 "Slipping or skidding?" – Duncan Angwin. It contains elements from "The history of Rover P4" (www.roverP4.com) and the BBC documentary *Rover – the last chance saloon*.

1.6 "Thinking the future . . ." – David Wilson.*

1.7 "Olympics, SARS, and the Government" – Duncan Angwin and Michael Wang.

2.1 "Disney versus Disney" – Derek Condon.

2.2 "Changing the face of industry" – Duncan Angwin.

2.3 "Shareholder revolution" – Duncan Angwin.

2.4 "Fiorina's folly" – Duncan Angwin. It contains elements from "An acquisition too far topples leading lady," *Financial Times* (February 10, 2005); "Director departures weaken Fiorina's position," *Financial Times* (February 10, 2005); "Group failed to keep top talent after merger," *Financial Times* (February 10, 2005), "A struggle over strategy: HP counts the cost of 'playing the other guy's game'," *Financial Times* (February 11, 2005).

2.5 "Repel borders!" – Duncan Angwin.

2.6 "Merry men and virgins" – Stephen Cummings. It contains elements from "Health Service Damned by Virgin Report," *The Scotsman* (July 22, 2000); "Virgin Team Highlights NHS Shambles," *The Guardian* (July 22, 2000); "How Labour has Blown £1 billion on Consulting Outside 'Experts'," *Independent on Sunday* (May 28, 2000); "Britain asks Virgin's Branson for Advice on Hospitals: Workers Sceptical," *Financial Post* (May 8, 2000).

2.7 "Fad power" – Stephen Cummings. It contains elements of "Mozart and Management: Why companies fall for myths", *Financial Times* (June 15, 2005).

3.1 "Power is money" – Chris Smith. Adapted from the report "Fair Play at the Olympics" by Oxfam GB, available at www.fairolympics.org. See also www.cleanclothes.org.

3.2 "The price of entry" – Duncan Angwin.

3.3 "The golden arches" – Chris Smith. This case is drawn from various newspaper and magazine articles and a number of websites including the McDonald's company website and www.mcspotlight.org.

3.4 "High-tech hell" – Duncan Angwin. It is based on "A struggle over strategy: HP counts the cost of 'playing the other guy's game'," *Financial Times* (February 11, 2005).

3.5 "Bouncing back" – Stephen Cummings and David Stewart.

3.6 "The 'lows' of 'highs'" – Chris Smith. This case is drawn from various public websites; *Fortune* (January 24, 2005); and particularly *The Economist* (November 27, 2004, April 16, 2005).

3.7 "Barbershop harmonies" – Stephen Cummings. This case contains elements of "Barbershops with a Twist: Get a Haircut and New CDs," *Wall Street Journal* (September 27, 2002).

3.8 "Crumbling palaces" – Duncan Angwin.

4.1 "Parenting problems" – Chris Smith. This is a heavily disguised, actual company. "Thank you" to the managers – you know who you are ☺.

4.2 "A conglomerate by any other name?" – Chris Smith. Sources: Reuters, Associated Press and other websites; GE website and 2005 annual report.

4.3 "Follow the Hurd?" – Chris Smith. As well as specific attributions in the body of the text, various websites; newspaper and magazine articles.

4.4 "easyEmpire" – Duncan Angwin. It is based on easyGroup annual reports for 2001/2002, 2002/2003; easyGroup website; a BBC documentary from "Trouble at the Top" series; BBC news report (March 10, 2005); netimperative.com (January 4, 2005); *Sunday Times* (February 29, 2004).

4.5 "Pendulum swings..." – Stephen Cummings. Names and places have been disguised.**

4.6 "Red, green and blue" – Stephen Cummings.

5.1 "The train pulling in is Tesco" – Chris Smith.

5.2 "Living with the Amazons" – Stephen Cummings.**

5.3 "Can hybrids fly?" – Stephen Cummings. The case is based on: "Restructuring will target cutting costs and airfares," *The Birmingham Post* (November 12, 2001); "EU denies slots to low-fare airlines: Markets rate £3bn Ryanair number 1 in Europe," *The Guardian* (November 13, 2001); "BMI launches 'low-cost, full-frills' restructuring," *The Independent* (November 13, 2001); and, "Outlook: Sir Michael plots new path through turbulence," *The Independent* (November 13, 2001).*

5.4 "Anticipation" – Duncan Angwin. This case is based on a discussion with a firm of strategy consultants about how they received instructions for strategy assignments.

5.5 "Two brews" – Stephen Cummings.

5.6 "Customers – those bastards!" – Chris Smith.*

5.7 "Mirage?" – Duncan Angwin, Wael Eid, and Ben Knight. This case focuses on the struggles of an Islamic bank to survive in the UK market. It draws on data kindly provided by the Islamic Bank of Britain during 2005, and Al Omar, F. and Abdel-Haq, M. (1996) *Islamic Banking: theory, practice and challenges*, London: Zed; Ariff, M. (1988) Islamic banking, *Asia Pacific Economic Literature*, 2 (2): 46–62; Karbhari, Y., Naser, K., and Shahin, Z. (2004) Problems and challenges facing the Islamic Banking System in the West: The case of the UK, *Thunderbird International Business Review*, 46 (5): 521; Khan, M. S. and Mirakhor, A. (1987) *Theoretical Studies in Islamic Banking and Finance*, Houston, TX: Institute for Research and Islamic Studies; Zaher, T. S. and Hassan, M. K. (2001) A comparative literature survey of Islamic Finance and Banking, *Financial Markets, Institutions and Instruments*, 10 (4): 155–99.

5.8 "Out of the frying pan . . ." – Stephen Cummings.**

5.9 "Get Cata" – Stephen Cummings.

5.10 "Cereality" – Stephen Cummings. The case includes elements from "Snap, Crackle, Cash," *People* (November 22, 2004); "A store for cereal (seriously)," *Business* (October 20, 2004); and "Cereal: It's what's for lunch, dinner," *USA Today* (May 21, 2004).

6.1 "Schumacher's success" – Stephen Cummings.

6.2 "The band" – David Wilson.*

6.3 "Bringing back the branch" – Stephen Cummings. It contains elements of "Rooting for Branches" and "Trust me, I'm a Banker," both from *The Economist*'s Survey of International Banking (April 17, 2004) and "Bigger Usually isn't Better in Banking," *Atlanta Business Chronicle* (November 21, 2003).

6.4 "Helping old people eat" – Stephen Cummings. With special thanks to Mark Wood.

6.5 "The power of the WEB" – Stephen Cummings.

6.6 "Breathing fresh air into business" – Stephen Cummings.**

6.7 "Practice above content" – Stephen Cummings. It contains elements of "Science body snubs 'impractical' ethics oath," from the *Times Higher Education Supplement* (March 2, 2001).

6.8 "Emergence" – Stephen Cummings.

7.1 "Pokemon versus The Little Engine That Could" – Stephen Cummings. It contains elements from "The Child is 'Father' to the Manager: Images of Organization," V. H. Ingersoll and G. B. Adams, *Organization Studies*, 1992 (vol. 13, no.4: 497–520); "Pokemania v. Globophobia," *The Economist* (November 18, 2003); M. E. Porter, "What is Strategy," *Harvard Business Review*, 1996; and "Debunking Japan's Model," *The Wall Street Journal* (January 15, 2001).

7.2 "Vikings and Anglos" – David Wilson and Duncan Angwin.

7.3 "Sydney chainsaw massacre" – Duncan Angwin and Richard Dunford. It is adapted from a case called "Merger in Adland" from the book *Organizational Behaviour: An Organizational Analysis Perspective* (Addison-Wesley, Sydney, 1992: 12–13). © Richard Dunford.

7.4   "Virtue Finance: bore values" – Stephen Cummings. The identity of this company has been disguised.

7.5   "From Jack Dee to 2-D and back" – Stephen Cummings. It contains elements from "Lager Than Life," *Marketing* (April 23, 1998); "John Smith's in £10m Sales Push," *Marketing* (September 9, 1998); "Media Case Study: John Smith's," *Marketing* (September 23, 1998); "Cardboard Cut-out With Cult Status." *The Scotsman* (September 24, 1998); "Live Update," *Campaign* (September 25, 1998); "Design and Advertising Brave an Uneasy Alliance," *Campaign* (May 14, 1999); "John Smith's Unveils £20m Comedy Ads," *The Guardian* (May 8, 2002); and "John Smith's in Bitter Sweet Awards Triumph," *The Guardian* (September 19, 2003).**

7.6   "Safer communities together" – Stephen Cummings.*

7.7   "Natural History" – Stephen Cummings.

7.8   "5 to Five" – Stephen Cummings. It is based on reporting in *The Times* ("Who's Your Favourite Television Channel?," September 9, 1998), *The Guardian* (" 'Channel Filth' Plays the Family Card," August 12, 2000), *The Independent* ("Channel 5 Boss Demands Explicit Sex on Television," August 21, 2000), and *The Independent* ("Last Night's Television," September 19, 2002).**

8.1   "Do you feel lucky?" – Duncan Angwin. This case contains elements from "Kodak's strategy not black and white," *FT Global News Wire, Business Daily Update* (October 5, 2004); "Analysis – Kodak's China moment turns fuzzy, *Reuters News* (July 12, 2001); http://www.factiva.com; Ko, D. C. T. L., Manlu, L., Downing, M., and Tung, A. W. N. (2000) *Kodak in China*, INSEAD/CEIBS. With special thanks to Kalimah A. Priforce, Georgetown University.

8.2   "Biggles does Korea" – Stephen Cummings and Duncan Angwin. This case is based on the second author's trip to Korea just before the World Cup, and also contains elements from " 'Asian Culture' Link in Jet Crashes," *The Times* (March 19, 1998).

8.3   "Lo-glo Barbies" – Stephen Cummings, Duncan Angwin, Bob Galliers, and Sue Newell. With special thanks to Josephine Green for the example from Philips.

8.4   "Different Guyanas" – Duncan Angwin and Stephen Cummings.

8.5   "Cultural icebergs" – Duncan Angwin.*

8.6   "Burgers and cola" – Stephen Cummings. It contains elements from "Back to Classic Coke," *Financial Times* (March 27, 2000); "Ice-cold Times for an Icon," *The Independent* (January 20, 2000); "Cola: The New Political Statement," *The New Zealand Herald* (April 19, 2003); "Turkish Pop Culture," *Time* (September 15, 2003); and "Global ads buck local taste trend," *The Australian* (September 11, 2003).

8.7   "The world's local bank" – Stephen Cummings. It contains elements from www.hsbc.com.**

8.8   "The Trojan Rover" – Duncan Angwin. This case contains elements from "Chinese getting off their bikes as the car becomes king," *The Times* (September 24, 2004), "MG Rover thinks big in venture with Chinese carmaker," *Financial Times* (September 25, 2004).

9.1   "Hanging by a thread" – Stephen Cummings. It contains elements of "Pringle takes to the catwalk to shed its staid image," *The Independent* (September 16, 2002); "Luxury goods manufacturers face another season of belt tightening," *Sunday Times* (September 22, 2002); "The age of the immortals," *Financial Times*, (September 20, 2003); and the BBC video *Pringles – hanging by a thread* (episode 1 of series 5 of the popular "Trouble at the Top" series). It is recommended that this case be used in conjunction with the BBC video, which can be purchased at www.bbcworldwide.com.

9.2   "The awakening giant" – Andrew Pettigrew.*

9.3   "Leopards, tigers, and bears" – Stephen Cummings. The corporate and individual names in this case have been disguised.**

9.4   "The plastic pig" – Duncan Angwin.

9.5   "Four weddings and a funeral" – Stephen Cummings. It draws on reporting from "Jersey Beat," *The Times* (May 19, 1998); "Liverpool Show Way Forward," *The Times* (December 21, 1999); "Best League Table in the World . . . Ever!" *The Times* (January 1, 2000); "Managing to put the Side Back into Mersey," *Irish Sunday Tribune* (February 13, 2000); "IMF in Need of New Faith," *The Guardian* (April 17, 2000); "Eco Soundings," *The Guardian* (April 19, 2000); "Bill and Dave Show," *Human Resources* (January/February, 1996); "Cook Sells Britain's New Look Abroad," *The Times* (July 23, 1999). Special thanks to Tony Smith and the staff and students at Baraka College.*

9.6   "Three in one" – Duncan Angwin.

10.1   "McAttacked" – Chris Smith. Various newspaper and magazine articles and a number of websites including the McDonald's company website and www.mcspotlight.org.

10.2   "Growing the future?" – Chris Smith. Figures for the 2003/4 financial year from *Fortune* (May 18, 2005); various sources as indicated in the text, including "Growth though Global Sustainability: An Interview with Monsanto's CEO, Robert B. Shapiro," by Joan Magretta (1997) *Harvard Business Review*, January–February: 79–88.

10.3   "The Credo" – Stephen Cummings. The Credo shown courtesy of Johnson & Johnson.

10.4   "Codes and conduct" – Chris Smith.

10.5   "Handi Ghandi Curries" – Stephen Cummings. It contains elements of "Bapu with beef handi gets great-grandson's goat," by Satish Nandgaonkar, *Calcutta Telegraph* (June 16, 2005); "What's Next, Martin Luther Burger King Jr.?" by Constantine von Hoffman, *CMO Magazine* (June 17, 2005); and "Curry boycott," *Lismore Northern Star* (June 25, 2005).

10.6   "The Il Ngwesi: eco-warriors" – Stephen Cummings.

10.7   "Sustaining Postman Pat?" – Stephen Cummings. David Thomas's words are extracted from "Why Pat Must be Saved for the Nation," *The Independent* (November 28, 2000). This case also draws on "Post office that inspired 'Postman Pat' to close," *The Independent* (June 20, 2003).**

11.1   "Dumplings to villas" – Shiyong Fan and Stephen Cummings.

11.2   "Gray boxes" – Duncan Angwin. This case is based on an assignment I had early in my investment banking career involving the refinancing of Racal Electronics. The "gray box" in question was the first mobile phone. When it was launched, despite all the problems identified in the case, the product became hugely successful for the company and this business unit was subsequently de-merged as Vodafone – now the world's largest mobile phone company.

11.3   "21st century cars" – Stephen Cummings. It contains elements from "Curiouser and Curiouser," H. Pearman, *Sunday Times* (February 7, 1999); "A Vintage Harvest," R. Hutton, *Sunday Times* (January 7, 2001); "Bigger and Bolder," *Sunday Times* (July 15, 2001); "Good Car, Bad Car," *Sunday Times* (February 10, 2002); "French Revolution," *Sunday Star Times* (November 3, 2002); and "Designer Cars," *BusinessWeek* (February 16, 2004).

11.4   "Breaking the chain; joining the customer" – Stephen Cummings. It contains elements of "Build-A-Bear Workshop," by Roger Crockett in *BusinessWeek* (June 6, 2005).

11.5   "The curate's egg?" – Stephen Cummings. It contains elements from "Game Over! Back to Work," by Jonathan Bell, which appeared in *Wallpaper** (October, 2004); and *Willing Slaves: How the Overwork Culture is Ruining Our Lives*, by Madeline Bunting (2004) HarperCollins.

11.6 "Crafting strategy" – Stephen Cummings. It contains elements from *Recreating Strategy*, S. Cummings (2002); *Principles of Scientific Management*, F. W. Taylor (1911); *Reengineering the Corporation: A Manifesto for Business Revolution*, M. Hammer and J. Champy (1993); and "The Quest for Quality," *Time* (August 27, 2001) (at the time of writing, full copies of this story and the associated cases could be found at http://www.time.com/time/europe/specials/summerjourney/opener.html.) **Answers to "who wrote what in the case": Taylor = 2, 3, 6, 7, and 10; Hammer = 1, 4, 5, 8, and 9.**

11.7 "Picture this!" – Stephen Cummings and Duncan Angwin. Elements are abstracted from "Beautiful Strangeness," by Jonathan Glancy in *The Guardian* (November 4, 2000) and "The Organizational Advantages of Double Vision," by Stephen Cummings in the *Proceedings of the 1992 ANZAM Conference*, Sydney.

11.8 "Strategize that!" – Duncan Angwin and Stephen Cummings.

Earlier versions of asterisked cases appeared in
* *Images of Strategy (Blackwell, Oxford, 2003).*
** *Recreating Strategy (Sage, London, 2002).*

Acknowledgements

We would like to thank the following friends and colleagues for helping create this book.

Matthew Checkley, Warwick Business School
Derek Condon, Warwick Business School.
Richard Dunford, MacQuarie University, Sydney.
Wael Kamel Eid, MBA, Marketing Manager, Islamic Bank of Britain.
Josephine Green, Philips, NV.
Ben Knight, Warwick Business School.
Tim Scholes, Senior Partner, IAMCO Ltd.
Tony Smith and the staff and students at Baraka College.
Michael Wang, Warwick Business School.
Allun Williams, Director of Sales and Marketing, Islamic Bank of Britain.
David Wilson, Warwick Business School.
Mark Wood, MD, Prudential PLC.

The publishers thank the following for permission to reproduce copyright material:

Figure 1.1: Keith Davis and William C. Frederick, *Business and Society: Management, Public Policy, Ethics*, 5th edition. New York: McGraw-Hill, 1984. Copyright © 1984 by Keith Davis and William C. Frederick. Reprinted by permission of The McGraw-Hill Companies.

Figure 1.4: Henk Witze Volberda, *Building the Flexible Firm*. Oxford: Oxford University Press, 1998. Copyright © 1998 by Henk W. Volberda. Reprinted by permission of Oxford University Press.

Figure 3.6: Adam M. Brandenburger and Barry J. Nalebuff, *Co-opetition*. NY: Currency, 1996. Copyright © 1996 by Adam M. Brandenburger and Barry J. Nalebuff. Reprinted by permission of Doubleday, a division of Random House, Inc.

Figure 5.1: Michael E. Porter, *Competitive Advantage: Creating and Sustaining Superior Performance*, fig 1.3, p. 12. NY: The Free Press, 1998. Copyright © 1985, 1998 by Michael E. Porter. Reprinted by permission of The Free Press, a Division of Simon & Schuster Adult Publishing Group. All rights reserved.

Figure 5.2: Cliff Bowman, *Strategy in Practice*. Harlow: Prentice Hall, 1988. Copyright © 1998 by Prentice-Hall Europe. Reprinted by permission of Pearson Education Ltd.

Table 5.2: Henry Mintzberg, Generic strategies: toward a comprehensive framework, from R. B. Lamb and P. Shivastava, *Advances in Strategic Management*. JAI Press, 1998. Copyright © 1998 by JAI Press. Reprinted by permission of Elsevier.

Figure 5.3: Michael E. Porter, *Competitive Advantage: Creating and Sustaining Superior Performance*, Fig 2.2, p. 37. NY: Free Press, 1985. Copyright © 1985, 1998 by Michael E. Porter. Reprinted by permission of The Free Press, a Division of Simon & Schuster Adult Publishing Group. All rights reserved.

Figure 7.3: G. Johnson, K. Scholes, and R. Whittington, *Exploring Corporate Strategy*, 7th edition. Harlow: Prentice Hall, 2005. Copyright © 1998 by Prentice-Hall Europe. Reprinted by permission of Pearson Education Ltd.

Figure 8-1.1, US v. China: Geert Hofstede, *Cultures and Organizations: Software of the Mind*, Revised and Expanded 2nd Edition. New York: McGraw-Hill, 2005. Copyright © 2005 by Geert Hofstede BV. Adapted by permission of the author.

Figure 9.2: Henry Mintzberg and Y. Westley, Strategic changes related to organizational changes pp. 39–59, from *Strategic Management Journal* 13, 1992. Copyright © 1992 by John Wiley & Sons Limited. Reprinted by permission of the publisher.

Figure 9.3: David C. Wilson, *A Strategy of Change: Concepts and Controversies in the Management of Change*. Routledge, 1992. Copyright © 1992 by David C. Wilson. Reprinted by permission of Thomson Publishing Services on behalf of Thomson Learning and Routledge.

Figure 9.4: Dexter C. Dunphy and D. A. Stace, *Under New Management: Australian Organizations in Transition*. McGraw Hill, 1990. Copyright © 1990 by Dexter C. Dunphy. Reprinted by permission of McGraw-Hill Education, Australia & New Zealand.

Figure 9.5: Brian Leavy and David C. Wilson, *Strategy and Leadership*. Routledge, 1994. Copyright © 1994 by Brian Leavy and David C. Wilson. Reprinted by permission of Thomson Publishing Services on behalf of Thomson Learning and Routledge.

Figure 9.6: J. P. Kotter and L. A. Schlesinger, pp. 106–14, *Harvard Business Review*, March/April 1979. Copyright © 1979 by the Harvard Business School Publishing Corporation. Reprinted by permission of Harvard Business Review. All rights reserved.

Santish Nandgaonkar, Bapu with beef handi gets great-grandson's goat, from *The Calcutta Telegraph* 16 June, 2005. Copyright © 2005. Reprinted by permission of The Telegraph, Calcutta, India.

Curry Boycott, from *Lismore Northern Star* 25 June, 2005. Copyright © 2005. Reprinted by permission of The Northern Star Newspaper, Lismore, NSW Australia. Copyright reserved.

David Thomas, "Postman Pat: Why he must be saved for the nation," from *The Independent* 28 November, 2000. Copyright © 28 November 2000 by *The Independent*. Reprinted by permission.

The publishers apologize for any errors or omissions in the above list and would be grateful to be notified of any corrections that should be incorporated in the next reprint or edition of this book.

ACKNOWLEDGEMENTS

Index

INDEX

INDEX

354